Applying Harvard Graphics:

A PROJECT APPROACH

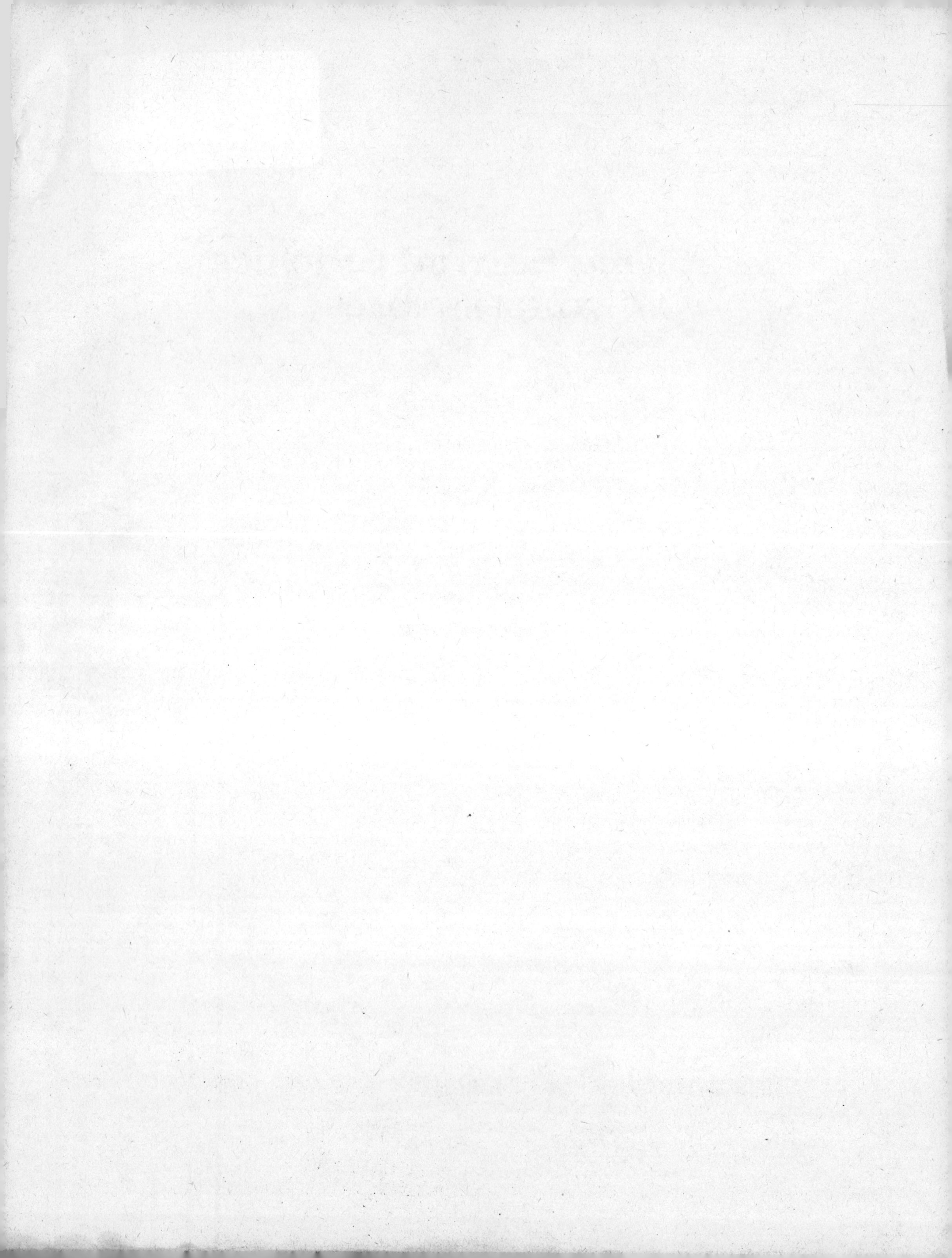

Applying Harvard Graphics:
A PROJECT APPROACH

CAROL M. CRAM

Capilano College
No. Vancouver, B.C.

HOUGHTON MIFFLIN COMPANY   BOSTON   TORONTO

Geneva, Illinois   Palo Alto   Princeton, New Jersey

Supervising Development Editor: **Joanne Dauksewicz**
Senior Project Editor: **Margaret M. Kearney**
Production/Design Coordinator: **Caroline Ryan-Morgan**
Manufacturing Coordinator: **Marie Barnes**
Marketing Manager: **Bob Wolcott**

This book is dedicated to my parents, Tom and Ruby Cram, who gave me the confidence and support to continue, and to my husband and daughter for their constant love.

Printed in the U.S.A.

ISBN: 0-395-662206

123456789-B-97 96 95 94 93

CONTENTS

PREFACE — xi

INTRODUCTION — 1
PART 1 TEXT OVERVIEW — 1
PART 2 GETTING IN — 2
PART 3 GUIDED TOUR — 2
Menus 2
Tools 7
PART 4 QUICK PRACTICE — 9
PART 5 TEXT ORGANIZATION — 14

SECTION ONE TEXT CHARTS — 17

LESSON ONE TITLE PAGE — 22

ACTIVITY 1 TITLE PAGE PURPOSE — 22
ACTIVITY 2 TITLE PAGE 1 — 25
Change Your Chart Orientation 25
Enter and Format Your Text 27
Enhance Your Title Page 31
Save and Print Your Title Page 32

ACTIVITY 3 TITLE PAGE 2 — 34
Edit Your Text 34
Add a New Symbol 38
Save and Print Your Title Page 40

ACTIVITY 4 CHALLENGE ASSIGNMENT — 41
Determine Your Document Type 41
Write Your Title Page Information 42
Create and Format Your Title Page 43

ACTIVITY 5 LESSON ONE REVIEW — 44
SUPPLEMENTARY EXERCISES — 45

LESSON TWO   **BULLET CHART**   **46**

ACTIVITY 1   **BULLET CHART INFORMATION**   **46**

ACTIVITY 2   **BULLET CHART 1**   **48**

Create Your Bullet Chart   48
Enhance Your Bullet Chart   51
Save and Print Your Bullet Chart   54

ACTIVITY 3   **BULLET CHART 2**   **56**

Edit Your Chart Data   56
Enhance Your Bullet Chart   59
Save and Print Your Chart   66

ACTIVITY 4   **CHALLENGE ASSIGNMENT**   **67**

Choose Your Bullet Chart Topic   67
Plan Your Chart Information   68
Create and Format Your Chart   69

ACTIVITY 5   **LESSON TWO REVIEW**   **72**

SUPPLEMENTARY EXERCISES   **72**

LESSON THREE   **ADVERTISING FLYER**   **73**

ACTIVITY 1   **DESIGN A FLYER**   **73**

ACTIVITY 2   **FLYER 1**   **75**

Enter Your Text Blocks   75
Add Symbols   80
Save and Print Your Flyer   85

ACTIVITY 3   **FLYER 2**   **87**

Create the Curved Text and Wave Lines   87
Copy Text and Curves to Your Flyer   94
Revise the Flyer Format   96
Save and Print Your Flyer   98

ACTIVITY 4   **CHALLENGE ASSIGNMENT**   **99**

Choose Your Product/Service/Event   99
Determine Your Flyer's Purpose   99
Plan Your Flyer Information   100
Create and Format Your Flyer   101

ACTIVITY 5   **LESSON THREE REVIEW**   **103**

SUPPLEMENTARY EXERCISES   **103**

<table>
<tr><td>SECTION TWO</td><td>NUMBER CHARTS</td><td>105</td></tr>
</table>

LESSON FOUR   **PIE CHART**   **110**

ACTIVITY 1   **PIE CHART INFORMATION**   **110**

ACTIVITY 2   **PIE CHART 1**   **113**

Create Your Pie Chart   113
Enhance Your Pie Chart   117
Save and Print Your Pie Chart   121

ACTIVITY 3   **PIE CHART 2**   **122**

Get and Link Pie Chart 1   123
Enter Your Data for Pie Chart 2   123
Enhance Your Linked Pie Charts   125
Save and Print Your Pie Chart   129

ACTIVITY 4   **CHALLENGE ASSIGNMENT**   **130**

Select Your Company/Organization   130
Determine Your Pie Chart Purpose   130
Plan Your Pie Chart Information   131
Create and Format Your Pie Chart   132

ACTIVITY 5   **LESSON FOUR REVIEW**   **134**

SUPPLEMENTARY EXERCISES   **134**

LESSON FIVE   **BAR CHART**   **135**

ACTIVITY 1   **BAR CHART INFORMATION**   **135**

ACTIVITY 2   **BAR CHART 1**   **138**

Create Your Bar Chart   138
Enhance Your Bar Chart   141
Save and Print Your Bar Chart   144

ACTIVITY 3   **BAR CHART 2**   **146**

Edit Your Chart Data   146
Enhance Your Bar Chart   149
Save and Print Your Chart   159

ACTIVITY 4   **CHALLENGE ASSIGNMENT**   **160**

Determine Your Bar Chart Purpose   161
Plan Your Bar Chart Information   161
Create and Format Your Chart   163

ACTIVITY 5   **LESSON FIVE REVIEW**   **165**

SUPPLEMENTARY EXERCISES   **166**

LESSON SIX   **AREA CHART**   **167**

ACTIVITY 1   AREA CHART INFORMATION   **167**

ACTIVITY 2   AREA CHART 1   **172**

Create Your Area Chart   172
Enhance Your Area Chart   175
Add an Evolved Symbol   180
Save and Print Your Area Chart   184

ACTIVITY 3   AREA CHART 2   **186**

Edit and Save Your Area Chart   186
Convert Your Area Chart to a Table Chart   188
Place Charts in Draw and Enhance   192
Save and Print Your Chart   198

ACTIVITY 4   CHALLENGE ASSIGNMENT   **198**

Select Your Company/Organization   199
Plan Your Chart Information   199
Create and Format Your Chart   202

ACTIVITY 5   LESSON SIX REVIEW   **205**

SUPPLEMENTARY EXERCISES   **205**

SECTION THREE   PICTORIAL CHARTS   **206**

LESSON SEVEN   **ORGANIZATION CHART**   **210**

ACTIVITY 1   ORGANIZATION CHART INFORMATION   **210**

ACTIVITY 2   ORGANIZATION CHART 1   **212**

Create Your Organization Chart   212
Enhance Your Organization Chart   217
Save and Print Your Organization Chart   220

ACTIVITY 3   ORGANIZATION CHART 2   **222**

Edit Your Chart Data   222
Enhance Your Chart   227
Save and Print Your Chart   231

ACTIVITY 4   CHALLENGE ASSIGNMENT   **232**

Select Your Company/Organization   233
Plan Your Chart Information   233
Create and Format Your Chart   234

ACTIVITY 5   LESSON SEVEN REVIEW   **235**

SUPPLEMENTARY EXERCISES   **236**

Contents **ix**

LESSON EIGHT   **GEOGRAPHICAL CHART**   **237**

ACTIVITY 1   GEOGRAPHICAL CHART INFORMATION   **237**

ACTIVITY 2   GEOGRAPHICAL CHART 1   **240**

Enter Your Chart Heading   240
Create Your Map and Legend   243
Fill Your Map Areas   249
Save and Print Your Chart   259

ACTIVITY 3   GEOGRAPHICAL CHART 2   **260**

Create and Enhance Your Bar Chart   261
Save Bar Chart as Symbol   265
Combine Bar Chart with Map Symbol   266
Save and Print Your Chart   276

ACTIVITY 4   CHALLENGE ASSIGNMENT   **277**

Select Your Map   277
Determine Your Chart Purpose   278
Plan Your Chart Information   278
Display Method   279
Create and Format Your Chart   280

ACTIVITY 5   LESSON EIGHT REVIEW   **282**

SUPPLEMENTARY EXERCISES   **283**

LESSON NINE   **DIAGRAM**   **284**

ACTIVITY 1   DIAGRAM CONTENT   **284**

ACTIVITY 2   DIAGRAM 1   **286**

Draw Your Floor Plan Lines   286
Add Boxes   293
Add Labels   294
Save and Print Your Diagram   301

ACTIVITY 3   DIAGRAM 2   **302**

Draw, Duplicate, and Position Shapes   304
Draw an Arrow   308
Duplicate and Position Arrows   310
Enter and Position Labels   314
Enter Title and Legend   316
Save and Print Your Diagram   319

ACTIVITY 4   CHALLENGE ASSIGNMENT   **320**

Choose Your Diagram Topic   320
Plan Your Diagram Information   321
Create and Format Your Diagram   321

ACTIVITY 5   LESSON NINE REVIEW   **324**

SUPPLEMENTARY EXERCISES   **324**

x Contents

SECTION FOUR **PRESENTATIONS** **325**

LESSON TEN **SCREEN SHOW** **328**

ACTIVITY 1 **SCREEN SHOW CONTENT** **328**

ACTIVITY 2 **SCREEN SHOW CHARTS** **329**
Create the Title Chart 338
Create Bullet Chart 1 340
Create the Organization Chart 342
Create Pie Chart 1 345
Create Pie Chart 2 347
Create the Bar Chart 349
Create Bullet Chart 2 351

ACTIVITY 3 **SCREEN SHOW PRODUCTION** **353**
Create Presentation Background 353
Apply Presentation Attributes 357
Add Transition Effects 360
Display Your Screen Show 361

ACTIVITY 4 **CHALLENGE ASSIGNMENT** **362**
Determine Your Show Subject 362
Prepare Your Charts 362
Edit Your Presentation 363
Produce Your Screen Show 364

ACTIVITY 5 **LESSON TEN REVIEW** **364**

APPENDIX A **ADVANCED FEATURES** **366**

ACTIVITY 1 **CREATING TEMPLATES** **366**

ACTIVITY 2 **IMPORTING AND EXPORTING FILES** **368**

INDEX **373**

Applying Harvard Graphics®: A Project Approach will teach you the concepts and techniques you need to produce effective presentation graphics. In addition, the book encourages you to go beyond simple mastery of Harvard Graphics to *apply* the skills you learn to the creation of documents that reflect your own needs and interests.

The basic philosophy behind the book is that learning software occurs most effectively when each user can find and fulfill his or her own purposes for using the software. In fact, *why* a software program is used goes hand-in-hand with *how* the software program is used. When software users are actively involved with the content of their own documents, they quickly develop the essential problem-solving skills they need to work with any software program.

The book's emphasis on a project approach to teaching Harvard Graphics is based on my experience as a college instructor of many different courses in computer software. In the past, I used the traditional "feature-by-feature" approach to teach a new program. For example, I'd start by teaching students how to draw a line, or retrieve a symbol, or show percents in a bar chart. This approach, however, did not really teach the software in a meaningful way. Students could understand the techniques presented but lacked the confidence to apply these techniques to the creation of useful business documents. The project approach, however, *challenges* students to use new features in a way that reflects their personal needs and develops their layout, formatting, and communication skills.

Individuals who are likely to find this text particularly useful include:

- Students and office professionals who wish to learn the basics of presentation graphics.
- Students enrolled in a marketing or business communication class.
- Students in graphics arts programs that emphasize the development of layout and formatting skills.

FEATURES OF THE BOOK

- Each lesson presents the concepts and techniques required to produce *specific business documents.*
- *A five-activity format* presents the materials in each lesson in an easy-to-learn and manageable form.
- *Step-by-step instructions* are clearly presented to help you work through each activity in a logical and productive manner.
- *Frequent illustrations* are provided to help you check your work as you progress through each lesson.
- Each lesson includes several *review questions* to help you test your understanding of the concepts and techniques you have learned.
- *Supplementary exercises* are included to provide you with more opportunities to apply the lesson materials.

WHAT YOU NEED TO GET STARTED

- An IBM or 100% compatible 80286, 80386, or 80486 computer.
- A minimum of 640K of memory.
- A hard disk and one disk drive.
- Graphics card; a color monitor is also recommended.
- Laser printer recommended or dot-matrix printer capable of printing graphics.
- DOS version 3.0 or later.
- Harvard Graphics 3.0.

ACKNOWLEDGMENTS

I would like to thank my students in the Office Administration Department at Capilano College in North Vancouver, B.C., Canada. Their enthusiastic acceptance of the project approach to learning software convinced me of the need for this text. I also wish to thank Ray Deveaux and Joanne Dauksewicz of Houghton Mifflin for their incredible help and encouragement, and Darrell Uhearn of Houghton Mifflin Canada for helping me get started in the first place.

I also wish to acknowledge the following people in particular for their assistance in reviewing the manuscript: Pat Graves, *Easter Illinois University;* Alan Rowland, *Indiana Vocational Technical College;* Nancy Johnson Theran, *Boston Computer Society;* Fannie E. Johnson, *Western Oklahoma State College;* Dr. Joyce Kupsh, *California State Polytechnic University, Pomona;* Harvey Blessing, *Essex Community College.*

Applying Harvard Graphics:
A PROJECT APPROACH

INTRODUCTION

TOPICS

- Text Overview
- Getting In
- Guided Tour
- Quick Practice
- Text Organization

PART 1   TEXT OVERVIEW

Applying Harvard Graphics®: A Project Approach teaches you the concepts and skills you need to develop effective presentation graphics. You will learn how to communicate information through text charts, graphs, and diagrams *and* how to develop your ability to design visual aids that are eye catching and easy to understand.

You can use *Applying Harvard Graphics: A Project Approach* as your text for a course in Harvard Graphics presented by an instructor or you can work through the text on your own as part of a self-study program.

The text focuses on production—on applying the Harvard Graphics features to real business situations. Rather than learning one feature after another in isolation, you will learn *why* you produce a certain type of document and *how* you can apply basic design principles to communicate your message effectively.

First, let's focus on the basic purpose of Harvard Graphics—the development of effective presentation graphics.

Presentation Graphics

The term *presentation graphics* refers to the visual aids used to highlight information presented in meetings, sales presentations, seminars, or lectures. Visual aids may consist of printed handouts, slides, overheads, flip charts, or even projections of images directly from a computer screen. Computer software programs such as Harvard Graphics were developed so that businesspeople could create visual aids that would quickly and effectively communicate information to both small and large groups.

Using Harvard Graphics

Harvard Graphics uses the term *charts* to refer to the graphs, drawings, and text documents you create as visual aids. You can think of the types of charts available as falling into three broad categories:

1

- text charts (title, bullet, table)
- number charts (pie, bar, area, line)
- pictorial charts (organization, drawing, diagram)

Once you learn how to create these charts, you can then *combine* them into a presentation on a specific theme and display your presentation as a slide show, computer screen show, or print-out.

With any new software program, your first question is probably "How do I get in?" followed closely by your second question, "What do I do next?" In this Introduction, you will first learn how to access Harvard Graphics. You can then try the hands-on Guided Tour of the basic features and finally complete two Quick Practices to create your first Harvard Graphics documents.

PART 2   GETTING IN

If you work on a network, your instructor will show you how to access Harvard Graphics, or you can ask the computer resource person in your office. If you see a list of programs on your screen when you turn on your computer, press your cursor to highlight **Harvard Graphics** and press **Enter**.

To access Harvard Graphics from a hard drive, position your cursor opposite the prompt (usually C> or D>).

1.   Type *cd\HG3* and press **Enter** to access the Harvard Graphics directory.
2.   Type *HG3* and press **Enter**.

The Harvard Graphics Title Screen appears. After a few seconds the Main Menu appears. You are now ready to start the Guided Tour.

PART 3   GUIDED TOUR

In the Guided Tour, you will take a look at the two principal elements used in Harvard Graphics to create and enhance charts. These two elements are menus and drawing tools.

Let's start with menus.

Menus

If you have just accessed Harvard Graphics as described above, you will see the Main Menu on your screen. Here's what it looks like:

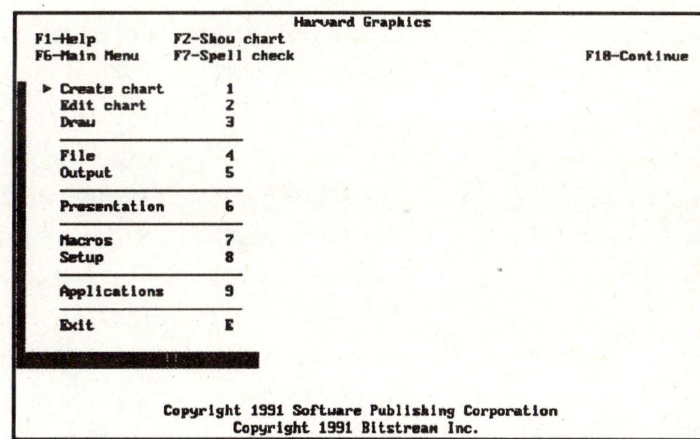

In the following activities you will learn about the first three options: Create Chart, Edit Chart, and Draw.

Selecting Menu Items

Your first task is to learn how to select and deselect an item from the menu. Three methods are available. To familiarize yourself with these methods, try the following activities.

Number Method

1. Press **1** for **Create Chart.** The Create Chart Menu appears:

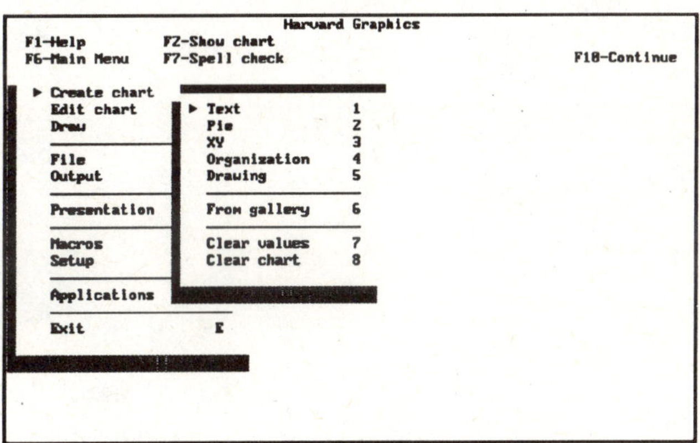

2. Now press the **ESC** key to return to the Main Menu.

The instructions throughout *Applying Harvard Graphics* specify the number method to access menu items. You can also choose to use either the Cursor/ Enter method or the Mouse method. Try the Cursor/Enter method now.

Cursor/Enter Method

1. Press your ↓ arrow until **File** is highlighted.
2. Press **Enter.** The File Menu appears. You will learn more about this menu when you start the lessons.
3. Press the **ESC** key to return to the Main Menu.

Mouse Method

You can also use your mouse to select menu items. In this text, the instructions to access most menu items refer only to the keyboard. Because your fingers are already on the keyboard typing in chart data, you will generally find that using the keyboard is more convenient than using the mouse to access the various menus.

However, you certainly can use the mouse to select a menu item. Try the following activity.

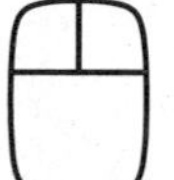

1. Move your mouse until **Create Chart** is highlighted.
2. Click your **left** mouse button. The Create Chart Menu appears.
3. Click your **right** mouse button to return to the Main Menu.

When you access the Draw Screen to use the Draw Tools, you will work much more efficiently with a mouse. The instructions for draw functions, therefore, are always preceded with a note to switch to mouse use. You'll learn more about how to use the mouse when you access the Draw Screen later in the Guided Tour.

Menu Selection Summary

To summarize the selection process, here are the three methods again:

Number method:

Press the number that follows the menu item you wish to access. Press the **ESC** key to exit from the menu.

Cursor/Enter method:

Cursor to the menu item and press **Enter.** Press the **ESC** key to exit from the menu.

Mouse method:

Move your mouse to a menu item and click the **left** button. Click the **right** button to exit from the menu.

Now let's find out more about the Create Chart selection.

Create Chart

You select **Create Chart** when you want to create a specific type of chart such as a pie chart, bar chart, or organization chart. When you want to create a drawing, you choose item **3** for **Draw.** For now, however, let's just look at Create Chart.

1. Press **1** for **Create Chart.** The Create Chart Menu appears. In this menu you select the *type* of chart you wish to create.
2. Press **2** for **Pie.** The Pie Chart Edit Screen appears.

You will learn more about this screen when you try the Quick Practice activities following this Guided Tour. For now, let's examine some of the menu commands you will use when working with Harvard Graphics.

Menu Commands

In the following activity, you will learn about the two most common menu commands: **F8** for **Options** and **F3** for **Choices.**

F8 (Options)

1. Press **F8** to access the **Options** Menu in the Pie Chart Edit Screen you have just entered. Here's what the Options Menu looks like:

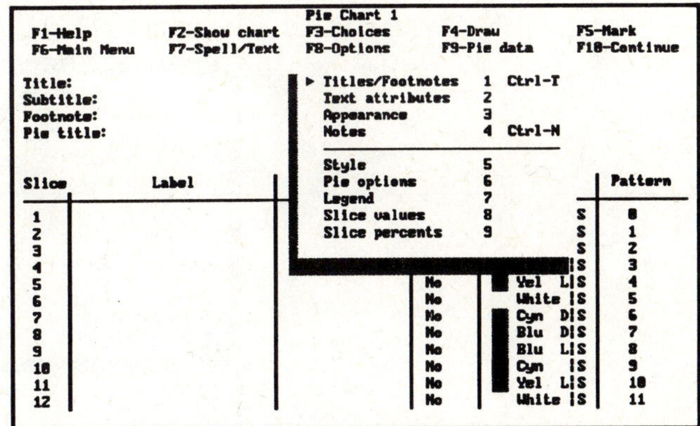

The Options Menu provides you with a variety of selections that you can use to enhance the look of your chart. For example, if you wanted to change the overall appearance of your chart, you would choose **3** for **Appearance.** Let's try it now.

2. Press **3** for **Appearance.** Another menu—the Appearance Menu—appears. Here's what it looks like:

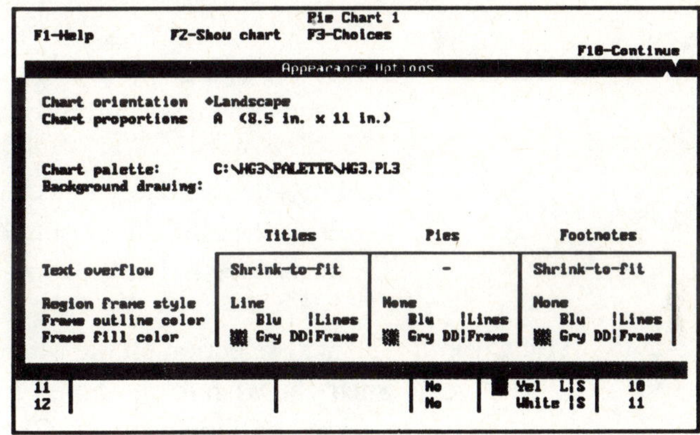

F3 (Choices)   Often, a specific Harvard Graphics feature includes a variety of choices. For example, you can choose to display your chart in either Landscape or Portrait orientation.

1. Press **F3** to see the list of choices available for Chart Orientation. A small "pop-up" menu appears over the Appearance Menu:

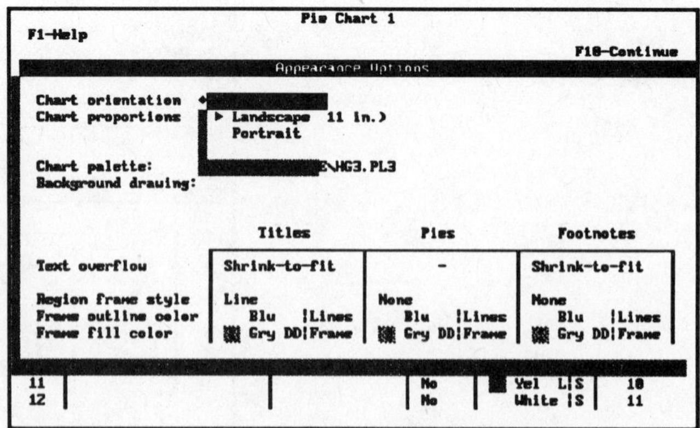

Throughout *Applying Harvard Graphics*, you will see the directions "Press F8 for Options" or "Press F3 for Choices." You will soon find that you first determine *what* changes you want to make to a chart (for example, placing a box around a chart title) and then *how* to make these changes by studying the choices listed in the menus.

With a bit of practice, you will discover that the Harvard Graphics menus are logically structured and easy to follow.

Exit Menus

Before you can go on to learn about the Edit Chart selection, you need to exit the menus you have currently accessed. Here's how.

1. Press the **ESC** key to exit the Choices Pop-up.
2. Press the **ESC** key again to exit the Appearance Menu.
3. Press the **ESC** key again to return to the Main Menu.

Edit Chart

The next selection on the Main Menu is **2** for **Edit Chart**. You would select **2** when you wish to enter the Chart Edit Screen for the chart you are currently working on. You use **Edit Chart** if you either intentionally or mistakenly return to your Main Menu when you are in the middle of entering the data for your chart.

Draw

To conclude our Guided Tour of some of the Harvard Graphics menus, let's look at the Draw selection.

1. Press **3** for **Draw**. The Harvard Graphics Draw Screen appears. Here's what it looks like:

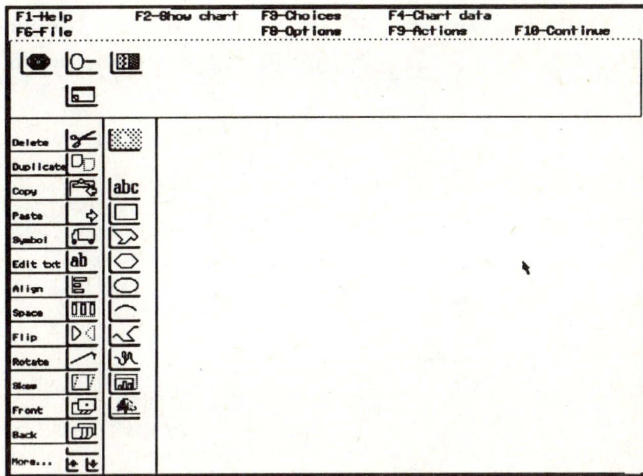

At first, the Draw Screen may look a bit bewildering. To make sense of the Draw Screen, you need to know about the selection of tools you use to create Draw Charts. The next part of the Guided Tour introduces you to some of these tools.

Tools

To the left of your Blank Draw screen, you'll see a selection of *tools*. You use these tools to draw objects such as lines, boxes, and circles; to enter blocks of text; and to retrieve preset drawings called *symbols*. All of these elements are called *objects*.

Once you have placed an object such as a box or text block on your Draw Screen, you can use the Draw Tools to *manipulate* your object. For example, you can rotate it, copy it, resize it, or even enhance it with a shadow. *Applying Harvard Graphics* teaches you a wide variety of ways you can use the tools to enhance your charts and drawings.

In the Draw Screen, you will use your mouse almost exclusively to select tools and create objects. Try the following activities to develop your mouse technique.

Selecting Tools   1. Move the mouse pointer to the **Circle Tool.** Here's what it looks like:

2. Click your **left** mouse button to select the Circle Tool. You always *select* a tool by clicking the left mouse button.
3. Move your mouse into the center of your Draw Screen. Notice that your mouse pointer now appears as a **+**.

4. Click your **right** mouse button to *deselect* the circle tool. The + is re-placed by a pointer.

Trouble Note  If you clicked your right mouse button twice, you will return to the Main Menu. Just point to **Draw** and click **left** to return to the Draw Screen.

Try selecting and deselecting another drawing tool.

1. Move your mouse pointer to the **Box Tool.** Here's what it looks like:

2. Click your **left** mouse button to select the box tool.
3. Click your **right** mouse button to deselect the box tool.

Mouse Review   You have just used the mouse to perform two of its three functions: selecting and deselecting or finishing. You can also press and hold the left mouse button to perform an activity called *dragging*. The following illustration demonstrates these techniques:

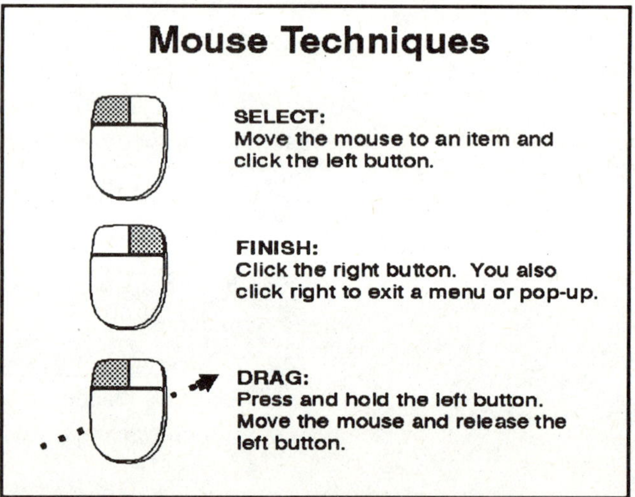

Exiting   You can exit from the Draw Screen by clicking the **right** mouse button until the Main Menu appears. You can also exit as follows:

1. Point your mouse to **F6 File** that appears at the top left corner of your Draw Screen.
2. Click the **left** mouse button to select **F6 File.**
3. Now move your mouse to **Exit to Main Menu.**
4. Click your **left** mouse button again.

You have now returned to the Main Menu. After reading the following note about color, go on to the Quick Practice.

A Note About Color

You are probably using a color screen with your Harvard Graphics program. However, you may not have access to a color printer. As a result, all of the documents you produce with *Applying Harvard Graphics* are designed to print as clearly as possible on a black-and-white printer. In fact, you will often be asked to change the colors displayed on your screen to ensure a sharp black-and-white print-out.

If you are able to print in color, you can substitute colors that look good on your screen. A color printer will reproduce these colors as you see them.

PART 4 QUICK PRACTICE

In the following Quick Practice, you will first access the Pie Chart Edit Screen to create a simple pie chart and then access the Draw Screen to create a text block and symbol.

Practice 1: Pie Chart

Let's create a Pie Chart that shows three of the main uses for Pie Charts in business graphics. In Lesson Four, you will learn much more about Pie Charts and their uses.

1. At the Main Menu, press **1** for **Create Chart.**
2. Press **2** for **Pie.**

The Pie Chart Edit Screen appears:

```
                              Pie Chart 1
   F1-Help          F2-Show chart   F3-Choices      F4-Draw       F5-Mark
   F6-Main Menu     F7-Spell/Text   F8-Options      F9-Pie data   F10-Continue

   Title:
   Subtitle:
   Footnote:
   Pie title:


   Slice        Label           Value      Cut        Color        Pattern

     1                                       No      ▌ Cyn  D|S        0
     2                                       No      ▌ Blu  D|S        1
     3                                       No      ▌ Blu  L|S        2
     4                                       No      ▌ Cyn   |S        3
     5                                       No      ▌ Yel  L|S        4
     6                                       No        White |S        5
     7                                       No      ▌ Cyn  D|S        6
     8                                       No      ▌ Blu  D|S        7
     9                                       No      ▌ Blu  L|S        8
    10                                       No      ▌ Cyn   |S        9
    11                                       No      ▌ Yel  L|S       10
    12                                       No        White |S       11
```

In this screen, you will enter all the data that will appear on your Pie Chart. Note that your cursor is positioned next to **Title.**

1. Type the Title of your Pie Chart in all caps: *PRACTICE PIE CHART.* Press **Enter.**
2. Now type the Subtitle of your Pie Chart in upper/lower case: *Pie Chart Uses.* Press **Enter.**

Enter Label Information   You need to define each of the three slices of your pie.

Label Headings
1. Press **Enter** three times to move your cursor to the **Label** column next to Slice 1.
2. Type *Cost Breakdown* and press **Enter.**
3. Type *Dept. Organization* and press **Enter.**
4. Type *Age Groups.*

Slice Values
1. Press your ↑ arrow twice to return to the **Cost Breakdown** line.
2. Press **Tab** to move your cursor into the **Value** column.
3. Type *33* and press **Enter.**
4. Type *51* and press **Enter.**
5. Type *24.*

Your Pie Chart Edit Screen now looks like this:

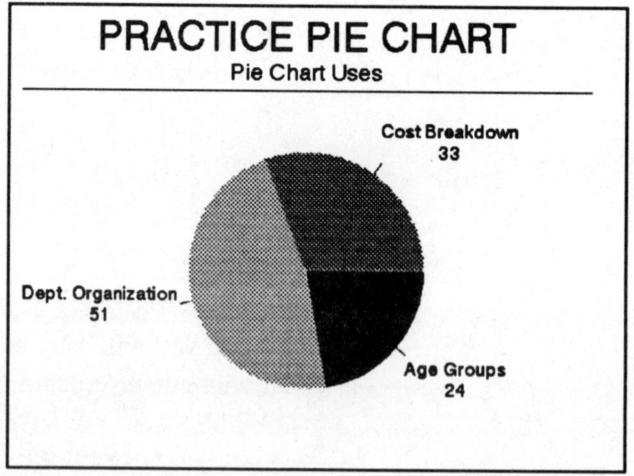

Now press **F2** to display your Chart. Here's what it will look like:

After you've looked at your Pie Chart, press **Enter** to return to your Chart Edit Screen.

In Lesson Four, you will create a Pie Chart as you've just done *and* access the F8 Options Menu to make such changes as enclosing the title in a box, adding percents to the pie slices, cutting a slice, etc.

Before you go on to Practice 2, *clear* your Practice 1 Chart from your screen. You don't need to save it.

1. Press **F6** for **Main Menu.**
2. Press **1** for **Create Chart.**
3. Press **8** for **Clear Chart.** The following message appears on your screen:

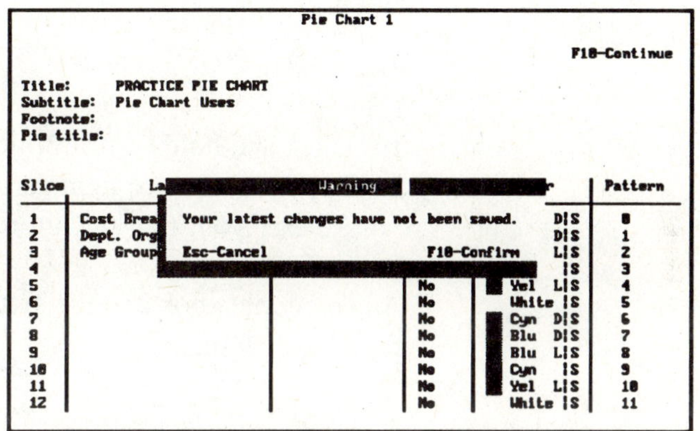

4. Press **F10** to confirm that you don't want to save your Practice Chart.

Now go on to Practice 2.

Practice 2   For Practice 2, you will use your mouse to enter a block of text and retrieve a preset picture or *symbol.*

Mouse Reminders    Remember that you click your **left** button to *select* a function and your **right** button to *finish* a function. To *drag* your mouse, click and hold your **left** button, move your mouse, and then release the mouse button.

If you click the right button twice, you may return to the Main Menu. If this happens, just press or click on **3** for **Draw** to return to your Draw Screen.

1. At the Main Menu, press **3** for **Draw.**

As you discovered during the Guided Tour, the pictures or icons on the left of your screen represent the various Harvard Graphics *tools* you use to create and manipulate objects. For Practice 2, you will use two tools: the Text Tool and the Symbol Tool.

Text Tool   **Symbol Tool**

Text Tool   First, you need to enter a block of text.

1. Move your mouse to the **Text Tool.**
2. Click your **left** button to select the **Text Tool.**
3. Move your mouse back to your Draw Screen. You will notice that a yellow + appears on your screen.
4. Move your mouse so that the + is positioned in the top left corner of your screen.

Trouble Note ▶   If you wait too long to enter your text, a message appears telling you to draw a box or click on a point. Click **right** to remove this message.

You need to *drag* a box.

1. Click and hold your **left** mouse button.
2. Drag your mouse right across your screen and then down about one inch. Release your mouse button.

An empty blue box and the Text Pop-up appears. Now you will type the text for your drawing.

1. Type *Mountain Resorts*.
2. Press **F10** to return to your drawing.

Your next step is to move your text block so that it is centered at the top of your screen.

Pointer Tool   1. Move your mouse to the **Pointer Tool.**
2. Click your **left** button to select the **Pointer Tool.**

Notice that your text block is now surrounded with a series of small orange boxes. These boxes are called *handles*. Notice also that the + has changed back to a pointer.

1. Position the pointer *inside* your text block. Be careful not to touch any of the orange handles.
2. Click and hold your **left** mouse button. Notice that a box appears around your text. When you move your mouse, this box will also move.
3. Move your mouse up to position your text block in the top middle of your screen. Release your mouse button.

Trouble Note ▶   If you release your mouse button before you have positioned your text block, just click and hold the **left** mouse button again to reposition your text.

Your Draw Screen should look like this:

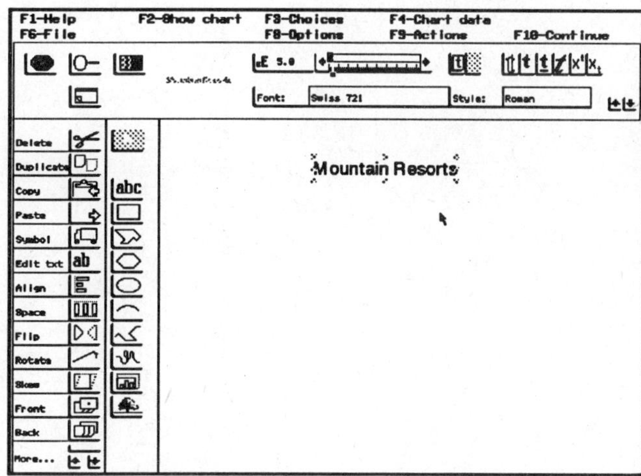

Symbol Tool   Your next step is to retrieve one of the Harvard Graphics preset symbols.

1. Move your mouse to the **Symbol Tool** at the left of your Draw Screen.
2. Click your **left** button to select the **Symbol Tool.**
3. Click your **left** button again on **Get Symbol.**

A list of the Harvard Graphics Symbol Directories appears on your screen.

1. Press **F8** to list the Directories in alphabetical order.
2. Move your mouse to the **BUILD3** Directory.
3. Click your **left** mouse button to select the **BUILD3** Directory.

All the symbols in the BUILD3 Directory appear on your screen.

1. Move your mouse to the picture of the **Chalet.**
2. Click your **left** mouse button on the **Chalet.**
3. Click on **F10** twice to return to your Draw Screen.

Notice that your Chalet is enclosed by a series of small orange boxes
(handles).

1. Press your **right** mouse button to remove these handles.

Compare your screen to the following illustration:

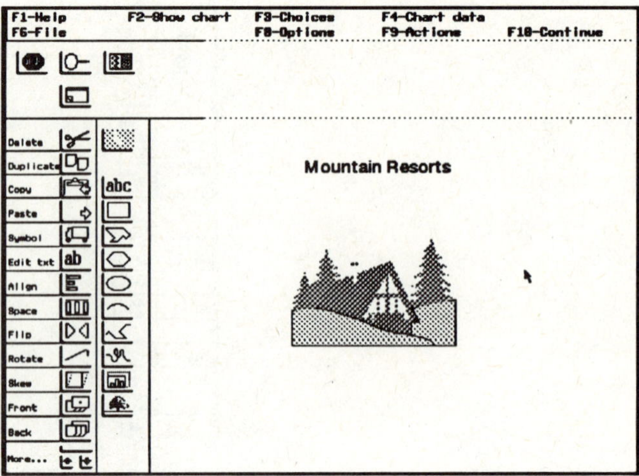

In Lesson One, you will again access the Draw Screen and retrieve a symbol that you can then position and size.

Finish your practice session by clearing your drawing from the screen. You don't need to save your practice drawing.

1.   Press **F6** for **File.**
2.   Press **E** for **Exit to Main Menu.**
3.   Press **1** for **Create Chart.**
4.   Press **8** for **Clear Chart.** The following message appears on your screen:

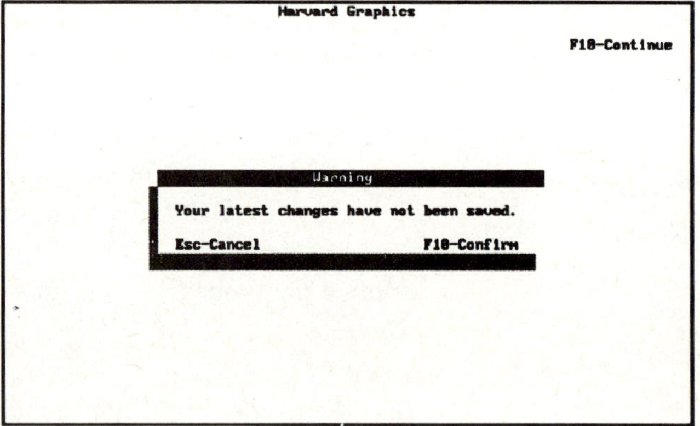

5.   Press **F10** to confirm.

Go on now to Part 5 and read how *Applying Harvard Graphics* is organized to help you create clear and exciting visual aids.

PART 5   TEXT ORGANIZATION

Applying Harvard Graphics takes a project approach to teaching you the skills you need to use Harvard Graphics with confidence. The term *project ap-*

proach means that in each lesson you will have the opportunity to *apply* the skills you have learned to create your own documents.

Text Divisions   The ten lessons are divided into four sections—each representing a document *type* commonly used for presentation graphics.

SECTION ONE: TEXT CHARTS
Lesson One: Title Page
Lesson Two: Bullet Chart
Lesson Three: Advertising Flyer

SECTION TWO: NUMBER CHARTS
Lesson Four: Pie Chart
Lesson Five: Bar Chart
Lesson Six: Area Chart

SECTION THREE: PICTORIAL CHARTS
Lesson Seven: Organization Chart
Lesson Eight: Geographical Chart
Lesson Nine: Diagram

SECTION FOUR: PRESENTATIONS
Lesson Ten: Screen Show

You can choose to start with any lesson you wish, although if you are new to Harvard Graphics, you would be wise to start with Lesson One. However, each lesson is self-contained and provides all the instructions you need to produce the lesson documents.

Lesson Activities   Five activities are required for each lesson:

ACTIVITY 1:   Learn *why* and *when* you use the lesson document and develop the *information* you need to create the two lesson documents.

ACTIVITY 2:   Follow the instructions provided to create the first lesson document.

ACTIVITY 3:   Follow the instructions provided to create the second lesson document (often involves editing or enhancing the first lesson document).

ACTIVITY 4:   Develop, design, and produce a document based on information you determine.

ACTIVITY 5:   Test your new skills with a Lesson Review.

Supplementary Exercises   At the end of each lesson, you will find two Supplementary Exercises. Complete these exercises to provide you with more practice and to reinforce the skills you have learned.

On Your Own   As you progress through each lesson, you will find yourself increasingly able to adapt the instructions for Activities 2 and 3 to produce interesting documents of your own in Activity 4.

The key to success with Harvard Graphics lies in your willingness to experiment with its many functions. Frequently study the menus you will be using. You will soon discover a variety of ways in which you can present your information to reflect your personal needs.

SECTION ONE

TEXT CHARTS

Purpose In a text chart, readers perceive your primary message through words. Graphic elements such as symbols, lines, or boxes enhance the words, but do not detract from the reader's focus on the meaning of the words.

Typical presentations use text charts more frequently than number charts or pictorial charts to highlight important information.

Required Terms To produce an effective text chart, you need to know the following terms:

- Attributes
- Frames
- Symbols

You will encounter all these terms throughout *Applying Harvard Graphics*. For now, let's look at how they apply to text charts.

Attributes In Harvard Graphics, *attributes* is the "blanket term" used to describe the *look* of your text characters. The attributes available are: size, color, alignment, font, and font style.

Size Harvard Graphics calculates text size as a percentage of the narrowest side of your screen. A character with a text size of 9, for example, would take up 9% of the screen depth. As a result, a text size of 9 is quite large—suitable for a major title.

Note that text size in Harvard Graphics is not related to the "point" sizes you may encounter in word processing programs. For example, a 12-point text size in WordPerfect would be a standard text size similar to the characters you are reading here. A character with a text size of 12 in Harvard Graphics, however, would take up 12% of the horizontal page size—that's over one-tenth of the available space!

Color You can select from a wide variety of text colors. Usually, Harvard Graphics sets the text color as light yellow, which prints black on a black-and-white printer.

Alignment You can choose to align your text to the left, right, center, or spread. A spread alignment means that all the text on a line will extend from margin to margin. For most charts, you will choose left, right, or center alignment.

Here's an illustration of the alignment options:

Alignment Options

Left   **Right**   **Center**   **Spread**

Font   The term *font* refers to the type of text character you use to present your words. In Harvard Graphics, you can use the following eight fonts:

Harvard Graphics Fonts

Swiss 721

Dutch 801

Geo Slab 712

HG Gothic

HG Roman

HG Sans Serif

HG Script

Monospace 821

When you first encounter a variety of fonts, you may be tempted to use several of them in one chart. Resist the impulse! Too many fonts on a page can confuse readers and diminish the impact of your message. Your safest bet is to use *one* font only in a text chart and add variations through the use of different sizes and styles such as *italics* or **bold.**

Font Style To vary the look of the font you choose for a document, you can specify a variety of styles, depending on the font. The Swiss 721 font, for example, can be displayed as bold, bold italic, italic, roman (no bold or italic), thin, or thin italic as illustrated:

> **FONT STYLES**
>
> **Swiss 721 Bold**
>
> ***Swiss 721 Bold Italic***
>
> *Swiss 721 Italic*
>
> **Swiss 721 Roman**
>
> Swiss 721 Thin
>
> *Swiss 721 Thin Italic*

Limit the number of font styles to two or three at most in a typical document. Generally, you are safe using bold for titles and subtitles and italics or plain roman for labels, footnotes, and any additional text. However, don't feel you *have* to vary your font styles. Some of the most effective charts use only one font and font style and achieve variation by changing the text size.

Frames The term *frame* refers to how a block of text is enclosed or set off from other chart elements such as symbols or graphs. For example, you can choose to enclose your text in a rounded frame, 3-D frame, or plain square frame. You can also choose to have a simple straight line separate a title/subtitle block from other chart elements. Here are some examples of the frame styles available.

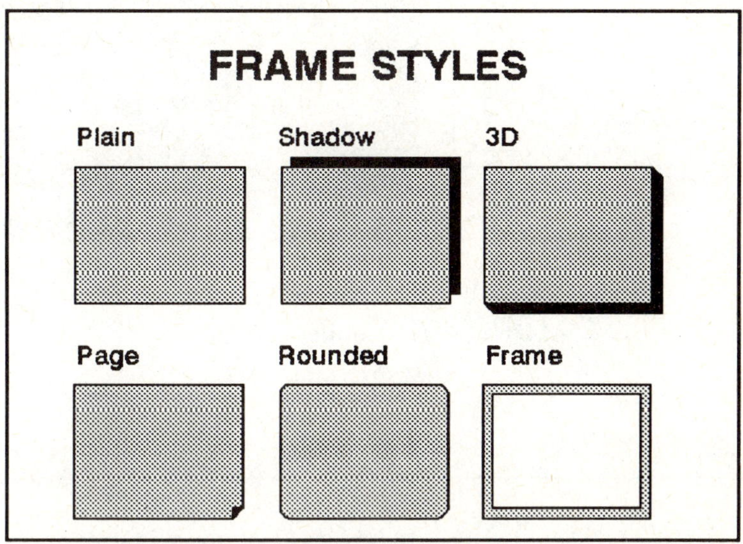

Use frames sparingly! If every text block on a chart is enclosed by a frame—particularly if these frames use different styles—the reader may feel as boxed in as your text appears. A frame should *highlight* important information, not overwhelm it. For most text charts, you can choose to frame the title/subtitle section or the main text section, but not both. Discretion is the key to the effective use of frames.

Symbols

In Harvard Graphics, a *symbol* is any type of picture. You can choose a symbol from the symbol directories or create an image yourself and then save it as a symbol. As with any graphic addition, a symbol should enhance but not overpower the principal message of a text chart. To see illustrations of the preset symbols included in Harvard Graphics, refer to Appendix B at the end of the text.

In addition to or instead of symbols or pictures, you can add graphic objects such as lines, boxes, circles, etc., to your text chart. Again, use such elements sparingly. A shaded line under a title, for example, anchors a page and draws the reader's eye to the title as the most important element.

Section One Charts

In Section One, you will start off by creating a simple Title Page, followed by a Bullet Chart, and finally an advertising Flyer. You will create both the Title Page and the Flyer in the Draw Screen and the Bullet Chart with the Text Chart feature.

<table>
<tr><td>LESSON ONE</td><td>TITLE PAGE</td></tr>
</table>

TITLE PAGE

FEATURES

- Adding Text in Draw
- Marking Text
- Adding and Sizing Symbols

- Changing Fonts and Attributes
- Using Portrait Format
- Using Zoom

INTRODUCTION

In Lesson One, you will use the Draw features of Harvard Graphics to create an attractively formatted Title Page. Here are the lesson activities.

ACTIVITY 1:   Determine the purpose of your Title Page.

ACTIVITY 2:   Follow the instructions given to create the Title Page illustrated on page 26.

ACTIVITY 3:   Follow the instructions given to adapt your Title Page for another type of document (see page 35).

ACTIVITY 4:   Create a Title Page based on your own information.

ACTIVITY 5:   Complete the Lesson Review Questions on Title Page creation and enhancement.

ACTIVITY 1   TITLE PAGE PURPOSE

An attractively formatted Title Page adds style and interest to a report, proposal, or presentation. Your aim is to attract attention with simple but effective blocks of text and one or two well-placed drawings or symbols.

A Title Page should intrigue your readers. You want them to feel confident that the information they find in the body of your report or presentation will be as clear and easy to understand as your Title Page.

Look at the difference between a cluttered, poorly organized report Title Page and one that effectively balances "white space" with concise text.

A Report
on the Analysis of Marketing Trends
in the
Word Processing Software Industry
with Specific Focus on
Comparing WordPerfect
and
Microsoft Word Users

Presented By
John Adams
Marketing Director

SoftCorp Distributors
918 West 11th Avenue
Toronto, Ontario, M5H 1A8
Phone: 987-3319 Fax: 987-9912

Cluttered Title Page

WordPerfect 5.1
Vs.
Microsoft Word

A Market Analysis

John Adams
Marketing Director
SoftCorp Distributors

Clear and Concise Title Page

Notice how the information in the clear and concise Title Page is reduced to the bare essentials. The title is short and has an immediate impact on the reader, while the subtitle informs the reader exactly what kind of document or presentation to expect. Extra information such as the company address is not required for most Title Pages, although sometimes you may wish to include a company logo.

Once you have reduced your text to the minimum amount of words, you can then apply Harvard Graphics features to create a Title Page that not only communicates the required information but also pleases the eye with simple, but effective, enhancements such as boxes, symbols, and different type fonts.

Here is a Title Page that introduces a slide presentation for businesspeople interested in purchasing one of Thrifty Rent-A-Car's franchise operations.

Summary of Activities 2 and 3

In Activities 2 and 3, you will create Title Pages for two documents required by The Photo Stop, a photography business specializing in custom illustrations for books and magazines. Alice Banks, The Photo Stop's sole proprietor, wishes to expand her company from two employees to ten. To do this, she needs to write a business plan to gain funding from investors and a proposal to obtain a large photography contract from *Nature First* magazine.

The Title Pages she creates for these two documents should accomplish three principal purposes.

- Present a professional company image
- Attract attention and intrigue investors and magazine editors
- Be easy to understand

Alice Banks's goal is to obtain funding from investors and a contract from the magazine. An effectively formatted Title Page will form a significant first impression for these readers.

ACTIVITY 2	## TITLE PAGE 1

You can create a Title Page in Harvard Graphics in two ways: with the Text Chart feature or on the Draw Screen. You choose the Draw Screen method when you want to move text around more easily than is possible with the Text Chart method.

For Lesson One you will create your entire Title Page in the Draw Screen so that you can learn how to manipulate text blocks and combine them with graphic symbols. You will use the Text Chart feature when you create a Bullet Chart in Lesson Two.

Four major steps are required to produce Title Page 1.

Step One:	Change Your Chart Orientation
Step Two:	Enter and Format Your Text
Step Three:	Enhance Your Title Page
Step Four:	Save and Print Your Title Page

Follow the step-by-step instructions in this Activity to reproduce Title Page 1 (see page 26). As you complete a function, place a check mark in the box that appears in the right-hand margin.

Change Your Chart Orientation

You can create a chart to display in either Landscape or Portrait orientation. In Landscape orientation, the chart appears in 11" × 8.5" format, while the Portrait orientation displays the chart in 8.5" × 11" format as illustrated:

Landscape
11" × 8.5"

Portrait
8.5" × 11"

The Photo Stop

Business Plan

Alice Banks
Sole Proprietor

By default, all Harvard Graphics charts and drawings are displayed in Landscape orientation. Because the Title Page you will create in Lesson One will be used as the first page of a document that will be printed in 8.5" × 11" format, you need to change your chart orientation from Landscape to Portrait.

Your first step is to access the Draw Screen.

Access Draw Screen

1.   At the Main Menu, press **3** for **Draw.**

You are now in the Harvard Graphics Draw Screen. On your left is the selection of drawing tools. You will use these tools to create and manipulate all the text and symbols on your Title Page.

Change Page Format

1.   Press **F8** for **Options.**
2.   Press **8** for **Appearance.**

The Appearance Menu appears. In this menu, you will change the Chart Orientation from Landscape to Portrait. Note that **Landscape** is currently displayed.

1.   Press **F3** for **Choices.**
2.   Press your ↓ arrow once to select **Portrait.**
3.   Press **Enter.**

Your Appearance Menu looks like this:

```
                                    Appearance Options

  Chart orientation:     *Landscape
  Chart proportions:     A  (8.5 in. x 11 in.)


  Chart palette:         C:\HG3\PALETTE\HG3.PL3
  Background drawing:
```

4.   Press **F10** to return to the Draw Screen.

Notice how your Draw Screen has narrowed to reflect the 8.5" × 11" Portrait format.

Chart Orientation Complete

The following functions require the use of the mouse. Remember to click the **left** button to perform functions and the **right** button to finish functions. If you click the right button twice, you may return to the Main Menu. If this happens, just press or click on **3** for **Draw** to return to your Draw Screen.

Enter and Format Your Text

Now you can use the Text Tool to enter, size, and position your Title, Document Type, and Author Information.

Title   Start with the Title.

1. Position your mouse on the **Text Tool** and click the **left** mouse button.

   Note that your mouse pointer now appears on the screen as a **+**.

2. Position the **+** in the upper left corner of your screen.
3. Click and hold your **left** mouse button and drag it all the way across your screen and down about 1.5".
4. Release your mouse button.

The Text Pop-up appears on the screen. You will type your Title in this box.

1. Type *The Photo Stop*. If you make a mistake, just press your backspace key to delete the error and then retype.
2. Press **F10** to exit the Pop-up and return to your Draw Screen.

> **NOTE:**   You can also click your **right** mouse button to exit the Text
> Pop-up.

Trouble Note    If you exit from the Pop-up and then notice that your text is incorrectly typed, *immediately* click on the **Undo Tool** located in the top left corner of your screen. You can then re-enter the text correctly.

Font Style   Your title appears quite small. However, before you adjust its size, you need to change the Font to Dutch 801.

1. Click on the **Pointer Tool** at the top of the tool box.

   Note that orange handles appear around your text block.

2. Move your mouse above the Draw Screen to the Text Attributes Pop-up.

3. Click on the **Font** box. The selection of available fonts appears.
4. Click on **Dutch 801.**
5. Now move your mouse to the **Style** box and click on the **Style** box.
6. Click on **Bold.**

> **NOTE:**   This font and style will remain Dutch 801 and Bold for any
> subsequent text blocks until you specify otherwise.

Title Size

Your next step is to enlarge your Title so that it extends across the top of your screen.

1. Click and *hold* your **left** mouse button on the bottom right handle of your Title.
2. Press **Shift** and, at the same time, drag your mouse to the opposite side of your screen.
3. Release the Shift key and left mouse button.

You press **Shift** when you size an object because you want to retain the correct proportions.

Title Position

1. Position your mouse in the middle of your Title.
2. Click and hold the **left** mouse button.
3. Move your mouse to center your Title at the top of the page.
4. Release your mouse button when you are satisfied with the position of your Title.

Compare your Title size and positioning to the following illustration:

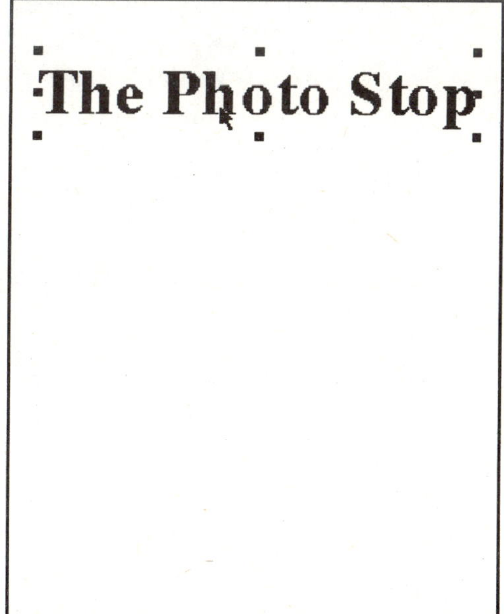

If you are satisfied with the size and position of your Title, click **right** to remove the orange handles and go on to enter your Document Type.

Title Size and Position Complete   ☐

Document Type   You need to enter, size, and position the Document Type next.

Text Enter   1. Click on the **Text Tool.**
2. Position the + slightly more than halfway down the page and at the left margin.
3. Click your **left** button and drag the mouse across and down to create a box.
4. At the Text Pop-up, type *Business Plan.*
5. Press **F10** to exit the Text Pop-up.

Size   Your next step is to enlarge *Business Plan.*

1. Click on the **Pointer Tool** to select your text.
2. Click and hold your **left** mouse button on the bottom right handle.
3. Press **Shift** and, at the same time, drag your mouse approximately 3" across the screen.
4. Release the Shift key and mouse button.

> **NOTE:**   Remember that you press **Shift** when you size an object because you want to retain the correct proportions.

Position   Adjust the positioning of *Business Plan* as follows:

1. Position your mouse in the middle of *Business Plan.*
2. Click and hold the **left** mouse button.
3. Move your mouse to position *Business Plan* so that it is centered about two-thirds of the way down the page as illustrated:

The Photo Stop

Business Plan

If you are satisfied with the size and position of *Business Plan,* click the **right** mouse button to remove the handles.

Document Type Complete

Author Text

Your last step is to enter the Author Text.

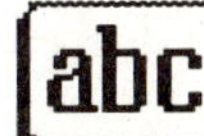

1. Click on the **Text Tool.**
2. Position the **+** at the bottom of the page and draw a box about 3" wide and 1" deep.
3. At the Text Pop-up, type *Alice Banks* and press **Enter.**
4. Now type *Sole Proprietor.*
5. Press **F10** to exit the Text Pop-up.

Center

You need to *center* the two lines of your Author Text.

1. Click on the **Pointer Tool** to select your text block.
2. Move your mouse up to the Text Attributes Pop-up. Note the arrows at the right.
3. Click on the **Down Arrow** to view the second of three Text Attributes "pages."
4. Click on the box that shows **centered** text as illustrated:

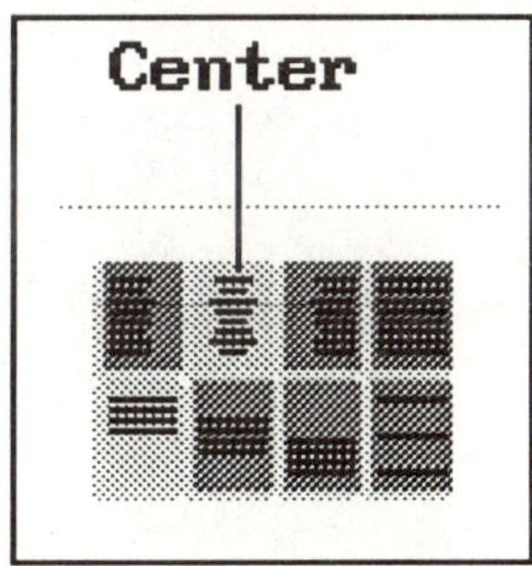

Position

You don't need to change the size of the Author Text. Just click on the text block and position it at the bottom center of your page.

When you are satisfied with the position of the Author Text, click **right** to remove the handles.

Author Text Complete

Enhance Your Title Page

Now all you need to do is get the preset picture (called a *symbol*) of the camera and then size and position it on your Title Page.

Get Camera Symbol

Your first step is to display the list of Symbol Directories so that you can retrieve the Camera Symbol.

1. Click your **left** mouse button on the **Symbol Tool.**
2. Click again on **Get.**
3. At the Symbol Files Screen, press **F8** to sort the Symbol Directories alphabetically.
4. Press your ↓ arrow until **COMNOBJ1** is highlighted.
5. Press **Enter** to see the symbols in the COMNOBJ1 Directory.
6. Click on the **Camera** Symbol.
7. Click on **F10** twice to return to your Draw Screen.

Camera Symbol Retrieved ☐

Size and Position Camera

Notice how your camera appears in the center of your Draw Screen. Your first step is to resize it slightly.

Size

1. Click and hold your **left** mouse button on the top left corner handle.
2. Press and hold the **Shift** key and drag the mouse down and to the right to slightly reduce the size of your camera.

Remember: You use the **Shift** key when you want to maintain the correct proportions of your symbol.

Position

1. Position your mouse anywhere on the camera *except* on one of the orange handles.
2. Click and hold the **left** button and then move your mouse to position your camera midway between the Title and the Document Type.
3. When you are satisfied with the position of your camera, click **right** to remove the handles.

Camera Symbol Sized and Positioned ☐

Save and Print Your Title Page

You will save your Title Page on your data disk and then access the Output command to print. You can then either exit from Harvard Graphics or get started on Activity 3.

Save

1. Press **F6** for **File** and **E** for **Exit to Main Menu.**
2. Press **4** for **File.**
3. Press **4** for **Save Chart.**

The Save Chart Menu appears. Your cursor is currently positioned next to **Filename.** The default Directory (usually C:\HG3\DATA) is displayed. You will save your file on a data disk in Drive A or B (depending on your system).

1. Press your ↑ arrow to position your cursor on the Directory.
2. Type *a:\ or b:* and then press **Delete** to erase the old Directory.
3. Press **Enter.** Your cursor is now opposite **Filename.**

4. Type *Title1* and press **Enter.**

> **NOTE:** Do not press the space bar between *Title* and *1*. Filenames
> may consist of up to eight letters with no spaces.

5. At **Description**, type *Title Page #1: Lesson 1.* You can type the description as you would any block of text.

Compare your Save Chart Screen with the following illustration:

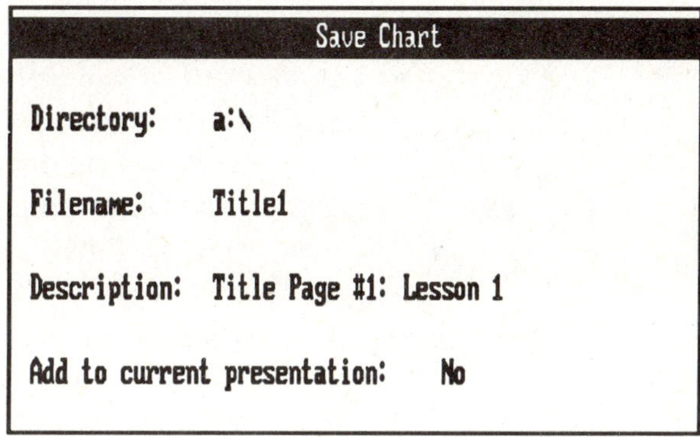

6. Press **F10** to save and return to the Main Menu.

> **NOTE:** If the problem message *"Insert diskette in Drive A (or B)"*
> appears, just press **Enter.**

Title Page 1 Saved

Turn on your printer and print your Title Page as follows:

Print   1. Press **5** for **Output.**
2   Press **Enter** to accept **Printer 1.**
3. Press **F2** to view how your document will appear in printed form.

> **NOTE:** If you do not like the look of your Title Page, press **ESC** to
> return to the Main Menu and **3** for **Draw** to return to your
> Draw Screen. Resize and position your text and objects as required.

4. If you are satisfied with the look of your Title Page, press **F10** twice to accept the Default Settings.

The Output to Printer Screen appears:

```
┌─────────────────────────────────┐
│        Output To Printer        │
│                                 │
│   Page: 1      Copy: 1   of 1   │
│                                 │
│        Press Esc to cancel      │
└─────────────────────────────────┘
```

Your Title Page has now been sent to the printer. Wait until the above screen disappears and you are returned to your Main Menu.

Title Page 1 Printed   ☐

You now have three options:

- Exit Harvard Graphics if you are finished with your learning session.
- Clear the current drawing.
- Keep Title Page 1 on the Draw Screen and begin Title Page 2. After making your changes to Title Page 1, you will save Title Page 2 under a different name so that Title Page 1 remains unaffected by the new changes.

Exit Harvard Graphics

1. At the Main Menu, press **E** to exit Harvard Graphics.

Clear the Current Chart

1. At the Main Menu, press **1** for **Create Chart.**
2. Press **8** for **Clear Chart.**

Keep Title Page 1 on Screen

If you choose this option, you can continue immediately to Activity 3. Omit the Get Title1 from Disk section under Edit Your Text and press **3** at the Main Menu before starting with Edit Title Page Text.

ACTIVITY 3   TITLE PAGE 2

Three major steps are required to produce Title Page 2.

Step One:	Edit Your Text
Step Two:	Add a New Symbol
Step Three:	Save and Print Your Chart

Follow these step-by-step instructions to edit and enhance your Title Page as illustrated on page 35. Remember to place a check mark in the box next to each function you complete.

Edit Your Text

Get Title1 from Disk

If you have exited out of Harvard Graphics and are starting fresh at your Main Menu, bring Title1 (saved on your data disk) to the screen as follows:

The Photo Stop

Proposal
Nature First Magazine

Alice Banks
Sole Proprietor

1. Press **4** for **File** and **1** for **Get Chart.** Either the default HG3 Data Direc-
    tory or your data drive appears on screen.
2. If necessary, type the letter of your data disk drive (*a:* or *b:*) over the
    current Directory and press **Delete** to erase the extra letters.
3. Press **Enter.**
4. At the list of files on your data disk, choose **Title1** and press **Enter** twice.

If you have not exited out of Harvard Graphics, press **3** for **Draw.**

Edit Title Page Text Your first step is to replace *Business Plan* with *Proposal/Nature First Magazine.*

Select the Edit Tool
1. Click on **Business Plan** to select it.
2. Click on the **Edit Text Tool.**

3. Click again on the **Edit** box. The Text Pop-up with *Business Plan* entered
    appears.
4. Press your **Delete** key to erase *Business Plan.*

Enter New Text
1. Type *Proposal.*
2. Press **Enter.**
3. Type *Nature First Magazine.*

Mark Text You want *Nature First Magazine* to appear in italics. To make only a portion
of the text in a text block appear in a different style, you use the **F5 Mark
Text** feature.

> **NOTE:** Marking text is easier to do with the cursor keys than with the
> mouse. Therefore, use your keyboard to highlight the text and
> then use your mouse to click on the Font and Font Style
> boxes.

1. Press your ← arrow to position your cursor under the "N" in *Nature.*
2. Press **F5.**
3. Press your → arrow until the entire second line is highlighted.
4. Click on the **Font Style** box above your Draw Screen.
5. Click on **Italic.**
6. Press **F10** twice to exit the Text Pop-up and Edit mode and to return to
    your Draw Screen.

Text Edit Complete

Center Text
1. Click on the **Pointer Tool** to select your text block.
2. Move your mouse to the Text Attributes Pop-up above your Screen.
3. Click on the **Down Arrow** symbol at the right to view the second of three
    "pages" in the Text Attributes Menu.

Note that the second "page" of options appears.

4. Click on the box that shows centered text.

Size Text
1. Click and hold your **left** mouse button on the bottom right handle.
2. Press **Shift** and, at the same time, drag your mouse up and to the right to reduce the size.
3. Release the mouse button and Shift key.

Remember: You press **Shift** when you size an object because you want to retain the correct proportions.

Position Text   Adjust the positioning of your text block as follows:

1. Position your mouse in the middle of the text block.
2. Click and hold the **left** mouse button.
3. Move your mouse to position your text block so that it is centered about two-thirds of the way down the page.
4. Release the mouse button.

Compare your screen to the following illustration:

If you are satisfied with the size and positioning of your text block, click the **right** mouse button to remove the handles.

Text Sized and Positioned   □

Add a New Symbol

Now all you need to do is display the Tree Symbol and place it in the camera lens.

Get Tree Symbol   Your first step is to access the Symbol Directories to retrieve the Tree Symbol.

1. Click your **left** mouse button on the **Symbol Tool.**
2. Click again on **Get.**
3. At the Symbol Files Screen, press **F8** to sort the Symbol Directories alphabetically.
4. Click on **ANIPLANT.**
5. Click on the **Cypress Tree** Symbol.
6. Click on **F10** twice to return to your Draw Screen.

Size and Position Tree   Notice how your tree appears in the center of your Draw Screen. Your first step is to make it small enough to fit into your camera lens.

Size

1. Click on the bottom left corner handle and use the **Shift** key to make your tree about .5" square.

> **NOTE:**   Remember that you use the **Shift** key when you want to maintain the correct proportions of your symbol.

2. Position your mouse anywhere on the tree *except* on one of the orange handles.
3. Click **left** and move your tree until it is in the middle of your camera lens.

Zoom

You will now need to resize your tree to ensure it fits exactly in the middle of the camera lens. To simplify the task of positioning the tree in the middle of the camera lens, you will access the Zoom feature.

1. Click on the **Zoom Tool** (located in the top left corner of your screen). Your screen appears as illustrated:

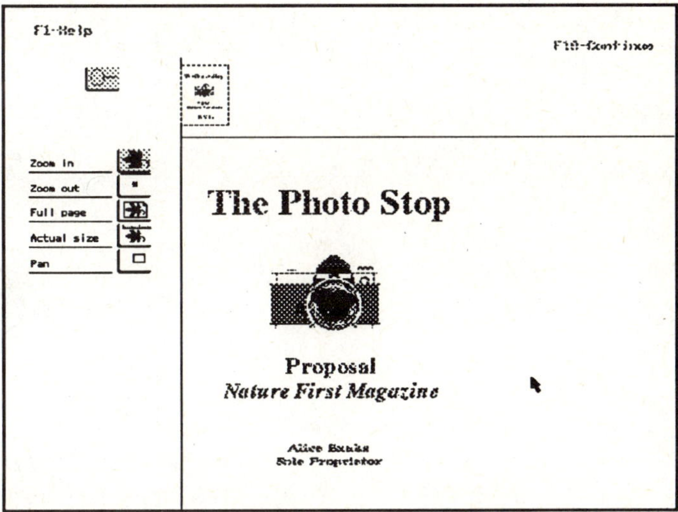

2. Click on the **Zoom In** box. Your pointer is replaced by a **+.**
3. Position the + above and to the left of the camera.
4. Click and hold your **left** mouse button and drag the mouse down and to the right to draw a box around the camera and tree.
5. Click **right** to return to the Draw Screen.

You have now "zoomed in" on the camera and tree as illustrated:

Resize and Reposition Tree
1. Click your **left** mouse button on one of the corner handles and use the **Shift** key to reduce the size of your tree so that it will fit in the center of the camera lens.
2. Reposition the tree as required.

Exit Zoom
1. Click on the **Zoom Tool.**
2. Click on the **Full Page** box. Your screen returns to the full page format.

Compare your Title Page to the following illustration and then click **right** to remove the handles.

The Photo Stop

Proposal
Nature First Magazine

Alice Banks
Sole Proprietor

Tree Symbol Sized and Positioned ☐

Save and Print Your Title Page

You will save your Title Page on your data disk and then choose the Output command to print. You can then either exit from Harvard Graphics or get started on creating your own Title Page in Activity 4.

Save

1. Press **F6** for **File** and then **E** for **Exit to Main Menu.**
2. Press **4** for **File** and then **4** for **Save Chart.**

The Save Chart Menu appears. Your cursor is currently positioned next to **Filename.** Either the default Directory (usually C:\HG3\DATA) or your data Drive A or B will be displayed.

1. If necessary, type *a:* or *b:* and then press **Delete** to erase the old Directory.
2. Press **Enter.**
3. At **Filename,** type *Title2* and press **Enter.**
4. At **Description,** type *Title Page #2: Lesson 1.*
5. Press **F10** to return to the Main Menu.

Title Page 2 Saved ☐

Print

1. Press **5** for **Output.**
2. Press **Enter** to accept **Printer 1.**
3. Press **F2** to view how your document will appear in printed form.
4. If you are satisfied with the look of your Title Page, press **F10** twice to accept the Default Settings.

> **NOTE:** If you do not like the look of your Title Page, press **ESC** to
> return to the Main Menu and **3** for **Draw** to return to your
> Draw Screen. Resize and position your text and objects as re-
> quired.

The Output to Printer Screen appears. Your Title Page has now been sent to
the printer. Wait until the Output to Printer Screen disappears and you are returned to the Main Menu.

Title Page 2 Printed   ☐

You now have two options:

- Exit Harvard Graphics if you are finished with your learning session.
- Clear the current drawing and get started on Activity 4.

Exit Harvard Graphics   1. At the Main Menu, press **E** to exit Harvard Graphics.

Clear the Current Chart   1. Press **1** for **Create Chart.**
                              2. Press **8** for **Clear Chart.**

ACTIVITY 4   CHALLENGE ASSIGNMENT

Read through the following sections for suggestions on content and then adapt
the instructions given for your own material. Use the boxes provided to record
information about your Title Page.

The Challenge Assignment requires three major steps.

Step One: Determine Your Document Type
Step Two: Write your Title Page Information
Step Three: Create and Format Your Title Page

Determine Your Document Type

First, determine the type of document or presentation that requires a Title
Page. Choices include an annual report, a proposal, a business plan, a sales
presentation, or even a term project. If your Title Page refers to a company, be
sure you include the company name.

<table>
<tr><td>

Type of Document or Presentation:

Name of Company:

</td></tr>
</table>

Write Your Title Page Information

The text you include in your Title Page should be very clear and easy to understand. Avoid cluttering the page with long titles or irrelevant information. Your aim is to intrigue your readers, not overwhelm them.

Three main blocks of information are required.

- Title
- Subtitle: Document or Presentation Type
- Author

Title Summarize the subject of your report, proposal, presentation, etc., in as few words as possible. Think of advertising slogans—generally, they use no more than five words to powerfully convey their message.

Enter the Title of your document/presentation subject.

<table>
<tr><td>

Title:

</td></tr>
</table>

Subtitle Your subtitle should specify the *type* of document or presentation your Title Page introduces—for example, a market analysis, proposal, business plan, sales presentation, etc. Your aim is to prepare your readers for the information that lies ahead.

Specify the type of document/presentation your Title Page will precede.

<table>
<tr><td>

Type of Document:

</td></tr>
</table>

Author In addition to your name as author of the report, you will probably need to include one or two additional pieces of information that either identify you further or specify the recipient of your document or the audience for your presentation.

For example, a Title Page for an academic report would include the course title, section, and the instructor's name. If your Title Page introduces a proposal on behalf of a company, you will generally include your position title and the name of your company.

Just remember to limit the author identification to the bare essentials.

Author Information:

Create and Format Your Title Page

Refer to the selection of commands and functions that follows to help you create and format your Title Page.

Experiment with the size and position of the various elements in your Title Page until you are sure it introduces your document or presentation in an eye-catching and professional manner.

Enter the Draw Screen   At the Main Menu, press **3** for **Draw.**

Portrait Format
1. Press **F8** for **Options** and **8** for **Appearance.**
2. Press **F3** for **Choices** and select **Portrait.**

Enter Text
1. Click on the **Text Tool.**
2. Position the **+** at the top left corner of where you want your text to appear.
3. Click **left** and draw a box for your text.
4. At the Text Pop-up, type your text and press **F10.**

Change Fonts/Attributes
1. Select the text block by either clicking on the **Pointer,** if you have just exited from the Text Pop-up, or by clicking on the text block itself.
2. Move your mouse up to the Text Attributes Pop-up at the top of your screen.
3. Click on the attribute you wish to change; for example, font, size, alignment, etc.

> **NOTE:** The Text Attributes Pop-up consists of three "pages." To access the other two pages, click on the ▼ symbol at the top right of your screen. Note that you can also enclose your text with a box. Simply click on the **T** that is enclosed in a box and then choose your box style from the options provided.

Size Text
1. Click on the **Pointer Tool** to select your text.
2. Click and hold your **left** mouse button on the bottom right handle.

3. Press **Shift** and drag your mouse to the size required.

You press **Shift** when you size text or objects because you want to retain the correct proportions.

Position Text

1. Position your mouse anywhere on the text block *except* on one of the orange handles.
2. Click **left** and move your text.

Get Symbol

1. Click on the **Symbol Tool** and again on **Get.**
2. At the Symbol Directory, choose the appropriate Directory, click on the symbol you want, and then click on **F10** twice to return to your Draw Screen.

Zoom

Use Zoom to help you make precise adjustments to small objects.

1. Click on the **Zoom Tool.**
2. Click on the **Zoom In** box.
3. Draw a box around the portion of your drawing you wish to expand.
4. Click your **right** mouse button to return to the Draw Screen.
5. To exit Zoom, click on the **Zoom Tool**, and click again on the **Full Page** box.

Save

Press **F6** for **File** and then **2** for **Save Chart.** Change to the Directory in which you wish to save your file (usually Drive A or B) and then type a file-name for your Title Page.

Fast Save: Press **Ctrl + S** to bypass the Main Menu.

Print

1. Press **F6** and **E** to exit to the Main Menu.
2. At the Main Menu, press **5** for **Output**, press **Enter** to accept **Printer 1**, and then press **F10**.

Clear Chart

If you wish to start a new chart and have saved your current chart, first press **F6** and **E** for **Exit.** Now choose **1** for **Create Chart** and then **8** for **Clear Chart.** If you haven't saved your current chart, a message will appear. You can then press **ESC** to save your chart before clearing it. If you do not wish to save your chart, press **F10**.

Exit Harvard Graphics

Press **F6** and **E** for **Exit to Main Menu** and then **E** again to exit the program.

ACTIVITY 5   LESSON ONE REVIEW

Test your understanding of the functions and concepts you learned in Lesson One by completing the following Review Questions:

1. What are the three principal components of a Title Page?
2. How do you change your page orientation to Portrait format?
3. How many "pages" are available in the Text Attributes Pop-up in the Draw Screen?
4. How do you enter text in Draw?
5. Describe how to position a text block in Draw.
6. How do you delete a block of text?
7. What is the purpose of the Mark Text feature?
8. What are the fast save keys? (Refer to page 44 in Activity 4.)
9. How do you clear an existing chart or drawing so you can start work on a new chart?
10. Describe how to print a chart or drawing.

SUPPLEMENTARY EXERCISES

Exercise 1 Create a Title Page in Portrait format for the annual report of a mail-order office supply company. You determine the name of the company and the author information. Add symbols as appropriate.

Exercise 2 Adapt the Title Page you created in Exercise 1 for a sales presentation to a major client. Change the text fonts, style, and alignment and change the chart orientation to Landscape. Add new symbols or combine the symbols used for Exercise 1 in a different way.

<table>
<tr><td>LESSON TWO</td><td># BULLET CHART</td></tr>
</table>

FEATURES

- Creating a Bullet Chart
- Adding Secondary Bullets
- Changing Fonts and Attributes
- Changing Bullet Options
- Adding a Background
- Creating and Shading a Box

INTRODUCTION

In Lesson 2, you will learn how to use the Text Chart feature to create a Bullet Chart. Here are the lesson activities.

ACTIVITY 1: Determine the information required for your Bullet Chart.

ACTIVITY 2: Follow the instructions given to create the Bullet Chart on page 49.

ACTIVITY 3: Follow the instructions given to draw a shaded box under your Chart Title/Subtitle and to add a background as illustrated on page 57.

ACTIVITY 4: Create a Bullet Chart based on your own information.

ACTIVITY 5: Complete the Lesson Review Questions on Bullet Chart creation and enhancement.

ACTIVITY 1   BULLET CHART INFORMATION

You use a Bullet Chart to convey important information in point or list form. For the reader, an effectively formatted Bullet Chart should provide an easy-to-understand summary of the vital points made in a presentation, lecture, or report.

Here are just some of the many uses for the Bullet Chart.

- Outline for a sales presentation
- Agenda for a meeting
- Major points to be covered in a lecture or seminar
- Overview of the major points in a report

Bullet Definition   The term *bullet* refers to the symbol placed at the beginning of each item in a list. The most common type of bullet is the black dot. Harvard Graphics also provides a number of other bullet symbols as illustrated:

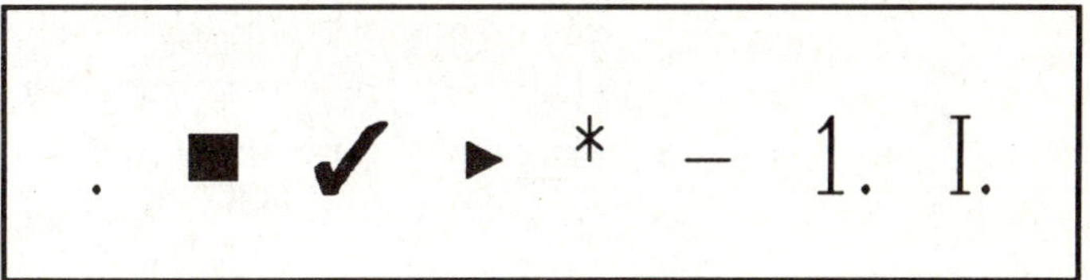

Bullet Chart Information   Three blocks of information are typically required for a Bullet Chart.

- Title
- Subtitle
- List of Items

Note, however, that not all Bullet Charts must include a title and subtitle. You can often choose to omit the title and subtitle and include only the list of items.

Here is an example of a Bullet Chart that includes both a title and a subtitle and lists the major points to be covered in a travel lecture on climbing in North America.

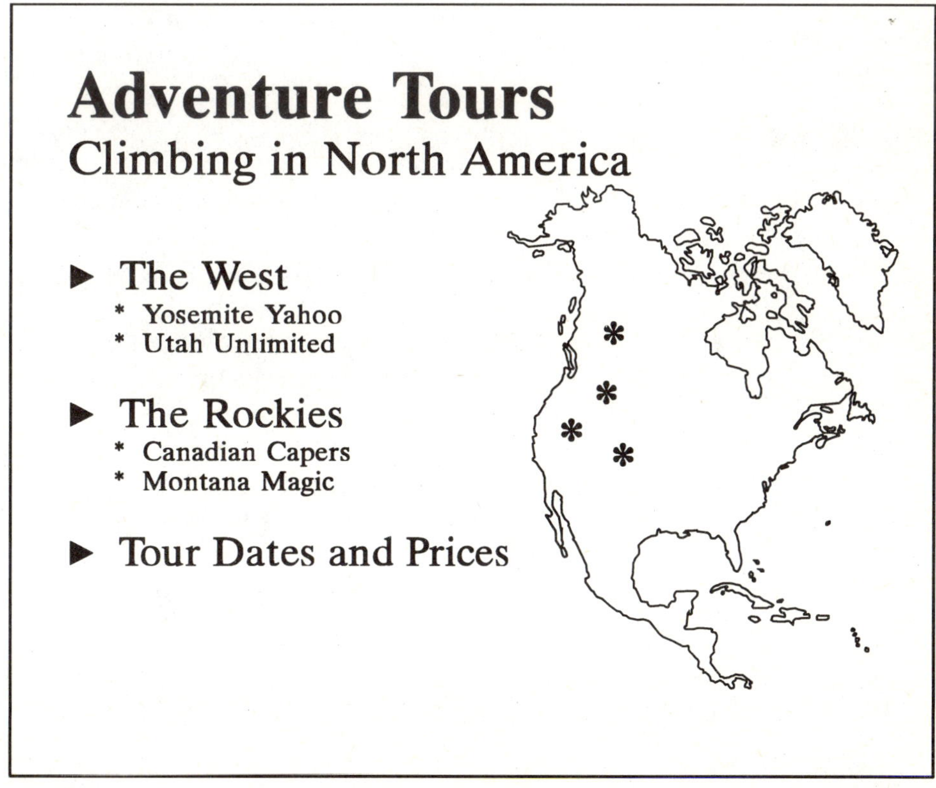

Note that the points to be covered in the lecture evoke the exciting materials to come in a short and easy-to-understand format. The goal of an effective

Bullet Chart is to give your readers a quick overview—a blueprint of your subject that emphasizes the main points.

Summary of Activities 2 and 3

Joan Martin, president of Greenart Landscaping, plans to use the Bullet Charts you create for Activities 2 and 3 as part of a sales presentation to potential clients. She requires charts that convey information about her presentation in a clear and simple format that communicates the professional approach she takes to marketing her landscaping services.

For Activity 2, you will create a chart listing the four major points to be covered in the Greenart Landscaping sales presentation.

In Activity 3, you will present just two of the four major points along with secondary points that highlight important information about Greenart's services. You will then add a preset background drawing and use the Harvard Graphics Draw feature to place a shaded box under the Title/Subtitle.

ACTIVITY 2   BULLET CHART 1

Three major steps are required to produce Bullet Chart 1.

Step One: Create Your Bullet Chart
Step Two: Enhance Your Bullet Chart
Step Three: Save and Print Your Bullet Chart

Follow the step-by-step instructions to reproduce Bullet Chart 1 (see page 49). As you progress through the lesson, remember to place a check mark in the box next to each function you complete.

Create Your Bullet Chart

You will first create your Bullet Chart and then enter the Title and Subtitle and the information for each bulleted point.

Create Chart

1. At the Main Menu, press **1** for **Create Chart.**
2. Press **1** for **Text Chart.**
3. Press **2** for **Bullet Chart.**

The Bullet Chart Data Form appears. Note that your cursor is currently next to **Title.**

GREENART LANDSCAPING
Sales Presentation
▲ Service Description
▲ Customer Profile
▲ Area Considerations
▲ Price Options

```
                                    Bullet Chart
   F1-Help           F2-Show chart                   F4-Draw         F5-Mark
   F6-Main Menu      F7-Spell/Text   F8-Options       F9-Edit bullet  F10-Continue

   Title:        ←————————  [Cursor Position]
   Subtitle:
   Footnote:
```

Enter Title/Subtitle

1. Type the Title of your Bullet Chart in all caps: *GREENART LANDSCAP-ING*. Press **Enter.**
2. Now type the Subtitle of your Bullet Chart in upper/lower case: *Sales Presentation*. Press **Enter** twice.

Title/Subtitle Complete

> **NOTE:**   If you make a typing error, press Backspace or the Delete key
> to erase the error, and then retype the correct characters.

Bullet Data

Your cursor should be positioned *under* the Title/Subtitle line. If not, press **Enter.** Note that a dot for your first bullet point appears on the screen.

Bullet 1

1. Type *Service Description.*
2. Press **Enter** twice.

The second bullet appears.

Bullets 2–4

Type the following three bullets. Remember to press **Enter** twice after each entry *except* the last entry.

- *Customer Profile* (**Enter** twice)
- *Area Considerations* (**Enter** twice)
- *Price Options*

Bullet Data Complete

Enhance Your Bullet Chart

Your Bullet Chart contains all the required text. Here's what you need to do next.

Required Enhancements

> → Modify the Text Attributes:
> - Change the Text Size
> - Change the Text Font and Style
>
> → Change the Bullet Options:
> - Change the Bullet Type
> - Change the Bullet Size
> - Change the Bullet Alignment
>
> → Enhance the Chart Appearance:
> - Change the Region Frame Style for the Title/Subtitle and the Bullet Text

Text Attributes

1. Press **F8** for **Options.**
2. Press **2** for **Text Attributes.**

The Text Attributes Menu appears. Note that your cursor is currently resting under the **9** in the **Size** column next to **Title.**

Text Size

1. Press your ↓ arrow once so that your cursor rests on the **5** next to **Subtitle 1.**
2. Type 7.

Title Font/Style

1. Press your ↑ arrow once and press **Tab** three times to move your cursor into the **Font Name** column opposite **Title.**
2. Press **F3** for **Choices.**
3. Cursor up to **Dutch 801** and press **Enter.**
4. Press **Tab** once to move to the **Font Style** column.
5. Press **F3** for **Choices.**
6. Cursor up to **Bold** and press **Enter.**

Subtitle and Bullet Text Font Fast Method

Now use the fast method to change the text font for the Subtitle and Bullet Text:

1. Press your ↓ and ← arrows to move your cursor into the **Font Name** column opposite **Subtitle1.**
2. Press **D** for **Dutch 801.**
3. Now press your ↓ arrow to move your cursor opposite **Bullet Text.**
4. Press **D** for **Dutch 801** again. Compare your screen with the following illustration:

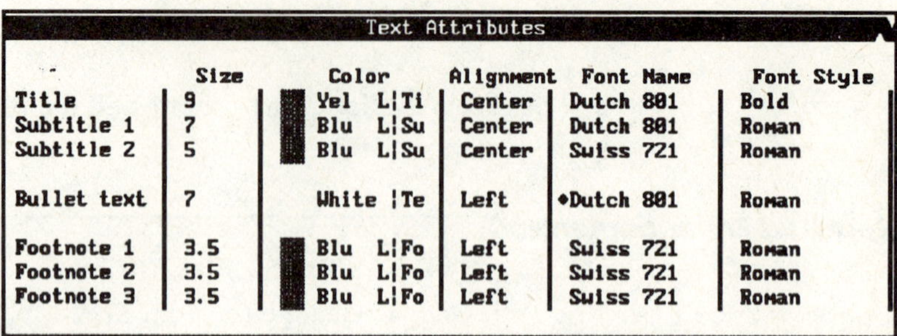

5. Press **F10** to return to your Chart Edit Screen.

Text Attributes Complete

Bullet Options

You now need to change your bullet style from ● to ▶, your bullet size to large, and the vertical alignment of your bullets to middle. You make all of these changes in the Bullet Options Menu.

1. Press **F8** for **Options.**
2. Press **5** for **Bullet Options.**

The Bullet Options Menu appears. Your cursor is next to **Bullet Type.** Make the following changes.

Bullet Type

1. Press **F3** for **Choices.**
2. Cursor to the ▶ character and press **Enter.**

Bullet Size

1. Press your ↓ arrow once to move opposite **Bullet Size.**
2. Press **F3** for **Choices.**
3. Cursor to **Large** and press **Enter.**

Vertical Alignment

You want your Bullet Text to be vertically aligned to the center or middle of your page.

1. Press your ↓ arrow to move opposite **Vertical Alignment.**
2. Press **F3** for **Choices.**
3. Cursor to **Middle** and press **Enter.** Compare your screen to the following illustration.

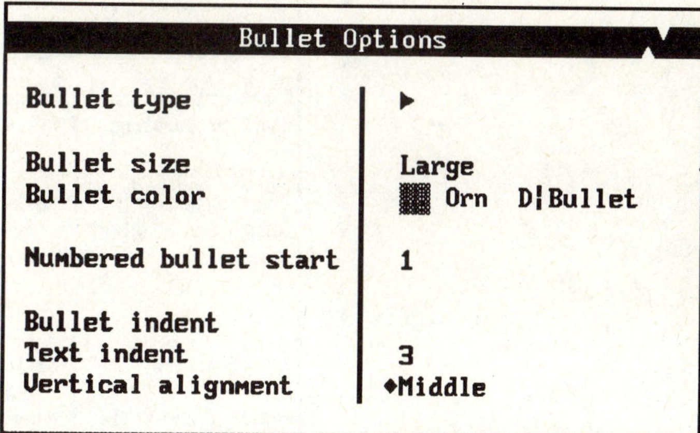

4. Press **F10** to return to your Chart Edit Screen.

Bullet Options Complete

Enhance Chart Appearance

You now need to access the Appearance Menu in F8 Options so that you can specify "no frame" around the Title/Subtitle and a rounded frame around the Bullet Text. First, access the Appearance Menu.

1. Press **F8** for **Options.**
2. Press **3** for **Appearance.**

Title Region Frame Style

1. Press your ↓ arrow to position your cursor next to **Region Frame Style** in the **Titles** column. **Line** is currently highlighted.
2. Press **F3** for **Choices.**
3. Press your ↑ arrow until **None** is highlighted and press **Enter.**

Bullet Text Frame Style

1. Press your → arrow to position your cursor next to **Region Frame Style** in the **Bullet Text** column.
2. Press **F3** for **Choices.**
3. Cursor to **Rounded** and press **Enter.** Your Appearance Menu should look like this:

```
┌──────────────────────────────────────────────────────────────────┐
│                       Appearance Options                          ▲│
│                                                                    │
│  Chart orientation    Landscape                                    │
│  Chart proportions    A  (8.5 in. x 11 in.)                        │
│                                                                    │
│                                                                    │
│  Chart palette:       C:\HG3\PALETTE\HG3.PL3                        │
│  Background drawing:                                               │
│                                                                    │
│                                                                    │
│                        Titles        Bullet text      Footnotes    │
│                    ┌────────────┬────────────────┬────────────┐    │
│  Text overflow     │Shrink-to-fit│Shrink-to-fit  │Shrink-to-fit│   │
│                    │             │               │             │   │
│  Region frame style│None         │◆Rounded       │None         │   │
│  Frame outline color│   Blu  |Lines│   Blu  |Lines│   Blu  |Lines│  │
│  Frame fill color  │▓ Gry DD|Frame│▓ Gry DD|Frame│▓ Gry DD|Frame│  │
│                    └────────────┴────────────────┴────────────┘    │
└──────────────────────────────────────────────────────────────────┘
```

4. Press **F10** to return to your Chart Edit Screen.

Chart Appearance Enhanced ☐

Display Chart ▶ Press **F2** to display your Chart. To return to your Chart Edit Screen, press
Enter.

Save and Print Your Bullet Chart

You will save your Bullet Chart on your data disk and then choose the Output
command to print your Chart. Once you are satisfied with your Chart, you can
either exit from Harvard Graphics or get started on Activity 3.

Save 1. Press **F6** for **Main Menu.**
2. Press **4** for **File** and then **4** for **Save Chart.**

The Save Chart Menu appears. Your cursor is currently positioned next to
Filename. The default Directory (usually C:\HG3\DATA\) is displayed. You
will save your file on a data disk in Drive A or B.

1. Press your ↑ arrow to position your cursor next to **Directory.**
2. Type *a:* or *b:* and then press **Delete** to erase the old Directory.
3. Press **Enter.**
4. At **Filename** type *Bulchrt1* and press **Enter.**
5. At **Description** type *Bullet Chart #1: Lesson 2.*

```
┌──────────────────────────────────────────────┐
│                  Save Chart                    │
├──────────────────────────────────────────────┤
│  Directory:      a:\                            │
│                                                 │
│  Filename:       Bulchrt1                       │
│                                                 │
│  Description:    Bullet Chart #1: Lesson 2      │
│                                                 │
│  Add to current presentation: No                │
│                                                 │
│  Auto-Build:   No                               │
└──────────────────────────────────────────────┘
```

6.   Press **F10** to save and return to the Chart Edit Screen.

Bullet Chart 1 Saved

Print
1.   Press **F6** for **Main Menu.**
2.   Press **5** for **Output.**
3.   Press **Enter** to accept **Printer 1.**
4.   Press **F2** to view how your document will appear in printed form.

> **NOTE:** If you do not like the look of your Chart, press **ESC** to return
> to the Main Menu and **2** for **Edit Chart.** You can then press
> **F8 Options** to change your Chart's **Appearance (3)** or **Bullet
> Options (5).**

When you are satisfied with the look of your Chart, continue as follows:

5.   Press **F10** twice to accept the Default Settings.

The Output to Printer Screen appears. Your Bullet Chart has now been sent to
the printer. Wait until the Output to Printer Screen disappears and you are returned to your Chart Edit Screen.

Bullet Chart 1 Printed

You now have three options:

- Exit Harvard Graphics if you are finished with your learning session.
- Clear the current chart.
- Keep the Bullet Chart 1 Edit Screen and begin Bullet Chart 2. After making
  your changes to Bullet Chart 1, you will save Bullet Chart 2 under a different name. Bullet Chart 1 will therefore remain unaffected by the new
  changes.

Exit Harvard Graphics
1.   Press **F6** for **Main Menu** and **E** to exit Harvard Graphics.

Clear the Current Chart
1. Press **F6** for **Main Menu**.
2. Press **1** for **Create Chart.**
3. Press **8** for **Clear Chart.**

Keep Bullet Chart 1 on Screen
If you choose this option, you can continue immediately to Activity 3. Omit Get Bulchrt1 from Disk and start with Edit Bullet Text.

ACTIVITY 3   BULLET CHART 2

Three major steps are required to produce Bullet Chart 2:

Step One: Edit your Chart Data
Step Two: Enhance Your Chart
Step Three: Save and Print Your Chart

Follow the step-by-step instructions to edit and enhance your Bullet Chart (see page 57). Remember to place a check mark in the box next to each function you complete.

Edit Your Chart Data

Get Bulchrt1 from Disk
If you have exited out of Harvard Graphics and are starting fresh at your Main Menu, bring Bulchrt1 (saved on your data disk) to the screen as follows:

1. Press **4** for **File** and **1** for **Get Chart.** Either the default HG3 Data Directory or your data drive appears on screen.
2. If necessary, type the letter of your data disk drive (*a*:\ or *b*:\) over the current Directory and press **Delete** to erase the extra letters.
3. Press **Enter.**
4. At the list of files on your data disk, choose **Bulchrt1** and press **Enter** to access the Bullet Chart Edit Screen.

Edit Bullet Text
Joan Martin, president of Greenart Landscaping, requires a Bullet Chart with only two bullets: Service Description and Area Considerations. She will then add two subpoints (called *secondary bullets*) to each of the two main bullets.

Secondary Bullets for *Service Description*
First insert the secondary bullets under *Service Description.*

To insert Secondary Bullet 1:

1. Position your cursor one line below the "S" in *Service Description.*
2. Press **Ctrl + Ins** to insert one line.
3. Press **Ctrl + B** to access the Special Characters Pop- up.
4. Cursor to the √ character and press **Enter.**

GREENART LANDSCAPING
Sales Presentation

► **Service Description**
√ Landscape Design
√ Maintenance Contracts

► **Area Considerations**
√ Lakeshore District
√ Mountain Heights District

5. Press your space bar twice and type *Landscape Design.*
6. Press **Enter.**

To insert Secondary Bullet 2:

1. Press **Ctrl + B.**
2. The √ character is already highlighted. Press **Enter.**
3. Press your space bar twice and type *Maintenance Contracts.*
4. Press **Enter.**

Delete *Customer Profile*   1. Press **Ctrl + Del** to delete *Customer Profile.*

Secondary Bullets for *Area Considerations*   Now insert the secondary bullets under *Area Considerations.*

To insert Secondary Bullet 1:

1. Position your cursor one line below the "A" in *Area Considerations.*
2. Press **Ctrl + Ins** to insert one line.
3. Press **Ctrl + B** and **Enter.**
4. Press your space bar twice and type *Lakeshore District.*
5. Press **Enter.**

To insert Secondary Bullet 2:

1. Press **Ctrl + B** and **Enter.**
2. Press your space bar twice and type *Mountain Heights District.*
3. Press **Enter**.

Delete *Price Options*   1. Press **Ctrl + Del** to delete *Price Options.*

Your Chart Edit Screen should look like this:

```
BULCHRT1.CH3                        Bullet Chart
 F1-Help          F2-Shou chart                   F4-Drau       F5-Mark
 F6-Main Menu     F7-Spell/Text  F8-Options       F9-Edit bullet F18-Continue

Title:     GREENART LANDSCAPING
Subtitle:  Sales Presentation
Footnote:

       ►  Service Description
          √  Landscape Design
          √  Maintenance Contracts

       ►  Area Considerations
          √  Lakeshore District
          √  Mountain Heights District
```

Bullet Text Edited

Enhance Your Bullet Chart

Required Enhancements

To enhance your Bullet Chart, you will first make changes in the Chart Edit Screen to the Chart's Appearance and Text Attributes. Then you will access Draw to add the final formatting touches. Start with the Chart Edit changes.

> → Enhance the Chart Appearance:
> - Add a preset background of shaded falling leaves
> - Change the Chart Palette to match the new background
> - Change the Region Frame Style and Fill for the Bullet Text
> → Change the Title/Subtitle Alignment

Enhance Chart Appearance

First access the Appearance Menu.

1. Press **F8** for **Options.**
2. Press **3** for **Appearance.**

Background Drawing

1. Press your ↓ arrow to position your cursor opposite **Background Drawing.**
2. Press **F3** for **Choices.**

The Harvard Graphics Directory containing the preset background drawings appears.

> **NOTE:** You may need to change the Directory from A to C. Place your cursor opposite Directory, type *C:\HG3\DATA* (or the Directory you've designated for Harvard Graphics) and press **Enter.**

1. Cursor to **LEAVES.CH3.**

> **NOTE:** To the right of the LEAVES.CH3 filename, you will see the message: *"Use 7 or 7SH.PL3."* This message refers to the best Chart Palette to use with the LEAVES background. A *palette* is the color combinations Harvard Graphics uses on a screen. The 7 and 7SH.PL3 palettes will suit the Leaves background because they include more gray tones than the default palette.

2. Press **Enter** to accept the **LEAVES.CH3** filename.

Chart Palette

1. Press your ↑ arrow to position your cursor next to **Chart Palette.**
2. Press **F3** for **Choices.**

3. Cursor to **7.PL3** and press **Enter**.

Display Chart ▶ Press **F2** to display your Chart. Notice how the background drawing gives the chart an interesting look that reflects the nature concerns of Greenart Landscaping. Press **Enter** to return to the Appearance Options Screen.

Bullet Text Frame Style

1. Press your ↓ and → arrows to position your cursor next to **Region Frame Style** in the **Bullet Text** column.
2. Press **F3** for **Choices**.
3. Press your ↑ arrow to highlight **Plain** and press **Enter**.

Bullet Text Frame Fill

1. Press your ↓ arrow to move opposite **Frame Fill Color**.
2. Press **F3** for **Choices**.
3. Select **Blue** and press **Enter**. Your Appearance Menu should look like this:

4. Press **F10** to return to your Bullet Chart Edit Screen.

Chart Appearance Enhanced   ☐

Change Title/Subtitle Alignment

In Bullet Chart 2, you will change the alignment of the Title and Subtitle to left.

Title

1. Press **F8** for **Options**.
2. Press **2** for **Text Attributes**.
3. Press **Tab** twice to position your cursor in the **Alignment** column opposite **Title**.
4. Press **F3** for **Choices**.
5. Select **Left** and press **Enter**.

Subtitle

1. Press your ↓ arrow once. Your cursor is now positioned in the **Alignment** column opposite **Subtitle**.
2. Press **L** for **Left**.
3. Press **F10** to return to your Chart Edit Screen.

Text Attributes Complete   ☐

Access the Draw Screen

You will now place your Bullet Chart in the Draw Screen so that you can add a shaded box under the Title/Subtitle and reposition the Bullet Text area.

1. Press **F4** to place your Bullet Chart in the Draw Screen. Notice that your Leaves background is not visible. You can only see a background when you press **F2** for **Show Chart.**

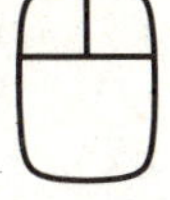

The following functions require the use of the mouse. Remember to click the **left** button to select functions and the **right** button to finish functions. If you click the **right** button twice, you may return to the Main Menu. If this happens, just press or click on **3** for **Draw** to return to your Draw Screen.

Add Shaded Box

1. Move your mouse to the Tool Box Area of your Draw Screen.
2. Click your **left** mouse button on the **Box Tool.**

The Box Attributes Pop-up appears at the top of your screen and your cursor appears as a +.

The following diagram illustrates how to draw a box.

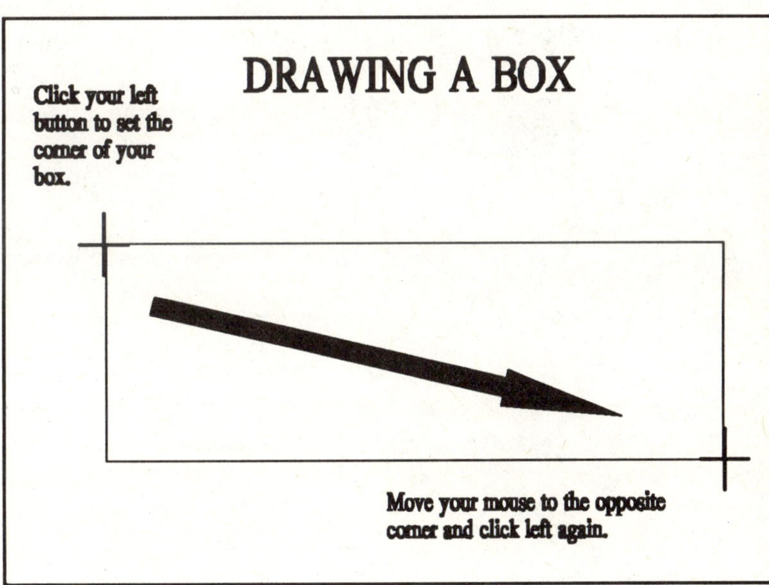

1. Use your mouse to position the + directly below the "S" in *Sales Presentation,* as illustrated:

2.   Click and release your **left** mouse button.
3.   Move your mouse to the opposite side of your screen and approximately .5" down.
4.   Click your **left** mouse button to set the end of the box.

Trouble Note ▶   If your box is too big or not big enough, you can try again as follows:

1.   Move your mouse to the top left of your screen and click **left** on the **Undo Tool.**
2.   Try drawing your box again.

Compare your screen to the following illustration:

Box Drawing Complete

Box Shading   To fill your box with shading, you will first select your box and then select the
Color Tool at the top left of your Draw Screen.

1. Click on the **Pointer Tool** at the top of your Draw Tools. Handles appear
    around your box to indicate that it has been selected.

2. Move your mouse up to the **Color Tool** and click your **left** button to se-
    lect it.

    The Color Pop-up appears. Note that the **Fill** box at the top of the Pop-up
    is currently highlighted.

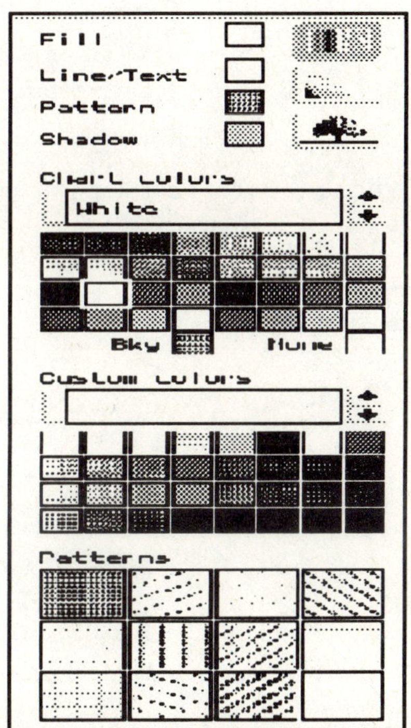

3. Click on the **Shade Tool**. Two things will happen:

    - The label Gradient and three boxes (one large and two small) appear at the
      bottom of your Color Pop-up.
    - Your box now appears shaded white to black from top to bottom.

    Compare your screen to the following illustration:

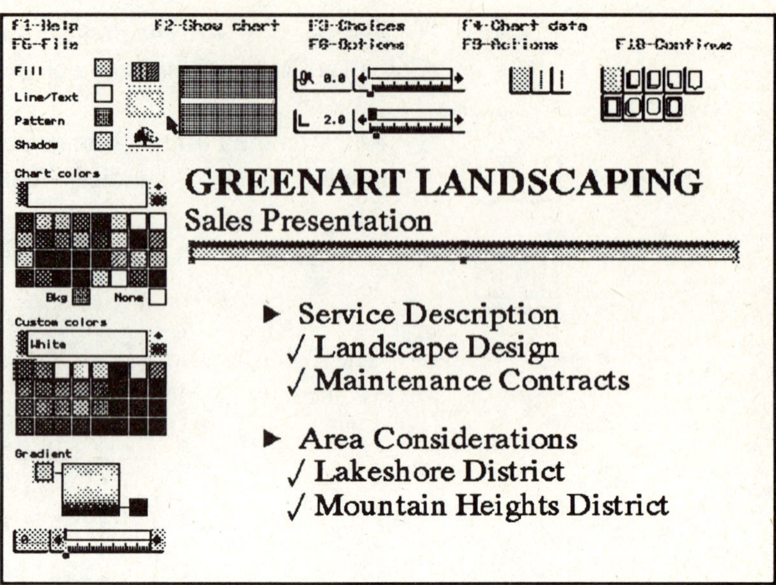

Shade Direction

Your next step is to change the *direction* of the shading so that it extends from left to right.

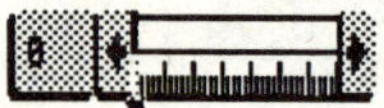

1. Click on the **0** in the scale at the bottom of the Color Pop-up.
2. Type *100* and press **Enter.**

Notice how the shading shifts direction.

> **NOTE:** You can also change shade direction by clicking on one of the arrows at either end of the shade direction scale and dragging the yellow bar left or right. In this way, you can quickly determine the shaded look you want.

Now you will change the Box Line Color to none.

Box Line

1. Click on the **Line/Text** box at the top of your Color Pop-up.
2. Click on the **None** box underneath the series of Chart Color boxes, as illustrated:

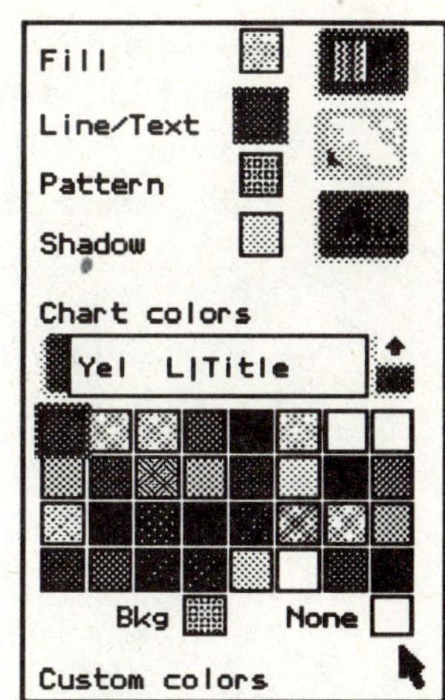

3. Click your **right** button twice to return to your Draw Screen.

Position

If you are not satisfied with the positioning of your box, move it as follows:

1. Position your pointer anywhere on the box and click **left** to select it.
2. Click and hold down your **left** mouse button to reposition your box so that its left side is directly below the "S" in *Sales Presentation.*
3. Click **right** to remove the handles.

Box Shaded and Positioned

Move Bullet Chart Area

To move the box containing your bulleted list, you must separate it from the Title/Subtitle. To do this, you select the entire Chart, click on the Ungroup Tool, and then select and reposition the box containing the Bullet List. Here's how:

Chart Select

1. Position your cursor anywhere on your screen *except* on your shaded box.
2. Click your **left** button. Note that handles appear around your entire chart area.

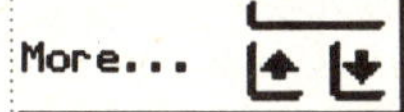

3. Position your mouse on the ▼ symbol at the very bottom of your Tool Box.
4. Click on the ▼ symbol.

A new selection of tools appears. When you want to return to the first selection of tools, you merely click on the ▲ symbol.

Ungroup Tool

1. Click on the **Ungroup Tool.**

Notice how handles now appear around both the Title/Subtitle area and the Bullet List box.

2. Click **right** to remove all the handles.

Now you will select and move just the box containing the Bullet List.

1. Position your cursor in the middle of the Bullet List box and click **left** to select it. Handles appear around the box.
2. Click and hold your **left** mouse button and drag your mouse to right-align the box under the shaded box as illustrated:

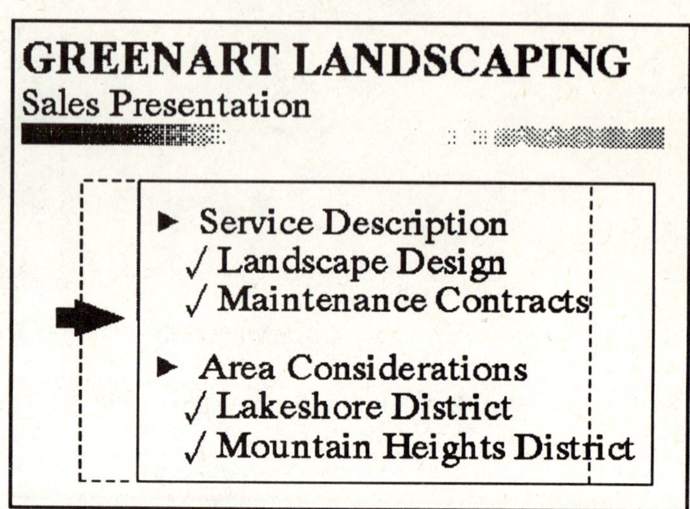

3. Click **right** to remove the handles.

Bullet List Positioned

Display Chart ▶ Press **F2** to display your completed Chart and then **Enter** to return to your Chart Edit Screen. You are now ready to save and print your Chart. Remember that the colors you see on your display screen will appear in black and white when you print.

Save and Print Your Chart

You will save Bullet Chart 2 on your data disk and then access the Output command to print your Chart. Once you are satisfied with your Chart, you can either exit from Harvard Graphics or get started on Activity 4.

Save
1. Press **F6** for **File.**
2. Press **E** for **Exit to Main Menu.**
3. Press **4** for **File** and then **4** for **Save Chart.**

The Save Chart Menu appears. Either the default Directory or your data drive will be displayed next to Directory. Change your Directory if necessary and then replace Bullet Chart 1 with Bullet Chart 2.

1. At **Filename,** type *Bulchrt2* over *Bulchrt1* and press **Enter.**
2. At **Description,** type *Bullet Chart #2: Lesson 2.*
3. Press **F10** to save and return to the Main Menu.

Bullet Chart 2 Saved

Print   1. Press **5** for **Output.**
2. Press **Enter** to accept **Printer 1.**
3. Press **F2** to view how your document will appear in printed form.
4. If you are satisfied with the look of your Chart, press **F10** twice to accept the Default Settings.

The Output to Printer Screen appears. Your Bullet Chart has now been sent to the printer. Wait until the Output to Printer Screen disappears and you are returned to the Main Menu.

Bullet Chart 2 Printed   ☐

You now have two options:

- Exit Harvard Graphics if you are finished with your learning session.
- Clear the current Chart and get started on creating your own Bullet Chart in Activity 4.

Exit Harvard Graphics   1. Press **E** to exit Harvard Graphics.

Clear the Current Chart   1. Press **1** for **Create Chart.**
2. Press **8** for **Clear Chart.**

ACTIVITY 4   CHALLENGE ASSIGNMENT

Read through the following sections for suggestions on content and then adapt the instructions given for your own material. Use the boxes provided to record information about your Bullet Chart.

The Challenge Assignment requires three major steps.

Step One: Choose Your Bullet Chart Topic
Step Two: Plan Your Bullet Chart Information
Step Three: Create and Format Your Bullet Chart

Choose Your Bullet Chart Topic

First, you need to decide what kind of event or topic your Bullet Chart will represent. For example, you could create a Bullet Chart that summarizes the principal points of a college lecture on marketing, the Civil War, or any other topic of your choice. You could also use a Bullet Chart to list the items covered in the annual or general meeting of a local union, company, or charitable organization.

Determine the name of your company/organization and the topic of your bullet chart and record them in the following box.

<table>
<tr><td>

Company/Organization Name:

Bullet Chart Topic:

</td></tr>
</table>

Plan Your Chart Information

Once you have determined your Bullet Chart topic, you need to write the material you will include. Remember the three elements of the Bullet Chart: Title, Subtitle, and Bulleted List.

Title/Subtitle

Keep your Title short and easy to understand. Your Subtitle should supplement your Title with a few brief words that define the *type* of list your Bullet Chart will present.

For example, here is the Title and Subtitle for a Bullet Chart that defines the steps required to get a job:

Title: GETTING A JOB

Subtitle: Six Steps to Success

Write your Bullet Chart Title and Subtitle in the following box.

<table>
<tr><td>

Title:

Subtitle:

</td></tr>
</table>

Bullet Items

Now you need to make a list of the bulleted items your Chart will present. Include no more than five major points or two major points and two minor points. Keep each entry short.

Parallel Structure

Pay particular attention to the grammatical structure of each entry in your list. To avoid errors, use *parallel structure* for each item. For example, if the first step in the Bullet Chart on getting a job is "Evaluate Your Skills," then every following step must also begin with a verb and be followed by a pronoun and noun.

Look what happens when one item in a list uses a different grammatical structure from the other items:

- Evaluate Your Skills
- Research Your Options
- **Resume Writing**
- Organize Your Approach
- Put Your Best Foot Forward

Notice that "Resume Writing" uses a different grammatical structure from the other four steps. As a result, you feel "jarred" by the contrast—something you want to avoid when presenting information to your readers. To revise the list, write *Prepare Your Resume* so that this step conforms to the same structure used by the other five steps.

List your major/minor points in the following box.

```
Point 1:
        Minor Point:
        Minor Point:
Point 2:
        Minor Point:
        Minor Point:
Point 3:
Point 4:
Point 5:
```

NOTE: Do not record an entry for *all* the items in the box. For example, if your chart will consist of only three major points, omit the minor points and points 4 and 5. Only create a 5-point Bullet Chart if you do not include any minor points.

Create and Format Your Chart

Refer to the following selection of commands and functions to help you create and format your Bullet Chart. Once you are satisfied with the information and format of your Bullet Chart, press **F4** to place your chart in the Draw Screen. Try adding a shaded vertical or horizontal box as you did for Bullet Chart 2.

Experiment until you are sure your Bullet Chart communicates your points clearly and with style.

Create Chart   At the Main Menu, press **1** for **Create Chart**, **1** for **Text Chart**, and **2** for **Bullet Chart**.

Enter Bullet Data
1. Position your cursor under the **Title/Subtitle** line.
2. Type the information you wish to include in your first bullet.
3. Press **Enter** twice to add the next bulleted item.

Add Secondary Bullets
1. Position your cursor one line below the bullet you wish to precede the secondary bullet.
2. Press **Ctrl + B.**
3. Choose a bullet character and press **Enter.**
4. Press the **space bar** once and type the information for the secondary bullet.

Insert Bullets
1. Position your cursor where you want a new line to appear.
2. Press **Ctrl + Ins.**

Delete Bullets
1. Position your cursor on the bullet you wish to delete.
2. Press **Ctrl + Del.**

Change Bullet Options

To change the style of your major bullets:

1. Press **F8** for **Options** and then **5** for **Bullet Options.**

In this menu, you can change the bullet type, size, color, indent spacing, and vertical alignment. If you choose numbered bullets, you can access this menu to choose a number other than "1" to start your list. This feature is useful for two-page Bullet Charts.

Text Attributes
1. Press **F8** for **Options** and then **2** for **Text Attributes.**

At the Text Attributes Menu, you can change the size, color, alignment, and font of your text.

Chart Appearance
1. Press **F8** for **Options** and then **3** for **Appearance.**

At the Appearance Menu, you can change the region frame style and color for the Title/Subtitle and chart regions.

Backgrounds
1. Press **F8** for **Options** and then **3** for **Appearance.**
2. Position your cursor opposite **Background Drawing.**
3. Press **F3** for **Choices** and select a background drawing from the list provided. Note the suggested palette.

Palettes
1. Position your cursor opposite **Palette.**
2. Press **F3** for **Choices** and select the palette suggested for the background drawing you chose.

Draw Screen
Press **F4** to place your chart in the Draw Screen. Press **F4** again if you wish to return to the Chart Edit Screen.

Draw Box   1. In Draw, use your mouse to click on the **Box Tool.**
                2. Move your cursor to the point where you want one corner of your box to appear.
                3. Click and release your **left** button.
                4. Drag your mouse in a diagonal line until you have the box height and width you want.
                5. Click your **left** button again.
                6. Click on the **Pointer** to select the box.

Shading   If you start work on your box *after* you have performed tasks with other objects, you must first click **left** on your box to select it.

                1. Select the **Color Tool.**
                2. In the Color Pop-up, select the **Shade Tool.**
                3. Change your shade direction and colors as desired.

Ungroup   To separate a chart into two sections:

                1. Click on the **Ungroup Tool** (press the ▼ symbol to view the second Tool Box level). Handles now appear around both the Title/Subtitle Area and the Bullet List Area.
                2. Click **right** to remove the handles and then click **left** on the chart area you wish to move or size.

Save   From the Draw Screen, press **F6** for **File** and then **E** for **Exit to Main Menu.** Now press **4** for **File** and **4** for **Save Chart.** Change to the directory in which you wish to save your file (usually Drive A or B) and then type a filename for your Bullet Chart.

                Fast Save: Press **Ctrl + S** to bypass the Main Menu.

Print   At the Main Menu, press **5** for **Output**, **Enter** to accept **Printer 1**, and then **F10.**

Clear Chart If you wish to start a new chart and have saved your current chart, first press **F6** and **E** for **Exit.** Now choose **1** for **Create Chart** and then **8** for **Clear Chart.** If you haven't saved your current chart, a message will appear. You can then press **ESC** to save your chart before clearing it.

Exit Harvard Graphics From the Chart Edit Screen; press **F6** for **Main Menu** and then **E** to exit the program.

                From the Draw Screen; press **F6** and **E** to return to the Main Menu and then **E** to exit the program.

ACTIVITY 5   LESSON TWO REVIEW

Test your understanding of the functions and concepts you learned in Lesson
Two by completing the following Review Questions:

1.   List two uses for a Bullet Chart.
2.   How do you access the Bullet Chart Edit Screen from the Main Menu?
3.   How do you enter a bulleted item?
4.   How do you change the bullet style from ● to ▶?
5.   How do you delete a bullet?
6.   How do you add a secondary bullet under a major bulleted item?
7.   What is parallel structure? (See Activity 4 introduction.)
8.   How do you draw a box?
9.   How do you add a preset background drawing?
10.   How do you change the shading *direction* in a box?

SUPPLEMENTARY EXERCISES

Exercise 1   Create a Bullet Chart outline for a slide show presented by a company that
offers wilderness canoe trips. You determine the name of the company and
include *four* main topics.

Exercise 2   Edit the Bullet Chart you created in Exercise 1 as follows:

- Delete two main topics and add two subtopics to each of the remaining two
  topics.
- Change the title and subtitle alignment.
- Place the Chart in the Draw Screen and ungroup it.
- Reposition the Title/Subtitle and Bullet Chart regions.
- Add the map symbol for North America.
- Add stars (in the STARS Symbol Directory) to the map to indicate canoe
  trip areas. Note: Retrieve one star and resize it and then use the Duplicate
  Tool to copy several stars.

Refer to the sample Bullet Chart included in Activity 1 at the beginning of this
lesson for formatting ideas.

<table><tr><td>

LESSON THREE

</td><td>

ADVERTISING FLYER

</td></tr></table>

FEATURES

- Adding Text in Draw
- Connecting Text to Objects
- Drawing Curves and Boxes
- Copying and Pasting

- Using the Align Tool
- Rotating and Flipping Symbols
- Using the Scratchpad
- Applying the Group Tool

INTRODUCTION

In Lesson Three, you will use the Harvard Graphics Draw features to create an Advertising Flyer. Here are the lesson activities.

ACTIVITY 1: Design a Flyer.

ACTIVITY 2: Follow the instructions provided to create the Flyer on page 76.

ACTIVITY 3: Follow the instructions given to enhance your Flyer with curved text as illustrated on page 88.

ACTIVITY 4: Create an Advertising Flyer based on your own information.

ACTIVITY 5: Complete the Lesson Review Questions on Draw features.

ACTIVITY 1   DESIGN A FLYER

The wide variety of Draw features available with Harvard Graphics provides you with plenty of options for the creation of distinctive advertising flyers. You can display text as slanted or curved, add preset symbols to highlight your points, and place a "burst" across one side of your Flyer to contain extra contact information.

Flyer Elements

No matter what features you use to create your Flyer, you have basically two elements to work with:

- Text
- Objects and Symbols

Flyer Purpose

Your first priority is to determine the *purpose* of your Flyer so that you can then work on the most important element—the text. A Flyer generally advertises a specific event, sale, or special offer. For example, you could design a Flyer to advertise an antique car rally being held to raise funds for the local children's hospital.

Flyer Text

Limit the text in a Flyer to short titles and point form lists. Readers should be able to quickly understand the purpose of your Flyer and the information it contains. Just make sure you include *enough* information so that an interested reader knows where to go or whom to call for more information.

Here is a Flyer advertising the antique car rally:

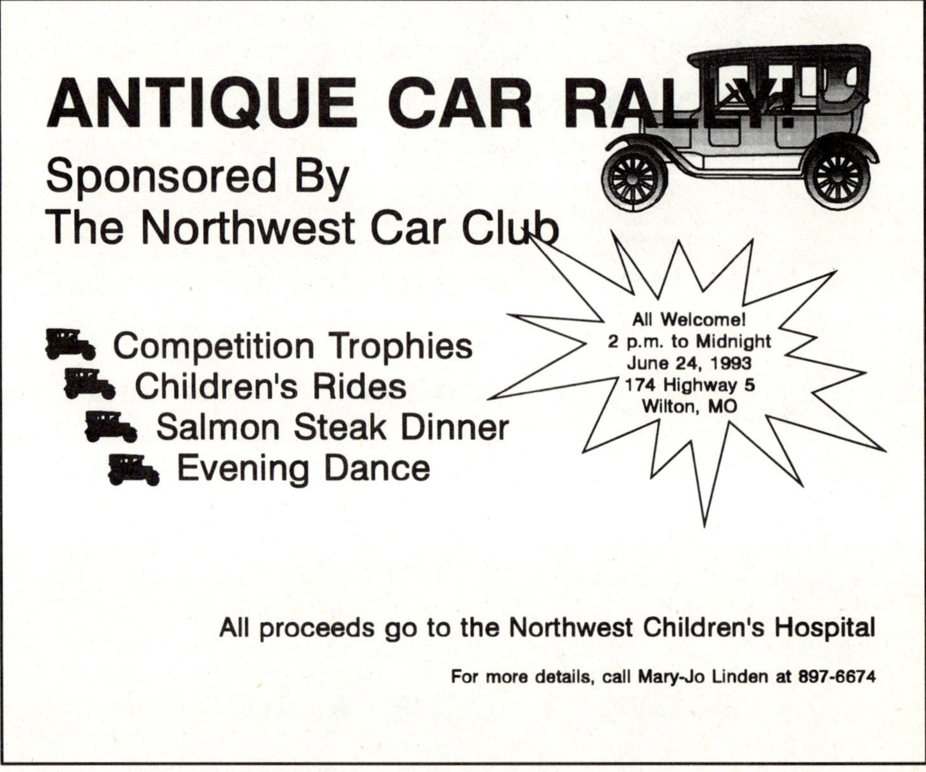

Summary of Activities 2 and 3

For Activities 2 and 3, you will use the Harvard Graphics Draw Screen to create and enhance a Flyer advertising the Special Alaska Cruises being offered by Travel Time Inc. The travel agents at Travel Time will include this Flyer in a packet sent to all regular customers.

Here are the elements your Flyer must include.

1.   Company name and phone number
2.   Cruise information
3.   Price range

You need to position each of these blocks of information on the page with a selection of symbols that draws attention to the text without overwhelming it.

For Activity 2, you will create the text blocks and add a variety of symbols.

In Activity 3, you will use the Scratchpad and Connect features to display a section of the text in a curved format.

ACTIVITY 2   **FLYER 1**

Three major steps are required to produce Flyer 1.

Step One: Enter Your Text Blocks
Step Two: Add Symbols
Step Three: Save and Print Your Flyer

Follow the step-by-step instructions to reproduce Flyer 1 (see page 76). Remember to place a check mark in the box next to each function you complete.

Enter Your Text Blocks

You will first access the Draw Screen and enter the text for the Title, Subtitle, and information points.

Access Draw   1.   Press **3** for **Draw.**

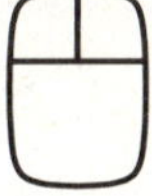

The following functions require the use of the mouse. Remember to click the **left** button to select functions and the **right** button to finish functions. If you click the right button twice, you may return to the Main Menu. If this happens, just press or click on **3** for **Draw** to return to your Draw Screen.

Enter Title   1.   Move your pointer to the **Text Tool** and click **left** to select it.

Before you enter your text, you need to change the text size, font, and font style.

1.   Move your mouse above the Draw Screen to the Text Attributes Pop-up.

Trouble Note ▶   While you are making the following changes, a message box may appear on your screen to instruct you to "Drag a box or click on a point." Just click **right** to remove this box.

Make the following changes in the Text Attributes Pop-up:

1.   Click on the **5.0** in the **Text Size Ruler.**
2.   Type *14.0* and press **Enter.**

Travel Time Inc.

Special Alaskan Cruises

 *Sightseeing Excursions*

 *Wildlife Photography*

 *Packages From Only $2,376*

Special Family Rates

3. Click on the **Font** box and select **Dutch 801.**
4. Click on the **Style** box and select **Bold.**

Your Text Attributes Pop-up should now look like this:

Enter your text as follows:

1. Position the **+** at the top left corner of your screen.
2. Click and hold your **left** mouse button to draw a box that extends across the screen and about 2" down.
3. At the Text Pop-up, type *Travel Time Inc.*
4. Press **F10** to exit the Text Pop-up.

Title Position

1. Click on the **Pointer Tool** to select your text.
2. Position your mouse in the middle of your title.
3. Click and hold your **left** mouse button and move your Title so that it appears at the top left of your screen as illustrated:

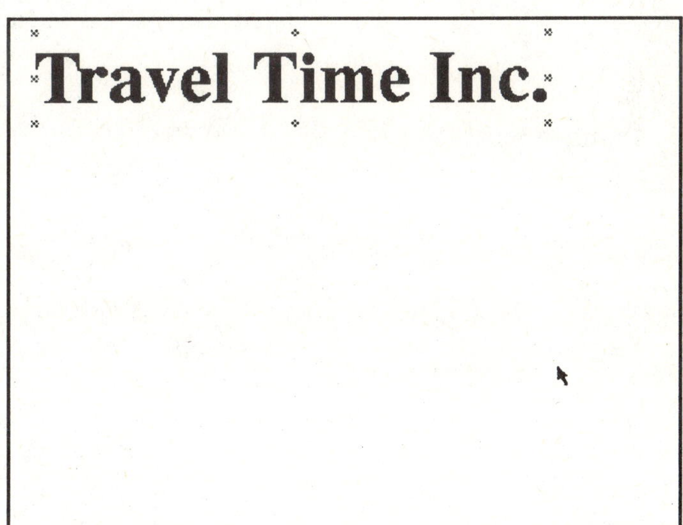

4. Click **right** to remove the handles.

Subtitle   Your next step is to enter the Subtitle.

1. Click on the **Text Tool.**
2. Move your mouse pointer up to the Text Attributes Pop-up.
3. Click on **14.0** in the **Text Size Ruler** at the top of your screen.

4. Type *7.0* and press **Enter.**
5. Click on the **Style** box and select **Roman.**

Now enter your text.

1. Position your **+** at the extreme left of your screen *under* the Title.
2. Click **left** and draw a box across the screen and about 1" down.
3. At the Text Pop-up type *Special Alaskan Cruises.*
4. Press **F10** to exit the Pop-up.

Trouble Note ▶

If your text appears on two·lines, click on the **Undo Tool** at the top left of your Draw Screen. Make sure you position the **+** as far left as possible. Click **left** and draw a box that extends to the opposite side of the screen. You want to allow plenty of room so that the text fits on one line.

You need to position your Subtitle directly below the Title. To ensure that your Title and Subtitle align, first select both items and then apply the Align Tool.

Select Title & Subtitle

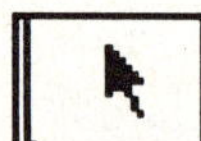

1. Click on the **Pointer Tool** to select your Subtitle.
2. Move your mouse to the Title.
3. Press and hold the **Shift** key and click the **left** mouse button.

Note that handles now appear around both the Title and Subtitle. You can use the Shift + Mouse method when you want to select more than one item at a time.

Trouble Note ▶

If both items are not selected, move your mouse to the Subtitle and press **Shift** and your **left** mouse button to select it.

Now apply the Align Tool:

1. Click on the **Align Tool.**
2. Click on the box labeled **Left** (top box).

Compare your screen to the following illustration:

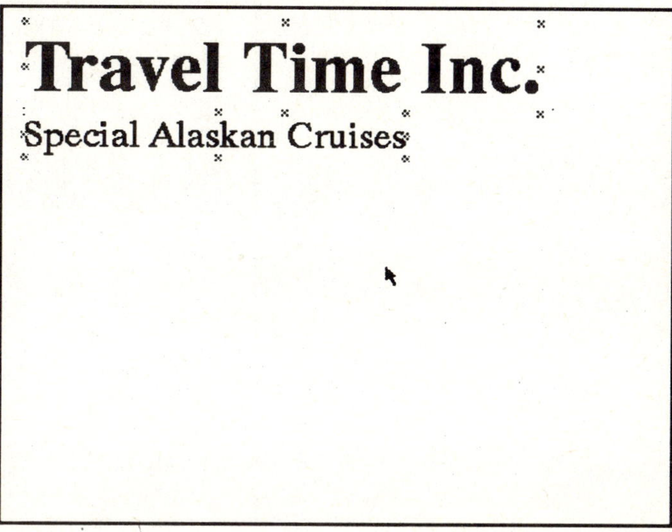

3.   Click **right** to remove the handles.

Title/Subtitle Complete

Now go on to specify the Text Attributes for the information points.

Enter Information Points

1.   Click on the **Text Tool.**
2.   Move your mouse up to the Text Attributes Pop-up.
3.   Click on the number in the **Text Size Ruler** at the top of your screen.
4.   Type *5.0* and press **Enter.**
5.   Click on the **Style** box and select **Italic.**

Now you can enter your text.

1.   Position your **+** under the Subtitle and as far left as possible.
2.   Click and hold the **left** button to draw a box across the screen and as far down as you can go.
3.   At the Text Pop-up, type

     Sightseeing Excursions (**Enter** twice)
     Wildlife Photography (**Enter** twice)
     Packages from Only $2,376 (**Enter** twice)
     Special Family Rates

4.   Press **F10** to exit the Pop-up.

Position

Click on the **Pointer** and position your information points as illustrated:

Travel Time Inc.

Special Alaskan Cruises

Sightseeing Excursions

Wildlife Photography

Packages From Only $2,376

Special Family Rates

2. Click **right** to remove the handles.

Information Points Complete   ☐

Add Symbols

Get Information Symbols

Now you need to get each of the four symbols that will appear to the left of your information points. First, get the Plane Symbol.

Get Plane Symbol

1. Click your **left** mouse button on the **Symbol Tool.**
2. Click again on **Get.**
3. At the Symbol Files Screen, press **F8** to sort the files alphabetically.
4. Scroll down to **TRANSPT1** and click **left** to select it.
5. Click on the **Plane.**
6. Click on **F10** twice.

Flip, Size, and Position Plane

Notice how your plane appears in the center of your Draw Screen. Now "flip" the plane so that its propeller faces right and then reduce the plane size.

Flip

1. Click on the **Flip Tool.**
2. Click on the **Horizontal** box.

The plane now faces in the opposite direction. Your next step is to reduce the size of your plane.

Size

1. Click first on the bottom left handle.
2. Press **Shift** and reduce the size of your plane until it is approximately .5" wide.

Position

1. Click on the middle of your plane and move it to the left of *Sightseeing Excursions.*

Trouble Note ▶ Be careful not to click on a handle. If you do click on a handle and as a result start to resize your plane, click on the **Undo Tool** and try again.

2. Adjust the sizing and positioning so that your plane appears as illustrated:

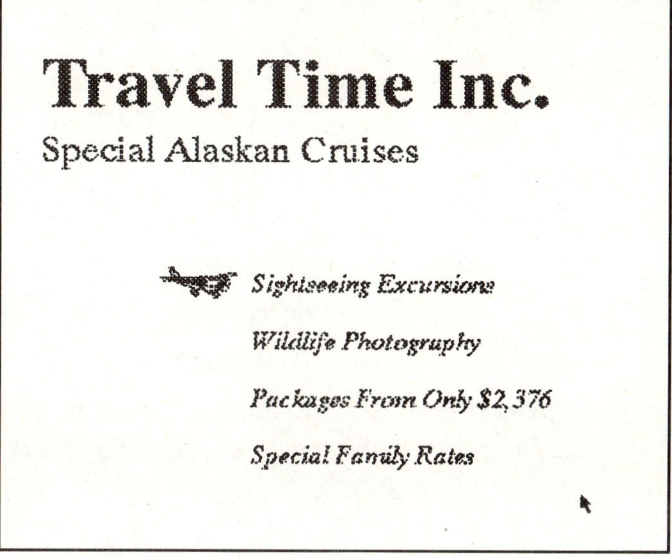

3. Click **right** to remove the handles.

Plane Symbol Sized and Positioned

Now get, size, and position the other three symbols. Note that you will have to flip the eagle symbol. You will also have to adjust the sizing when you move your symbols opposite the information points. Take your time with the sizing and positioning—fine mouse movements require some practice.

Here is the list of symbols required:

Eagle: ANIMALS Directory

Coins: MONEY Directory (select Coins1)

Family: HUMANS4 Directory.

Your screen should appear as illustrated on the next page after you have retrieved, sized, and positioned your symbols.

Travel Time Inc.

Special Alaskan Cruises

Sightseeing Excursions

Wildlife Photography

Packages From Only $2,376

Special Family Rates

Group Information Area

Now you need to adjust the size of your entire information area and then align the area to the left so that it lines up with the Title and Subtitle.

Your first step is to group the four symbols and information points so that you can size and position them as a block.

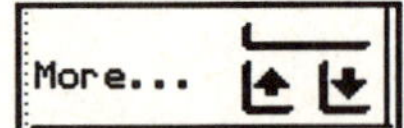

Note the ▼ symbol at the very bottom of your Tool Box.

1. Click on the ▼ symbol.

A new selection of tools appears. When you want to return to the first selection of tools, merely click on the ▲ symbol.

First, select the Information Area, which contains the symbols and text block.

1. Position your mouse above and to the left of your Information Area.
2. Click and hold the **left** button to draw a box around the entire Information Area to select it.

Note that orange handles now appear around all four symbols and the text block.

Group Tool 1. Click on the **Group Tool.**

Notice how orange handles now appear only around the Information Area as a whole. You now want to elongate the Information Area slightly.

1. Click on the middle right handle and drag your box to the right about .5".

Align Tool Now align the Information Area to the left as follows:

1. Move your mouse up to the Subtitle and press **Shift** and your **left** mouse button to select it. Handles now appear around both the Subtitle and the grouped Information Area.
2. Click on the **Align Tool.**
3. Click on **Left** (top selection).

Compare your screen to the following illustration:

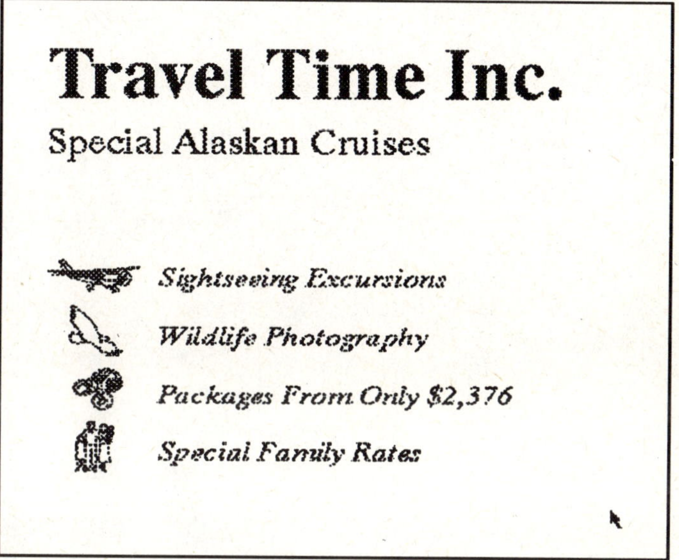

4. Click **right** to remove the handles.

Information Area Complete

Create Starburst and Text Your last step is to get the Starburst Symbol and fill it with text. First, you'll get your Starburst Symbol and then flip, position, and rotate it. You can then use the Text Tool to enter your text in the middle of the starburst.

Get Starburst
1. Click on the ▲ symbol at the bottom of your Tool Box to access the first tool level.
2. Click on the **Symbol Tool** and then click again on **Get.**
3. Press **F8** to sort the files alphabetically.
4. Scroll down to the **STARS1** Directory and click **left** to select it.
5. Click on **Star 9** and click on **F10** twice.

Flip The starburst will look better if it is "flipped" vertically.

1. Click on the **Flip Tool.**
2. Click on the **Vertical** box.

Rotate   You need to rotate the starburst 30° to the left.

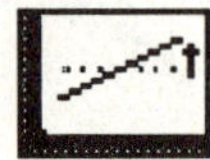

1. Click on the **Rotate Tool.**
2. Click on the **0.00** next to **Degrees.**
3. Type *30.0* and press **Enter.**
4. Click on the **Reverse** box to rotate your graph 30° to the left.
5. Click **right** to return to the Draw Screen.

Position   1. Click on the middle of your starburst and position it as illustrated:

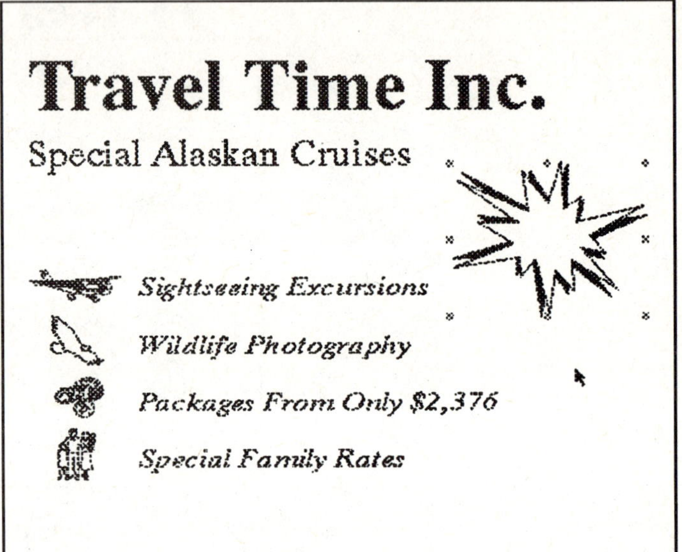

2. Click **right** to remove the handles.

Starburst Complete

Enter Starburst Text   Your last step is to enter the text in the starburst.

1. Click on the **Text Tool.**
2. Move your mouse up to the Text Attributes Pop-up. In this Pop-up, you
    need to change the size, style, and alignment of your text.
3. Click on the number in the **Text Size Ruler.**
4. Type *3.0* and press **Enter.**
5. Click on the ▼ symbol at the top right of the Text Attributes Pop-up to
    view the second "page" of attributes.
6. Click on the page that shows **Centered** text.

Now you are ready to type the text.

1. Click on a point above your starburst and draw a box about 2" square.
2. At the Text Pop-up, type:

Call (**Enter**)
786-4457 (**Enter**)
Now!

3. Press **F10** to exit the Pop-up and return to your Draw Screen.

Starburst Text Complete

Size/Position   1. Click on the **Pointer** to select the text block. Then resize and position it as illustrated:

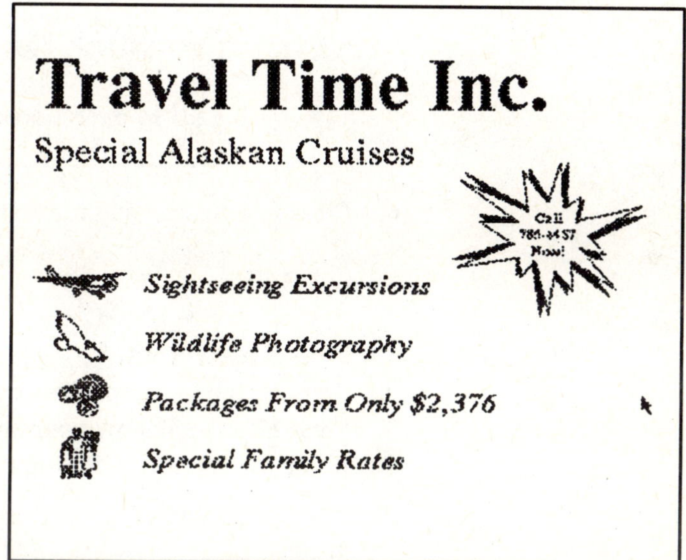

2. Click **right** to remove the handles.

Text Block Sized and Positioned

Save and Print Your Flyer

You will save Flyer 1 on your data disk and then access the Output command to print your Flyer.

Save   1. Press **F6** for **File.**
2. Press **E** for **Exit to Main Menu.**
3. Press **4** for **File** and then **4** for **Save Chart.**

The Save Chart Menu appears. Your cursor is currently positioned next to Filename. The Directory displays the default drive (usually C:\HG3\DATA). You will save your file on a data disk in Drive A or B.

1. Press your ↑ arrow to move opposite **Directory.**
2. Type *a:* or *b:* and then press **Delete** to erase the old Directory.
3. Press **Enter.**

4. At **Filename**, type *Flyer1* and press **Enter.**
5. At **Description,** type *Flyer #1: Lesson 3.*

Your Save Chart Menu should look like this:

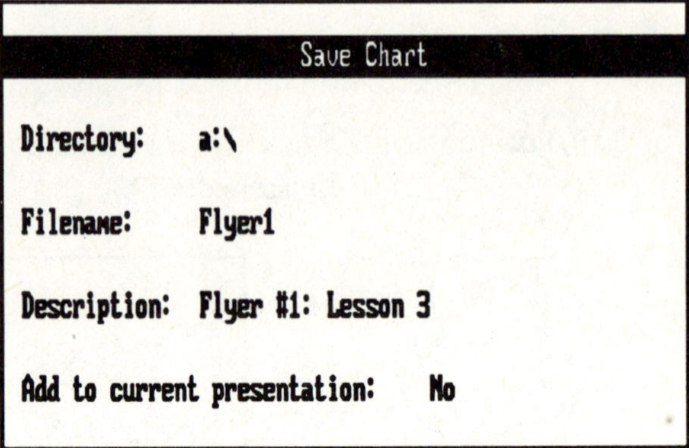

6. Press **F10** to save and return to the Main Menu.

Flyer 1 Saved

Print
1. Press **5** for **Output.**
2. Press **Enter** to accept **Printer 1.**
3. Press **F2** to view how your document will appear in printed form.
4. If you are satisfied with the look of your Flyer, press **F10** twice to accept the Default Settings.

The Output to Printer Screen appears. Your Flyer has now been sent to the printer. Wait until the Output to Printer Screen disappears and you are back at the Main Menu.

Flyer 1 Printed

You now have three options:

- Exit Harvard Graphics if you are finished with your learning session.
- Clear the current chart.
- Keep Flyer 1 on your screen and get started on Activity 3.

Exit Harvard Graphics
1. At the Main Menu, press **E** to exit Harvard Graphics.

Clear the Current Chart
1. Press **1** for **Create Chart.**
2. Press **8** for **Clear Chart.**

Keep Flyer 1 on Screen
If you want to continue directly to Activity 3, press **3** for **Draw** to return to your Draw Screen. Omit the Get Flyer1 from Disk section.

ACTIVITY 3   FLYER TWO

Four major steps are required to produce Flyer 2.

Step One:	Create the Curved Text and Wave Lines
Step Two:	Copy Text and Curves to Your Flyer
Step Three:	Revise the Flyer Format
Step Four:	Save and Print Your Flyer

Follow the step-by-step instructions to create Flyer 2 (see page 88). Remember to place a check mark in the box next to each function you complete.

Create the Curved Text and Wave Lines

Get Flyer1 from Disk

If you have exited out of Harvard Graphics and are starting fresh at your Main Menu, bring Flyer1 (saved on your data disk) to the screen as follows:

1. Press **4** for **File** and **1** for **Get Chart.** Either the default Data Directory or your data drive appears.
2. If necessary, type the letter of your data disk drive (*a:* or *b:*) over the current Directory and press **Delete** to erase the extra letters.
3. Press **Enter**.
4. At the list of files on your data disk, choose **Flyer1** and press **Enter** twice to bring your file to the Draw Screen.

If you have not exited out of Harvard Graphics, press **3** for **Draw.**

Delete *Special Alaskan Tours*

First, delete *Special Alaskan Tours* so that you can replace it with the curved lines and text.

1. Position your mouse on *Special Alaskan Tours* and click **left** to select it.
2. Click on the **Delete Tool.**

Access Scratchpad

The Scratchpad provides you with a blank Draw Screen to work on while you create the curved lines and text. After creating the curved lines and text, you will cut and paste them into your Flyer.

1. Click on the **Scratchpad Tool.**

Your Draw Screen is replaced by a blank "working" screen.

Enter Text

You will first enter the text again as three separate blocks and then draw three curves to represent waves. You will then use the Connect Tool to join the text block to the curves.

Travel Time Inc.

Special Alaskan Cruises

Sightseeing Excursions

Wildlife Photography

Packages From Only $2,376

Special Family Rates

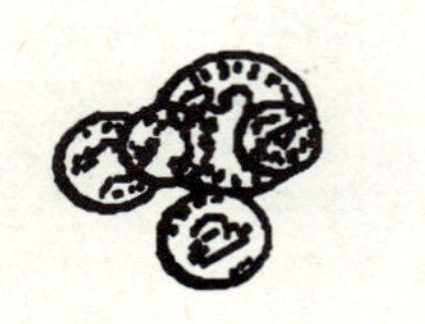

1. Click on the **Text Tool.**
2. Move your pointer up to the Text Attributes Pop-up.
3. Click on the number in the **Text Size Ruler.**
4. Type *6.0* and press **Enter.**
5. Your Font and Font Style should still be Dutch 801 and Roman. If not, click on **Font** and **Style** to select **Dutch 801** and **Roman.**

Now move your mouse on to the Draw Screen and position the + in the upper left corner of your screen.

1. Click **left** and draw a box that extends across the screen.
2. At the Text Pop-up, type *Special.*
3. Press **F10** to exit the Pop-up.
4. Position your + below and to the right of *Special* and draw another box.
5. At the Text Pop-up, type *Alaskan* and press **F10.**

Your screen should look like this:

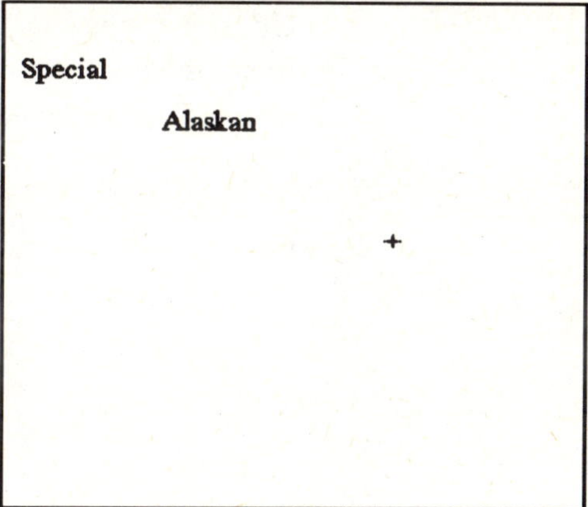

6. Go on to enter the final text block *Cruises.*

Text Blocks Complete

Draw Curves   You need to draw three curved lines to represent the waves. Draw the first curve as instructed and then use the Duplicate Tool to copy the other two curves.

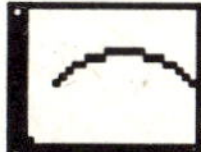

1. Click on the **Curve Tool.**
2. Change the size of your curve line as follows:

- Move your mouse up to the **Line Size Ruler** in the Attributes Pop-up at the top of your screen.
- Click on the **0.0.** Type *1.0* and press **Enter.**

Now draw the curve.

1. Position your mouse under *Special.*
2. Click and release your **left** mouse button.
3. Move your mouse about 2" to the right as illustrated:

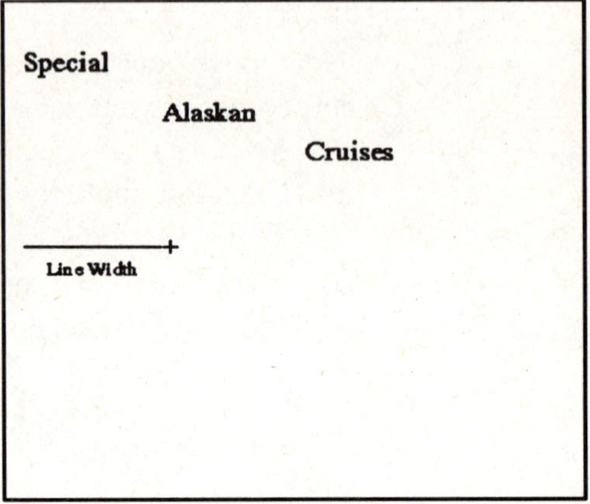

4. Click and release your **left** mouse button.
5. Position your mouse at the center of the line and pull your mouse down about .5" to make your curve.
6. Click **right** to set your curve.

Your curve should look like this:

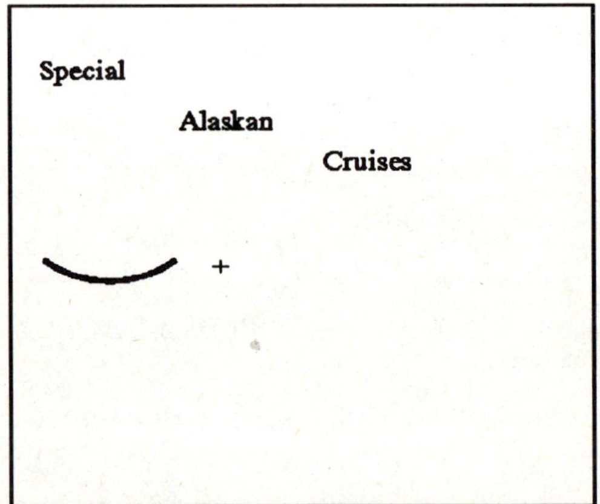

If you are not satisfied with your curve, click on the **Undo Tool** and try again. The following illustration reviews how to draw a curve.

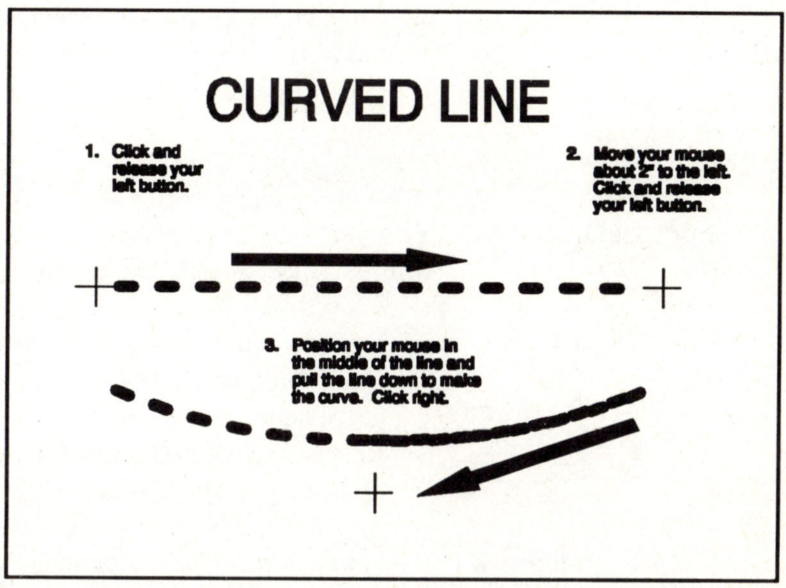

> **NOTE:** You may have to try several times to draw the curve. Take your time; drawing objects requires some practice.

Duplicate Curve

To ensure all three curves are exactly the same, you will *duplicate* the curve you just drew.

1. Click on the **Pointer** to select your curve.
2. Click on the **Duplicate Tool.** A second curve appears slightly down and to the right of your first curve.
3. Click and hold your **left** mouse button on the second curve. (Be careful not to click on one of the handles.)
4. Move the second curve to the right so that it just touches your first curve as illustrated:

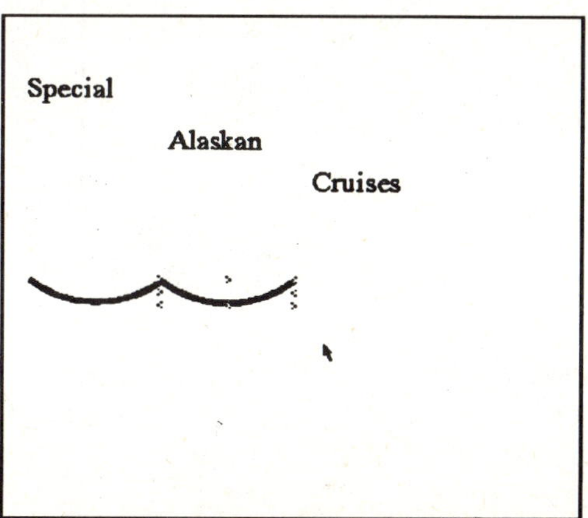

5. When you are satisfied with the position of your second curve, release your mouse button.

6. Click on the **Duplicate Tool** again. A third curve will appear attached to the second curve. If the third curve is not attached, adjust its positioning.
7. Click **right** to remove the handles.

Curved Lines Complete

Connect Text to Curves

Your next step is to connect each of the text blocks to a curve. To do this, you will first select *Special* and the first curve and then access the Connect Tool.

1. Position your mouse pointer above and to the left of *Special*.
2. Click and hold the **left** button to draw a box *only* around *Special* and the curve below it.
3. Release the mouse button. Orange handles will appear around both *Special* and your first curve to show they have been selected.

Trouble Note ▶ If handles do not appear around both objects, reposition your mouse above and to the left of the curve and *Special* and try drawing a slightly larger box.

Connect Tool   1. Click on the ▼ symbol at the bottom of your **Tool Box** to access the second level of tools.

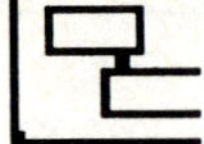

2. Click on the **Connect Tool.**
3. Click **right** to remove the handles.

The *Special* text block and the curve are now "connected" as illustrated:

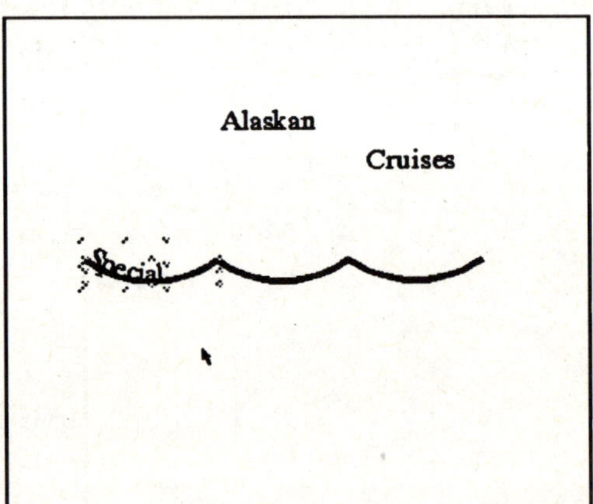

The *Special* text is too far left and too close to the curve. You need to move and rotate the *Special* text to place it in the center of the curve.

Move Text Block   1. Click on the middle of the *Special* text and move it to the center of the curve and up a fraction as illustrated:

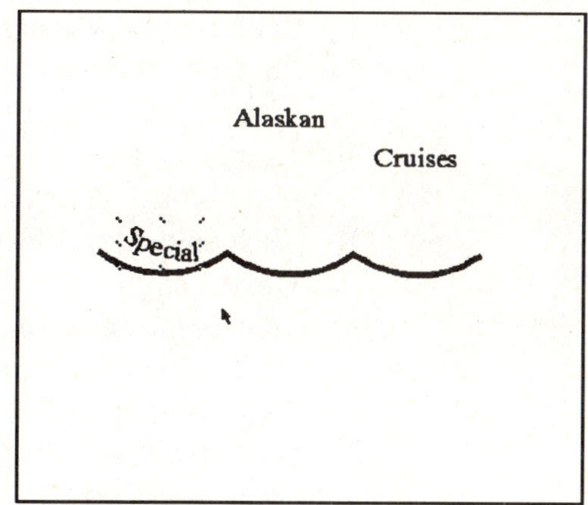

Rotate
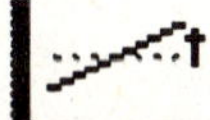

1. Click on the ▲ symbol at the bottom of your Tool Box to access the first level of tools.
2. Click on the **Rotate Tool.**
3. Click on the **Degrees** box.
4. Type *10.0* and press **Enter.**
5. Click on the **Reverse** box.

Click **right** to return to the Scratchpad Screen.

Your text block has rotated slightly to better match the curve. Reposition your text if necessary and then compare your screen to the following illustration:

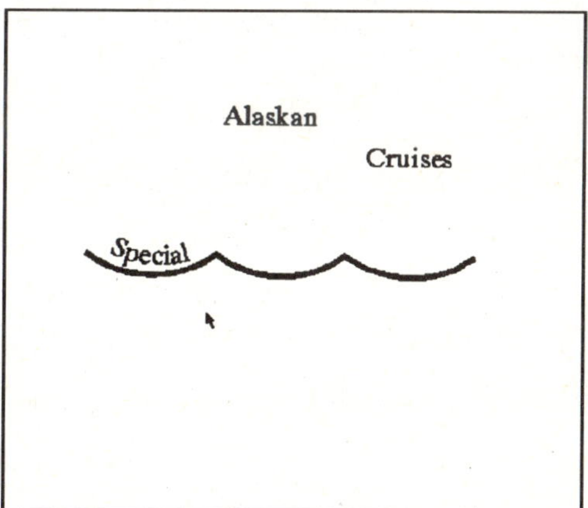

Click **right** to remove the handles around *Special* and go on now to connect *Alaskan* with the second curve and *Cruises* with the third curve. You will then need to move and rotate *Alaskan* and *Cruises* as you did for *Special*.

The following instructions review the Connect and Rotate/Move process. To Connect:

1. Click and hold your **left** button on a point above the text block you want to connect.
2. Draw a box around the text block and the curve to which it will connect. Make sure handles appear around *both* objects.
3. Click on the ▼ symbol to access the second tool level.

4. Click on the **Connect Tool.**
5. Click **right** to remove the handles.

To Move and Rotate:

1. Click on the text block to select it.
2. Move it slightly above the center of the curve.
3. Click on the ▲ symbol to access the first tool level.
4. Click on the **Rotate Tool.**
5. Click on the **Degrees** box.
6. Type *10.0* and press **Enter.**
7. Click on the **Reverse** box.
8. Click **right** to return to the Draw Screen.
9. Make any positioning adjustments necessary.

> **NOTE:** You can use two methods to adjust the text block rotation:
> 1. Click on the **Rotate Tool,** type the number of degrees to rotate, press **Enter,** and then click on a direction box.
> 2. Click on the **Rotate Tool** and then click and hold on the handle at the right of your text block. *Drag* the handle up or down.

Your screen should look like this when you have connected, moved, and rotated all three text blocks:

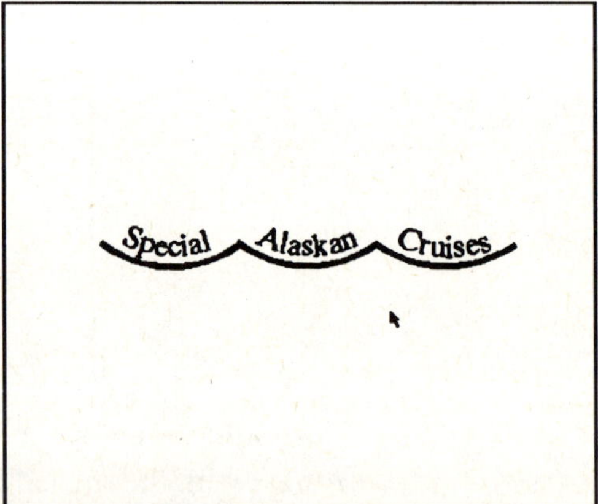

Curves and Text Connected

Copy Text and Curves to Your Flyer

Select All Objects   To copy the text blocks and curves to your Draw Screen, you first need to select all of them at once.

1. Press **F9** for **Actions.**
2. Press **3** for **Select Objects.**

3. Press **Enter** to accept **All.**

Note that handles now appear around all six objects. Your next step is to use the Group Tool to join them into one object so that you can then Copy and Paste them into your Draw Screen.

Group   1. Click on the ▼ symbol at the bottom of the tool box to view the second tool box level.

2. Click on the **Group Tool.**

Handles now appear around all six objects as a whole.

1. Click on the ▲ symbol to view the first tool level.

> **NOTE:**   To see both Tool Box levels at once, click on the horizontal bar above the ▲ and ▼ symbols. Both tool levels appear side-by-side *without* identifying text. Use this option when you can recognize the correct tools without the definitions. To view the levels with definitions, just click on either the ▲ or ▼ symbol.

2. Click on the **Copy Tool.**

3. Now click on the **Scratchpad Tool.** Your Scratchpad is replaced by your Draw Screen showing your Flyer.

4. Click on the **Paste Tool.**

Your text/curve block appears in the center of your Draw Screen.

Size and Position   1. Move the block so that it is centered under the Title.
2. Click and hold on one of the corner handles, press and hold **Shift,** and move the mouse to slightly increase the block size.
3. Reposition the block as illustrated:

Text/Curve Block Copied and Positioned

Revise the Flyer Format

In this step, you need to reposition all the Flyer elements to ensure an attractive format.

Align Text Blocks

First, reposition the three main text blocks so that they are centered in relation to each other and to the left and right margins of the page. You have already used the Align Tool to align the text blocks to the left. Now you can use the same tool to center align the text blocks.

Your Text/Curve block should still be selected. If not, click the **left** mouse button on the Text/Curve block.

1. Press **Shift** and your **left** mouse button on the Title.
2. Press **Shift** and the **left** mouse on the Information Area.

Handles appear around all three text blocks.

Align Tool

1. Click on the **Align Tool.**
2. Click on the box labeled **H.Center.**

The three text blocks are now centered horizontally in relation to each other.

Text Blocks Aligned

Position Text Blocks

All three text blocks remain selected.

1. Position your mouse on one of the text blocks and click **left.**
2. Move your mouse to center all three text blocks in relation to the left and right margins as illustrated:

3. Click **right** to remove the handles.

Text Blocks Centered ☐

Position Starburst   Your last task is to reposition the starburst.

1. Move your mouse to the starburst text and click **left** to select it.
2. Move your mouse out to the starburst itself and press **Shift** and your **left** mouse button to select it.
3. Drag your mouse to reposition the starburst as illustrated:

4. Click **right** to remove the handles.

Starburst Positioned ☐

Save and Print Your Flyer

You will save Flyer 2 on your data disk and then access the Output command to print your Flyer. You can then either exit from Harvard Graphics or get started on Activity 4.

Save
1. Press **F6** for **File.**
2. Press **E** for **Exit to Main Menu.**
3. Press **4** for **File** and then **4** for **Save Chart.**

The Save Chart Menu appears. Either the default Directory or your data drive will be displayed next to Directory. Change your Directory if necessary and then replace Flyer 1 with Flyer 2.

1. At **Filename,** type *Flyer2* over *Flyer1* and press **Enter.**
2. At **Description,** type *Flyer #2: Lesson* 3.
3. Press **F10** to save and return to the Main Menu.

Flyer 2 Saved   ☐

Print
1. Press **5** for **Output.**
2. Press **Enter** to accept **Printer 1.**
3. Press **F2** to view how your document will appear in printed form.
4. If you are satisfied with the look of your Flyer, press **F10** twice to accept the Default Settings.

The Output to Printer Screen appears. Your Flyer has now been sent to the printer. Wait until the Output to Printer Screen disappears and you are returned to your Main Menu.

Flyer 2 Printed   ☐

You now have two options:

- Exit Harvard Graphics if you are finished with your learning session.
- Clear the current Flyer and get started on creating your own Flyer in Activity 4.

Exit Harvard Graphics
1. Press **E** to exit Harvard Graphics.

Clear the Current Chart
1. Press **1** for **Create Chart.**
2. Press **8** for **Clear Chart.**

ACTIVITY 4   CHALLENGE ASSIGNMENT

Read through the following sections for suggestions on content and then adapt the instructions given for your own material. Use the boxes provided to record information about your Flyer.

The Challenge Assignment requires four major steps.

Step One:	Choose Your Product/Service/Event
Step Two:	Determine Your Flyer's Purpose
Step Three:	Plan Your Flyer Information
Step Four:	Create and Format Your Flyer

Choose Your Product/Service/Event

First, you need to choose the product, service, or event your Flyer will advertise. For example, you could decide to advertise a spring clearance sale for a furniture store or perhaps a Christmas bazaar at a local community center.

Write a brief description of your product, service, or event in the following box.

> Type of Product, Service, Event:

Determine Your Flyer's Purpose

What do you expect your Flyer to accomplish? Do you want to bring in more customers for your retail operation? attract interest in a new product? inform the public of a special event?

Remember that the purpose of the Flyers you created in Activities 2 and 3 was to inform customers of Travel Time's Special Alaskan Cruises. The secondary purpose was, of course, to encourage customers to call Travel Time and book an Alaskan Cruise.

Complete the following sentence to state the purpose of your Flyer:

> The Purpose of My Flyer Is To:

Plan Your Flyer Information

In Activity 1, you learned that a Flyer should contain the following elements:

- Name of the company or organization
- Contact information such as a phone number and/or an address
- Point form information about the product, service, or event
- Information about prices, if appropriate

Make sure you keep your point form information short. Use parallel structure as you did for your own Bullet Chart in Activity 4 of Lesson 2. Include only the information required to attract attention and encourage action.

Complete the following box with information about your Flyer.

Company/Organization Name:

Information Points (limit to 5 or less):

-
-
-
-
-

Price Information (if required):

Contact Information (address, phone number, name of contact, etc.):

Once you determine *what* your Flyer should say, you need to decide *how* you will format your information on the page. Use a pencil and paper to sketch various text block positions. For example, you could place your title at the top left corner and include a starburst containing contact information in the lower right corner.

Your principal goal is to leave plenty of *white space* on your Flyer. Don't fill every available area with text and symbols. Strive for a feeling of *balance* and *unity* by using only one font type and a minimum of symbols.

Place a completed sketch of your Flyer in the following blank box. You can then refer to this sketch as you format your Flyer.

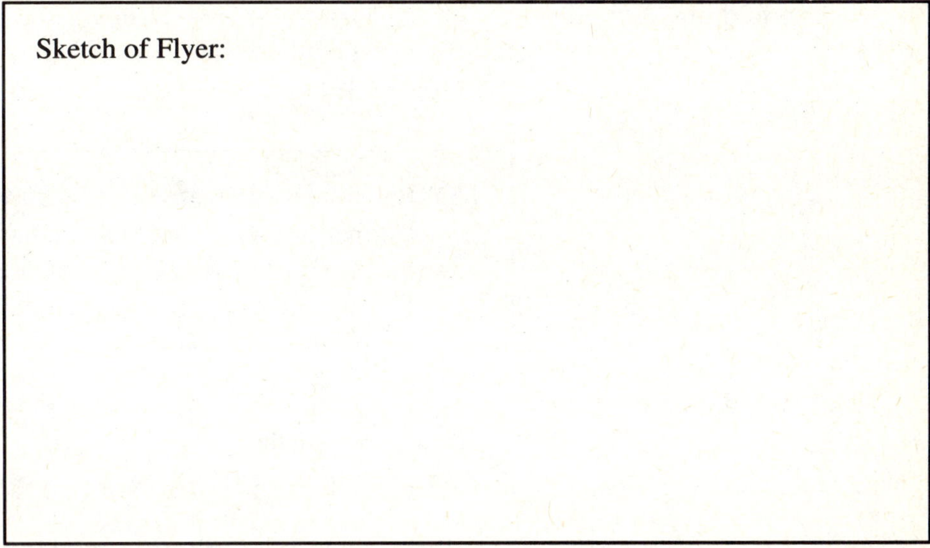

Create and Format Your Flyer

Refer to the following selection of commands and functions to help you create your Flyer.

Experiment with the size and position of the various elements in your Flyer until you are satisfied that it makes a clear and exciting advertisement for your product, service, or special event.

Access the Draw Screen   At the Main Menu, press **3** for **Draw.**

Enter Text

1. Click on the **Text Tool.**
2. Position the + at the top left corner of where you want your text to appear.
3. Click **left** and draw a box for your text.
4. At the Text Pop-up, type your text and press **F10.**

Change Fonts/Attributes

1. If you have just entered your text, click on the **Pointer** to select the text block.
2. Move your mouse up to the Text Attributes Pop-up at the top of your screen.
3. Click on the attribute you wish to change—for example, font, size, alignment, etc.

> **NOTE:** The Text Attributes Pop-up consists of three "pages." To access the other two pages, click on the ▼ symbol at the top right of your screen. Note that you can also enclose your text with a box. Simply click on the **T** that is enclosed in a box and then choose your box style from the options provided.

Size Text and Symbols
1. Click on the **Pointer** to select your text or symbol.
2. Click and hold your **left** mouse button on the bottom right handle.
3. Press **Shift** and drag your mouse to the size required.

> **NOTE:** Remember that you press **Shift** when you size text or symbols because you want to retain the correct proportions. You can also distort your images by *not* pressing **Shift** when you click on and drag one of the handles.

Position Text and Symbols
1. Position your mouse anywhere on the text/symbol block *except* on one of the orange handles.
2. Click and hold the **left** button to move the block.

Align
1. Select two or more objects or text blocks to align.
2. Click on the **Align Tool.**
3. Click on the type of alignment required—for example, left, right, top, bottom, etc.

Get Symbol
1. Click on the **Symbol Tool** and then click again on **Get.**
2. At the Symbol Directory, choose the appropriate Directory, click on the Symbol you want, and then click on **F10** twice to return to your Draw Screen.

Rotate Tool
1. Select the object to rotate and then click on the **Rotate Tool.**
2. Enter the degree of rotation required, press **Enter**, and then click the **Forward** or **Reverse** box. You can also just click on the right handle and drag your mouse.

Connect Text to Objects
1. Create the text block and then create an object such as a curve, box, or pyramid.
2. Click on a point above the text block and object and select both by drawing a box around them.
3. Click on the **Connect Tool.**

Flip Tool
1. Select the object to flip and click on the **Flip Tool.**
2. Click on either the **Vertical** or **Horizontal** box.

Select
1. Press **F9** for **Actions** and choose either **All** or **Similar.**

Group
1. Make sure you have selected the two or more objects you wish to group and then click on the **Group Tool.**

Scratchpad
1. Click on the **Scratchpad Tool** to access a blank Draw Screen. You can then use this screen to experiment with different effects before copying and pasting your completed object into your Draw Screen.

Copy and Paste   1. To copy from the Scratchpad, select the object to copy and then click on the **Copy Tool.**
2. Click on your **Scratchpad** to return to your Draw Screen.
3. Click on the **Paste Tool.**

Save   Press **F6** for **File** and then **2** for **Save Chart**. Change to the directory in which you wish to save your file (usually Drive A or B) and then type a filename for your Flyer.

Fast Save: Press **Ctrl + S**.

Print   At the Main Menu, choose **5** for **Output**, press **Enter** to accept **Printer 1**, and then **F10**.

Clear Chart   If you wish to start a new chart and have saved your current chart, first press **F6** and **E** for **Exit.** Now choose **1** for **Create Chart** and then **8** for **Clear Chart.** If you haven't saved your current chart, a message will appear. You can then press **ESC** to save your chart before clearing it.

Exit Harvard Graphics   Press **F6** and **E** for **Exit to Main Menu** and then **E** again to exit the program.

ACTIVITY 5   LESSON THREE REVIEW

Test your understanding of the functions and concepts you learned in Lesson Three by completing the following Review Questions.

1. What is the most important element of a Flyer?
2. Why should you limit your text to short titles and point form lists?
3. How do you change the size of your text in the Text Attributes Pop-up in Draw?
4. How do you flip an object or symbol?
5. Describe how to size a symbol in Draw.
6. How do you group a selection of text, symbols, or objects?
7. List the types of information required for a Flyer.
8. What is the purpose of the Connect Tool?
9. When do you need to use the Scratchpad?
10. Describe how to copy and paste an object from the Scratchpad to the Draw Screen.

SUPPLEMENTARY EXERCISES

Exercise 1   Create a Flyer to advertise a special 100th Anniversary Sale for a local department store. You determine the name of the department store and the Flyer content. Make sure you include the store location, sale dates, information about some of the sale items, and one or two symbols to add interest.

Exercise 2   Revise the Flyer you created in Exercise 1 as follows:

- Advertise a January "Blow-out" Sale.
- Revise the sale items.
- Offer a special discount for the first 100 customers who attend the sale's opening day.
- Revise the sale dates and use different symbols.

NUMBER CHARTS

Introduction

Pick up any newspaper and you will find number charts representing statistics about everything from housing markets to the national deficit. Number charts *show* you how specific categories of information vary and compare over a defined scale. You use number charts when you want your information to make an immediate *visual* impact on your reader that you cannot duplicate in words or lists of numbers.

Comparison to Table Chart

You can immediately see the greater impact of a number chart over other types of charts when you compare it with a straight table chart. For example, the following table chart compares the popularity of three Lake City radio stations over a five-year period.

LAKE CITY LISTENING
Five-year Comparison of Radio Station Audiences

Year	CKRX Classic Rock	CQRL Top Ten	CNC Public Radio
1989	24,000	21,000	18,000
1990	27,000	25,000	12,000
1991	33,000	22,000	15,000
1992	37,000	26,000	17,000
1993	40,000	14,000	22,000

You read and understand all the data displayed in this table, but you do not necessarily pay close attention to the data variations.

Now look at the same data displayed as a bar chart.

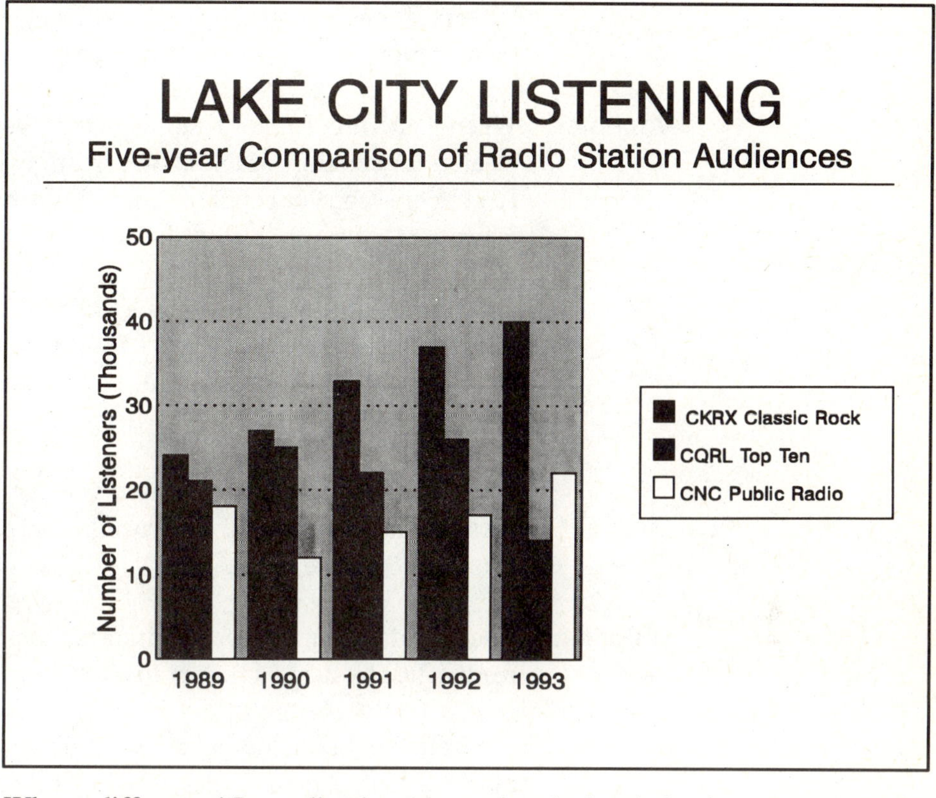

What a difference! Immediately, you see that the local classic rock station dominates the listening market in Lake City while the listening audience for the "Top Ten" station has started to decline. If you were giving a presentation on behalf of the classic rock station, such a bar chart would support your claim to an increased listening audience much more readily than would the table chart.

You choose a number chart, therefore, when you want to display numerical information in a form that your readers can immediately comprehend. In business graphics, you will find that number charts are used frequently to help readers visualize often complex data.

Required Terms   To produce the number charts in Section Two, you need to be familiar with the following terms:

- Data
- Variables
- Distortion
- Series
- Values

Data   You use the word *data* to mean information that you have counted or measured. This information may consist of money amounts, time periods, customer groups, usage levels, etc. For example, the data in the bar chart on Lake City

Listening consisted of the number of people who listened to each of the three radio stations over a period of five years.

Variables   When gathering data for a number chart, you need to use precise methods and be alert for certain variables that can affect the validity of the data. A *variable* is a circumstance or condition that affects how one series of information compares to another.

For example, the reason why more people in Lake City tune into the classic rock station could be that Lake City is a bedroom community that attracts a large percentage of young families. The adults in these families range in age from 30 to 45 years old—the prime target market for classic rock.

When you display a number chart, you can explain the influence of certain variables in a note on the chart itself or as part of the verbal presentation or text that accompanies the chart.

Distortion   You can often change *how* the information in a number chart affects your readers just by using a format that allows *distortion*.

For example, the following pie chart displays the 1993 data on the Lake City radio stations as percentages. The 40,000 listeners to WKRX classic rock, therefore, become 46 percent of the listening audience.

Each of the three pie "slices" correctly represents the percentages specified. However, you see immediately that the distorting effect of the 3-D format makes the slice that represents the public radio station *look* like it is more important than the other two slices even though the *number* it represents is smaller.

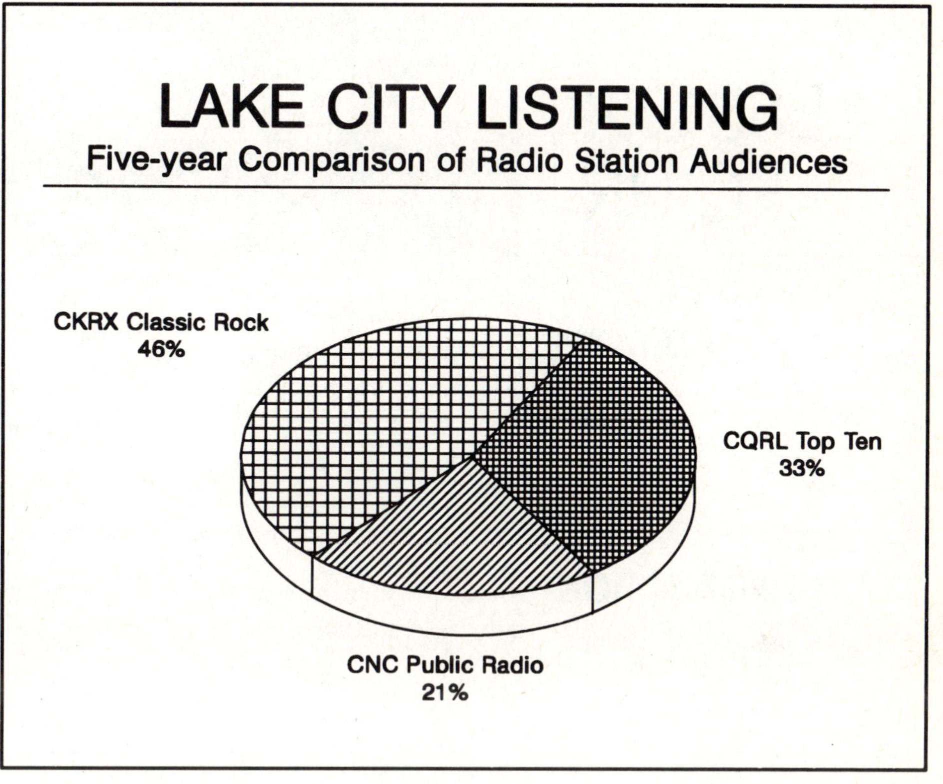

Series   The word *series* refers to each group of data points in a chart. In the Lake City bar chart, each of the three radio stations represents one series. A number chart can display only one series of data or a dozen or more, depending on the information you want to communicate. Generally, you want to limit the number of different series you present to three or four. Too many series on one chart diminishes the overall impact of the chart and makes greater demands on your readers.

Values   A *value* is the number represented by a series. For example, the value of the pie chart slice that represents the number of listeners to WQRL Top Ten is 33%.

Section Two Charts   In Section Two, you will create a simple pie chart followed by a bar chart and finally an area chart. You will first create the charts in the Harvard Graphics Chart Edit Screen and then place them into the Draw Screen to add symbols and other enhancements.

<table>
<tr><td>

LESSON FOUR

</td><td>

PIE CHART

</td></tr>
</table>

FEATURES
- Creating and Editing
- Adding 3-D Effects
- Using Patterns
- Adding Title Boxes
- Cutting a "Slice"
- Adding Symbols
- Changing Fonts and Attributes
- Linking Two Pie Charts

INTRODUCTION

In Lesson Four, you will learn how to create and enhance a Pie Chart. Here are the lesson activities:

ACTIVITY 1:   Determine the information required for your Pie Chart.

ACTIVITY 2:   Follow the instructions given to create the simple Pie Chart on page 114.

ACTIVITY 3:   Follow the instructions given to link one slice of your Pie Chart with another Pie Chart and then add a preset drawing (called a symbol). See page 124.

ACTIVITY 4:   Create a Pie Chart based on your own data.

ACTIVITY 5:   Complete the Lesson Review Questions on Pie Chart creation and enhancement.

ACTIVITY 1   **PIE CHART INFORMATION**

You choose a Pie Chart format when you want to display your data as parts of a whole—just like when you cut an apple pie into various-sized slices.

Pie Chart Data   Each slice of a Pie Chart represents one segment of data. For example, each slice in a pie chart that divides all the students at a college according to age group would represent one age group.

Pie Charts are especially useful for displaying data that, taken together, represent one complete entity. You could use a Pie Chart to show how five product groups for one company break down according to sales or to show the percentage of a company's operating budget used by each department.

Here is a sample of a Pie Chart that shows how the students at Lakeside College break down into five age groups.

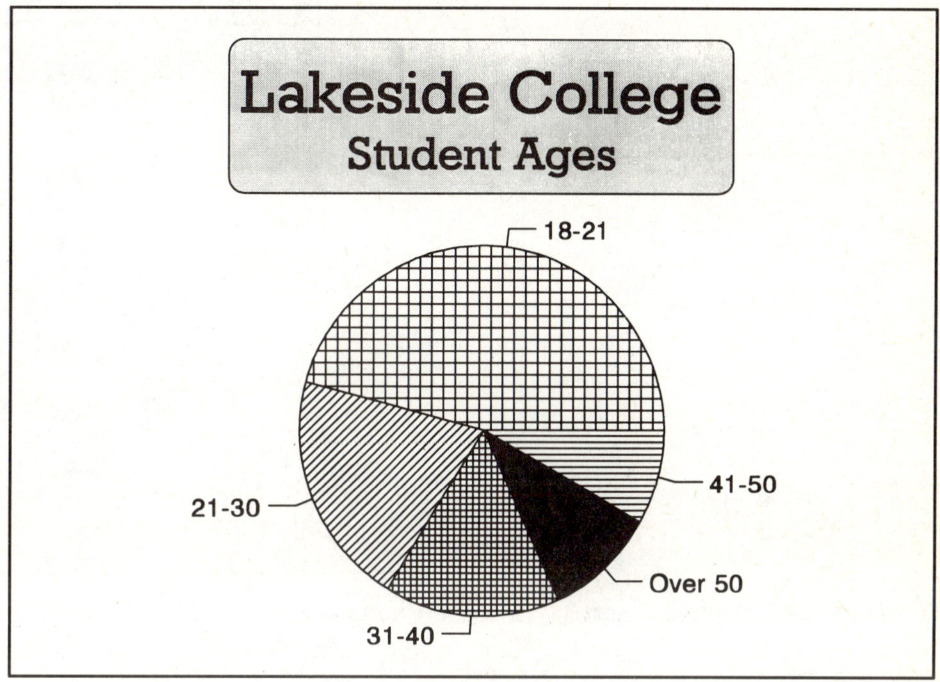

The minute you look at the sample Pie Chart, you recognize that the vast majority of students at Lakeside College are less than 30 years old. Such a conclusion is not surprising.

However, you may be intrigued at the size of the Over 50 slice—indicating, perhaps, that the college population is changing as more older people return to finish their educations.

Slice Emphasis   Sometimes you may wish to emphasize one particular slice of a Pie Chart. For example, if you were a college administrator speaking at a meeting of senior citizens, you may want to stress how your college now attracts a significant portion of over-50 students.

To emphasize your point, you would then display a Pie Chart with the Over 50 slice cut out as illustrated:

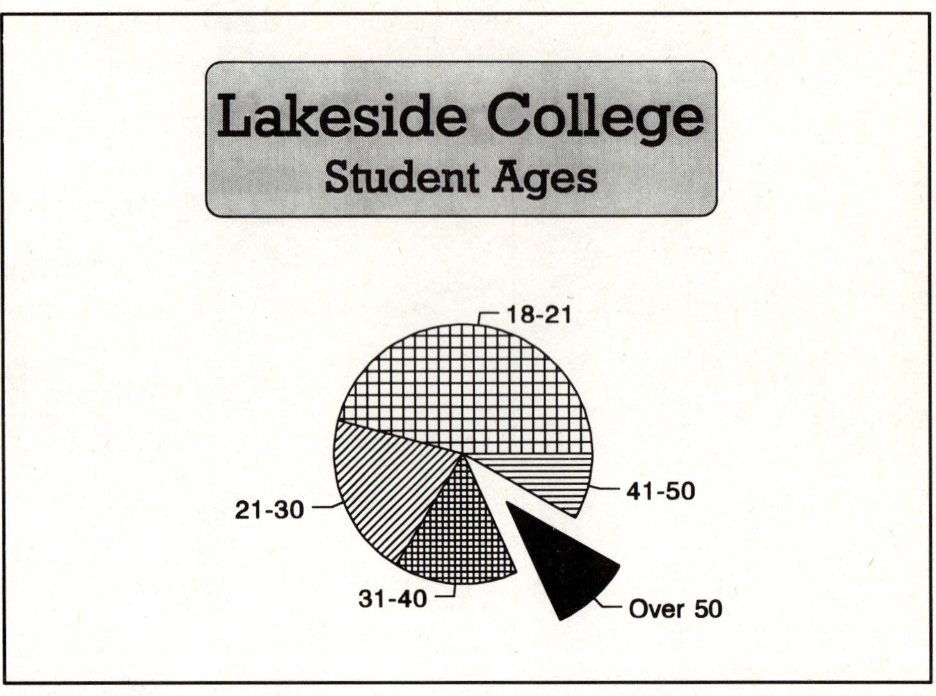

Summary of Activities 2 and 3

The Pie Charts you will create in Activities 2 and 3 are based upon information gathered from Travel Time, Inc.—a medium-sized travel agency.

The vice president of Travel Time, George Prentiss, needs to illustrate the percentage of clients who purchased five different types of travel service. Here's the information he discovered:

Cruises		21%
Sun Spot Package Tours		36%
European Package Tours		6%
Flights		13%
Other (Hotels, Car Rentals, etc.)		24%

George now needs to display these percentages in two Pie Charts he will use as part of an employee training presentation to inform sales personnel of Travel Time's current sales position.

In Activity 2, you will create a Pie Chart to display the percentage of customers who purchased each of the five different types of travel service. You will also *cut* the slice that represents "Cruises."

Your Pie Chart will accomplish two goals.

- Illustrate the breakdown of services
- Emphasize the percentage of clients who booked cruises

In Activity 3, you will further concentrate on the Cruises slice by *linking* it to another chart that shows the breakdown of Cruise types sold by Travel Time.

ACTIVITY 2   ## PIE CHART 1

Three major steps are required to produce Pie Chart 1.

Step One:	Create Your Pie Chart
Step Two:	Enhance Your Pie Chart
Step Three:	Save and Print Your Pie Chart

Follow the step-by-step instructions to reproduce Pie Chart 1 (see page 114). Remember to place a check mark in the box next to each function you complete.

Create Your Pie Chart

You will first create your Pie Chart and then enter the required information.

Create Chart
1. At the Main Menu, press **1** for **Create Chart.**
2. Press **2** for **Pie.**

A Pie Chart Edit Screen appears. In this screen, you will enter all the data that will appear on your Pie Chart. Note that your cursor is positioned next to **Title.**

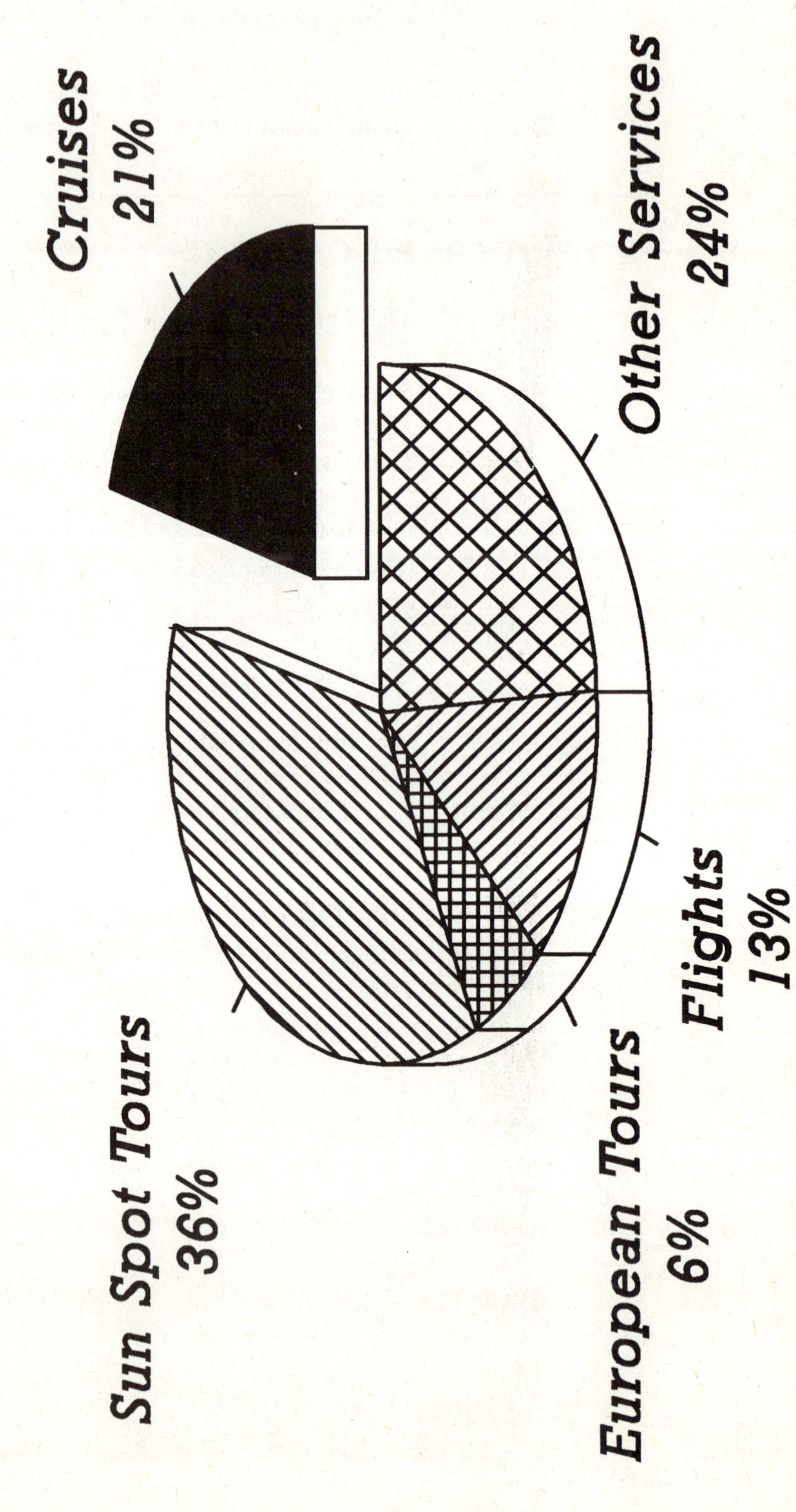

TRAVEL TIME SALES
Client Preferences: 1993
Cruises
21%
Other Services
24%
Sun Spot Tours
36%
European Tours
6%
Flights
13%

```
                              Pie Chart 1
  F1-Help          F2-Shou chart   F3-Choices      F4-Draw          F5-Mark
  F6-Main Menu     F7-Spell/Text   F8-Options      F9-Pie data      F18-Continue

  Title:       <------  [Cursor Position]
  Subtitle:
  Footnote:
  Pie title:

  Slice         Label            Value       Cut      Color       Pattern
    1                                         No     Cyn  D|S        8
    2                                         No     Blu  D|S        1
    3                                         No     Blu  L|S        2
    4                                         No     Cyn   |S        3
    5                                         No     Yel  L|S        4
    6                                         No     White |S        5
    7                                         No     Cyn  D|S        6
    8                                         No     Blu  D|S        7
    9                                         No     Blu  L|S        8
   10                                         No     Cyn   |S        9
   11                                         No     Yel  L|S       10
   12                                         No     White |S       11
```

Enter Title/Subtitle

1. Type the Title of your Pie Chart in all caps: *TRAVEL TIME SALES*. Press **Enter.**
2. Now type the Subtitle of your Pie Chart in upper/lower case: *Client Preferences: 1993*. Press **Enter.**

Title/Subtitle Entered □

Enter Slice Labels

You need to enter the labels that represent the five slices of your Pie:

1. Press **Enter** three more times to move your cursor into the **Label** column next to Slice 1.
2. Type *Cruises* and press **Enter.**
3. Type *Sun Spot Tours* and press **Enter.**
4. Type *European Tours* and press **Enter.**
5. Type *Flights* and press **Enter.**
6. Type *Other Services.*

Slice Labels Entered □

Enter Value Data

Now you will enter the *value* that will represent each slice label.

1. Press ↑ your arrow until *Cruises* is highlighted.
2. Press **Tab** to move your cursor into the **Value** column.
3. Type *21* and press **Enter.**
4. Type *36* and press **Enter.**
5. Type *6* and press **Enter.**
6. Type *13* and press **Enter.**
7. Type *24.*

Compare your screen to the following illustration:

```
                                  Pie Chart 1                                    ▲
 F1-Help          F2-Show chart   F3-Choices        F4-Draw         F5-Mark
 F6-Main Menu     F7-Spell/Text   F8-Options        F9-Pie data     F10-Continue

 Title:      TRAVEL, TIME SALES
 Subtitle:   Client Preferences: 1993
 Footnote:
 Pie title:


 Slice          Label              Value       Cut       Color         Pattern

  1      Cruises                    21          No     ▌ Cyn  D|S         0
  2      Sun Spot Tours             36          No     ▌ Blu  D|S         1
  3      European Tours             6           No     ▌ Blu  L|S         2
  4      Flights                    13          No     ▌ Cyn   |S         3
  5      Other Services             24          No     ▌ Yel  L|S         4
  6                                             No       White |S         5
  7                                             No     ▌ Cyn  D|S         6
  8                                             No     ▌ Blu  D|S         7
  9                                             No     ▌ Blu  L|S         8
 10                                             No     ▌ Cyn   |S         9
 11                                             No     ▌ Yel  L|S        10
 12                                             No       White |S        11
```

Slice Values Entered ☐

Show Data as Percents — You want to display your slice values as percentages. To do this, you first access Slice Values in the F8 Options Menu and then Show Percents.

Slice Values

1. Press **F8** for **Options.**
2. Press **8** for **Slice Values.**
3. At the Slice Values Menu, press **N** for **No** on the **Show Values** line.
4. Press **F10** to return to your Chart Edit Screen.

Show Percents

1. Press **F8** for **Options.**
2. Press **9** for **Slice Percents.**
3. Press **Y** for **Yes** on the **Show Percents** line.
4. Press **F10** to return to your Chart Edit Screen.

Percent Data Complete ☐

Display Chart ▶ — Press **F2** to display your Chart. Your Pie Chart should look like this:

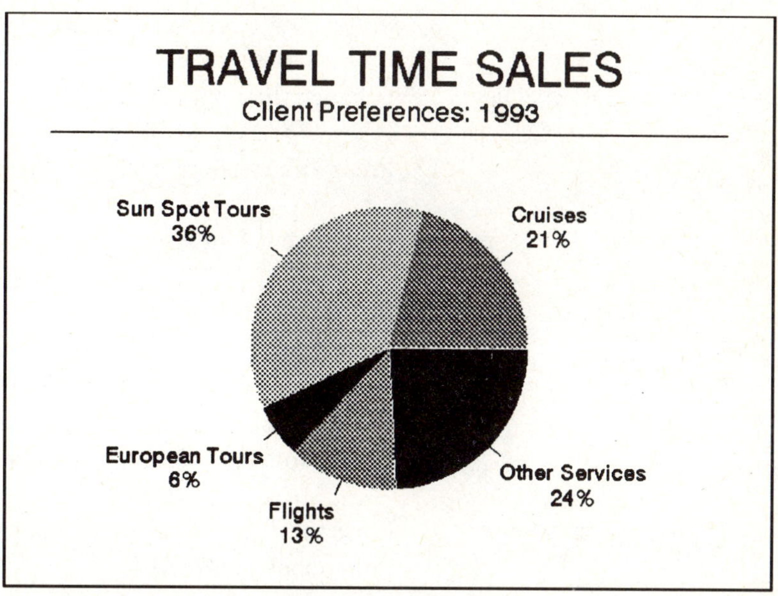

Press **Enter** to return to your Chart Edit Screen.

Enhance Your Pie Chart

While your chart looks pretty impressive, it could still use some enhancements. Here's what you need to do.

> → Change the Fonts/Attributes for the Title, Subtitle, and Pie Labels
> → Select a box style for the Title/Subtitle
> → Display the Pie Chart in a 3-Dimensional format
> → Fill the pie slices with patterns
> → Cut the Cruises slice away from the main Pie

Enhance Title/Subtitle You need to access the Text Attributes Menu so that you can change the size, font, and color of your Title and Subtitle.

Text Attributes

1. Press **F8** for **Options.**
2. Press **2** for **Text Attributes.**
3. Press **1** for **Titles/Footnotes.**

The Text Attributes Titles/Footnotes Screen appears. Your cursor is currently resting under the **9** in the **Size** column next to **Title.**

Title Size

1. Key in *8* to make the Text size slightly smaller.

Text Color Now change the color of the Title.

1. Press **Tab** to move the cursor to the **Color** column.
2. Press **F3** to see a list of **Choices.**

3. Press your ↓ arrow to **White** and press **Enter.**

Title Font Name and Style

Next change the Font Name and Font Style for your Title.

1. Press **Tab** twice to position your cursor in the **Font Name** column.

   The current font is Swiss 721. Let's change this font to Geo Slab 712.

2. Press **F3** for **Choices.**
3. Press your ↑ arrow to move your cursor to **Geo Slab 712** and press **Enter.**
4. Press **Tab** to move to the **Font Style** column.
5. Press **F3** for **Choices.**
6. Cursor to **Medium** and press **Enter.**

Subtitle Font Name and Style

1. Press the ↓ and ← arrows to position your cursor in the **Font Name** column opposite **Subtitle.**
2. Press **G** for **Geo Slab 712.**
3. Press **Tab** to the **Font Style** column and press **M** for **Medium.**

Your Text Attributes Menu should look like this:

Text Attributes Titles/Footnotes	Size	Color	Alignment	Font Name	Font Style
Title	8	White |Te	Center	Geo Slab 71	◆Medium
Subtitle 1	5	Blu L¦Su	Center	Geo Slab 71	Medium
Subtitle 2	5	Blu L¦Su	Center	Swiss 721	Roman
Footnote 1	3.5	Blu L¦Fo	Left	Swiss 721	Roman
Footnote 2	3.5	Blu L¦Fo	Left	Swiss 721	Roman
Footnote 3	3.5	Blu L¦Fo	Left	Swiss 721	Roman
Pie 1 title	4	Blu L¦Su	Below	Swiss 721	Roman
Pie 2 title	4	Blu L¦Su	Below	Swiss 721	Roman
Pie 3 title	4	Blu L¦Su	Below	Swiss 721	Roman
Pie 4 title	4	Blu L¦Su	Below	Swiss 721	Roman
Pie 5 title	4	Blu L¦Su	Below	Swiss 721	Roman
Pie 6 title	4	Blu L¦Su	Below	Swiss 721	Roman

4. Press **F10** to return to your Chart Edit Screen.

Text Attributes Complete

☐

Enhance Labels

Now you need to choose the same Font for the Pie Labels as you used for your Title and Subtitle.

1. Press **F8** for **Options.**
2. Press **2** for **Text Attributes.**
3. Press **2** for **Labels.**
4. Press **Tab** twice to move to the **Font Name** column.
5. Press **G** for **Geo Slab 712.** (The labels will appear in the default setting of Medium Italic.)
6. Press **F10** to return to your Chart Edit Screen.

Label Attributes Complete

Select Title/Subtitle Box

Your next step is to enclose the Title/Subtitle in an attractive box.

1. Press **F8** for **Options.**
2. Press **3** for **Appearance.** The Appearance Menu appears.
3. Press your ↓ arrow to move to **Region Frame Style** in the **Titles** column. **Line** is currently highlighted.
4. Press **F3** for **Choices.**
5. Press your ↑ arrow to move to **3-D** ⌐.
6. Press **Enter.** Your Appearance Menu now looks like this:

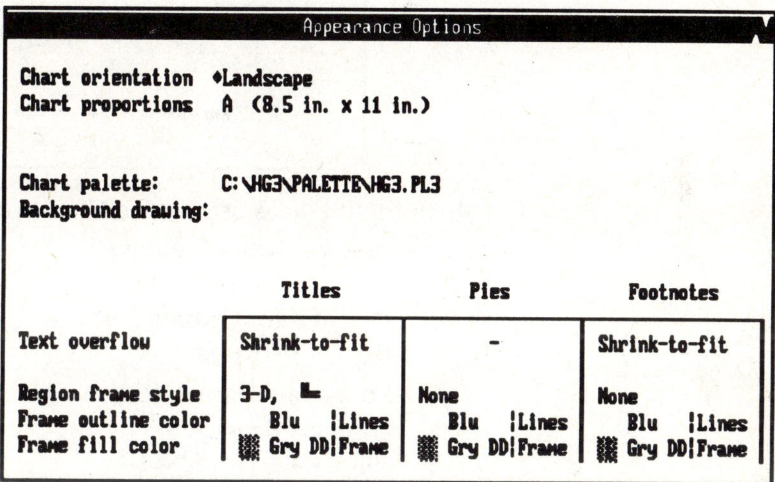

7. Press **F10** to return to your Chart Edit Screen.

Chart Appearance Enhanced

Display in 3-D Format

You now want to display your Pie Chart in a 3-Dimensional format.

1. Press **F8** for **Options.**
2. Press **5** for **Style.**
3. Press your ↓ arrow once to position your cursor opposite **3D Effect.**
4. Press **Y** for **Yes.**
5. Press **F10** to return to your Chart Edit Screen.

3-D Effect Selected

Define Slice Patterns

For a more effective print-out in black and white, you need to specify patterns for each slice. Note the column labeled Pattern at the far right of the Pie Chart Edit Screen. The numbers displayed refer to the 12 preset patterns available with Harvard Graphics.

The following illustration displays the 12 pattern types.

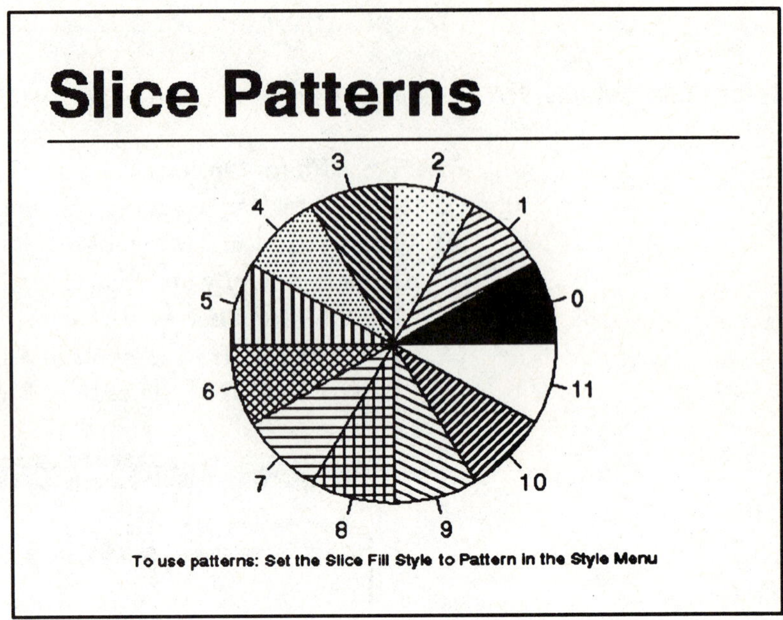

To fill the slices of your Pie Chart with patterns, you first need to access the F8 Options Menu as follows:

1. Press **F8** for **Options.**
2. Press **5** for **Style.**
3. Press your ↓ arrow to move your cursor opposite **Slice Fill Style. Color** is currently displayed.
4. Press **F3** for **Choices.**
5. Cursor to **Pattern** and press **Enter.**
6. Press **F10** to return to the Chart Edit Screen.

Slice Patterns Complete   ☐

Cut Cruises Slice   To emphasize the Cruises slice, you need to *cut* it from the main Pie.

1. Press your ↑ arrow and **Tab** to position your cursor in the **Cut** column to the right of *Cruises.*
2. Press **Y** for **Yes.**

Cruises Slice Cut   ☐

Display Chart ▶   Press **F2** to see your completed Chart as illustrated:

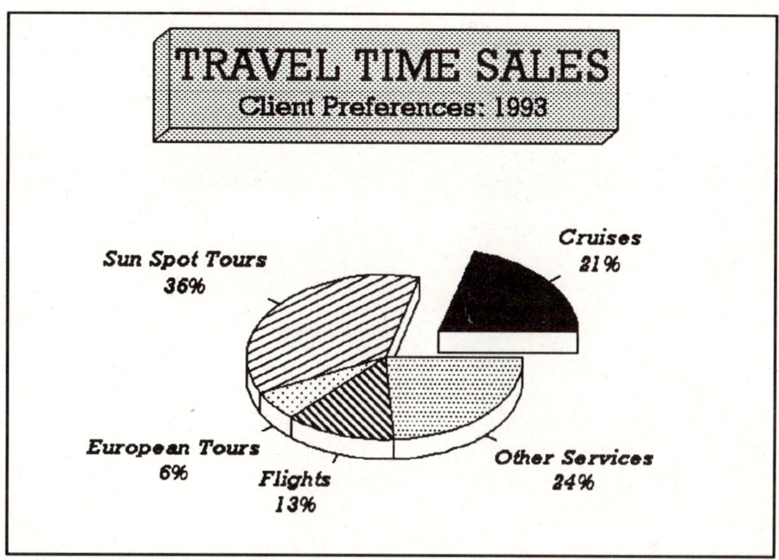

Press **Enter** to return to your Chart Edit Screen.

Save and Print Your Pie Chart

You now need to save your Pie Chart on your data disk and then access the
Output command to print your chart. Once you are satisfied with your Chart,
you can either exit from Harvard Graphics or get started on Pie Chart 2 in Activity 3.

Save
1. Press **F6** for **Main Menu.**
2. Press **4** for **File.**
3. Press **4** for **Save Chart.**

The Save Chart Menu appears. The default Directory (usually C:\HG3\DATA)
is displayed. You will save your file on a data disk in Drive A or B.

1. Press your ↑ arrow to position your cursor next to **Directory.**
2. Type *a:* or *b:* and then press **Delete** to erase the old Directory.
3. Press **Enter.**
4. At **Filename**, type *Piechrt1* and press **Enter.**
5. At **Description**, type *Pie Chart #1: Lesson 4.* Your Save Chart Screen
   should look like this:

```
┌─────────────────────────────────────────────────┐
│                   Save Chart                      │
│                                                   │
│ Directory:    a:\                                 │
│                                                   │
│ Filename:     Piechrt1                            │
│                                                   │
│ Description:  Pie Chart #1: Lesson 4              │
│                                                   │
│ Add to current presentation:    No               │
│                                                   │
└─────────────────────────────────────────────────┘
```

6.   Press **F10** to save and return to the Chart Edit Screen.

Pie Chart 1 Saved

Print
1.   Press **F6** for **Main Menu.**
2.   Press **5** for **Output.**
3.   Press **Enter** to accept **Printer 1.**
4.   Press **F10** to accept the Default Settings.

The Output to Printer Screen appears. Your Pie Chart has now been sent to the printer. Wait until the Output to Printer Screen disappears and you are returned to your Chart Edit Screen.

Pie Chart 1 Printed

You now have three options:

- Exit Harvard Graphics if you are finished with your learning session.
- Clear the current chart.
- Keep the Pie Chart 1 Edit Screen and begin Pie Chart 2. When you make the changes to Pie Chart 1 to turn it into Pie Chart 2, you will save it with a different name so that Pie Chart 1 remains unaffected by the new changes.

Exit Harvard Graphics
1.   Press **F6** for **Main Menu** and then **E** to exit Harvard Graphics.

Clear the Current Chart
1.   Press **F6** for **Main Menu.**
2.   Press **1** for **Create Chart** and **8** for **Clear Chart.**

Keep Pie Chart 1 on Screen
If you choose this option, you can continue immediately to Activity 3. Omit Get Piechrt1 from Disk and start with Link Pies.

ACTIVITY 3   PIE CHART 2

Pie Chart 2 will break the Cruise slice into five segments so that you can show the percentage of clients who booked each of five different types of cruises.

To show the relationship between the Cruise slice and the types of cruises, you need to *link* Pie Chart 1 with a new Pie Chart that lists the five cruise types. You will then display the slice breakdown in a column format rather than a pie format.

Four major steps are required to produce Pie Chart 2.

Step One:	Get and Link Pie Chart 1
Step Two:	Enter Your Data for Pie Chart 2
Step Three:	Enhance Your Linked Pie Charts
Step Four:	Save and Print Your Pie Chart

Follow the step-by-step instructions to link Pie Chart 1 with Pie Chart 2 and add a symbol (see page 124). Remember to place a check mark in the box next to each function you complete.

Get and Link Pie Chart 1

If you have exited out of Harvard Graphics and are starting fresh at your Main Menu, bring Piechrt1 (saved on your data disk) to the screen as follows:

Get Piechrt1 From Disk

1. Press **4** for **File** and **1** for **Get Chart.**
2. The default HG3 Data Directory appears on screen.
3. Type the letter of your data disk drive (*a:* or *b:*) over the current Directory and press **Delete** to erase the extra letters.
4. Press **Enter.**
5. At the list of files on your data disk, choose **Piechrt1** and press **Enter.**

Link Pie Charts 1 and 2

1. Press **F8** for **Options.**
2. Press **5** for **Style.**
3. Press your ↓ arrow twice to position your cursor opposite **Link Pies 1 & 2.**
4. Press **Y** for **Yes.**
5. Press **F10** to return to your Chart Edit Screen.

Pie Charts Linked   ☐

Enter Your Data for Pie Chart 2

Get Pie Chart 2

1. Press **F9** for **Pie Data.**
2. Press **2** for **Pie 2 Data.**

A second Chart Edit Screen appears. "Pie Chart 2" is displayed at the top of the screen.

Enter Slice Labels

1. Position your cursor in the **Label** column on the **Slice 1** line.
2. Type *Caribbean* and press **Enter.**

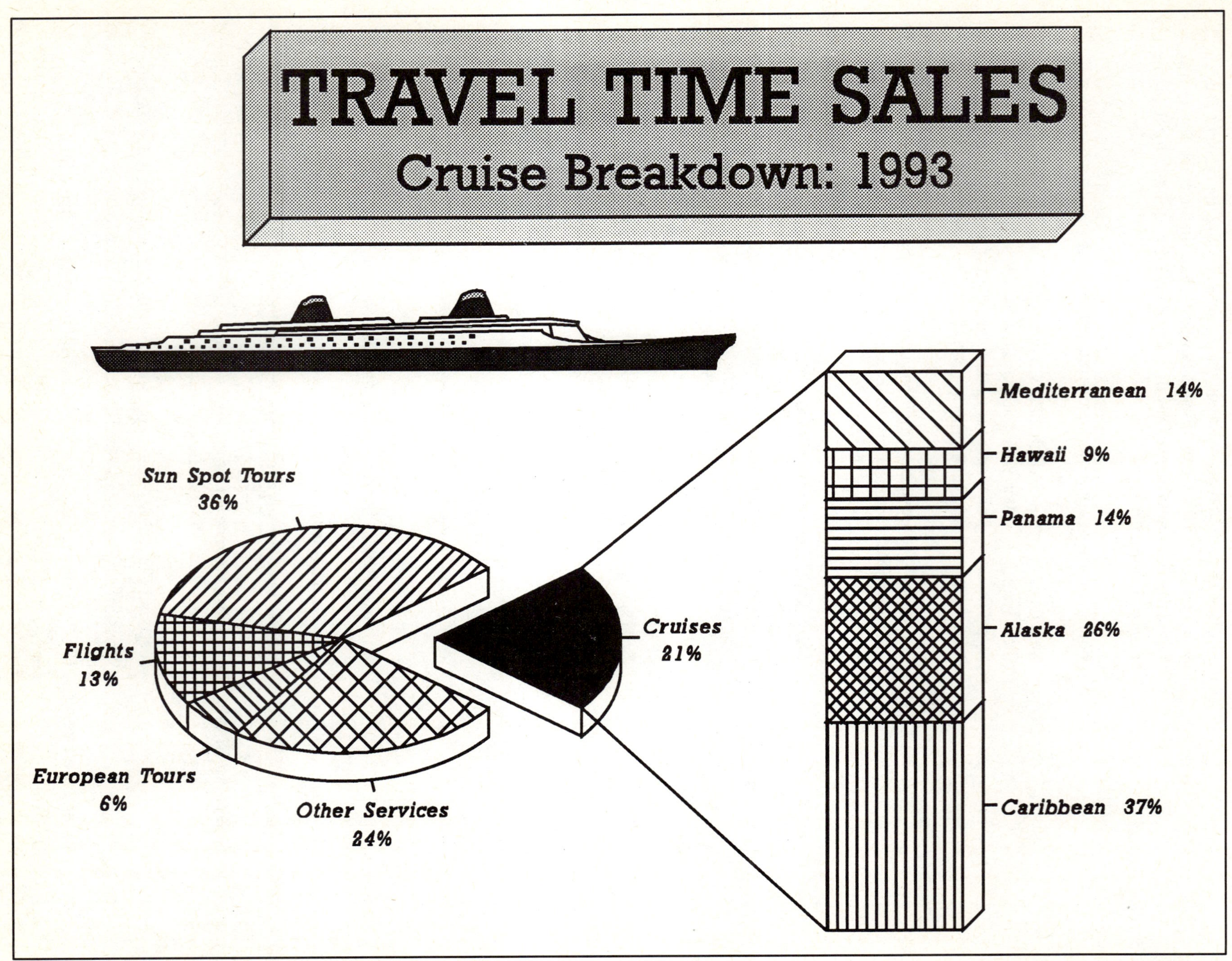

TRAVEL TIME SALES
Cruise Breakdown: 1993
Sun Spot Tours 36%
Flights 13%
European Tours 6%
Other Services 24%
Cruises 21%
Mediterranean 14%
Hawaii 9%
Panama 14%
Alaska 26%
Caribbean 37%

3. Type *Alaska* and press **Enter.**
4. Type *Panama* and press **Enter.**
5. Type *Hawaii* and press **Enter.**
6. Type *Mediterranean.*

Slice Labels Entered

Enter Value Data Now you will enter the value that will represent each slice label.

1. Press your ↑ arrow until *Caribbean* is highlighted.
2. Press **Tab** to move your cursor into the **Value** column.
3. Type *37* and press **Enter.**
4. Type *26* and press **Enter.**
5. Type *14* and press **Enter.**
6. Type *9* and press **Enter.**
7. Type *14.*

Your Pie Chart 2 Edit Screen should look like this:

```
PIECHRT1.CH3                        Pie Chart 2                              ▼
 F1-Help           F2-Show chart    F3-Choices      F4-Draw       F5-Mark   ▲
 F6-Main Menu      F7-Spell/Text    F8-Options      F9-Pie data   F10-Continue

Title:      TRAVEL TIME SALES
Subtitle:   Client Preferences: 1993
Footnote:
Pie title:


Slice         Label              Value      Cut       Color        Pattern
─────────────────────────────────────────────────────────────────────────
  1     Caribbean               37          No      ▌ Cyn  D|S        0
  2     Alaska                  26          No        Blu  D|S        1
  3     Panama                  14          No        Blu  L|S        2
  4     Hawaii                  9           No        Cyn   |S        3
  5     Mediterranean           14          No        Yel  L|S        4
  6                                         No        White |S        5
  7                                         No      ▌ Cyn  D|S        6
  8                                         No        Blu  D|S        7
  9                                         No        Blu  L|S        8
 10                                         No        Cyn   |S        9
 11                                         No        Yel  L|S       10
 12                                         No        White |S       11
```

Value Data Entered

Enhance Your Linked Pie Charts

Here's what you need to do to enhance your linked pie charts.

→ Change the Font Size for the Slice Labels
→ Display Pie Chart 2 in Column Format
→ Change the Slice Values to percentages
→ Specify Patterns for Pie Chart 2
→ Change the Subtitle of Pie Chart 1
→ Add, size, and position the Cruise Ship Symbol

Change Label Text Size   At present, the font size for the Labels is too large. Reduce the font size as follows:

1. Press **F8** for **Options.**
2. Press **2** for **Text Attributes** and then press **2** for **Labels.**
3. Type *2* in the **Size** column next to **Pie 1 Labels** and press **Enter.**
4. Type *2* in the **Size** column next to **Pie 2 Labels.**

You must also make the Font Name and Style the same as the Pie 1 Labels.

1. Press **Tab** twice to move to the **Font Name** column on the **Pie 2 Labels** line.
2. Press **G** for **Geo Slab 712.**
3. Press **F10** to return to your Pie 2 Edit Screen.

Label Attributes Complete   ☐

Show Pie 2 as a Column   1. Press **F8** for **Options.**
2. Press **6** for **Pie Options.**
3. Press your ↓ arrow once to move to the **Show As** column.
4. Press **F3** for **Choices.**
5. Cursor to **Column** and press **Enter.**
6. Press **F10** to return to your Pie 2 Edit Screen.

Column Format Specified   ☐

Change Slice Values to Percents   1. Press **F8** for **Options.**
2. Press **8** for **Slice Values.**
3. At the Slice Values Menu, press **N** for **No** next to **Show Values.**
4. Press **F10** to return to the Pie 2 Edit Screen.
5. Press **F8** for **Options** and then press **9** for **Slice Percents.**
6. Press **Y** for **Yes** next to **Show Percents.**
7. Press your ↓ arrow once to move opposite **Place Percents.**
8. Press **F3** for **Choices.**
9. Cursor to **Adjacent** and press **Enter.**
10. Press **F10** to return to your Pie 2 Edit Screen.

Percent Data Complete   ☐

Change Patterns   Patterns is already specified in the Style Menu because of the changes you made for Pie Chart 1. However, to prevent readers from thinking that slices and bars with the same patterns are related, you need to specify *different* patterns for the Column bars in Pie Chart 2.

1. Move your cursor into the **Pattern** column opposite *Caribbean.*
2. Type *5* and press **Enter.**
3. Type *6* and press **Enter.**

4. Type *7* and press **Enter.**
5. Type *8* and press **Enter.**
6. Type *9.*

Patterns Changed ☐

Display Chart ▶ Press **F2** to display your Chart and compare it with the following illustration:

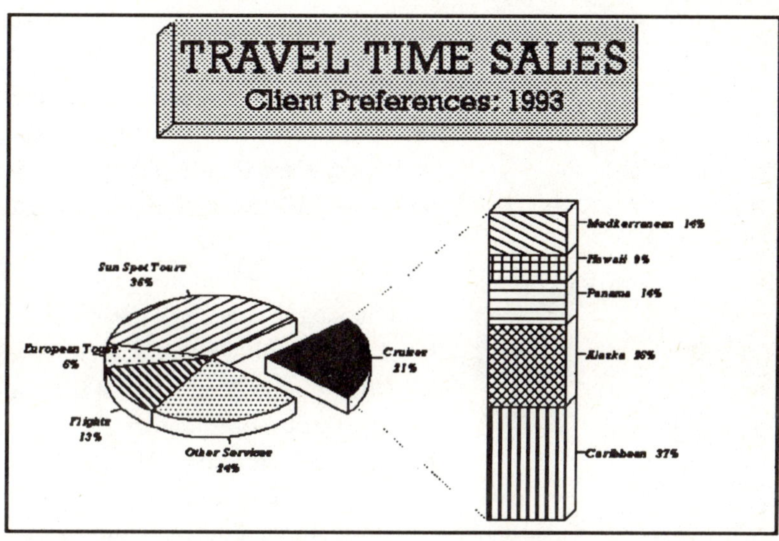

Two things are wrong with this chart. First, the Subtitle (Client Preferences: 1993) does not match the new data displayed by the linked pie charts and second, the European Tours label "runs into" the pie.

Press **F10** to return to your Pie 2 Edit Screen so that you can fix these problems.

Enter New Subtitle To enter a new subtitle, you need to return to the Pie Chart 1 Edit Screen and change the Subtitle from *Client Preferences: 1993* to *Cruise Breakdown.*

1. Press **F9** for **Pie Data.**
2. Press **Enter** to accept **Pie 1 Data.** Your Pie 1 Edit Screen reappears.
3. Position your cursor on the "C" in *Client Preferences.*
4. Type *Cruise Breakdown: 1993.* Press **Delete** to erase any extra letters.

Subtitle Changed ☐

Reposition European Tours To prevent *European Tours* from running into its pie slice, you can switch its position with *Flights.*

1. Position your cursor on *European Tours.*
2. Type *Flights* and press **Delete** to erase any extra letters.
3. Press **Tab** and type *13.*
4. Press your ↑ and ← arrows to move to *Flights.*

5.   Type *European Tours*.
6.   Press **Tab** and type *6*. Press **Delete** to erase the extra number.

Label Repositioned

Add Cruise Ship Symbol

Your last step is to access the Harvard Graphics Draw Screen and retrieve the Cruise Ship Symbol.

Access Draw

1.   Press **F4** to place your Pie Charts in the Draw Screen.

The following functions require the use of the mouse. Remember to click the **left** button to select functions and the **right** button to finish functions. If you click the right button twice, you may return to the Main Menu. If this happens, just press or click on **3** for **Draw** to return to your Draw Screen.

Add Symbol

1.   Click your **left** mouse button on the **Symbol Tool.**
2.   Click again on **Get.**
3.   At the Symbol Files Screen, press **F8** to sort the files alphabetically.
4.   Click on the ▼ symbol at the top right of your screen to scroll through the list of symbol directories.
5.   Click on **TRANSPT1.**
6.   Click on the **Ocean Liner.**
7.   Click on **F10** twice to return to your Draw Screen.

Symbol Retrieved

Size and Position Ocean Liner

Notice how your ocean liner appears in the center of your Draw Screen. Your first step is to reduce the size of your ocean liner.

Size

1.   Click first on the bottom right corner handle and use the **Shift** key to drag your ocean liner up and across so that it is approximately one-half its original size.
2.   Now click on the top middle handle to flatten your ocean liner.

Position

1.   Position your mouse anywhere on the ocean liner *except* on one of the orange handles.
2.   Click **left** and move your ocean liner under and to the left of the Subtitle.
3.   Adjust the sizing if required.
4.   Click **right** to remove the handles.

Compare the size and position of your ocean liner to the following illustration:

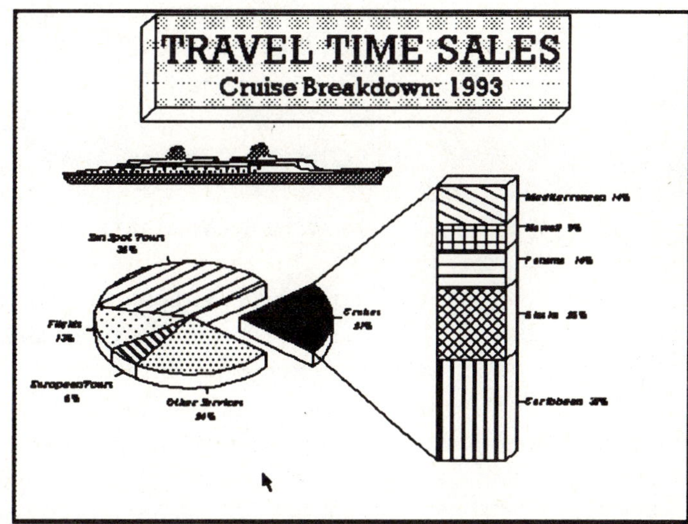

Ocean Liner Sized and Positioned

Save and Print Your Pie Chart

You now need to save your Pie Chart on your data disk as Piechrt2 and then access the Output command to print your Chart. Once you are satisfied with your Chart, you can either exit from Harvard Graphics or get started on the Challenge Assignment in Activity 4.

Save
1. Press **F6** for **File.**
2. Press **2** for **Save Chart.**

The Save Chart Menu appears. Either the default Directory or your data drive will be displayed next to Directory. Change your Directory if necessary and then replace Pie Chart 1 with Pie Chart 2.

1. At **Filename,** type *Piechrt2* over *Piechrt1* and press **Enter.**
2. At **Description,** type *Pie Chart #2: Lesson 4.*
3. Press **F10** to save and return to the Draw Screen.

Pie Chart 2 Saved

Print
1. Press **F6** for **Main Menu** and **E** for **Exit to Main Menu.**
2. Press **5** for **Output.**
3. Press **Enter** to accept **Printer 1.**

Press **F2** to view how your document will appear in printed form.

If you are satisfied with the look of your Pie Chart, press **F10** twice to accept the Default Settings.

The Output to Printer Screen appears. Your Pie Chart has now been sent to the printer. Wait until the Output to Printer Screen disappears and you are returned to your Draw Screen.

Pie Chart 2 Printed

You now have two options:

- Exit Harvard Graphics if you are finished with your learning session.
- Clear the current Pie Chart and get started on creating your own Pie Chart in Activity 4.

Exit Harvard Graphics

1.   At the Main Menu, press **E** to exit Harvard Graphics.

Clear the Current Chart

1.   At the Main Menu, press **1** for **Create Chart.**
2.   Press **8** for Clear Chart.

ACTIVITY 4   CHALLENGE ASSIGNMENT

Read through the following sections for suggestions on content and then adapt the instructions given for your own material. Use the boxes provided to record information about your Pie Chart.

The Challenge Assignment requires four major steps.

Step One:	Select Your Company/Organization
Step Two:	Determine Your Pie Chart Purpose
Step Three:	Plan your Pie Chart Information
Step Four:	Create and Format Your Pie Chart

Select Your Company/Organization

First, you need to decide on the kind of company or organization your Pie Chart will represent. For example, you could create a company that sells sports cars and then develop a Pie Chart to show the breakdown of sales according to sports car type. Give your company/organization a name.

Name and Type of Your Company/Organization:

Determine Your Pie Chart Purpose

You need to determine *why* you require a Pie Chart in the first place. For example, do you wish to inform the board of directors that your company needs to sell more units of a particular product? Or how about convincing your supervisor that your organization needs to target a new market segment?

Remember that the purpose of the Pie Charts you created in Activities 2 and 3 was to show the breakdown of travel services for Travel Time, Inc., and to motivate sales personnel to book more cruises.

Here are some other purposes of a Pie Chart.

- Inform customers that your product is preferred by the largest market segment
- Motivate public relations personnel to concentrate on eliminating the greatest source of complaints
- Inform a board of directors that 20% of your operating budget is spent on employee benefits

Specify the purpose of your Pie Chart in the following box.

> Pie Chart Purpose:

Plan Your Pie Chart Information

Now determine the information you will include in your Pie Chart. First, you need to give your Pie Chart a Title and a Subtitle, and then you need to list your Pie Chart Labels.

Title/Subtitle The Title and Subtitle you choose should reflect the purpose of your Pie Chart. For example, here is a Title/Subtitle for a Pie Chart that illustrates the relative ages of all women clients who use a local fitness center:

FITNESS INC. CLIENT PROFILE
Breakdown of Women Participants By Age

In the following box, specify your Pie Chart Title and Subtitle:

> Pie Chart Title:
>
> Pie Chart Subtitle:

Chart Labels Determine how many slices your Pie Chart will contain and then assign a name to each slice. For example, the Pie Chart to show the breakdown of women participants by age at Fitness, Inc. could have the following labels:

Slice	Label	Value
Slice 1	18–24	16
Slice 2	25–36	40
Slice 3	37–45	20
Slice 4	46–55	14
Slice 5	55 and over	10

Fill in the following box with your Pie Chart slice labels. Limit your pie to no more than five slices and assign a value to each slice. You can convert your values into percentages when you create your Pie Chart.

Slice 1: _________________________________Value: _________

Slice 2: _________________________________Value: _________

Slice 3: _________________________________Value: _________

Slice 4: _________________________________Value: _________

Slice 5: _________________________________Value: _________

Now go on to create your Pie Chart. If you wish, link two pies as you did in Activity 3.

Create and Format Your Pie Chart

The following selection of commands and functions will help you create and format your Pie Chart. Once you are satisfied with the format of your Pie Chart, press **F4** to place your chart in the Draw Screen and try adding one or two symbols.

Experiment until you are satisfied that your Pie Chart displays your information in an efficient—and attractive—format.

Create Chart At the Main Menu, press **1** for **Create Chart** and **2** for **Pie.**

Edit Chart At the Main Menu, press **2** for **Edit Chart** to return to the Chart Edit Screen. This option only works if you have already either created or retrieved a chart.

Display Chart   Press **F2** to look at your Pie Chart and then press **Enter** to return to the Chart Edit Screen.

Options   Press **F8** to see a list of Options provided in the Chart Edit Screen. Here are some of the functions you can access in Options:

1. Alter your text fonts and attributes: **2** for **Text Attributes**
2. Put a box around your Title/Subtitle: **3** for **Appearance**
3. Change your Chart to a 3-D format: **5** for **Style**
4. Link two Pies: **5** for **Style**
5. Specify patterns: **5** for **Style**
6. Change a Pie to a Column: **6** for **Pie Options**
7. Replace Chart Values with Percentages: **8** for **Slice Values** and **9** for **Show Percents**

Draw   Press **F4** to place your Pie Chart in the Draw Screen so that you can add symbols.

Get Symbol   Click your **left** mouse button on the **Symbol Tool.** Click again on **Get** and then choose a symbol from the files provided. Click **F10** twice to return to the Draw Screen.

Save   From the Chart Edit Screen, press **F6** for **Main Menu** and then **4** for **File** and **4** for **Save Chart.** From the Draw Screen, press **F6** for **File** and then **2** for **Save Chart.**

Fast Save: Press **Ctrl + S.**

When you access the Save Menu, change to the Directory in which you wish to save your file (usually Drive A or B) and then type a filename and description for your Pie Chart.

Print   At the Main Menu, choose **5** for **Output**, press **Enter** to accept **Printer 1**, and then press **F10.**

Clear a Chart   If you wish to start a new chart and have saved your current chart, first return to the Main Menu (**F6** from the Edit Screen or **F6** and **E** from the Draw Screen). Now choose **1** for **Create Chart** and then **8** for **Clear Chart.** If you haven't saved your current chart, a message will appear. You can then press **ESC** to save your chart before clearing it.

Exit Harvard Graphics   From the Chart Edit Screen, press **F6** to return to the Main Menu and then press **E** to exit the program.

ACTIVITY 5   LESSON FOUR REVIEW

Test your understanding of the functions and concepts you learned in Lesson
Four by completing the following Review Questions.

1. At the Main Menu, what two choices do you make to access the Pie
   Chart Edit Screen?
2. What information do you enter in the Label column?
3. What is the Options command?
4. In Options, what do you choose to alter Text Attributes?
5. In Options, what do you choose to link two pies?
6. What is the Choices command?
7. How do you place your Pie Chart in the Draw Screen?
8. How do you bring a picture or symbol to the screen?
9. At the Main Menu, what selection do you choose to print your Pie
   Chart?
10. How do you clear a Chart from your screen?

SUPPLEMENTARY EXERCISES

Exercise 1   Create a Pie Chart to show the budget categories of a local television station.
You determine the station name and five budget categories. Examples include
salaries, production, and advertising. Assign a value to each of the five slices.
Change the Pie Chart attributes, appearance options, etc., as required to create
a sharp and interesting document.

Exercise 2   Cut one of the slices for the Pie Chart you created in Exercise 1. Link the Pie
Chart to a second Pie Chart that shows the additional budget categories represented by the cut slice. Display the second Pie Chart as a column and change
your Chart Title and Subtitle to reflect the new information. Experiment with
different attribute, appearance, and style options.

<table>
<tr><td>LESSON
FIVE</td><td># BAR CHART</td></tr>
</table>

FEATURES

- Creating a Bar Chart
- Enhancing the Y Axis
- Using Group/Ungroup
- Entering X Data Automatically
- Adding and Shading Symbols
- Saving Charts as Symbols
- Using the Front Tool

INTRODUCTION

In Lesson Five, you will learn about one of the most common charts used to show relationships between data—the Bar Chart. Here are the lesson activities.

ACTIVITY 1: Determine the information required for your Bar Chart.

ACTIVITY 2: Follow the instructions provided to create the simple Bar Chart on page 139.

ACTIVITY 3: Follow the instructions given to add a second data series and a shaded background symbol to your Bar Chart as illustrated on page 147.

ACTIVITY 4: Create your own Bar Chart based on data you have developed.

ACTIVITY 5: Complete the Lesson Review Questions on Bar Chart creation and enhancement.

ACTIVITY 1 BAR CHART INFORMATION

You choose a Bar Chart when you wish to show how data compare over time or distance. In Harvard Graphics, the Bar Chart is called an *XY Chart* because data displayed on a Bar Chart relates to both a vertical and a horizontal *axis*. To plan an effective Bar Chart, you first need to understand the *anatomy* of a typical Bar or XY Chart.

Bar Chart Areas Let's look at the three principal areas of the Bar Chart:

- X Axis
- Y Axis
- Data Points (called *Series*)

The following Bar Chart displays the number of guests who stayed at Maplewood Resort over the four seasons of the year. Note the labels designating the three chart areas.

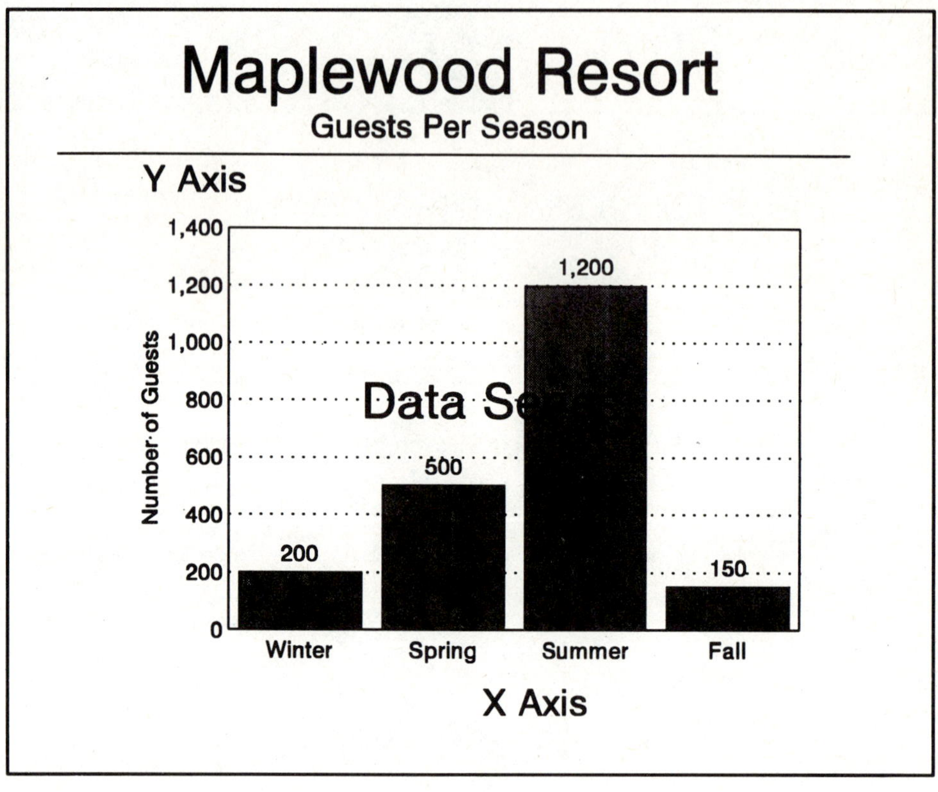

X Axis As you can see from the illustration, the *X Axis* is the horizontal line at the bottom of the Bar Chart. On this line are displayed the *categories* used to compare the Bar Chart data.

For most Bar Charts, the X Axis displays time series information such as years, months, weeks, etc. The chart illustrated uses the X Axis to define the four seasons of the year. Note that the number of guests in the summer far exceeds the number of guests who come to Maplewood Resort in the winter, spring, and fall.

Y Axis The *Y Axis* displays the numbers that define each data point. In the Maplewood Resort chart, these numbers represent the number of guests who came to the resort each season. In winter, for example, only 200 guests arrived. In the summer, however, the Resort hosted 1,200 guests.

Data Points (Series) The *Data Points* represent the *kind* of information being measured and are displayed as vertical bars. For the Maplewood Resort chart, these bars represent guests.

Multiple Series You can use a Bar Chart to compare one data series over time or to display two or more series for each time point on your X Axis. For example, here is a

Bar Chart that compares the number of visitors to Willow Bay who stay at the Maplewood Resort with the number of guests who stay at its nearest competitor, the Pink Sands Hotel.

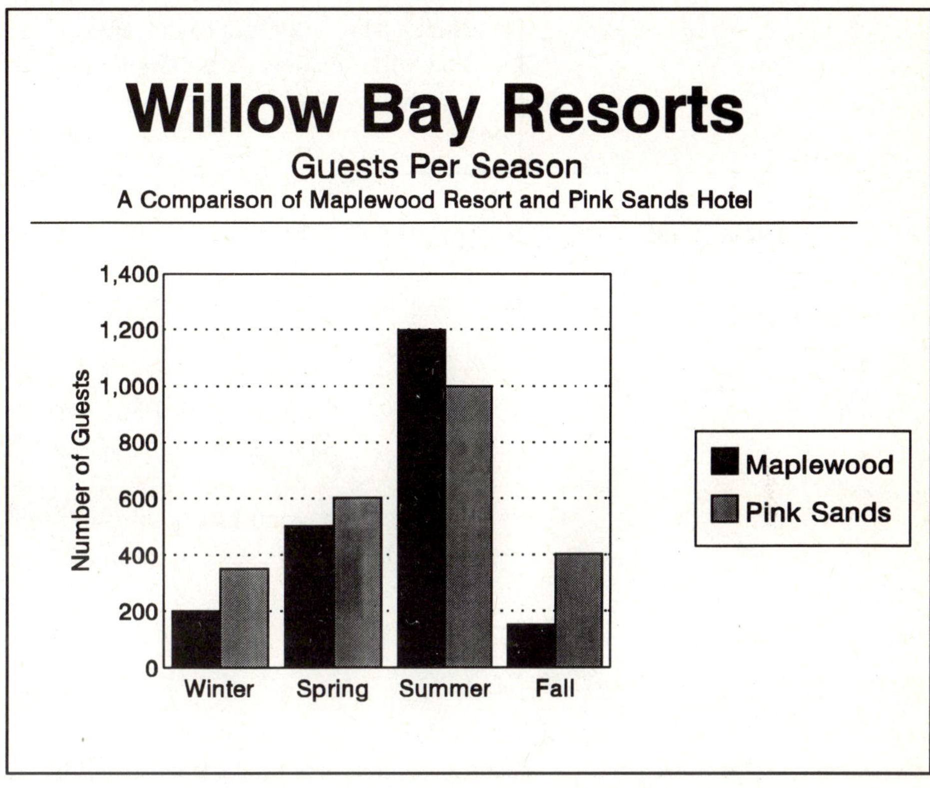

Bar Chart Purpose

An effective Bar Chart should lead readers to draw some kind of *conclusion* about the data presented. For example, the Bar Chart comparing Maplewood Resort to the Pink Sands Hotel informs readers that while both places are popular in the summer, the Pink Sands Hotel attracts more visitors year-round. If the reader of this chart was the owner of Maplewood Resort, he or she might then wish to investigate *why* the Pink Sands Hotel attracts more visitors in the off-season.

Number of Bars

Bar Charts convey the strongest impact when the number of time series is limited to five or less. For example, you could use a Bar Chart to compare a company's sales over five years. Your goal is to make the information you wish to convey as clear as possible so that your readers can understand the significance of the various bars at a glance.

Summary of Activities 2 and 3

In Activities 2 and 3, you will create two Bar Charts for DataLink Word Services—a medium-sized company of 15 employees that provides word processing, graphics, and writing services to local businesses.

The Bar Chart you create in Activity 2 will present DataLink's annual sales over a five-year period. This chart will be used as part of a sales presentation to potential investors. DataLink wishes to illustrate how sales have grown consistently from its beginnings five years earlier.

In Activity 3, you will add another data series to your Bar Chart to show how DataLink's sales compare to the sales of its nearest competitor, WordMaster, Inc. You will then access the Draw Screen to add a shaded symbol and to reposition the various areas of your chart.

ACTIVITY 2   BAR CHART 1

Three major steps are required to produce Bar Chart 1.

Step One: Create Your Bar Chart
Step Two: Enhance Your Bar Chart
Step Three: Save and Print Your Bar Chart

Follow the step-by-step instructions to reproduce Bar Chart 1 (see page 139). Remember to place a check mark in the box next to each function you complete.

Create Your Bar Chart

You will first create your Bar Chart and then use the Automatic Data Entry feature to enter your X-Axis information. You can then type the Title/Subtitle of your Bar Chart and the data for each series.

Create Chart
1.   At the Main Menu, press **1** for **Create Chart.**
2.   Press **3** for **XY Chart.**
3.   Press **1** for **Bar.**

The X Data Pop-up appears:

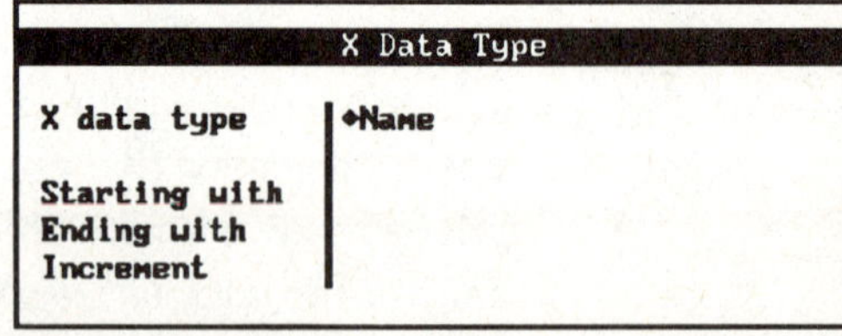

Enter X Data
In the X Data Pop-up, you will choose Year as your data type and then enter the beginning and ending years. Harvard Graphics will fill in the intervening years.

Data Type
1.   Press **F3** for **Choices.**
2.   Press your ↓ arrow to move to **Year** and then press **Enter.**

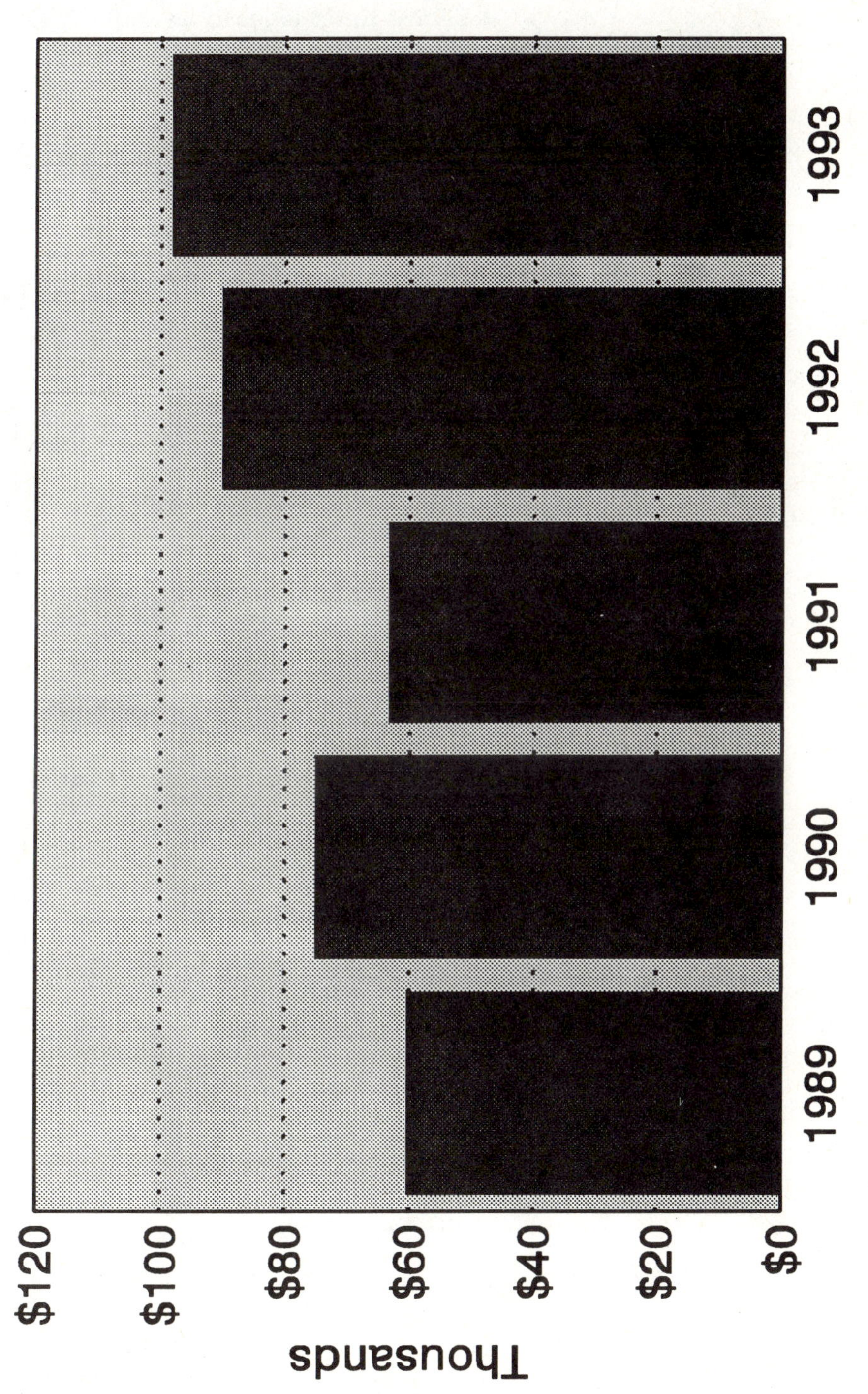

DataLink Word Services
Annual Sales: 1989-1993
1993
1992
1991
1990
1989
$120
$100
$80
$60
$40
$20
$0
Thousands

140   Lesson Five

Data Times

1. Press your ↓ arrow to position your cursor opposite **Starting With.**
2. Type *1989* and press **Enter.** Your cursor is now positioned next to **Ending With.**
3. Type *1993*.
4. Press **Enter** twice to reveal the XY Chart Edit Screen.

X Data Entered

In the Chart Edit Screen, you will see the years 1989–1993 entered in the X Axis column and your cursor positioned next to **Title.**

```
                                       XY Chart                              ◆▾
 ▌ F1-Help          F2-Show chart                      F4-Draw         F5-Mark
   F6-Main Menu     F7-Spell/Text   F8-Options         F9-XY data      F10-Continue

   Title:      ◄────────── ┌Cursor Position┐
   Subtitle:               └───────────────┘
   Footnote:

   ─────────────────────────────── 1 ────── 2 ────── 3 ────── 4 ─────
   Data│      X Axis
   Pt  │       Year         Series 1   Series 2   Series 3   Series 4
   ─────────────────────────────────────────────────────────────────
   1   │      1989
   2   │      1990
   3   │      1991
   4   │      1992
   5   │      1993
   6   │
   7   │
   8   │
   9   │
   10  │
   11  │
   12  │
```

Enter Title/Subtitle

Now you will enter the Title and Subtitle of your Bar Chart.

1. Type the Title of your Bar Chart: *DataLink Word Services.* Press **Enter.**
2. Now type the Subtitle of your Bar Chart: *Annual Sales: 1989–1993.* Press **Enter** twice.

Title/Subtitle Entered

Enter Series Data

Your next step is to enter the sales figures for each of the five years listed in the X Axis Year column. Your cursor currently appears on **1989.**

1. Press **Tab** to move to the **Series 1** column.
2. Type *60* and press **Enter.**

> **NOTE:** The *60* you just typed represents $60,000 worth of sales for 1989. When you enhance your Bar Chart in the next section, you will indicate that the *60* represents $60,000.

Fill in the rest of the series information:

1990:	78	1992:	85
1991:	62	1993:	98

Series Data Entered ☐

Enhance Your Bar Chart

Your Bar Chart contains all the required information. Here's what you need to do next.

Required Enhancements

> → Modify the Text Attributes:
> - Change the Text Size and Font
> - Align the Y-Axis Label vertically
>
> → Change the Region Frame Style for the Title/Subtitle
> → Enhance the Y Axis:
> - Display the $ sign and enter the Y-Axis Label
>
> → Hide the Legend Box
> → Change the Bar Colors

Modify Text Attributes

1. Press **F8** for **Options.**
2. Press **2** for **Text Attributes.**
3. Press **1** for **Titles/Footnotes.**

The Text Attributes Menu appears. Note that your cursor is currently resting under the **9** in the **Size** column next to **Title.**

Subtitle Text Size

Your Subtitle needs to be a few points larger to balance the Title.

1. Press your ↓ arrow once so that it rests on the **5** next to **Subtitle.**
2. Type *7*.

Title Font/Style

1. Press your ↑ arrow once and then **Tab** three times to move your cursor into the **Font Name** column opposite **Title.**
2. Press **F3** for **Choices.**
3. Cursor to **Geo Slab 712** and press **Enter.**
4. Press **Tab** to move to the **Font Style** column.
5. Press **F3** for **Choices.**
6. Cursor to **Medium** and press **Enter.**

Subtitle Font/Style
Fast Method

Now change the text font and style of the Subtitle with only two keystrokes:

1. Press your ↓ and ← arrows to move your cursor into the **Font Name** column opposite **Subtitle.**
2. Press **G** for **Geo Slab 712.**
3. Press **Tab** to move to the **Font Style** column and press **M** for **Medium.**

Y-Axis Alignment

You want the word *thousands* to appear vertically alongside the Y Axis to show that your two-digit Y-Axis numbers represent thousands. Your first step is to specify vertical alignment in the Text Attributes Menu.

1. Press your ↓ and ← arrows to position your cursor in the **Alignment** column opposite **Y1 Axis Title.**
2. Press **F3** for **Choices.**
3. Select **Side** and press **Enter.**

Compare your Text Attributes Menu to the following illustration:

Text Attributes Titles/Footnotes	Size	Color	Alignment	Font Name	Font Style
Title	9	Yel L|Ti	Center	Geo Slab 71	Medium
Subtitle 1	7	Blu L|Su	Center	Geo Slab 71	Medium
Subtitle 2	5	Blu L|Su	Center	Swiss 721	Roman
Footnote 1	3.5	Blu L|Fo	Left	Swiss 721	Roman
Footnote 2	3.5	Blu L|Fo	Left	Swiss 721	Roman
Footnote 3	3.5	Blu L|Fo	Left	Swiss 721	Roman
X axis title	3.5	Cyn LL|XT	Center	Swiss 721	Roman
Y1 axis title	3.5	Cyn LL|Y1	◆Side	Swiss 721	Roman
Y2 axis title	3.5	Yel L|Y2	Top	Swiss 721	Roman
Legend title	3.5	Cyn LL|XT	Center	Swiss 721	Roman

4. Press **F10** to return to your Chart Edit Screen.

Text Attributes Complete

Enhance Chart Appearance

You now need to select the Appearance Menu in F8 Options to change the Region Frame Style for the Title/Subtitle. First, access the Appearance Menu.

1. Press **F8** for **Options.**
2. Press **3** for **Appearance.**

Title Region Frame Style

1. Press your ↓ arrow to move your cursor next to **Region Frame Style** in the **Titles** column. **Line** is currently highlighted.
2. Press **F3** for **Choices.**
3. Press your ↑ arrow to move to **Octagonal** and press **Enter.**
4. Press **F10** to return to your Chart Edit Screen.

Chart Appearance Enhanced

Enhance Y Axis You want the dollar sign ($) to appear next to each number on your Y Axis and the word *thousands* to be displayed as the Y-Axis Title.

Currency Sign
1. Press **F8** for **Options.**
2. Press **A** for **Format.**
3. Press your ↓ arrow twice to move opposite **Currency.**
4. Press **Tab** to move your cursor into the **Y1 Axis** column.
5. Press **Y** for **Yes.**
6. Press **F10** to return to your Chart Edit Screen.

Y Axis Title
1. Press **F8** for **Options.**
2. Press **1** for **Titles/Footnotes.**
3. Press your ↓ arrow to move opposite **Y1 Axis Title.**
4. Type *Thousands*.
5. Press **F10** to return to your Chart Edit Screen.

Y Axis Enhanced   ☐

Hide Legend You require a Legend when you have two or more data series. For Bar Chart 1, you only have one series of bars. Therefore, you do not need the Legend box displayed. You will display the Legend box again when you modify your Bar Chart in Activity 3.

You hide your Legend as follows:

1. Press **F8** for **Options.**
2. Press **7** for **Legend.** Your cursor is opposite **Show Legend.**
3. Press **N** for **No.**
4. Press **F10** to return to your Chart Edit Screen.

Legend Hidden   ☐

Change Bar Color To print clearly in black and white, you need to select a darker color for the bars than the default setting.

1. Press **F8** for **Options.**
2. Press **6** for **Series.**
3. Press your ↓ arrow to move opposite **Fill Color** in the **Series 1** column.
4. Press **F3** for **Choices.**
5. Cursor to **Orange** and press **Enter.**
6. Press **F10** to return to the Chart Edit Screen.

Bar Color Changed   ☐

Display Chart ▶ Press **F2** to display your Chart. Compare your screen to the following illustration and then press **Enter** to return to your Chart Edit Screen.

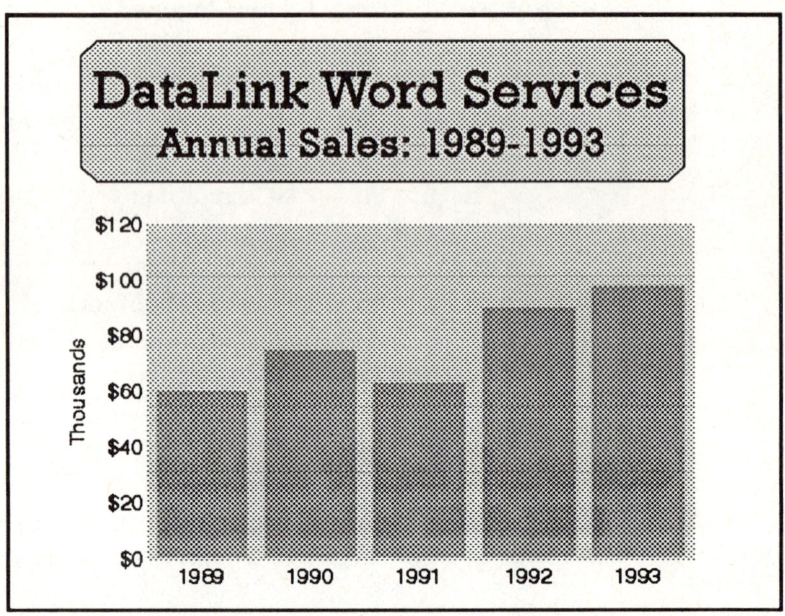

Save and Print Your Chart

You will save your Bar Chart on your data disk and then access the Output command to print your Chart. Once you are satisfied with your Chart, you can either exit from Harvard Graphics or get started on Activity 3.

Save   1.   Press **F6** for **Main Menu.**
      2.   Press **4** for **File** and then **4** for **Save Chart.**

The Save Chart Menu appears. Your cursor is currently positioned next to **Filename.** The default Directory (usually C:\HG3\DATA) is displayed. You will save your file on a data disk in Drive A or B.

1.   Press your ↑ arrow to move opposite **Directory.**
2.   Type *a:* or *b:* and then press **Delete** to erase the old Directory.
3.   Press **Enter.**
4.   At **Filename**, type *Barchrt1* and press **Enter.**
5.   At **Description**, type *Bar Chart #1: Lesson 5.*

Your Save Chart Menu should look like this:

```
┌─────────────────────────────────────────────────┐
│                                                  │
│  ███████████████████████████ Save Chart ████████ │
│                                                  │
│  Directory:      a:\                              │
│                                                  │
│  Filename:       Barchrt1                         │
│                                                  │
│  Description:    Bar Chart #1: Lesson 5           │
│                                                  │
│  Add to current presentation:      No            │
│                                                  │
└─────────────────────────────────────────────────┘
```

6. Press **F10** to save and return to the Chart Edit Screen.

Bar Chart 1 Saved   ☐

Print 1. Press **F6** for **Main Menu.**
    2. Press **5** for **Output.**
    3. Press **Enter** to accept **Printer 1.**
    4. Press **F2** to view how your document will appear in printed form.

> **NOTE:** If you do not like the look of your Chart, press **ESC** to return
> to your Chart Edit Screen. Access the F8 Options Menu to
> change your Chart's Appearance (3) or Text Attributes (2).

5. If you are satisfied with the look of your Chart, press **F10** twice to accept
the Default Settings.

The Output to Printer Screen appears. Your Bar Chart has now been sent to
the printer. Wait until the Output to Printer Screen disappears and you are returned to the Chart Edit Screen.

Bar Chart 1 Printed   ☐

You now have three options:

- Exit Harvard Graphics if you are finished with your learning session.
- Clear the current chart.
- Keep the Bar Chart 1 Edit Screen and begin Bar Chart 2. After making
  your changes to Bar Chart 1, you will save Bar Chart 2 under a different
  name so that Bar Chart 1 remains unaffected by the new changes.

Exit Harvard Graphics 1. Press **F6** for **Main Menu** and then **E** to exit Harvard Graphics.

Clear the Current Chart

1. Press **F6** for **Main Menu.**
2. Press **1** for **Create Chart.**
3. Press **8** for **Clear Chart.**

Keep Bar Chart 1 on Screen

If you choose this option, you can continue immediately to Activity 3. Omit Get Barchrt1 from Disk and start with Edit Bar Chart Data.

ACTIVITY 3   BAR CHART 2

Three major steps are required to produce Bar Chart 2.

Step One: Edit Your Chart Data
Step Two: Enhance Your Bar Chart
Step Three: Save and Print Your Chart

Follow the step-by-step instructions to edit and enhance your Bar Chart (see page 147). Remember to place a check mark in the box next to each function you complete.

Edit Your Chart Data

Get Barchrt1 from Disk

If you exited out of Harvard Graphics and are starting fresh at your Main Menu, bring Barchrt1 (saved on your data disk) to the screen as follows:

1. Press **4** for **File** and **1** for **Get Chart.**

   Either the default HG3 Data Directory or your Drive A or B appears next to **Directory.** If necessary, enter your data drive and press **Enter.**

2. At the list of files on your data disk, choose **Barchrt1** and press **Enter** twice to access the Chart Edit Screen.

Edit Bar Chart Data

DataLink needs to modify its Bar Chart to show how its sales compare to those of its nearest competitor, WordMaster. To illustrate this comparison, you need to add a second series of bars that represents WordMaster's sales.

Three activities are required:

- Change the Bar Chart Title.
- Key in titles for Series 1 and Series 2.
- Add the WordMaster sales information.

Bar Chart Title

Start with the Bar Chart Title.

1. Position your cursor on the "D" in *DataLink* opposite **Title.**
2. Type *DataLink & WordMaster* and press **Enter.**

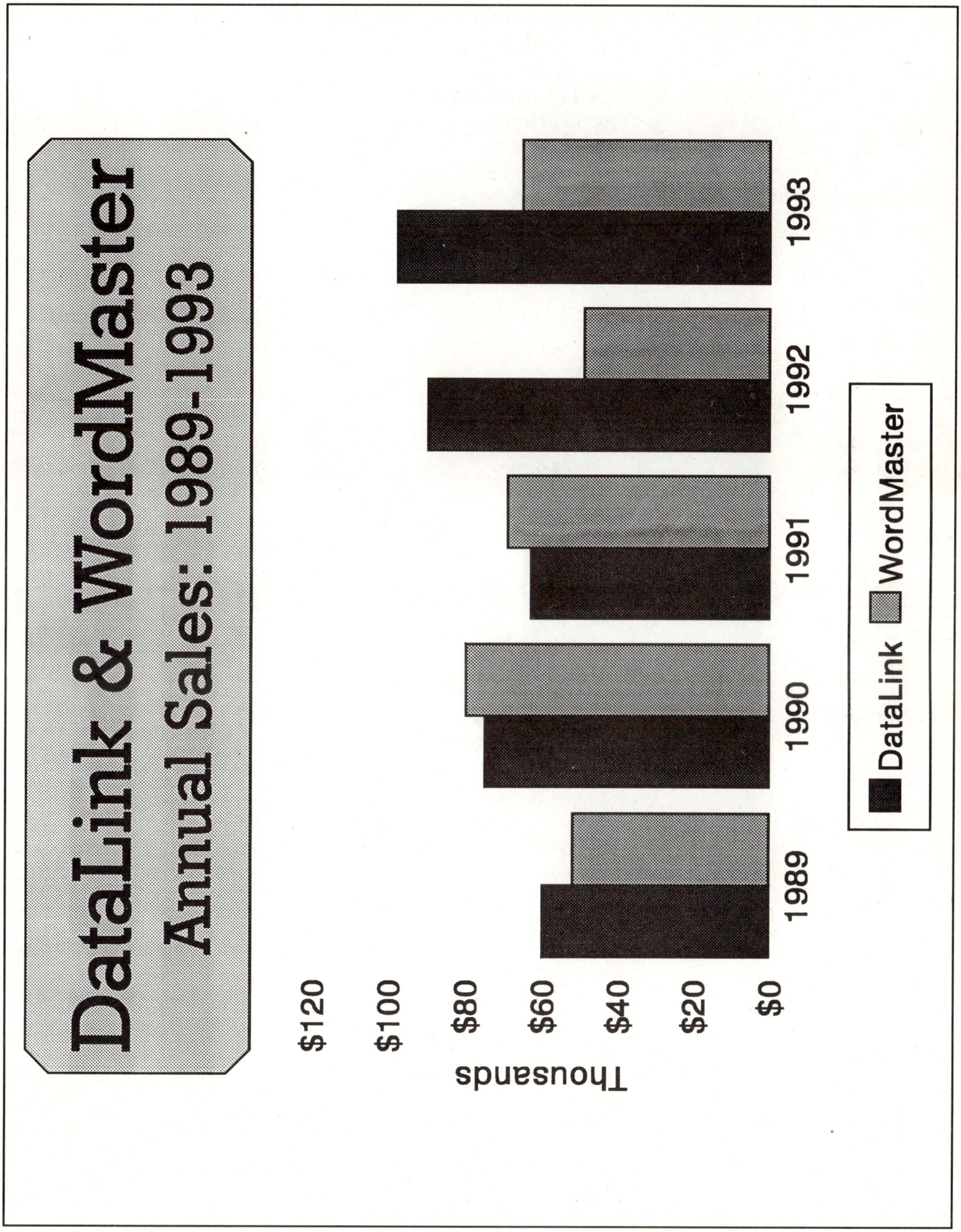

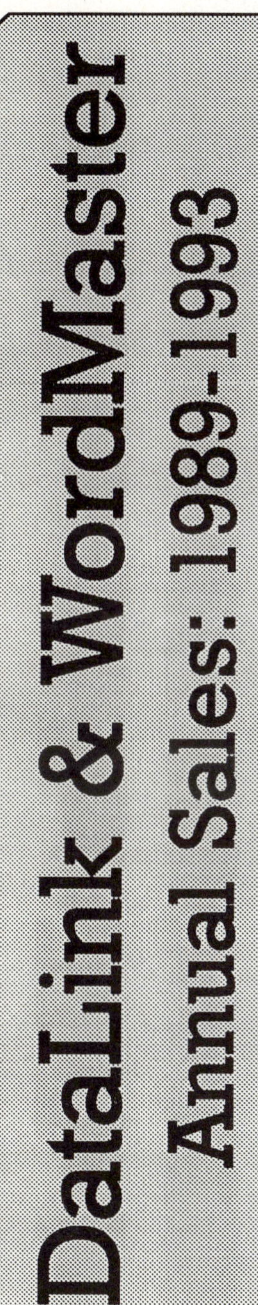

DataLink & WordMaster
Annual Sales: 1989-1993

$120
$100
$80
$60
$40
$20
$0
Thousands
1989
1990
1991
1992
1993
DataLink
WordMaster

Series Titles

1. Press your ↓ arrow twice, **Tab**, and ↑ arrow to move your cursor to the "S" in **Series 1.**
2. Type *DataLink*.
3. Press **Tab** to move to **Series 2.**
4. Type *WordMaster.*

WordMaster Sales Information

1. Press your ↓ arrow to position your cursor under *WordMaster* so that it appears on line 1.
2. Type *52* and press **Enter.**

Fill in the rest of the series information for WordMaster:

1990:   80   1992:   49
1991:   69   1993:   65

Your Chart Edit Screen should look like this:

```
                                        XY Chart
 F1-Help          F2-Show chart                    F4-Draw          F5-Mark
 F6-Main Menu     F7-Spell/Text  F8-Options         F9-XY data       F10-Continue

 Title:      DATALINK & WORDMASTER
 Subtitle:   Annual Sales: 1989-1993
 Footnote:

                              ---------- 1 --------- 2 --------- 3 --------- 4 -----
 Data|      X Axis        |           |           |           |
 Pt  |       Year         | Datalink  | WordMaster| Series 3  | Series 4
     |                    |           |           |           |
 1      1989                68          52
 2      1990                78          80
 3      1991                62          69
 4      1992                85          49
 5      1993                98          65
 6
 7
 8
 9
 10
 11
 12
```

Bar Chart Data Complete   ☐

Display Chart ▶ Press **F2** to display your Chart and compare it with the following illustration.

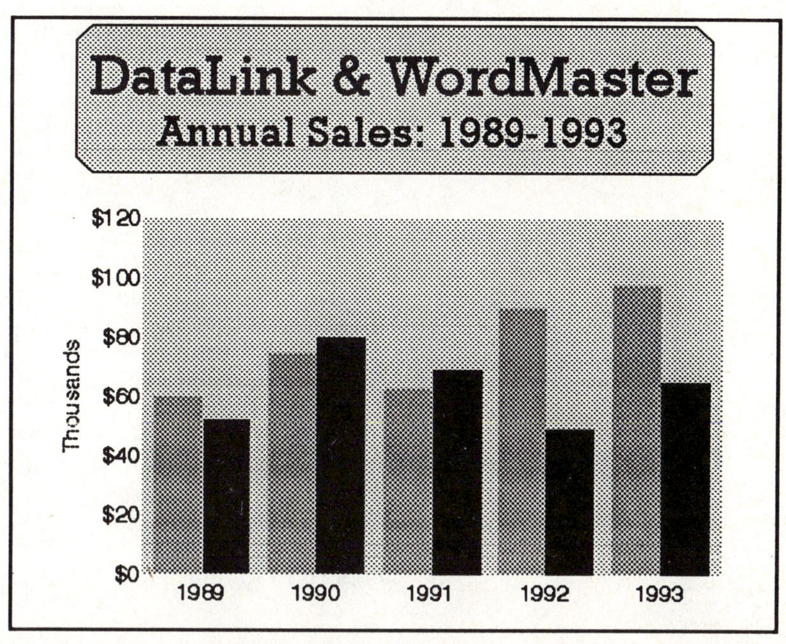

To return to the Chart Edit Screen, press **Enter.**

Enhance Your Bar Chart

Required Enhancements

To enhance your Bar Chart, you will first make changes in the Chart Edit Screen to add the Legend and delete the axis frame and grid lines. You will then save your Chart as a symbol, clear your screen, and access the Draw Screen. In Draw, you will "break apart" the various parts of your Bar Chart so that you can display a shaded symbol behind some of the bars.

Let's start with the Chart Edit changes.

→ Show the Legend and Move its Location
→ Hide the Axis Frame
→ Delete the Dotted Y-Axis Grid

Show Legend

1. Press **F8** for **Options.**
2. Press **7** for **Legend.**
3. Press **Y** for **Yes** to **Show Legend.**

Legend Location

1. Press your ↓ arrow to move your cursor to the box surrounded by dots as illustrated:

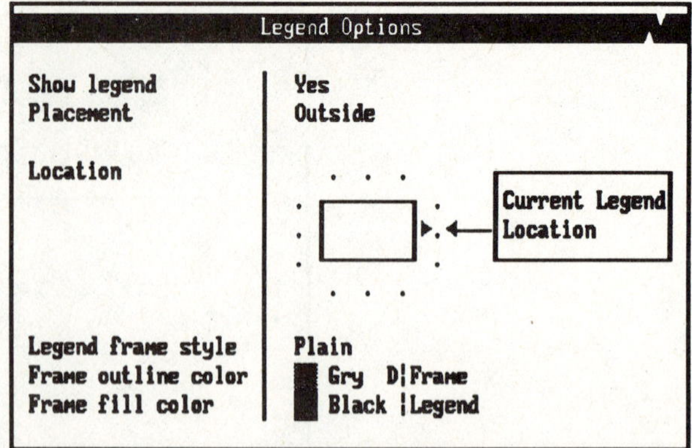

The dots correspond to various locations around the Chart. By default, your Legend box will appear to the right of your Chart.

Display Chart ▶ Press **F2** to display your Chart and see the current location of your Legend box. Press **F10** to return to your Legend Options Pop-up.

You need to move your Legend box so that it appears underneath your Bar Chart.

1. Press your **space bar** three times so that the arrow moves to the middle dot on the bottom.

Display Chart ▶ Press **F2** to display your Chart and see the new location of your Legend box as illustrated:

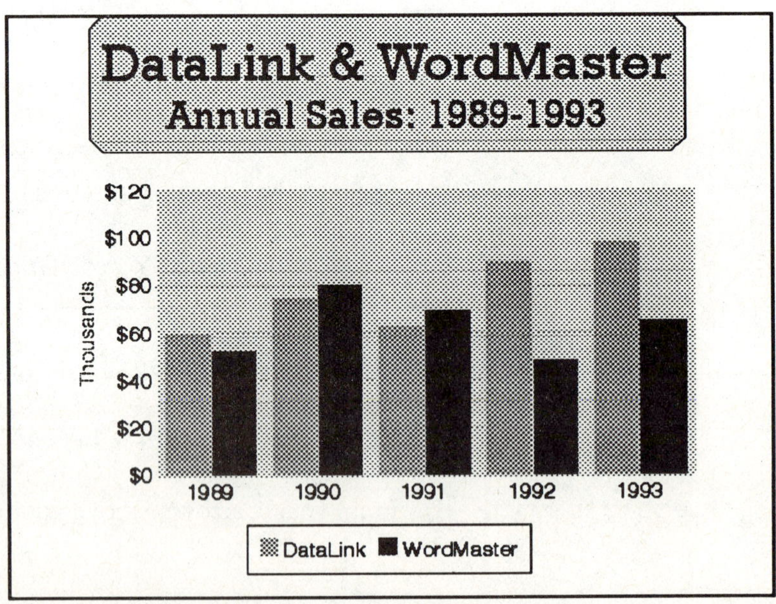

Press **Enter** to return to your Chart Edit Screen.

Legend Positioned

Hide the Axis Frame   In order to add a shaded symbol of the computer programmer, you need to "hide" the box that contains your Bar Chart data.

1.   Press **F8** for **Options.**
2.   Press **8** for **Axis Frame.**

The Axis Frame Pop-up appears. You need to change the Axis Frame Style to None and the Frame Outline and Fill Colors to Background.

Axis Frame Style   1.   Press **F3** for **Choices.**
2.   Cursor to **None** and press **Enter.**

Frame and Fill Colors   To change the Frame Outline Color:

1.   Press your ↓ arrow once to move opposite **Frame Outline Color.**
2.   Press **F3** for **Choices.**
3.   Cursor up to **Background** (the top selection) and press **Enter.**

To change the Frame Fill Color:

1.   Press your ↓ arrow once to move opposite **Frame Fill Color.**
2.   Press **F3** for **Choices.**
3.   Cursor up to **Background** (the top selection) and press **Enter.**

Compare your screen to the following illustration:

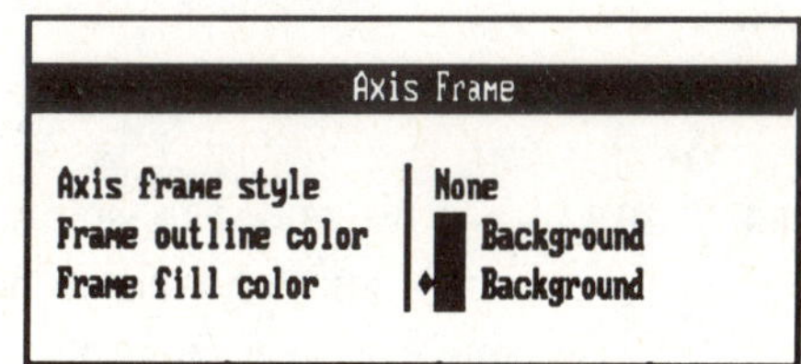

4.   Press **F10** to return to your Chart Edit Screen.

Axis Frame Changes Complete

Remove Grid Lines   Dotted lines appear on your Bar Chart to help your reader match the bar heights with the numbers on the Y Axis. To provide a clean background for the symbol you will add in Draw, you need to delete these grid lines.

1.   Press **F8** for **Options.**
2.   Press **9** for **Axis Options.**

The Axis Options Pop-up appears.

1.   Press **Tab** once to position your cursor in the **Y1 Axis** column.
2.   Press your ↓ arrow to move your cursor opposite **Grid Line Style.** The **Dotted** selection currently appears.

3. Press **F3** for **Choices.**
4. Cursor to **None** and press **Enter.**
5. Press **F10** to return to your Chart Edit Screen.

Grid Lines Removed

Display Chart ▶ Press F2 to display your Chart.

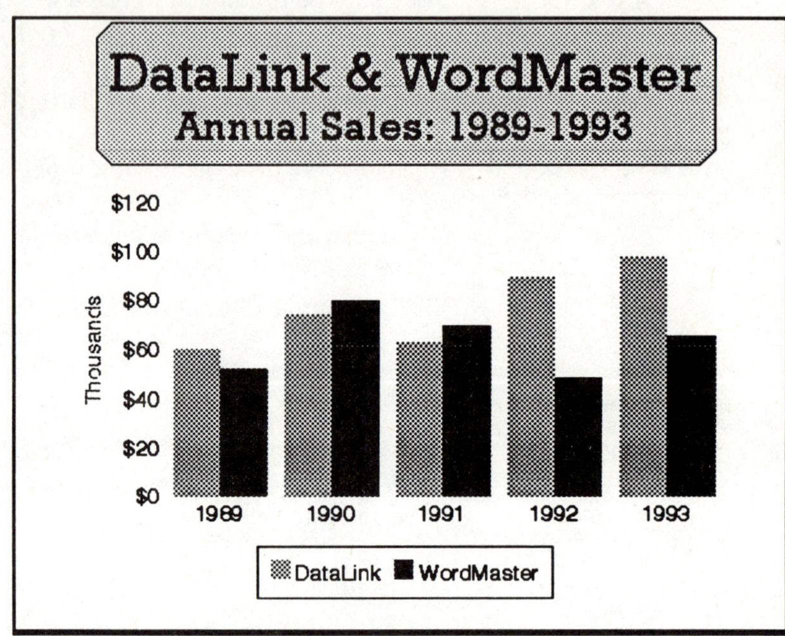

Press **Enter** to return to your Chart Edit Screen.

Save Chart as Symbol   You now need to save your Bar Chart as a symbol. You save a chart as a symbol when you want to be able to separate its various elements so that you can move or size them individually.

For Bar Chart 2, you need to place individual bars of your chart in front of the shaded symbol of the programmer. (Refer to the illustration of Bar Chart 2 on page 147).

Four steps are required to change your Bar Chart into a symbol and then access the Draw Screen.

- Save your Chart as a symbol.
- Save and clear Bar Chart 2 from your screen.
- Access the Draw Screen.
- Retrieve your Bar Chart Symbol into the Draw Screen.

Save as Symbol   1.   Press **F6** for **Main Menu.**
                  2.   Press **4** for **File** and **6** for **Save as Symbol.**

The Save Symbol File Pop-up appears. Notice that it is very similar to the Save Menu. Your cursor is currently positioned next to **Filename.** The default Directory (usually C:\HG3\DATA) is displayed. You will save your Bar Chart symbol on a data disk in Drive A or B.

1.   Press your ↑ arrow to move opposite **Directory.**
2.   Type *a:* or *b:* and then press **Delete** to erase the old Directory.
3.   Press **Enter.**
4.   At **Filename**, type *Barsym1* and press **Enter.**
5.   At **Description**, type *Bar Symbol #1: Lesson 5.*

Your Save Symbol File Menu should look like this:

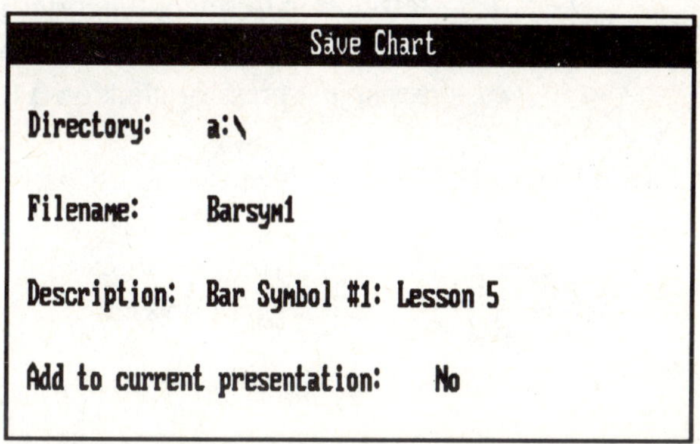

6.   Press **F10** to save your chart as a symbol and return to the Chart Edit Screen.

Bar Symbol Saved ☐

Save Chart   First, use the **Fast Save** method to save your chart as Barchrt2.

1.   Press **Ctrl + S** to take you directly to the Chart Save Menu.
2.   At **Filename**, type *Barchrt2* over *Barchrt1* and press **Enter.**
3.   At **Description**, type *Bar Chart #2: Lesson 5.*
4.   Press **F10** to save and return to the Chart Edit Screen.

Bar Chart 2 Saved ☐

Clear Chart   1.   Press **F6** for **Main Menu.**
              2.   Press **1** for **Create Chart.**
              3.   Press **8** for **Clear Chart.**

Access Draw   You are now ready to access the Draw Screen. Here's what you need to do.

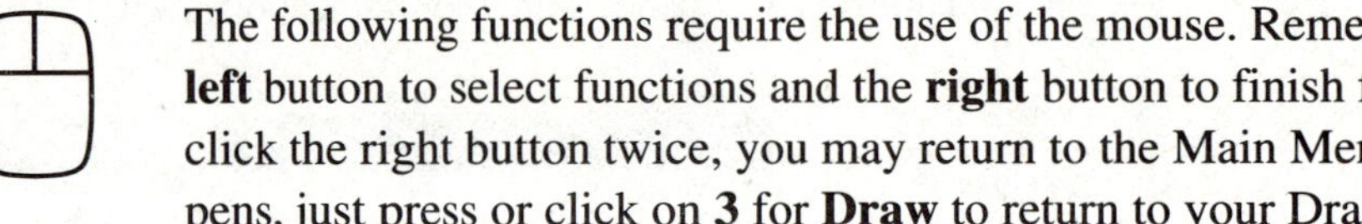

> - Retrieve your Bar Chart Symbol
> - Retrieve the Data Programmer Symbol:
>   - → Position the Programmer Symbol
>   - → Shade the Programmer Symbol
> - Ungroup your Bar Chart Symbol:
>   - → Select individual bars to place in front of the Programmer Symbol

First, access the Draw Screen from the Main Menu.

1.   Press **3** for **Draw.**

The following functions require the use of the mouse. Remember to click the **left** button to select functions and the **right** button to finish functions. If you click the right button twice, you may return to the Main Menu. If this happens, just press or click on **3** for **Draw** to return to your Draw Screen.

Retrieve Bar Chart Symbol   First, retrieve your Bar Chart Symbol to your Draw Screen.

1.   Click your **left** mouse button on the **Symbol Tool.**
2.   Click again on **Get.**

The Symbol Directory appears.

1.   Place your cursor opposite **Directory** and, if necessary, type *a:* or *b:* to access your data drive.
2.   Press **Delete** to erase the extra letters.
3.   Cursor to **Barsym1** and press **Enter.**
4.   Click on the picture of your **Bar Chart Symbol.**
5.   Click on **F10** twice to return to your Draw Screen.

Bar Chart Symbol Retrieved

Notice that orange handles appear around your Bar Chart Symbol to indicate it is selected.

1.   Click your **right** mouse button once to remove the orange handles.

Retrieve Programmer Symbol   You now need to get the Harvard Graphics Programmer Symbol.

1.   Click your **left** mouse button on the **Symbol Tool.**
2.   Click again on **Get.**
3.   If necessary, change your Directory to HG3\SYMBOL.
4.   At the Symbol Files Screen, press **F8** to sort the files alphabetically.

5. Press the ▼ symbol at the top right of your screen to scroll through the list of Symbol Directories.
6. Click on **HUMANS5**.
7. Click on the picture of the **Programmer**.
8. Click on **F10** twice to return to your Draw Screen.

Programmer Symbol Retrieved

Programmer Position

1. Position your mouse pointer anywhere on the programmer *except* on one of the handles.
2. Click and hold down your **left** mouse button and move your programmer up about 3/4" so that it is positioned as illustrated:

The orange handles remain around the Programmer Symbol to indicate it is still selected.

Programmer Shading

Five steps are required to shade your programmer.

- Select the Color Tool.
- Change the Fill Color to light gray.
- Change the Line/Text Color to none.
- Click on the Shade Tool.
- Choose dark gray to black as your shading range.

Color Tool

1. Move your mouse to the **Color Tool** and click your **left** button to select it.

The Color Tool Pop-up appears. Note that the **Line/Text** box (second box from the top of the Pop-up) is currently highlighted.

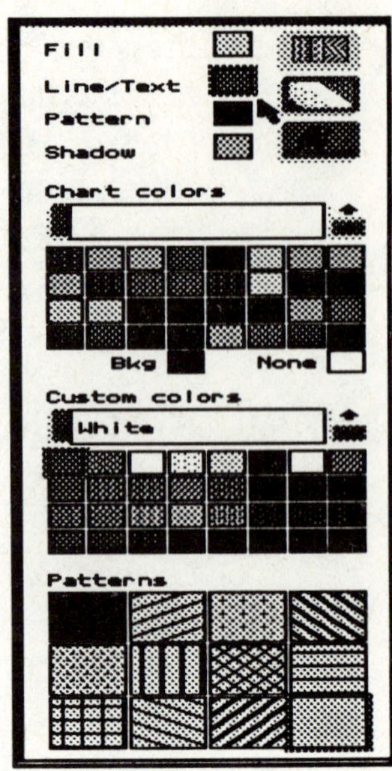

Fill Color
1. Move your mouse above the **Line/Text** box to the **Fill** box.
2. Click on the **Fill** box.
3. Move your cursor down to the color boxes below **Chart Colors.**
4. Click on the **White** box.

Note that both your Fill box and your programmer turn white.

Line/Text Color
1. Click on the **Line/Text** box under the **Fill** box at the top of the Color Pop-up.
2. Move your cursor down to the box that specifies **None.**
3. Click on the **None** box.

Shading
1. Click on the **Shade Tool.** Two things will happen:

- The label *Gradient* and three boxes (one large and two small) appear at the bottom of your Color Pop-up.
- Your programmer now appears shaded white to black from top to bottom.

Compare your screen to the following illustration:

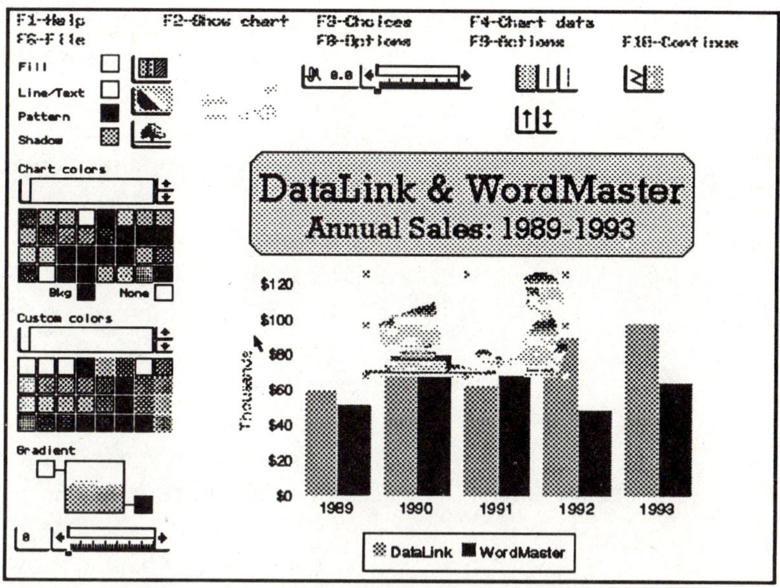

You want your programmer to appear lightly shaded in a black-and-white
print-out. With Harvard Graphics, your printer reads black text as white and
white text as black. Therefore, to ensure your programmer looks lightly
shaded at print-out time, you need to specify shading from dark gray to black.

1. Click on the small **White** box under **Gradient.**

    This box specifies the *starting color*. The small box at the bottom right of
    the large middle box specifies the *ending color.*

2. Move your cursor up to the **Dark Gray** color box to the left of the **Black**
    box in the group of Custom Color boxes.
3. Click on the **Dark Gray** color box to select it as the starting color.

The small box to the bottom right of the large middle box should already be
black.

Note how your programmer just about disappears against the black screen
background. Don't worry! When you print your Chart on a black-and-white
printer, your programmer will look just right.

4. Click **right** twice to exit the Color Pop-up and remove the handles around
    the Programmer Symbol.

Programmer Shading Complete   □

Ungroup Bar Chart   You are almost finished with Bar Chart 2! All you need to do now is ungroup your Bar Chart Symbol and place the central bars *in front* of the Programmer Symbol.

1. Position your cursor anywhere on your screen *except* on your programmer.
2. Click your **left** button. Note the orange handles that appear around your Bar Chart Symbol.

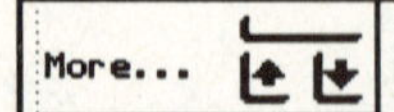

3. Click on the ▼ symbol at the very bottom of your Tool Box.

A new selection of tools appears. When you want to return to the first selection of tools, you merely click on the ▲ symbol.

Ungroup Tool   1. Click on the **Ungroup Tool.**

Notice how orange handles now appear around three areas of your Bar Chart Symbol: the Title/Subtitle, the Chart Region, and the Legend.

2. Click **right** to remove all the handles.

You now need to select just the chart region and ungroup it.

1. Click on any bar in your chart region. Orange handles appear around the entire chart region.
2. Click on the **Ungroup Tool** again. Your screen now looks like this:

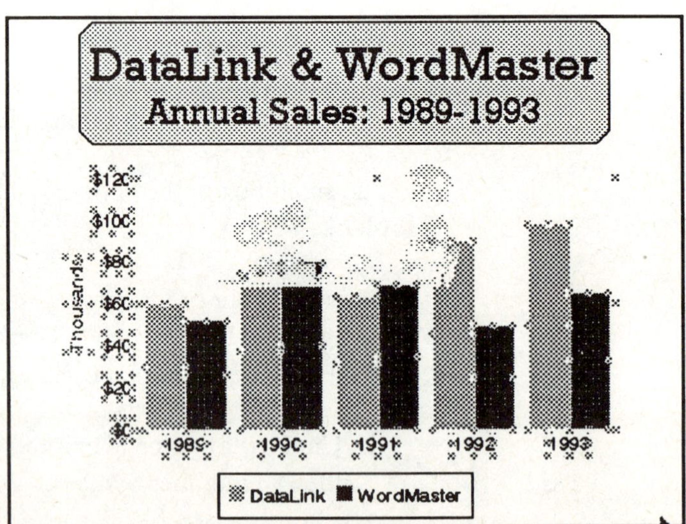

3. Click **right** to remove all the handles.

You need to place the four bars that currently obscure your programmer in front of the programmer.

To do this, you will select each bar in turn and then access the Front Tool. Here's how.

Bar Selection   1. Click on the first bar on the left that is currently *behind* the Programmer Symbol. Note that the orange handles now appear only around the bar you have selected.
2. Move your mouse to the next bar to the right.
3. Press **Shift** and at the same time click your **left** mouse button. Handles now appear around both bars.
4. Press **Shift** and your **left** mouse button to select the rest of the bars that are behind the Programmer Symbol.

Front Tool   1. Click on the ▲ symbol at the bottom of your Tool Box to view the first selection of tools.

2. Click on the **Front Tool.** Two **Front Tools** appear.
3. Click on the top **Front Tool.**

Notice how the bars you selected now appear in front of the Programmer Symbol as illustrated:

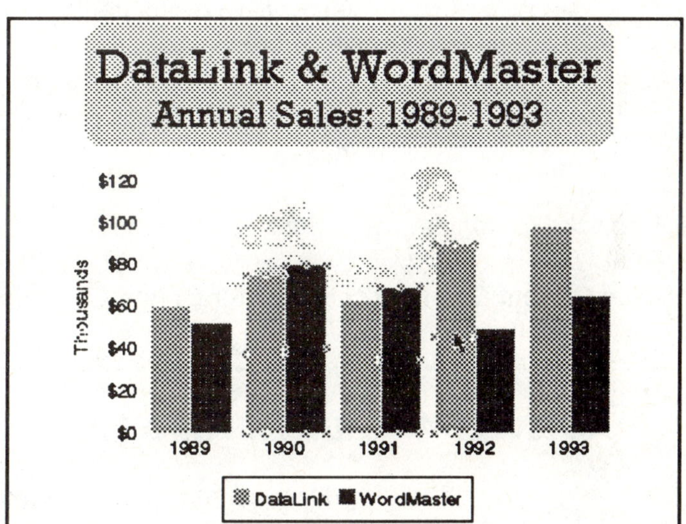

4. Click **right** to remove the handles from the bars.

Bar Placement to Front Complete

Save and Print Your Chart

You will save Bar Chart 2 on your data disk and then access the Output command to print your chart.

Save   1. Press **F6** for **File.**
2. Press **2** for **Save Chart.**

The Save Chart Menu appears. If necessary, enter your Drive A or B next to **Directory**.

3. At **Filename**, type *Barchrt2* and press **Enter.**
4. At **Description**, type *Bar Chart #2: Lesson 5* and press **Enter** twice. A message will appear warning you that Barchrt2 already exists.
5. Press **F10** to confirm.

Bar Chart 2 Saved

Print 1. Press **F6** for **File** and **E** for **Exit to Main Menu.**
2. Press **5** for **Output.**
3. Press **Enter** to accept **Printer 1.**

Press **F2** to view how your document will appear in printed form. If you are satisfied with the look of your Bar Chart, press **F10** twice to send your Chart to the printer.

Bar Chart 2 Printed

You now have two options:

- Exit Harvard Graphics if you are finished with your learning session.
- Clear the current chart and get started on creating your own Bar Chart in Activity 4.

Exit Harvard Graphics 1. At the Main Menu, press **E** to exit Harvard Graphics.

Clear the Current Chart 1. Press **1** for **Create Chart** and **8** for **Clear Chart.**

ACTIVITY 4 CHALLENGE ASSIGNMENT

Read through the following sections for suggestions on content and then adapt the instructions given for your own material. Use the boxes provided to record information about your Bar Chart.

The Challenge Assignment requires three major steps.

Step One: Determine Your Bar Chart Purpose
Step Two: Plan Your Bar Chart Information
Step Three: Create and Format Your Bar Chart

Determine Your Bar Chart Purpose

Remember that a Bar Chart shows data in relation to the time series displayed on the X Axis. Time series information includes years, months, weeks, or quarters.

Change Over Time

You need to show how a collection of data *changes* over time. For example, you could decide to show how the sales of two pet stores compare over a five-year period or how the monthly class averages for two related college courses fluctuate over a four-month term.

Complete the sentence in the following box.

My Bar Chart shows how ________.________________________________

____

has changed/fluctuated/altered/compared over a period of ___________

years/months/weeks/quarters.

Plan Your Bar Chart Information

To plan your Bar Chart information, you need to determine the following five components:

- Title and Subtitle
- X-Axis Labels
- Series Titles
- Y-Axis Title (if any)
- Series Data

Title/Subtitle

For a Bar Chart, your title will either be the name of the company or organization your Bar Chart represents or a summary of the information presented. The Subtitle generally specifies the *nature* of the data.

For example, here is the Title/Subtitle for a Bar Chart that compares how often three types of users check out library materials over the four quarters of one year:

Title: LIBRARY USE
Subtitle: Quarterly Comparison of Three User Groups

Write your Bar Chart Title and Subtitle in the following box.

```
Title:

Subtitle:
```

X-Axis Labels

Now you need to specify the *time series* information you will display on your X Axis. For the Library Use Bar Chart, the X-Axis information would be: Jan–Mar, Apr–Jun, Jul–Sep, and Oct–Dec to represent the four quarters of the year. You can also specify quarters as Q1, Q2, etc.

Remember to limit your time series to no more than *five* categories. Specify your X-Axis Labels in the following box.

```
X-Axis Labels:
1.
2.
3.
4.
5.
```

Series Titles

If you plan to show more than one bar per time category, you need to specify *titles* for each series. If, however, you wish to display only one series, as in Bar Chart 1, you do not need to specify a name. Your title will make the name of the one series obvious.

For the Library Use Bar Chart, three series titles are required to represent the three User Groups: Children, Teens, and Adults.

Limit the number of series to three or less. Too many bars on a page can confuse readers and detract from the overall impact of your Bar Chart.

List your series titles in the following box.

```
Series 1:
Series 2:
Series 3:
```

Y-Axis Title

Usually, you need to add a Y-Axis Title either to explain that the numbers shown represent thousands, millions, etc., or to define what the numbers refer to.

For the Library Use Bar Chart, the Y-Axis Title would be *Number of Users*.

Write your Y-Axis Title in the following box:

Y-Axis Title:

Series Data　Now you are at the point where you need to list the *values* of each of the bars. Here is the series data for the Library Use Bar Chart.

User Group	Jan–Mar	Apr–Jun	Jul–Sep	Oct–Dec
Children	170	160	130	180
Teens	160	190	100	220
Adults	210	150	120	140

The following table provides enough space to list the data for five time categories and three series names. Complete the boxes you require with your own data.

Series Name	X Axis Titles				

Create and Format Your Chart

Refer to the following selection of commands and functions to help you create and format your Bar Chart. Once you are satisfied with the information and format of your Bar Chart, press **F4** to place your Chart in the Draw Screen. Try adding a shaded symbol as you did for Bar Chart 2.

Experiment until you are sure your Bar Chart communicates your points clearly and with style.

Create Chart　At the Main Menu, press **1** for **Create Chart**, **3** for **XY Chart**, and **1** for **Bar.**

Enter X Data　1.　Press **F3** for **Choices.**
2.　Choose your X Data type and then enter the **Starting With** and **Ending With** information.

Text Attributes   1.   Press **F8** for **Options** and then **2** for **Text Attributes.**

At the Text Attributes Menu, you can change the size, color, alignment, and font of your Title, Subtitle, and Y Axis.

Chart Appearance   1.   Press **F8** for **Options** and then **3** for **Appearance.**

At the Appearance Menu, you can change the region frame style and color for the Title/Subtitle and chart regions.

Bar Style   1.   Press **F8** for **Options** and then **5** for **Box Options.**

In this menu, you can change your bar style to 3-D.

Format Y Axis   1.   Press **F8** for **Options** and **A** for **Format.**

In this menu, you can select a currency or percent sign to precede or follow your Y-Axis numbers.

Y-Axis Title   1.   Press **F8** for **Options** and **1** for **Titles/Footnotes.**
2.   Key in the title for your Y1 Axis (e.g., *Thousands, Number of Users,* etc.).

Legend Options   1.   Press **F8** for **Options** and **7** for **Legend.**
2.   For a one-series chart, choose **No** for **Display Legend.**
3.   To change the Legend location, cursor to the Box and press your space bar to move the pointer around the Box perimeter.

Draw Screen   Press **F4** to place your Chart in the Draw Screen. Press **F4** again if you wish to return to your Chart Edit Screen.

Get Symbol   1.   Click on the **Symbol Tool** and then click again on **Get.**
2.   At the Symbol Directory, choose the appropriate Directory, click on the symbol you want, and then click on **F10** twice to return to your Draw Screen.

Shading   1.   Position your mouse on the symbol you wish to shade and click **left** to select it.
2.   Select the **Color Tool**.
3.   In the Color Tool Pop-up, select the **Shade Tool.**

Remember that on a black-and-white printer, dark colors print light and light colors print dark.

Ungroup   To separate the Chart into sections:

1. Click on the **Ungroup Tool.**
2. Note that handles appear around the Title/Subtitle area, the Chart Text area, and the Legend. Click **right** to remove all the handles.
3. Select the area required and click on the **Ungroup Tool** again.

Bring to Front
1. Select the object you need to bring to the front.
2. Click on the **Front Tool** twice.

Save   Press **F6** for **File** and then press **2** for **Save Chart.** Change to the directory in which you wish to save your file (usually Drive A or B) and then type a file-name for your Bar Chart.

Fast Save: Press **Ctrl + S.**

Print   At the Main Menu, press **5** for **Output, Enter** to accept **Printer 1**, and then **F10.**

Clear Chart   If you wish to start a new chart and have saved your current chart, first press **F6** and **E** for **Exit to Main Menu.** Now choose **1** for **Create Chart** and then **8** for **Clear Chart.** If you haven't saved your current chart, a message will appear. You can then press **ESC** to save your chart before clearing it.

Exit Harvard Graphics   From the Draw Screen, press **F6** and **E** to return to the Main Menu and **E** to exit the program.

ACTIVITY 5   LESSON FIVE REVIEW

Test your understanding of the functions and concepts you learned in Lesson Five by completing the following Review Questions.

1. What type of information does the X Axis display?
2. How do you access the Bar Chart Edit Screen from the Main Menu?
3. How do you change the alignment of the Y-Axis Title to vertical?
4. How do you hide the Legend box?
5. What menu do you access to type the Y1-Axis Title?
6. How do you ungroup the chart region so that *every* element is selected?
7. What does the Front Tool do?
8. Describe how to get a symbol.
9. How do you select more than one object at a time?
10. Why do you save a chart as a symbol?

SUPPLEMENTARY EXERCISES

Exercise 1 Create a Bar Chart comparing the absenteeism rate of the employees in two company departments over a six-month period. You determine the name of the company, the two departments (for example, Purchasing and Finance), the months involved (for example, January to June), and the bar values.

Exercise 2 Add a series showing the absenteeism rate for a third department to the Bar Chart you created in Exercise 1. Save the Chart as a symbol and then access the Draw Screen to add a symbol. Remember to alter the chart attributes in the Chart Edit Screen so that your grid lines, background, etc. are not visible.

<table>
<tr><td>LESSON SIX</td><td>AREA CHART</td></tr>
</table>

FEATURES
- Creating an Area Chart
- Converting to a Table Chart
- Using Group/Ungroup
- Using the Scratchpad
- Evolving Symbols
- Enhancing a Table Chart
- Combining Charts
- Using the Align Tool

INTRODUCTION

In Lesson Six, you will learn how to create an Area Chart and then convert it to a Table Chart. Here are the lesson activities:

ACTIVITY 1:   Determine the information required for your Area Charts.

ACTIVITY 2:   Follow the instructions provided to create an Overlap Area Chart and then use the Evolve feature in Draw to modify a symbol as illustrated on page 173.

ACTIVITY 3:   Follow the instructions given to change your Area Chart to a Table Chart and then display them side by side in Draw (see page 187).

ACTIVITY 4:   Create your own Area Chart based on data you have developed.

ACTIVITY 5:   Complete the Lesson Review Questions on Area Chart creation and symbol enhancement.

ACTIVITY 1   AREA CHART INFORMATION

You use an Area Chart when you need to show how three or four different data groups relate to the same X Axis. Like the Bar Chart you created in Lesson Five, the Area Chart is also termed an XY Chart.

XY Data Types

Remember that the *X Axis* is the horizontal line at the bottom of your chart. Usually the X Axis shows time increments such as years, months, or even days. The vertical *Y Axis* displays the scale against which your data is measured. In business graphics, the Y Axis generally represents money amounts.

Line versus Area Charts

To understand the characteristics of an Area Chart, you need to be familiar with its close cousin: the Line Chart. A Line Chart displays data as simple lines extending across the chart grid. An Area Chart fills in the spaces between these lines with solid colors or patterns.

You can see how the visual impact of the same data varies depending on the choice of a Line or an Area Chart. Let's look first at how a Line Chart shows the average daily sales of three product lines over a typical week at Bob's Bike Shop.

Line Chart

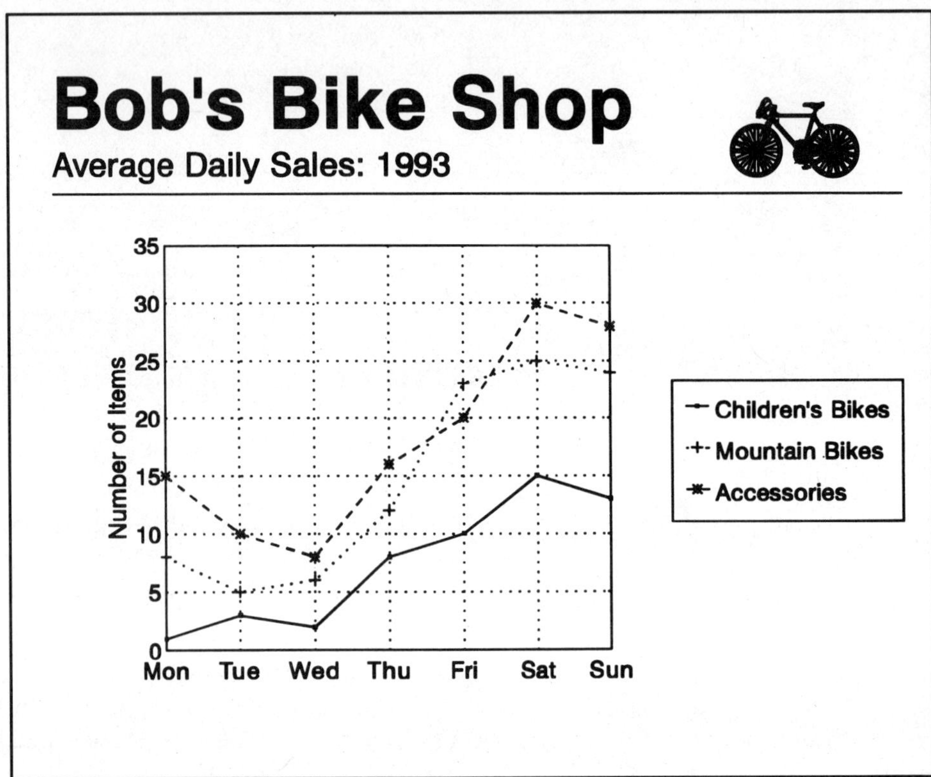

Overlap Area Chart   Now look at an Area Chart showing the exact same data.

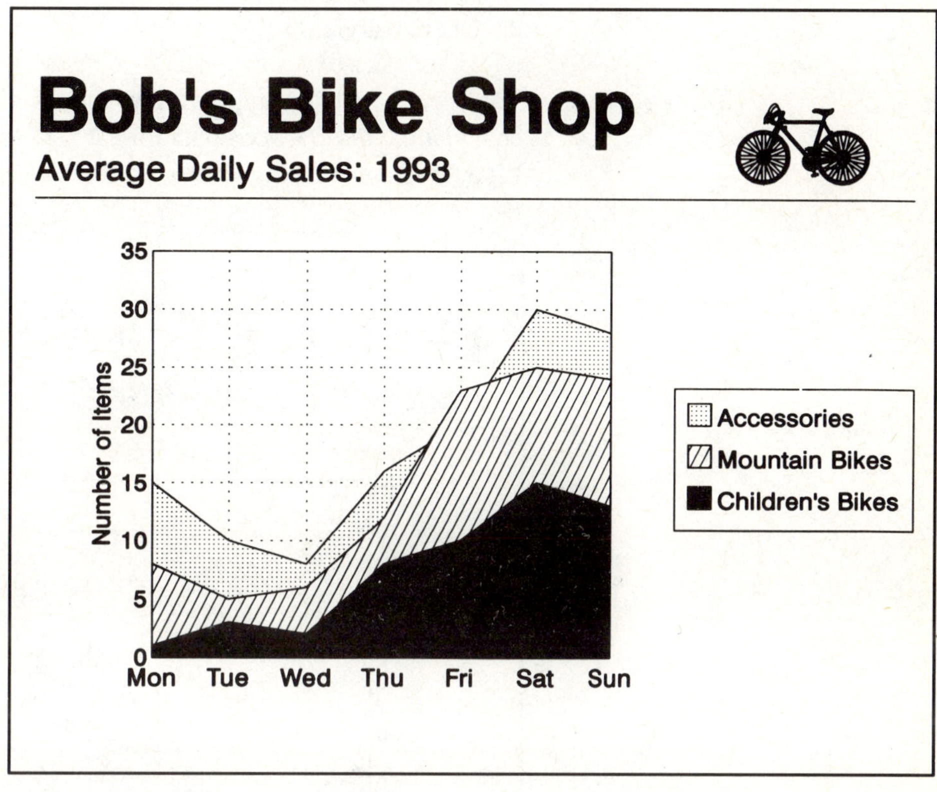

Notice how the use of an Area Chart changes the *look* of the chart dramatically. Three different pattern styles fill the space between the X Axis and the lines that represent the sales figures for each of the three product types. In one place, these patterns overlap—showing that on Friday, for example, the sales of Mountain Bikes exceeded the sales of Accessories.

Area Charts Styles   When you choose the Area Chart format to display your data, you can also select two Area Chart styles—depending on *how* you want your reader to perceive your data.

Overlap Style   The Overlap style was used to show the product sales for Bob's Bike Shop. You use the Overlap style when you want an area chart to display data exactly as a line chart would—but with the addition of colors or patterns to fill the space between the lines and the X Axis.

The Overlap style is useful when the data for each series vary widely. If the data are closely spaced and frequently intersecting, an overlap chart would obscure much of the data and be impossible to read. A Line Chart would be a more appropriate choice in such a case.

To create a clear and easy-to-understand Overlap Area Chart, you must enter the data for the series with the lowest numbers *first* and the data for the series with the highest numbers *last*. In addition, you need to ensure that the data for each series vary *consistently;* that is, each series is consistently more or less than each of the other series. The Area Charts you create in this Lesson use the Overlap style.

Stacked Style   You use the Stacked style to show data as individual bands that, taken together, equal the *total* Y-Axis data for each X-Axis category. Here is the Bob's Bike Shop data displayed as a Stacked Area Chart:

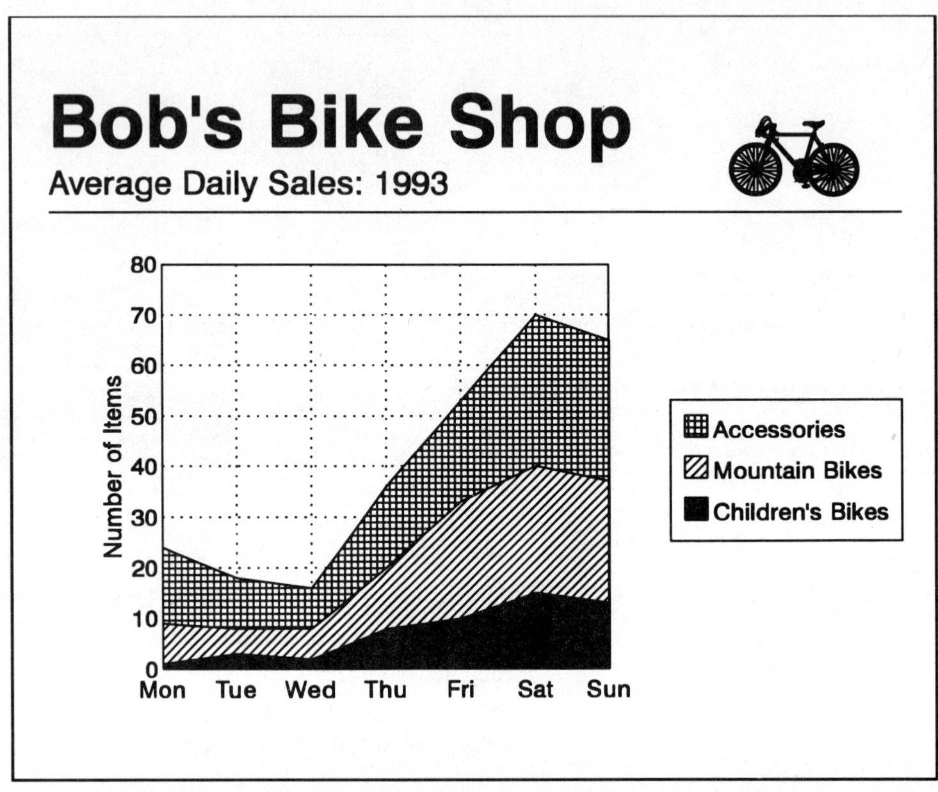

In the Stacked Area Chart, the information is displayed as bands stacked on top of each other. You can see how the *impact* of the data has changed with the use of a Stacked Area Chart. Now, a more careful reading is required to make sense of the data displayed.

Reading a Stacked Area   To read a Stacked Area Chart accurately, you need to understand that each
Chart   band of data is *self-contained.*

Look at the bottom left corner of the Stacked Area Chart for Bob's Bike Shop. The distance from the bottom of the graph to the beginning of the second band represents 1 sale of Children's Bikes. The next band—Mountain Bikes—represents 8 sales, *not* 9 sales as you might at first think. To determine the number of sales represented by the top band—Accessories—you need to calculate the number of increments between 9 and 24. Of course, this number is 15.

This Area Chart therefore tells us that on an average Monday, Bob sells 1 Children's Bike, 8 Mountain Bikes, and 15 Accessory items.

In addition, you can use a Stacked Area Chart to display the total sales made on each day. For example, the chart tells us that 24 sales *in total* are made on an average Monday.

You determine the daily sales total by looking at the amount represented by the distance between the top of the Accessory band to the bottom of the Children's band. For Monday, we see that the top of the Accessory band starts just a shade less than halfway between the 20 and 30 displayed on the Y Axis. We can estimate this number as 24.

You use a Stacked Area Chart, therefore, when you want to display *both* total sales and individual series sales.

Series Data Display

Harvard Graphics includes a feature that allows you to display the data for each series directly below the Area Chart. Here is the same Area Chart with the addition of a table that presents the number of items in each series that are sold each day.

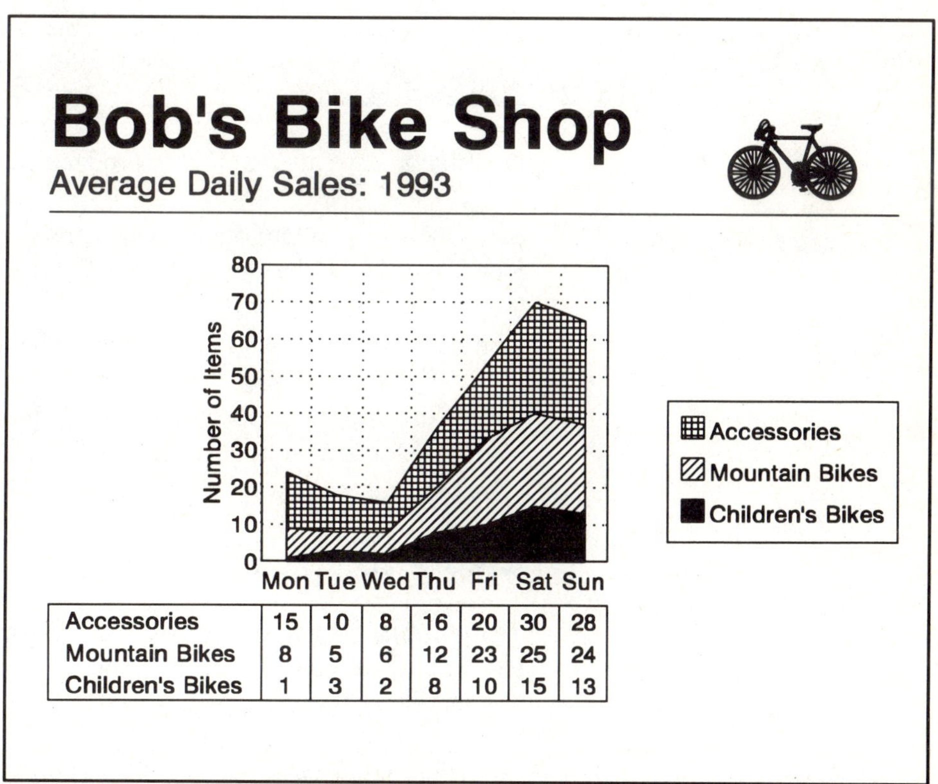

Accessories	15	10	8	16	20	30	28
Mountain Bikes	8	5	6	12	23	25	24
Children's Bikes	1	3	2	8	10	15	13

Create an Impression

As you can imagine, an Area Chart is best used to give an overall *impression* of how information compares, rather than precise calculations. The Line Chart, with its clear intersecting lines representing the three data series, is a much more accurate portrayal of certain data; however, it lacks the exciting visual impact of the Area Chart.

Area Charts are best used to convey a strong impression of data comparisons. The Overlap Area Chart for Bob's Bike Shop tells us that while Accessories are purchased most frequently, the sales of all three product lines rise dramatically on the weekend and plunge particularly low on Wednesdays. The Stacked Area Chart tells us that the total daily sales range from a low of approximately 17 on Wednesday to a high of 70 on Saturdays.

Summary of Activities 2 and 3

In Activities 2 and 3, you will create two documents that show the same data displayed in two different ways. These documents will be used by Fantastic Florists, Inc. to compare quarterly sales in four major North American cities: New York, Los Angeles, Toronto, and Miami.

For Activity 2, you will create an Overlap Area Chart to display the sales data and then enhance it with an "evolved" picture of a flower.

In Activity 3, you will change your Area Chart to a Table Chart and display both charts side by side in the Draw Screen.

ACTIVITY 2   AREA CHART 1

Four major steps are required to produce Area Chart 1.

Step One: Create Your Area Chart
Step Two: Enhance Your Area Chart
Step Three: Add an Evolved Symbol
Step Four: Save and Print Your Area Chart

Follow the step-by-step instructions to reproduce the Area Chart illustrated on page 173. Remember to place a check mark in the box next to each function you complete.

Create Your Area Chart

You will first create your Area Chart and then use the Automatic Data Entry feature to enter your X-Axis information. You can then type the Title/Subtitle of your Area Chart and the data for each series.

Create Chart

1. At the Main Menu, press **1** for **Create Chart.**
2. Press **3** for **XY Chart.**
3. Press **6** for **Area.**

The X Data Pop-up appears.

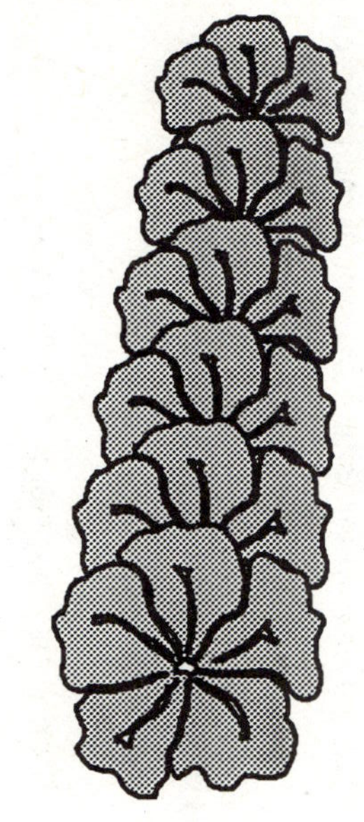

Fantastic Florists Inc.
1993 Quarterly Sales By City

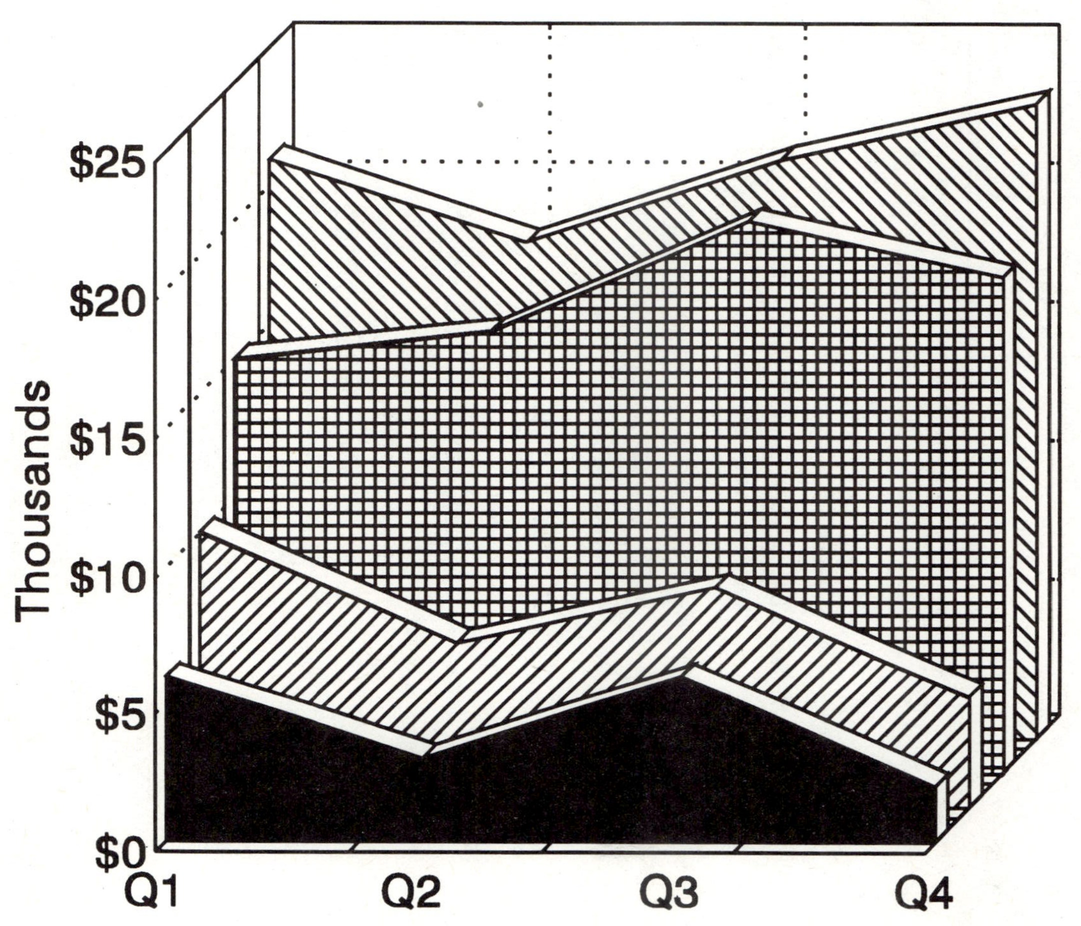

Enter X Data   In the X Data Pop-up, you will choose your data type (**Quarter**) and then enter the starting and ending quarters. Harvard Graphics will fill in the intervening quarters.

Data Type   1. Your cursor is positioned on the **X Data Type** line. Press **F3** for **Choices.**
2. Cursor to **Quarter** and press **Enter.**

Data Times   1. Press your ↓ arrow to position your cursor next to **Starting With.**
2. Type *Q1* and press **Enter.**
3. Your cursor is now positioned next to **Ending With.**
4. Type *Q4*. Your X Data Pop-up looks like this:

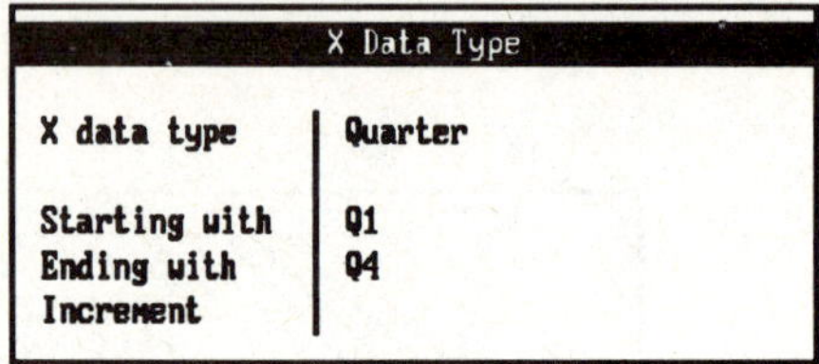

5. Press **Enter** twice to reveal the XY Chart Edit Screen.

X Data Entered

Enter Title/Subtitle   In the Chart Edit Screen, you will see the **Q1-Q4** entered in the **X Axis** column and your cursor positioned next to **Title.**

1. Type the Title of your Area Chart: *Fantastic Florists Inc.* Press **Enter.**
2. Now type the Subtitle of your Area Chart: *1993 Quarterly Sales By City.* Press **Enter.**

Title/Subtitle Complete

Enter Series   You need to enter the names of each of the four cities to be compared.

1. Press **Tab** to position your cursor on the "S" in **Series 1.**
2. Type *Toronto* and press **Delete** to erase any extra letters.
3. Press **Tab** to move to **Series 2.**
4. Type *New York.*

Fill in the other two series names:

Series 3:   Los Angeles
Series 4:   Miami

Series Names Complete

Series Data   Now you need to enter the quarterly sales figures for each city.

1. Press your ↓ and ← arrows to position your cursor in the **Toronto** column opposite **Q1.**
2. Type *6* and press **Enter.**
3. Type *3* and press **Enter.**
4. Type *5* and press **Enter.**
5. Type *2.*
6. Press **Tab** and your ↑ arrow to move opposite **Q1** in the **New York** column. Fill in the data specified in the following table for New York, Los Angeles, and Miami.

	New York	Los Angeles	Miami
Q1	10	15	21
Q2	6	16	18
Q3	8	19	21
Q4	4	18	23

Compare your screen to the following illustration:

```
                                    XY Chart                                 ◆▾
  F1-Help           F2-Show chart                    F4-Draw        F5-Mark   ▴
  F6-Main Menu      F7-Spell/Text   F8-Options       F9-XY data     F10-Continue

  Title:       Fantastic Florists Inc.
  Subtitle:    1993 Quarterly Sales By City
  Footnote:

                                     ─ 1 ──────── 2 ──────── 3 ─────── 4 ─
  Data│     X Axis
  Pt  │     Quarter        Toronto     New York    Los Angele   Miami

  1     Q1                 6           10          15           21
  2     Q2                 3           6           16           18
  3     Q3                 5           8           19           21
  4     Q4                 2           4           18           23
  5
  6
  7
  8
  9
  10
  11
  12
```

Series Data Complete   ☐

Enhance Your Area Chart

Your Area Chart contains all the required information. Now you will access F8 Options to make the following changes. Note that the changes are listed in the order they appear on the Options Menu. Scan the following list and then go on to follow the instructions provided to make the required enhancements.

Required Enhancements

> → **Titles/Footnotes (1):** Enter *Thousands* for the Y-Axis Label
> → **Text Attributes (2):** Align the Title and Subtitle Left and the Y-Axis Label vertically. Specify the Font Style for the Title
> → **Chart Appearance (3):** Change the Title Region Frame Style
> → **Style (5):** Select Overlap and 3-D Styles
> → **Series (6):** Change the Fill Style
> → **Legend (7):** Move the Legend location
> → **Axis Frame (8):** Change the Axis Frame Fill Color
> → **Axis Options (9):** Show X-Axis grid lines
> → **Format (A):** Display the dollar sign next to the Y-Axis numbers

Enter Y-Axis Title

1. Press **F8** for **Options.**
2. Press **1** for **Titles/Footnotes.**
3. Press your ↓ arrow to position your cursor next to **Y1 Axis Title.**
4. Type *Thousands*.
5. Press **F10** to return to your Chart Edit Screen.

Y-Axis Title Entered   ☐

Change Text Attributes

1. Press **F8** for **Options.**
2. Press **2** for **Attributes.**
3. Press **1** for **Titles/Footnotes.**

The Text Attributes Menu appears. Note that your cursor is currently resting under the **9** in the **Size** column next to **Title.**

Title/Subtitle Alignment

1. Press **Tab** to move to the **Alignment** column opposite **Title.**
2. Press **L** for **Left.**
3. Press your ↓ arrow once and press **L** again for **Subtitle 1.**

Title Font Style

1. Press your ↑ arrow and **Tab** to move to the **Font Style** column opposite **Title.**
2. Press **B** to specify the **Bold** style.

Y-Axis Alignment

You want the word *thousands* to appear vertically alongside the Y1 Axis to show that your two-digit Y-Axis numbers represent thousands.

1. Press your ↓ and ← arrows to position your cursor in the **Alignment** column opposite **Y1 Axis Title.**
2. Press **F3** for **Choices.**
3. Select **Side** and press **Enter.**
4. Press **F10** to return to your Chart Edit Screen.

Text Attributes Complete   ☐

Change Region Frame Style   You now need to access the Appearance Menu in F8 Options to change the
Region Frame Style for the Title/Subtitle.

1. Press **F8** for **Options.**
2. Press **3** for **Appearance.**
3. Press your ↓ arrow to position your cursor next to **Region Frame Style** in
   the **Titles** column. **Line** is currently highlighted.
4. Press **F3** for **Choices.**
5. Cursor up to **None** and press **Enter.**
6. Press **F10** to return to your Chart Edit Screen.

Chart Appearance Enhanced

Change Chart Style   You want to display the data in Area Chart 1 as *overlapping* from the city with
the smallest sales (Toronto) to the city with the largest sales (Miami). You also
need to specify the 3-D style.

> **NOTE:** When you choose the Overlap style, you should make sure
> that you enter your data from smallest to largest. For this rea-
> son, you entered the data for Toronto first because the Toronto
> sales were very low and then ended with the data for Miami—
> the city with the highest sales.

1. Press **F8** for **Options.**
2. Press **5** for **Style.**
3. Press your ↓ arrow to position your cursor opposite **Area Style.**
4. Press **F3** for **Choices.**
5. Cursor to **Overlap** and press **Enter.**
6. Press your ↓ arrow to position your cursor opposite **Chart Style.**
7. Press **3** for **3-D.**
8. Press **F10** to return to your Chart Edit Screen.

Overlap and 3-D Style Specified

Change Fill Style to Pattern   On a black-and-white printer, the colors specified for each of the four series
will print as various shades of gray. To ensure a sharper print-out in black and
white, you need to specify *patterns* instead of colors as the series fill style.

1. Press **F8** for **Options.**
2. Press **6** for **Series.**
3. Press your ↓ arrow to position your cursor opposite **Fill Style** in the **Series 1** column.
4. Press **F3** for **Choices.**
5. Cursor to **Pattern** and press **Enter.**

Now specify patterns for the other three series:

1. Press **Tab** to move into the **Series 2** column and press **P** for Pattern.
2. Press **Tab** to move into the **Series 3** column and press **P** for Pattern.
3. Press **Tab** to move into the **Series 4** column and press **P** for Pattern.
4. Press **F10** to return to your Chart Edit Screen.

Patterns Specified

Display Chart ▶ Press **F2** to display your Chart. Compare your Chart with the following illustration and then press **Enter** to return to your Chart Edit Screen.

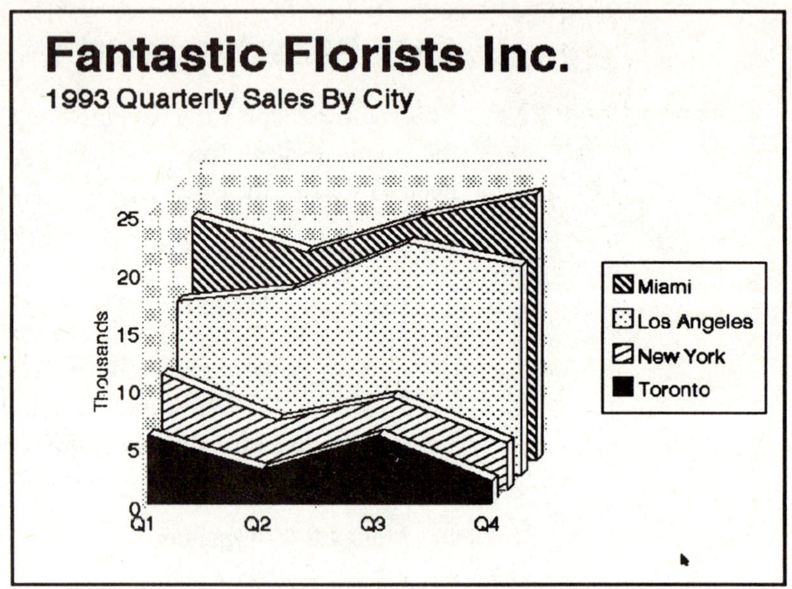

Change Legend Location   You need to change your Legend location so that it appears in the bottom right corner of your screen.

1. Press **F8** for **Options.**
2. Press **7** for **Legend.** Your cursor is opposite **Show Legend.**
3. Press your ↓ arrow to position your cursor at the **Location** box.
4. Press your **space bar** once to move the arrow down to the lower right corner.
5. Press **F10** to return to your Chart Edit Screen.

Legend Location Changed

Change Axis Frame Fill   Now you will change the Axis Frame Fill Color in order to ensure a sharp, uncluttered print-out.

1. Press **F8** for **Options.**
2. Press **8** for **Axis Frame.**
3. Cursor to **Frame Fill Color.**
4. Press **F3** for **Choices.**
5. Cursor up to **Background** and press **Enter.**

6. Press **F10** to return to your Chart Edit Screen.

Axis Frame Fill Changed ☐

Add X-Axis Grid Lines

To clearly indicate the points on the Area Chart that relate to Q2 and Q3, you can add vertical lines that extend from Q2 and Q3 to the top of the Chart frame.

1. Press **F8** for **Options.**
2. Press **9** for **Axis Options.**
3. Cursor to **Grid Line Style** in the X Axis column.
4. Press **F3** for **Choices.**
5. Cursor to **Dotted** and press **Enter.**
6. Press **F10** to return to your Chart Edit Screen.

X-Axis Grid Lines Displayed ☐

Display Dollar Sign

You want the dollar sign to appear next to each number on your Y Axis.

1. Press **F8** for **Options.**
2. Press **A** for **Format.**
3. Press **Tab** to move to the **Y1 Axis** column.
4. Press your ↓ arrow to position your cursor opposite **Currency.**
5. Press **Y** for **Yes.**
6. Press **F10** to return to your Chart Edit Screen.

Currency Sign Displayed ☐

Display Chart ▶

Press **F2** to display your Chart. Compare your chart with the following illustration and then press **Enter** to return to your Chart Edit Screen.

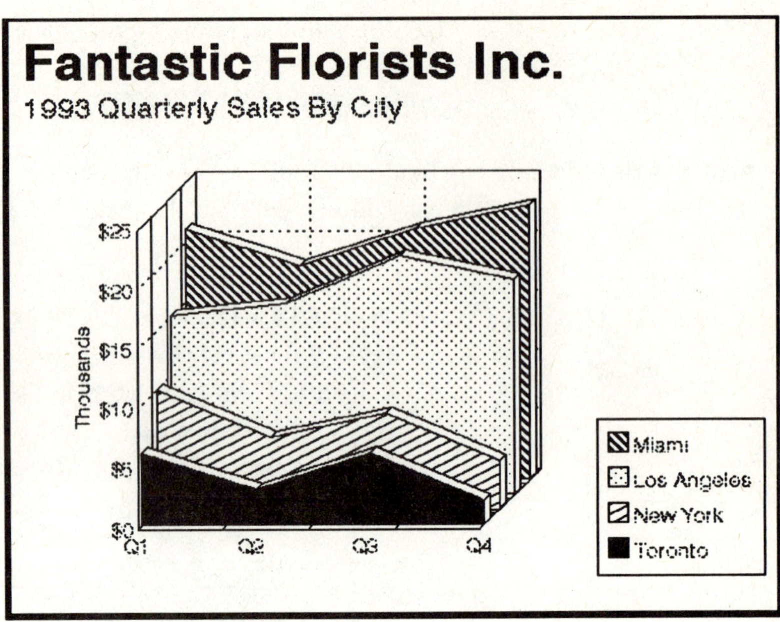

Add an Evolved Symbol

You are now ready to access the Draw Screen so that you can add the evolved Flower Symbol.

Access Draw   1.   Press **F4** to place your Area Chart in the Draw Screen.

The following functions require the use of the mouse. Remember to click the **left** button to select functions and the **right** button to finish functions. If you click the right button twice, you may return to the Main Menu. If this happens, just press or click on **3** for **Draw** to return to the Draw Screen.

Access Scratchpad

To get and then evolve the Flower Symbol, you need to access the Scratchpad so that you have plenty of room to move your symbols around before placing them in your Draw Screen.

1.   Move your mouse above the Tool Box area.
2.   Click your **left** mouse button on the **Scratchpad Tool.**

Notice how your Draw Screen disappears and is replaced by a blank screen. On this screen you can get and evolve your Flower Symbol and then copy it back to your Draw Screen.

Get Symbol   1.   Click your **left** mouse button on the **Symbol Tool.**

2.   Click again on **Get.**
3.   At the Symbol Files Screen, press **F8** to sort the files alphabetically.
4.   Click on **ANIPLANT.**
5.   Click on the picture of the **Flower.**
6.   Click on **F10** twice to return to your Draw Screen.

Your flower appears as illustrated:

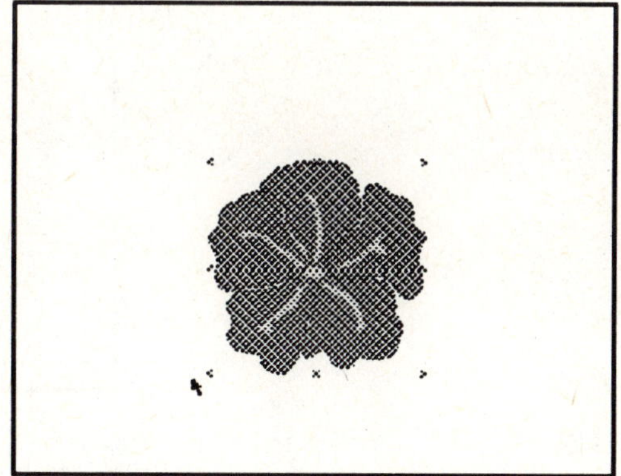

Flower Symbol Retrieved

Size Symbol   1.   Click on the bottom left corner handle and use the **Shift** key to resize your flower to approximately .5" square as illustrated:

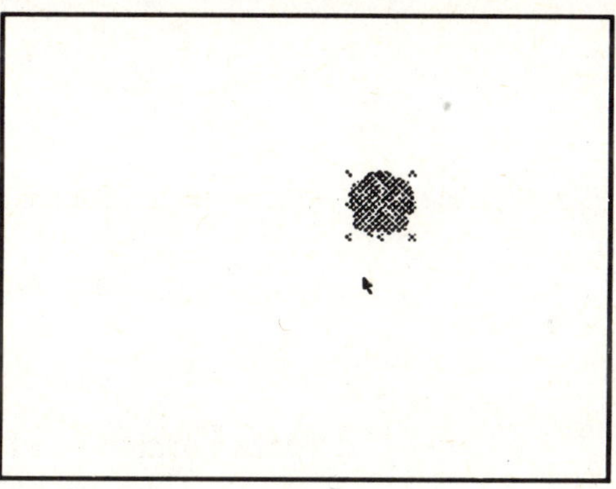

Remember: You use the **Shift** key when you want to maintain the correct proportions of your symbol.

Duplicate Flower   Now you need to *duplicate* your flower and increase its size. When you evolve objects, you *first* create the object you want to evolve from and then the object you wish to evolve to. We created the small flower first because we want the flower to evolve from smallest to largest.

1.   Click on the **Duplicate Tool.**

Notice how a second flower appears on top of the first flower. This second flower is now selected.

2.   Click and hold your mouse button to move your flower about 2" below and slightly to the left as illustrated:

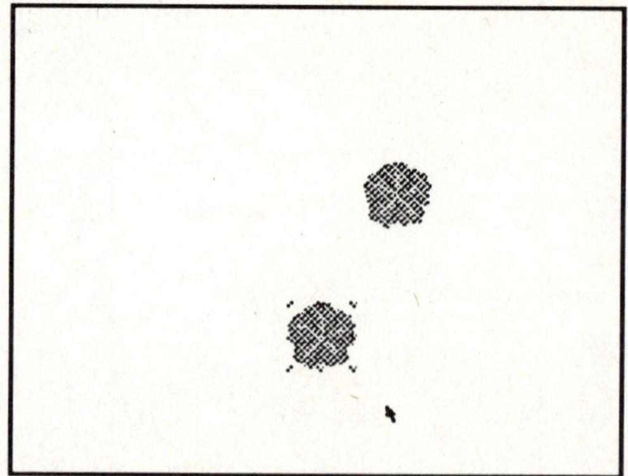

Resize Flower   You need to increase the size of the flower you just duplicated.

1. Click on the bottom left corner handle and press **Shift** to double the size of your flower. Your screen should look like this:

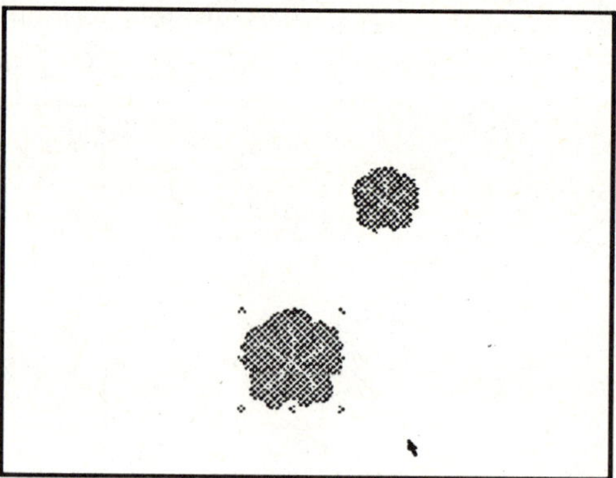

Position   Adjust the positioning of your bottom flower if necessary so that it is only *slightly* left of the small flower as illustrated:

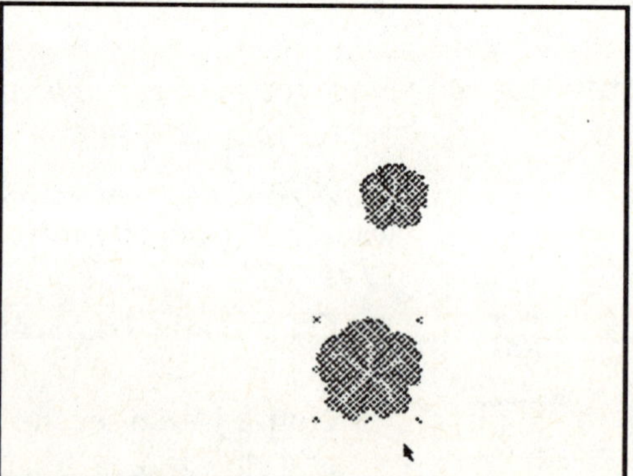

Click **right** to remove all handles.

Flowers Duplicated and Positioned

Evolve Flower   Now you are ready to evolve the flowers. First you need to select both flowers.

Select All   1.   Press **F9** for **Actions.**
              2.   Press **3** for **Select.**
              3.   Press **Enter** to accept **All.**

Orange handles now appear around both flowers.

Evolve Tool   1.   Click on the ▼ symbol at the very bottom of your Tool Box to access the
                   second level of tools.

              2.   Click on the **Evolve Tool.**
              3.   Click on the **Number of Steps** box.
              4.   Type *6* and press **Delete** to erase the zero.
              5.   Press **Enter.**
              6.   Click on the **Reverse** box.

Now you will have to wait about 30 seconds for the evolve feature to work.
When the evolve is complete, you will see six flowers on your screen—each
with orange handles as illustrated:

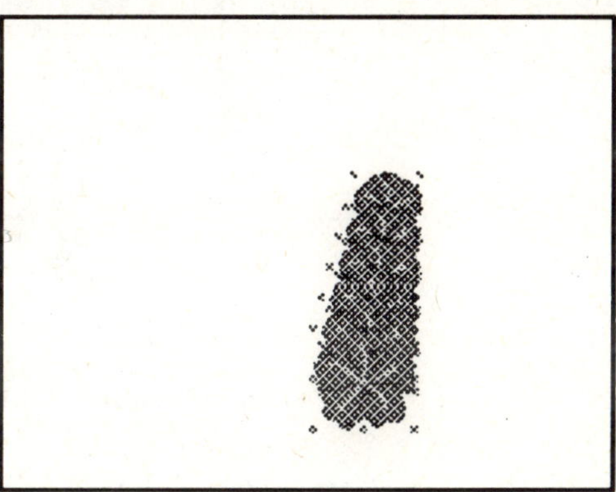

Flowers Evolved

Group Flowers   Before copying the evolved flowers to your Draw Screen, group them into
                one object.

                1.   Click on the **Group Tool.**

Copy to Draw Screen   Your next step is to copy your flowers back to your Draw Screen.

                1.   Click on the ▲ symbol at the bottom of your Tool Box to access the first
                     tool level.
                2.   Click on the **Copy Tool.**
                3.   Click on the **Scratchpad Tool.**

Now you have to paste your flowers into the Draw Screen.

                4.   Click on the **Paste Tool.**

Your flowers now appear in your Draw Screen. All you have to do now is to resize and position the flowers.

Resize and Position

1. Click on and move your flowers to the top right corner of your Draw Screen.
2. Click on one of the corner handles and hold down the **Shift** key to slightly resize your flowers to fit the space. Make any positioning adjustments necessary.

Your Draw Screen should look like this:

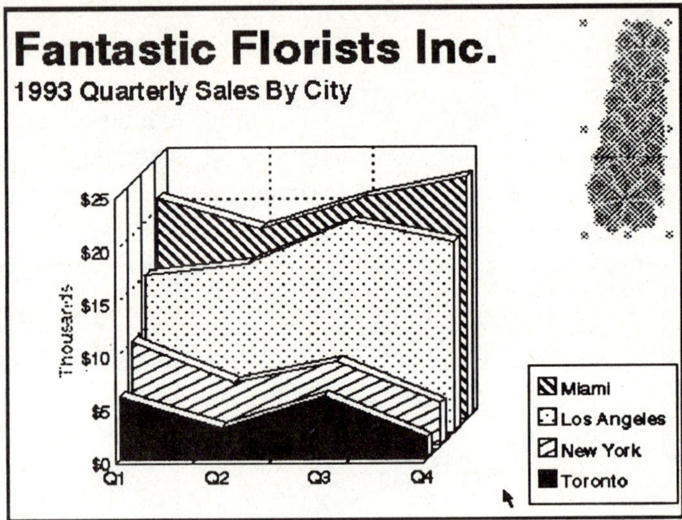

Flowers Resized and Positioned

Save and Print Your Area Chart

You will save your Area Chart on your data disk and then access the Output command to print your Chart. Once you are satisfied with your Chart, you can either exit from Harvard Graphics or get started on Activity 3.

Save

1. Press **F6** for **File.**
2. Press **2** for **Save Chart.**

The Save Chart Menu appears. Your cursor is currently positioned next to **Filename.** The HG3 Default Directory is displayed. You will save your file on a data disk in Drive A or B.

1. Press your ↑ arrow to move opposite **Directory.**
2. Type *a:* or *b:* and then press **Delete** to erase the old Directory.
3. Press **Enter.**
4. At **Filename**, type *Area1* and press **Enter.**
5. At **Description**, type *Area Chart 1: Lesson 6.*
6. Press **F10** to save and return to the Draw Screen.

Area Chart 1 Saved   ☐

Print
1. Press **F6** for **File** and **E** for **Exit to Main Menu**.
2. Press **5** for **Output**.
3. Press **Enter** to accept **Printer 1**.
4. Press **F2** to view how your document will appear in printed form.

> **NOTE:** If you do not like the look of your Chart, press **ESC** to return
> to the Main Menu and **3** for **DRAW** to return to your Draw
> Screen. You can then reposition or resize your flowers, if re-
> quired. If you want to make changes to your Area Chart, press
> **2** to return to the Chart Edit Screen. You can then access the
> **F8 Options Menu** to change your Chart's **Appearance (3)** or
> **Text Attributes (2)**.

5. If you are satisfied with the look of your Chart, press **F10** twice to accept
   the Default Settings.

The Output to Printer Screen appears. Your Area Chart has now been sent to
the printer. Wait until the Output to Printer Screen disappears and you are returned to the Main Menu.

Area Chart 1 Printed   ☐

You now have three options:

- Exit Harvard Graphics if you are finished with your learning session.
- Clear the current chart.
- Keep the Area Chart 1 Edit Screen and begin Area Chart 2. After making
  the required changes to Area Chart 1, you will save it as Area2 so that
  Area1 remains unaffected by the new changes.

Exit Harvard Graphics
1. At the Main Menu, press **E** to exit Harvard Graphics.

Clear the Current Chart
1. Press **1** for **Create Chart**.
2. Press **8** for **Clear Chart**.

Keep Area Chart 1 on Screen
If you choose this option, you can continue immediately to Activity 3. Omit
Get Area1 from Disk. Instead, press **2** for **Edit Chart** and go on to the in-
structions for Enhance Area Chart.

ACTIVITY 3   AREA CHART 2

In Activity 3, you will edit and then convert your Area Chart to a Table Chart, enhance the Table Chart, and then retrieve both charts into the Draw Screen so that you can add a Title, Subtitle, and Rose Symbol.

Four major steps are required to produce Area Chart 2:

Step One: Edit and Save Your Area Chart
Step Two: Convert Your Area Chart to a Table Chart
Step Three: Place Charts in Draw and Enhance
Step Four: Save and Print Your Drawing

Follow the step-by-step instructions to produce the charts illustrated on page 187. Remember to place a check mark in the box next to each function you complete.

Edit and Save Your Area Chart

Get Area1 from Disk   If you have exited out of Harvard Graphics and are starting fresh at your Main Menu, bring Area1 (saved on your data disk) to the screen as follows:

1. Press **4** for **File** and **1** for **Get Chart.**

    The default HG3 Data Directory appears on screen.

2. If necessary, type the letter of your data disk drive (*a:* or *b:*) over the current Directory and press **Delete** to erase the extra letters.
3. Press **Enter.**
4. At the list of files on your data disk, choose **Area1** and press **Enter** twice to access the Chart Edit Screen.

If you have not exited out of Harvard Graphics, press **2** at the Main Menu to place your Area Chart back into the Chart Edit Screen.

Enhance Area Chart   You need to change the Chart Style back to 2-D (two-dimensional), delete the Title and Subtitle of your Area Chart, and move the location of the Legend before accessing the Draw Screen to delete the evolved flowers.

Change to 2D Style   1. Press **F8** for **Options** and **5** for **Style.**
2. Cursor to **Chart Style** and press **2** for **2-D.**
3. Press **F10** to return to your Chart Edit Screen.

2-D Style Specified   ☐

Delete Title/Subtitle   1. Position your cursor on the "F" in *Fantastic.*

Fantastic Florists Inc.

1993 Quarterly Sales By City

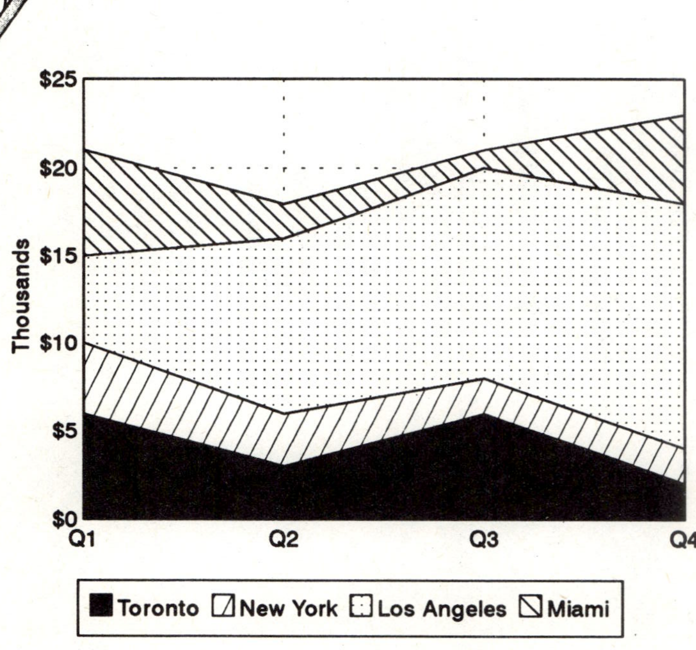

	Toronto	New York	Los Angeles	Miami
Q1	$6,000	$10,000	$15,000	$21,000
Q2	$3,000	$6,000	$16,000	$18,000
Q3	$6,000	$8,000	$20,000	$21,000
Q4	$2,000	$4,000	$18,000	$23,000

2. Press **Ctrl + Del** to erase the Title.
3. Move to Subtitle and press **Ctrl + Del** again.

Title/Subtitle Deleted ☐

Move Legend
1. Press **F8** for **Options.**
2. Press **7** for **Legend.**
3. Move down to the **Location** box.
4. Press your **space bar** twice to position your legend at the bottom center of your chart.
5. Press **F10** to return to your Chart Edit Screen.

Legend Location Changed ☐

Delete Flowers
1. Press **F4** to place your Area Chart in the Draw Screen.
2. Click on the **Flowers** to select them.
3. Click on the **Delete Tool.** Your flowers disappear!

Flowers Deleted ☐

Now you are ready to save your Area Chart and then convert it to a Table Chart.

Fast Save Area Chart
1. Press **Ctrl + S** to fast save your chart.
2. At **Filename**, type *Areasub* over *Area1.*
3. Change the **Description** to *Areasub: Lesson 6.*
4. Press **F10** to save and return to the Draw Screen.

Areasub Saved ☐

Convert Your Area Chart to a Table Chart

Convert to Table Chart
1. Press **F6** and **E** for **Exit to Main Menu.**
2. At the Main Menu press **1** for **Create Chart.**
3. Press **1** for **Text** and **3** for **Table.**

The message "Keep Current Data" appears.

4. Press **Enter** to accept **Yes.**

The Table Chart Edit Screen now appears. Note that the data displayed are the same as in your Area Chart:

```
                                    Table Chart                                    ◆▾
    F1-Help              F2-Show chart                     F4-Draw            F5-Mark
  ■ F6-Main Menu         F7-Spell/Text   F8-Options                          F10-Continue

    Title:
    Subtitle:
    Footnote:
  ─────────── 1 ──────────── 2 ─────────── 3 ─────────── 4 ─────────── 5 ──────
  1│                    Toronto        New York       Los Angeles   Miami

  2│ Q1                 6              10             15            21
  3│ Q2                 3              6              16            18
  4│ Q3                 5              8              19            21
  5│ Q4                 2              4              18            23
  6│
  7│
  8│
  9│
 10│
 11│
 12│
 13│
 14│
```

Add Thousands   Before enhancing your Table Chart, you need to add three zeros to each number so that the Table Chart will display the numbers as thousands.

1. Press your ↓ arrow, **Tab**, and → arrow to position your cursor to the right of the **6** in the **Toronto** column. Type *000* (zeros).
2. Press your ↓ arrow to the **3** under **Toronto** and again add three zeros.

Continue to add three zeros to every number in your Table Chart. Don't worry about commas; you will specify "thousands separator" when you enhance your Table Chart. Remember to press **Tab** to move to another column.

Display Chart ▶   Press **F2** to display your Table Chart. Note that the numbers and text are not centered and that the columns seem to be spaced too far apart as illustrated:

	Toronto	New York	Los Angeles	Miami
Q1	6000	10000	15000	21000
Q2	3000	6000	16000	18000
Q3	6000	8000	20000	21000
Q4	2000	4000	18000	23000

Press **Enter** to return to your Chart Edit Screen.

Required Enhancements   You need to make the following enhancements in the F8 Options menu:

> → **Chart Appearance (3):** Change the Title Region Frame Style to None and the Table Region Frame Style to Plain
> → **Table (5):** Show vertical lines between the Table columns
> → **Column (6):** Change the alignment of all text and numbers to Center, show the dollar sign, and insert a comma to show thousands

Chart Appearance
1. Press **F8** for **Options.**
2. Press **3** for **Appearance.**

Title Region Frame Style
1. Press your ↓ arrow to position your cursor opposite **Region Frame Style** in the **Titles** column.
2. Press **F3** for **Choices. Line** is currently highlighted.
3. Cursor up to **None** and press **Enter.**

Table Region Frame Style
1. Press **Tab** to move to **Region Frame Style** in the **Table** column.
2. Press **F3** for **Choices.**
3. Cursor to **Plain** and press **Enter.**
4. Press **F10** to return to your Chart Edit Screen.

Chart Appearance Enhanced   ☐

Table
1. Press **F8** for **Options.**
2. Press **5** for **Table.**

Vertical Grid
1. Press your ↓ arrow to position your cursor opposite **Vertical Grid.**
2. Press **F3** for **Choices.**
3. Cursor to **All Columns.**
4. Press **Enter.**
5. Press **F10** to return to your Chart Edit Screen.

Vertical Grid Displayed   ☐

Column
1. Press **F8** for **Options.**
2. Press **6** for **Column.**

Text Alignment
1. Press your ↓ arrow twice to move your cursor opposite **Text Alignment.**
2. Press **C** for **Center.**
3. Press your **Tab** key to move to the next column and press **C** again.
4. Tab to the next three columns and press **C** for Center.

Number Alignment
1. Press your ↓ and ← arrows to move your cursor to **Column 2** opposite **Number Alignment.**
2. Press **C** for **Center.**
3. **Tab** and press **C** for **Center** for the next three columns.

Dollar Sign 1. Press your ↓ and ← arrows to move your cursor to **Column 2** opposite **Currency.**
2. Press **Y** and **Tab** to **Column 3.**
3. Press **Y** for **Columns 3-5.**

Thousands Separator 1. Press your ↓ and ← arrows to move your cursor to **Column 2** opposite **Thousands Separator.**
2. Press **Y** and **Tab** to **Column 3.**
3. Press **Y** for **Columns 3-5.**

Compare your Columns Menu to the following illustration:

```
                          Column Options

                     Col 1    Col 2    Col 3    Col 4    Col 5
   Left position      0.78     11.76    31.29    54.2     82.39
   Right position     11.76    31.29    54.2     82.39    99.22

   Text alignment     Center   Center   Center   Center   Center
   Number alignment   Decimal  Center   Center   Center   Center

   Scale factor

   Percent            No       No       No       No       No
   Currency           No       Yes      Yes      Yes      Yes
   Negative no. format Minus   Minus    Minus    Minus    Minus
   Scientific notation No      No       No       No       No

   Decimal places
   Thousands separator  No     Yes      Yes      Yes     ◆Yes
```

4. Press **F10** to return to your Chart Edit Screen.

Column Options Complete   □

Display Chart ▶ Press **F2** to display your Table Chart and compare it with the following illustration:

	Toronto	New York	Los Angeles	Miami
Q1	$6,000	$10,000	$15,000	$21,000
Q2	$3,000	$6,000	$16,000	$18,000
Q3	$6,000	$8,000	$20,000	$21,000
Q4	$2,000	$4,000	$18,000	$23,000

To return to your Chart Edit Screen, press **Enter.**

You are now ready to save your Table Chart and then access Draw to retrieve it and your Area Chart 2 to the screen.

Fast Save Table Chart
1. Press **Ctrl + S** to fast-save your Table Chart.
2. At the Save Menu, key in your Directory, if required.
3. At **Filename**, type *Areatab* and press **Enter.**
4. At **Description**, type *Table: Lesson 6.*
5. Press **F10** to return to your Chart Edit Screen.

Table Chart Saved

Now you need to clear your Table Chart from the screen before accessing Draw.

1. Press **F6** for **Main Menu.**
2. Press **1** for **Create Chart.**
3. Press **8** for **Clear Chart.**

Place Charts in Draw and Enhance

Your first step is to access Draw and then retrieve your Area2 and Areatab files as Subcharts.

Access Draw
1. At the Main Menu, press **3** for **Draw.**

Get Area2 Chart
1. Press **F6** and **3** for **Get Subchart.**
2. At the list of files, choose **Areasub** and press **Enter.**

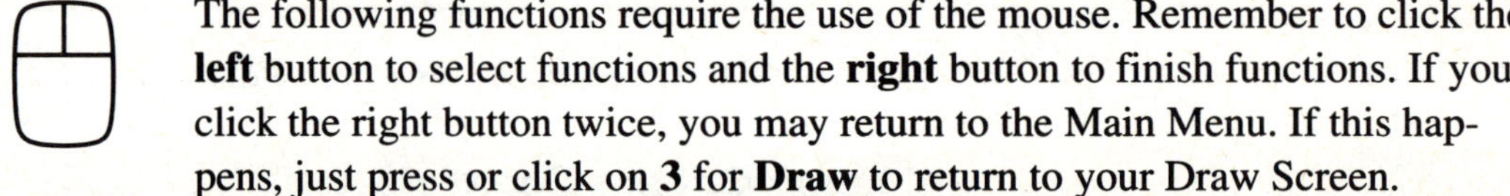

The following functions require the use of the mouse. Remember to click the **left** button to select functions and the **right** button to finish functions. If you click the right button twice, you may return to the Main Menu. If this happens, just press or click on **3** for **Draw** to return to your Draw Screen.

Your Areasub chart appears in the center of your Draw Screen. Before you get your Areatab chart, position your Area Chart as follows:

Position Area Subchart
1. Click your **left** mouse button on your chart and drag your mouse down and to the left to position your chart as illustrated:

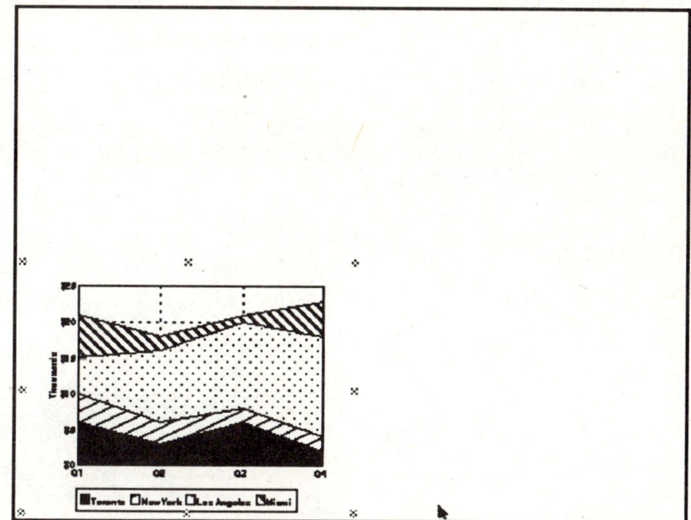

2.   Click **right** to remove the handles.

Area Subchart Positioned

Get Areatab Subchart

1.   Press **F6** and **3** for **Get Subchart.**
2.   At the list of files, choose **Areatab** and press **Enter.**

Position Table Subchart

1.   Click your **left** mouse button on your Table Chart and drag your mouse down and to the right to position your table next to your Area Chart as illustrated:

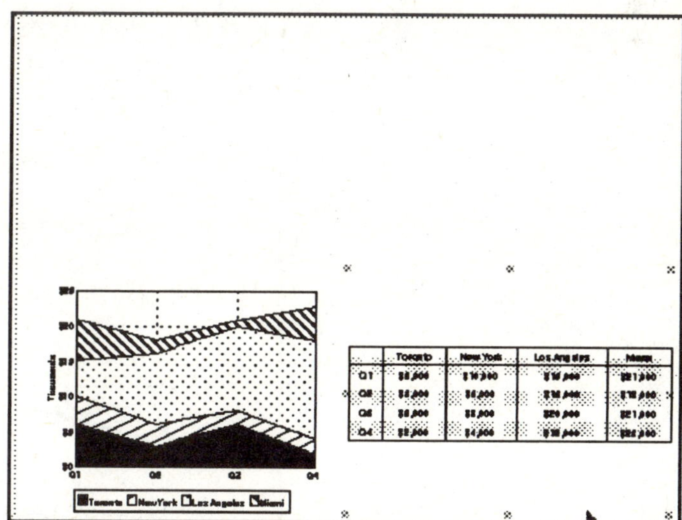

Size Table Chart

Your Table Chart appears a bit too "skinny" next to the Area Chart. Resize it as follows:

1.   Click and hold your **left** mouse button on the top middle handle.
2.   Drag your mouse up about 1" as illustrated:

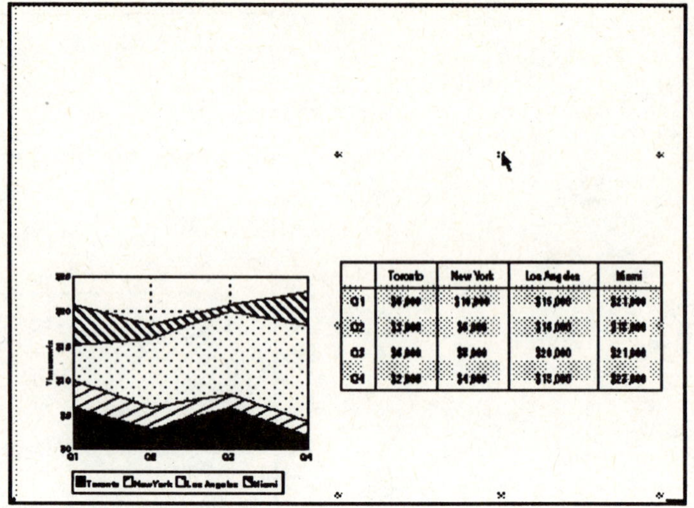

3. Now click and hold on the left middle handle.
4. Drag your mouse right about the width of the first column.

Table Chart Sized and Positioned

Align Charts   Use the Align Tool to vertically align your Table and Area Charts.

1. Move your mouse to the Area Chart.
2. Press **Shift** and the **left** mouse button to select the Area Chart. Handles now appear around both the Area and Table charts.
3. Click on the **Align Tool.**
4. Click on the box labeled **V. Center.**

Compare your chart positions to the following illustration:

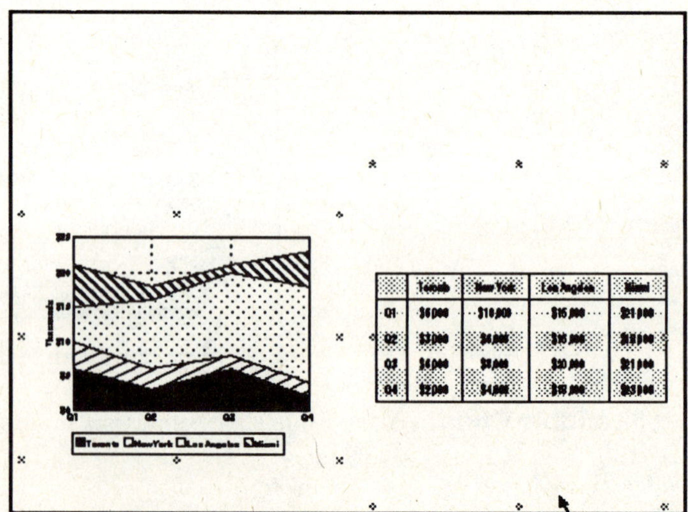

5. Click right to remove all the handles.

Charts Aligned

Enter Title and Subtitle   You now need to use the Text Tool to enter your Title and Subtitle.

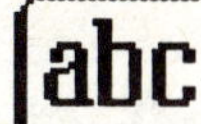

1. Click on the **Text Tool.**
2. Move your mouse to the Text Attributes Pop-up at the top of your screen.
3. Click on the **5.0** in the **Text Size Ruler.**
4. Type *10.0* and press **Enter.**
5. Click on **Style** and choose **Bold.**

Title Enter

1. Move your mouse to position the + in the top left corner of your Draw Screen and click **left.**
2. Draw a box that extends across your screen and down about 2".
3. At the Text Pop-up, type *Fantastic Florists Inc.*
4. Press **F10** to exit the Pop-up.

Title Position

1. Click on the **Pointer** to select the **Title.**
2. Position your Title at the top right of your screen as illustrated:

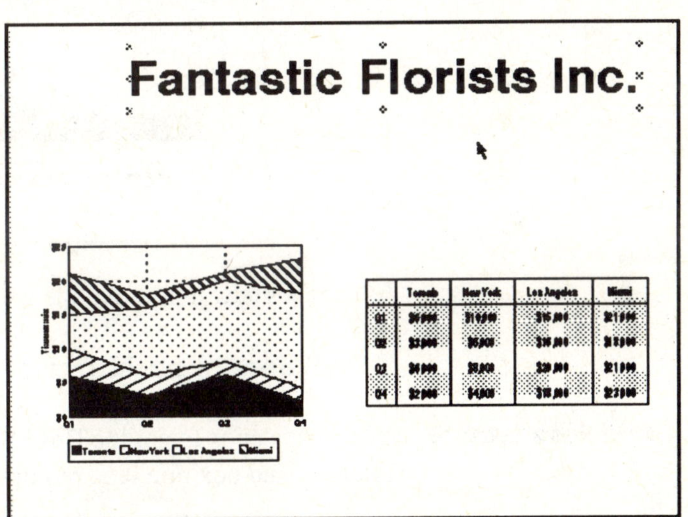

3. Click **right** to remove the handles.

Subtitle

1. Click on the **Text Tool.**
2. Click on the **10.0** in the **Text Size Ruler.**
3. Type *7.0* and press **Enter.**
4. Click on the **Style** box.
5. Click on **Roman.**

Now draw the box for the Subtitle.

1. Move your mouse to position the + under the "F" in *Fantastic Florists Inc.*
2. Click **left** and draw a box that extends across the screen and 2" down.

3. At the Text Pop-up, type *1993 Quarterly Sales By City.*
4. Press **F10** to exit the Pop-up.

Align Title and Subtitle

1. Click on the **Pointer.** Your Subtitle will be selected.
2. Move your Subtitle up so that it is positioned directly under the Title.
3. Move your mouse to the Title and press **Shift** and your **left** mouse button. Handles now appear around both the Title and the Subtitle.
4. Click on the **Align Tool.**
5. Click on the box labeled **Right.** Compare your screen to the following illustration:

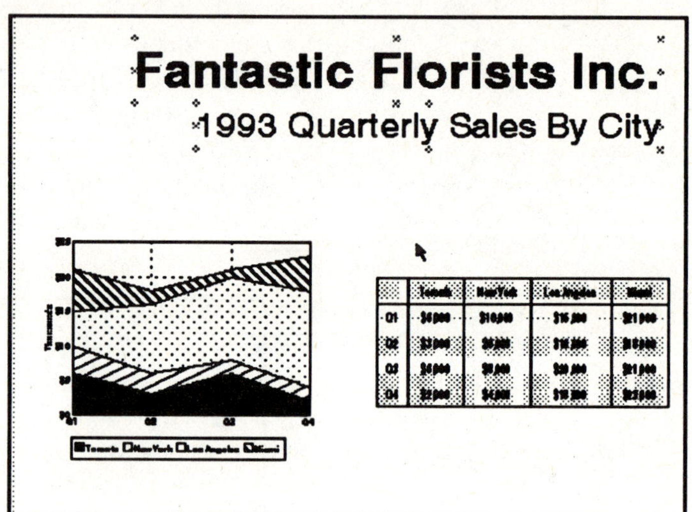

6. Click **right** to remove the handles.

Text Entered and Aligned

Add Rose Symbol

Your last step is to get the Rose Symbol and then flip it horizontally, size it, rotate it, and position it as required.

Get Symbol

1. Click your **left** mouse button on the **Symbol Tool.**
2. Click again on **Get.**
3. At the Symbol Files Screen, press **F8** to sort the Symbol Files alphabetically.
4. Click on **ANIPLANT.**
5. Click on the **Rose** Symbol and click on **F10** twice.

Size

1. Move the rose up to the top left corner of your screen.
2. Click on one of the corner handles.
3. Press **Shift** and reduce the size of your rose by approximately 1" as illustrated:

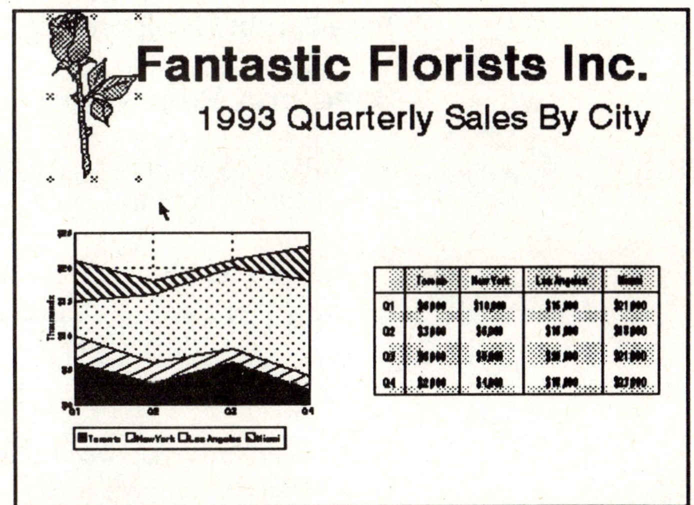

Flip Horizontally   You want your rose to face in the opposite direction.

1. Click on the **Flip Tool.**
2. Click on the **Horizontal Tool.**

Rotate   Now rotate your rose slightly.

1. Click on the **Rotate Tool.**
2. Click on the **0.0.**
3. Type *30.0* and press **Enter.**
4. Click on the **Forward** box.
5. Click **right** to exit **Rotate.**

Now position your rose under and to the left of your Title. You may wish to resize your rose to ensure it fits attractively in the space available as illustrated:

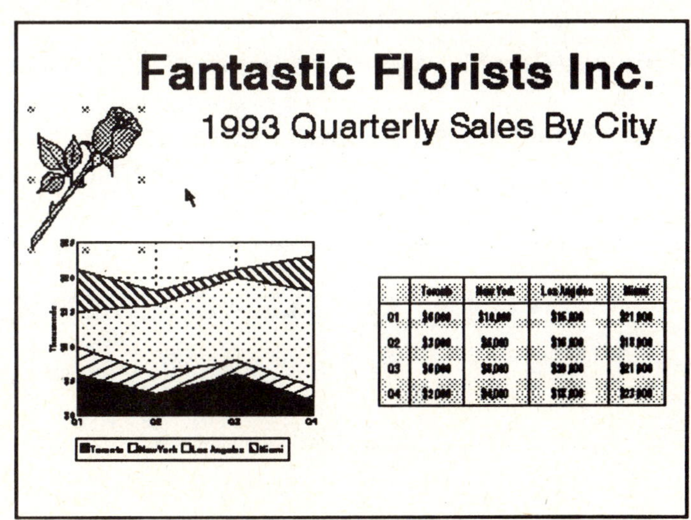

Rose Symbol Positioned   □

Save and Print Your Chart

You will save your drawing on your data disk as Area2 and then access the
Output command to print.

Save   1.   Press **F6** for **File** and **E** for **Exit to Main Menu.**
        2.   Press **4** for **File** and then **4** for **Save Chart.**

The Save Chart Menu appears. Key in your data drive (A or B) if required.

1.   At **Filename**, type *Area2* and press **Enter.**
2.   At **Description**, type *Area Chart 2: Lesson 6.*
3.   Press **F10** to save and return to your Main Menu.

Area Chart 2 Saved   □

Print   1.   Press **5** for **Output.**
        2.   Press **Enter** to accept **Printer 1.**

Press **F2** to view how your document will appear in printed form.

If you are satisfied with the look of your document, press **F10** twice to send it
to the printer.

Area Chart 2 Printed   □

You now have two options:

- Exit Harvard Graphics if you are finished with your learning session.
- Clear the current chart and get started on creating your own Area Chart in
  Activity 4.

Exit Harvard Graphics   1.   Press **E** to exit Harvard Graphics.

Clear the Current Chart   1.   Press **1** for **Create Chart.**
        2.   Press **8** for **Clear Chart.**

ACTIVITY 4   CHALLENGE ASSIGNMENT

Read through the following sections for suggestions on content and then adapt
the instructions given to create an Area Chart based on your own material.
Use the boxes provided to record information about your Area Chart.

The Challenge Assignment requires three major steps.

Step One: Select Your Company/Organization
Step Two: Plan Your Chart Information
Step Three: Create and Format Your Chart

Select Your Company/Organization

First, decide on the kind of company or organization your Area Chart will represent. For example, you could choose a charitable organization that raises money for the local children's hospital. You could then create a Stacked Area Chart that displays the total monies raised from corporate and private donors over a five-year period.

Give your company/organization a name.

Name and Type of Your Company/Organization:

Plan Your Chart Information

To plan your Chart information, you need to determine two principal requirements:

- Area Chart Style: Overlap or Stacked
- Chart Components

Chart Style   Your decision to select either the Overlap or Stacked style depends upon the nature of the data you wish to display. If each data series is spaced widely apart with very few intersections, choose an Overlap style. If, however, your data series show similar number ranges, choose a Stacked style.

If you can't decide which style to choose, wait until you have entered your data in the Chart Edit Screen. You can then see how your data displays in either the Overlap or Stacked style by pressing **F8** for **Options** and then **5** for **Style.** Choose the style you want and then press **F2** to display your chart. If you don't feel the Overlap style, for example, displays your data effectively, choose the Stacked style and press **F2** again.

Chart Components   Like the Bar Chart you created in Lesson Five, your Area Chart consists of the following five components:

- Title and Subtitle
- X-Axis Labels
- Series Titles

- Y-Axis Title (if any)
- Series Data

Title/Subtitle

Your title will either be the name of the company or organization your Area Chart represents or a summary of the information presented. The Subtitle generally specifies the *nature* of the data.

For example, here is the Title/Subtitle of an Area Chart that shows the dollar value of contributions received by the Children's Hospital Charity from two donor sources over a five-year period:

Title: CHILDREN'S HOSPITAL CHARITY
Subtitle: Donor Contributions: 1989-1993.

Write your Area Chart Title and Subtitle in the following box.

Title:

Subtitle:

X-Axis Labels

Now you need to specify the *time series* information you will display on your X Axis. For the Hospital Charity Area Chart, the X-Axis information would be the years 1989 to 1993. You could also specify quarters, months, weeks, or even days as in the Bob's Bike Shop Charts illustrated in Activity 1.

For an Area Chart, you can use more time series categories than you could for a Bar Chart. However, try not to exceed 12 categories (for example, the 12 months of the year) to ensure your chart can be easily understood. Specify your X-Axis Labels in the following box.

Type (year, quarter, month, etc.):

Starting With:

Ending With:

Series Titles

An Area Chart usually displays two or more data series. You need to specify a title for each of these series. For the Hospital Charity Chart, two series titles are required to represent the donor groups: Corporate and Private.

Limit the number of series to five or less. Area Charts, particularly Stacked Area Charts, can be difficult to read. If you include too many series, you may confuse your readers and diminish the overall impact of your chart.

List your series titles in the following box.

Series 1:
Series 2:
Series 3:
Series 4:
Series 5:

Y-Axis Title Usually, you need to add a Y-Axis Title either to explain that the numbers shown represent thousands, millions, etc. or to define what the numbers refer to. For the Hospital Charity Area Chart, the Y-Axis Title would be "Contributions in Thousands."

Write your Y-Axis Title in the following box.

Y-Axis Title:

Series Data Now you are at the point where you need to list the *values* for each series. Here is the series data for the Hospital Charity Chart.

Donor Group	1989	1990	1991	1992	1993
Private	17	14	30	20	12
Corporate	90	87	100	76	52

Note that the data for the series with the *lowest* overall numbers was entered *first* to ensure effective display in the Overlap style.

The following Table provides enough space to list the data for five time categories and five series names. Complete the boxes you require with your own data.

Series Name	X Axis Titles				

Create and Format Your Chart

Refer to the selection of commands and functions listed below to help you create and format your Area Chart. Once you are satisfied with the information and format of your Chart, press **F4** to place it in the Draw Screen. Try adding an evolved symbol or object (such as a circle or triangle) as you did in Activity 2. You can also choose to convert your Area Chart to a Table Chart and display them side by side as you did in Activity 3.

Experiment until you are sure your Area Chart communicates your data clearly and with style.

The following instructions specify the functions required to create an Area Chart and a Table Chart, and then a selection of the features you can access in the Draw Screen.

Create Chart
At the Main Menu, press **1** for **Create Chart**, **3** for **XY Chart,** and **6** for **Area.**

Enter X Data
1. Press **F3** for **Choices.**
2. Choose your X Data type and then enter the **Starting With** and **Ending With** information.

Text Attributes
1. Press **F8** for **Options** and then **2** for **Text Attributes.**

At the Text Attributes Menu, you can change the size, color, alignment, and font of your Title, Subtitle, and Y Axis.

Chart Appearance
1. Press **F8** for **Options** and then **3** for **Appearance.**

At the Appearance Menu, you can change the region frame style and color for the Title/Subtitle and chart regions.

Chart Style
1. Press **F8** for **Options** and then **5** for **Style.**

In this menu, you can change your Area Chart Style to Overlap or Stacked.

Format Y Axis   1. Press **F8** for **Options** and **A** for **Format.**

In this menu, you can select a Currency or Percent sign to precede or follow your Y-Axis numbers.

Y-Axis Title   1. Press **F8** for **Options** and **1** for **Titles/Footnotes.**
2. Key in the title for your Y1 Axis (e.g., *Thousands, Number of Users*, etc.)

Legend Options   1. Press **F8** for **Options** and **7** for **Legend.**
2. To change the Legend location, cursor to the box shown and press your space bar to move the pointer around the box perimeter.

The following instructions specify the functions required for conversion to and enhancement of a table chart:

Convert to Table Chart   First, edit your Area Chart to remove the Title/Subtitle and make any enhancement changes necessary. Convert your Area Chart to a Table Chart as follows:

1. Save your Area Chart (**Ctrl + S** for fast save).
2. Return to the Main Menu (**F6** from the Chart Edit Screen or **F6** and **E** from the Draw Screen).
3. Press **1** for **Create Chart**, **1** for **Text**, and **3** for **Table.**
4. Answer **Yes** to the "*Keep Current Data*" message.

Table Chart Enhancements   1. If necessary, enter 0's (zeros) after each entry in the Table Chart if you want your numbers to represent thousands.
2. In the **F8 Options** Menu:

- Choose **3** for **Appearance** to change the Region Frame Style for the Title and Table.
- Choose **5** for **Table Options**, change the Automatic Table Sizing to **No**, and show grid lines (if required).
- Choose **6** for **Column** to adjust the alignment of all the text and numbers, show the Currency sign, and insert a comma separator for thousands.

Save your Table Chart and then clear it at the Main Menu (**1** for **Create Chart** and **8** for **Clear Chart**). You can then retrieve the Table Chart into the Draw Screen as a subchart.

The following instructions specify the features you can access at the Draw Screen.

Draw Screen   Press **F4** to place your chart in the Draw Screen. Press **F4** again if you wish to return to your Chart Edit Screen.

Get Subcharts   Press **F6** and **3** for **Get Subchart.** At the list of files, choose your Area or Table chart and press **Enter.**

Get Symbol   1.   Click on the **Symbol Tool** and click again on **Get**.
2.   At the Symbol Directory, choose the appropriate Directory, click on the symbol you want, and then click twice on **F10** to return to your Draw Screen.

Scratchpad   1.   Click on the **Scratchpad Tool.** To return to the Draw Screen, click on the **Scratchpad Tool** again.

Evolve Symbol   1.   First create two symbols: one larger than the other.
2.   Select both symbols and then click on the **Evolve Tool** (second tool level).
3.   Specify the number of steps to evolve and the evolve direction.

Copy and Paste   1.   Select the object or objects to copy.
2.   Click on the **Copy Tool.** If you are in the Scratchpad, click on the **Scratchpad Tool** to access the Draw Screen.
3.   Click on the **Paste Tool.**

Group   To group a selection of objects:

1.   Click on a point above and to the left of the objects and draw a box around them.
2.   Click on the **Group Tool.**

Align   1.   Select the two or more objects you wish to align.
2.   Click on the **Align Tool** and then click on the box labeled with the *type* of alignment you require (Left, Right, Center, etc.).

Flip   1.   Select the object to flip. Then click on the **Flip Tool** and select either **Horizontal** or **Vertical** flipping.

Rotate   1.   Select the object to rotate and click on the **Rotate Tool.**
2.   Type the number of degrees to rotate and click on the forward or reverse box *or* click on the right handle and drag the mouse up or down to rotate the object as required.

Save   From Draw, either fast-save (**Ctrl + S**) or press **F6** for **File** and then **2** for **Save Chart.** Change to the Directory in which you wish to save your file (usually Drive A or B), and then type a filename for your Area Chart.

Print   At the Main Menu, choose **5** for **Output**, press **Enter** to accept **Printer 1.** Press **F2** to display your chart before printing to check how it will appear in black and white. Press **F10** twice to send your chart to the printer.

Clear Chart   To start a new chart after you have saved your current chart:

From Draw, press **F6** and **E** for **Exit to Main Menu.** Now choose **1** for
Create Chart and then **8** for **Clear Chart.** From the Chart Edit Screen, press
F6 and then **1** and **8.** If you haven't saved your current chart, a message will
appear. You can then press **ESC** to save your chart before clearing it.

Exit Harvard Graphics   From the Draw Screen, press **F6** and **E** to return to the Main Menu and then **E**
to exit the program.

From the Chart Edit Screen, press **F6** and **E.**

ACTIVITY 5   LESSON SIX REVIEW

Test your understanding of the functions and concepts you learned in Lesson
Six by completing the following Review Questions:

1. What are the two Area Chart styles?
2. What is the difference between a Line Chart and an Overlap Area Chart?
3. What kind of information does the X Axis *usually* show?
4. List the three types of information you enter in the X-Axis Automatic
   Data Entry Pop-up.
5. What does the Evolve Tool do?
6. Describe how to convert an Area Chart to a Table Chart.
7. How do you show grid lines in a Table Chart?
8. Sketch the Flip Tool.
9. Why would you choose the Stacked Area Chart style?
10. Describe two ways to rotate an object.

SUPPLEMENTARY EXERCISES

Exercise 1   Create a Stacked Area Chart comparing the production levels for three company departments over a five-year period. You determine the name of the
company and department and the series data.

Exercise 2   Convert the Area Chart you created for Exercise 1 into a Table Chart. Enhance your Table Chart and then retrieve both the Area Chart and the Table
Chart into the Draw Screen and add an evolved symbol.

PICTORIAL CHARTS

Introduction   The term *Pictorial Chart* covers a huge assortment of documents that use
graphics to communicate a message. The common component in all these
documents is the use of pictures, symbols, and geometric shapes to illustrate
information in a way that readers can immediately understand.

Think, for example, of the two methods you could use to explain a company's
organizational structure. First, you could fill a page with a description of the
company's personnel and lines of communication. After a delay of several
minutes to allow readers to study the text, your information would certainly
be understood.

Alternatively, you could present the same information with a collection of
boxes and interconnecting lines. The second option—an organization
chart—would communicate the names, titles, and relationships of company
personnel in a fraction of the time required to scan a page of text.

Pictorial Charts, therefore, can save readers time by providing them with an
identifiable *image* of the information presented.

To create an effective Pictorial Chart, you need to consider two factors:

- Purpose
- Format

Purpose   The purpose of a Pictorial Chart is to communicate information in "shorthand." Complex instructions or abstract ideas can often be demonstrated more
effectively with the use of pictorial charts. Even simple ideas can have a
greater impact when combined with pictorial elements.

For example, suppose you wanted to make the point that two-thirds of the
movies rented from Video Fun Ltd. are children's movies. You could create a
bar chart to show this information or simply write the message on a text chart.
Think how much more impact your message would have, however, if you
chose to display it as a Pictorial Chart. Here's one possibility:

This example illustrates a very basic use of the Pictorial Chart. You can create more complex Pictorial Charts to illustrate a sequence of events, a project overview, or even the scene of a crime. As long as your Pictorial Chart achieves its principal purpose of communicating information in a shorthand form that carries more impact than traditional number or text charts, you are bound only by the limits of your imagination.

Format

The Pictorial Chart is not constrained by the formatting requirements of a Number Chart or Text Chart. You can use a wide variety of methods to communicate your message. The only requirement is that the Pictorial Chart be clear and coherent. You achieve clarity through the use of simple labels and coherence through the use of strong lines and a simple, uncluttered appearance.

Section Three Charts

In Section Three, you will learn how to create three distinct types of Pictorial Chart.

- Organization Chart
- Geographical Chart
- Diagram

The Organization Chart uses a preset format that allows variation only in the number of organizational levels you add in the Harvard Graphics Organization Chart Edit Screen. The Geographical Chart uses map symbols to illustrate statistical information—similar to a Number Chart but not as confined by the Number Chart formats. The Diagram is created in the Draw Screen, which enables you to create an endless variety of designs. In Lesson Nine, you will create two Diagrams—a Floor Plan and a Process Diagram.

<table><tr><td>

LESSON SEVEN

</td><td>

ORGANIZATION CHART

</td></tr></table>

FEATURES
- Creating and Editing
- Adding Symbols
- Adding Boxes
- Changing Box Style
- Changing Fonts and Attributes
- Rotating Text

INTRODUCTION

In Lesson Seven, you will learn how to create and edit an Organization Chart. Here are the lesson activities:

ACTIVITY 1: Determine the information required for your Organization Chart.

ACTIVITY 2: Follow the instructions given to create the Organization Chart on page 213.

ACTIVITY 3: Follow the instructions given to edit and enhance your Organization Chart as illustrated on page 223.

ACTIVITY 4: Create an Organization Chart based on your own data.

ACTIVITY 5: Complete the Lesson Review Questions on Organization Chart creation and enhancement.

ACTIVITY 1 **ORGANIZATION CHART INFORMATION**

You use an Organization Chart when you want to display the relationships between positions and people in a company or organization.

For example, here's an Organization Chart that shows how responsibilities are delegated among the five members of the staff at Southside Theatre Company.

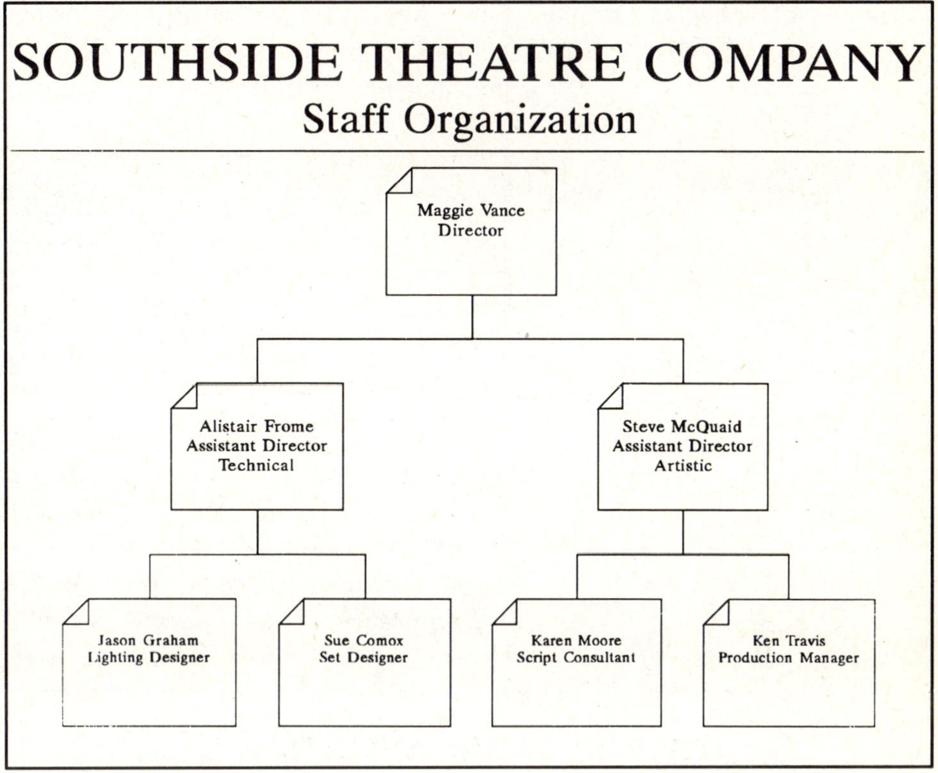

Lines of Communication

The lines that connect the boxes in an Organization Chart show the *relation-ships* between the various company positions. These relationships represent lines of communication.

For example, the Organization Chart for Southside Theatre Company shows that the two Assistant Directors report to the Director. In turn, each Assistant Director supervises two staff members.

Organization Chart Shape

An Organization Chart corresponds to the shape of a pyramid. At the top, or apex, is the highest position followed by two or three secondary positions, followed in turn by more positions until the base level is reached.

Chart Limitations

When you create an Organization Chart in Harvard Graphics, you need to be aware of certain limitations. For example, you cannot increase or decrease the size of the boxes displayed, nor can you change the size of the text displayed inside the boxes. As a result, the text in Organization Charts that consist of more than three levels can become difficult to read.

In addition, you cannot display two side-by-side boxes as the top level of an Organization Chart. If you wished to create a diagram of a family tree, for example, you could not display two boxes representing the mother and father at the top of the chart "pyramid." You should use the Organization Chart feature, therefore, when your top level consists of only one position or person.

Summary of Activities 2 and 3　　For Activity 2 you will create an Organization Chart for the Office Administration Department of Western Community College. This chart will require three organizational levels to represent nine faculty positions.

Level	Position	Number
One	Department Head	1
Two	Department Coordinators	2
Three	Full–Time Instructors	6

In Activity 3, you will augment your chart with two support staff positions and edit the data in your boxes to reflect staffing changes. In addition, you will access the Draw Screen to add a symbol and a line of slanted text.

The Organization Charts you create in Activities 2 and 3 will be used by the Department Head, Jane Dawson, as part of her presentation to new students.

ACTIVITY 2　ORGANIZATION CHART 1

Three major steps are required to produce Organization Chart 1:

Step One:　　Create Your Organization Chart
Step Two:　　Enhance Your Organization Chart
Step Three:　Save and Print Your Organization Chart

Follow the step-by-step instructions to reproduce Organization Chart 1 (see page 213). Remember to place a check mark in the box next to each function you complete.

Create Your Organization Chart

You will first create your Organization Chart and then enter the data for each box.

Create Chart　　1.　At the Main Menu, press **1** for **Create Chart.**
2.　Press **4** for **Organization.**

The Organization Chart Data Form appears. Your cursor currently appears next to **Title.**

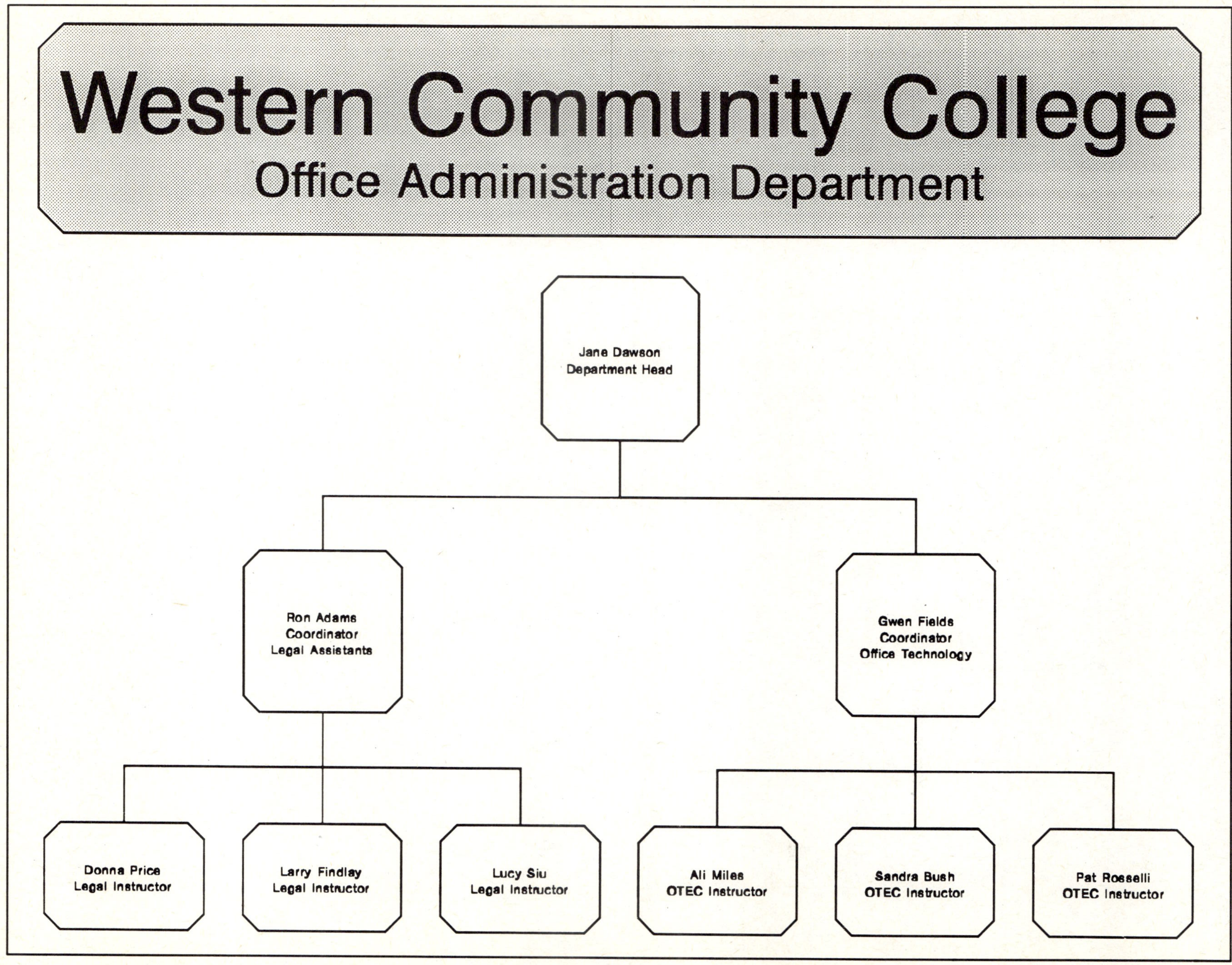
Western Community College
Office Administration Department
Jane Dawson
Department Head
Ron Adams
Coordinator
Legal Assistants
Gwen Fields
Coordinator
Office Technology
Donna Price
Legal Instructor
Larry Findlay
Legal Instructor
Lucy Siu
Legal Instructor
Ali Miles
OTEC Instructor
Sandra Bush
OTEC Instructor
Pat Rosselli
OTEC Instructor

Enter Title/Subtitle

1. Type the Title of your Organization Chart: *Western Community College.* Press **Enter.**
2. Now type the Subtitle of your Organization Chart: *Office Administration Department.* Press **Enter.**

Title/Subtitle Entered

> **NOTE:**   If you make a typing error, press the Backspace key to erase the error and then retype the correct characters.

Enter Data in Boxes

Your next step is to type the data required for each of the first three boxes.

Box 1

1. Press **Tab** once to move to the first box. Note that it is highlighted in white.
2. Press **Enter.** The Add/Edit Box Text Pop-up appears. You will enter the text for your first box in this Pop-up.
3. Next to **Name**, type *Jane Dawson* and press **Enter.**
4. Next to **Title**, type *Department Head* and press **Enter.**

Your Add/Edit Box Text Pop-up looks like this:

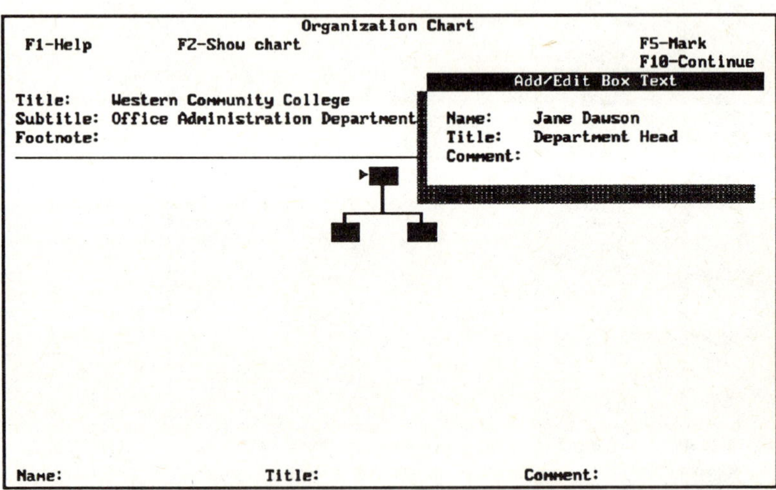

5. Press **Enter** again to return to your Chart Edit Screen. Note that the name and title you just entered appear at the bottom of the screen.

Box 1 Data Entered

Box 2   1. Press your ↓ arrow to move to the left box.
        2. Press **Enter** to access the Add/Edit Box Text Pop-up.
        3. Enter the information for this box as follows:

           Name: *Ron Adams* (**Enter**)
           Title: *Coordinator* (**Enter**)
           Comment: *Legal Assistants* (**Enter**)

Box 3   1. Press your → arrow to move to the right box.
        2. Press **Enter** to access the Add/Edit Box Text Pop-up.
        3. Enter the information for this box as follows:

           Name: *Gwen Fields* (**Enter**)
           Title: *Coordinator* (**Enter**)
           Comment: *Office Technology* (**Enter**)

Boxes 2 and 3 Data Entered

Add Boxes   You now need to add boxes to include data on the full-time instructors.

To add a box, you will first position your cursor on the box *above* where you want the new boxes to appear and then press **Ctrl + Ins.**

1. Position your cursor on the left box as illustrated:

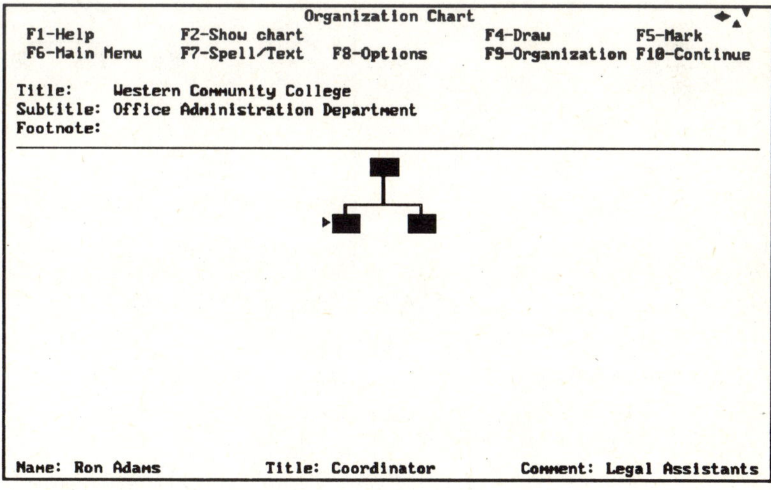

2. Press **Ctrl + Ins.** A new box will appear. The name of one of the three instructors in the Legal Assistants Program will be placed in this box.
3. To add the other two boxes, press **Ctrl + Ins** twice more. Your screen should now look like this:

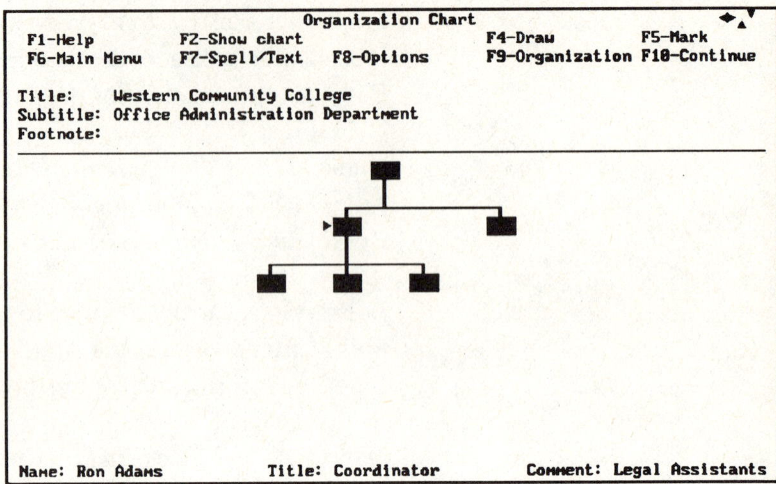

Now that you've added boxes to the Legal Assistants Coordinator, press your
→ arrow to move your cursor to the right box on level two.

1. Press **Ctrl + Ins** three times to insert three new boxes as illustrated:

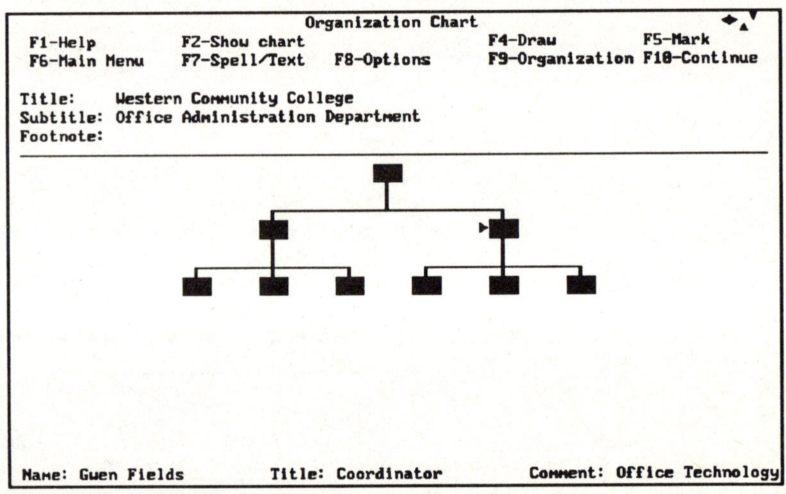

Level Three Box Additions Complete

Enter Level Three Data   Your next step is to place the names of the six instructors in the six new boxes
you've created.

1. Press your ↓ and ← arrows to position your cursor on the extreme left
    bottom box.
2. Press **Enter.**
3. At the Add/Edit Box Text Pop-up, type

    Name: *Donna Price* (**Enter**)
    Title: *Legal Instructor* (**Enter** twice).

4. Press your → arrow to move to the next box and press **Enter.**

5.   At the Add/Edit Box Text Pop-up, type

Name: *Larry Findlay* (**Enter**)
Title: *Legal Instructor* (**Enter** twice).

6.   Follow the same procedure to fill the rest of the boxes as follows:

Box 3:   Lucy Siu, Legal Instructor
Box 4:   Ali Miles, OTEC Instructor
Box 5:   Sandra Bush, OTEC Instructor
Box 6:   Pat Rosselli, OTEC Instructor

Level Three Box Data Complete

Display Chart ▶   Press **F2** to display your chart:

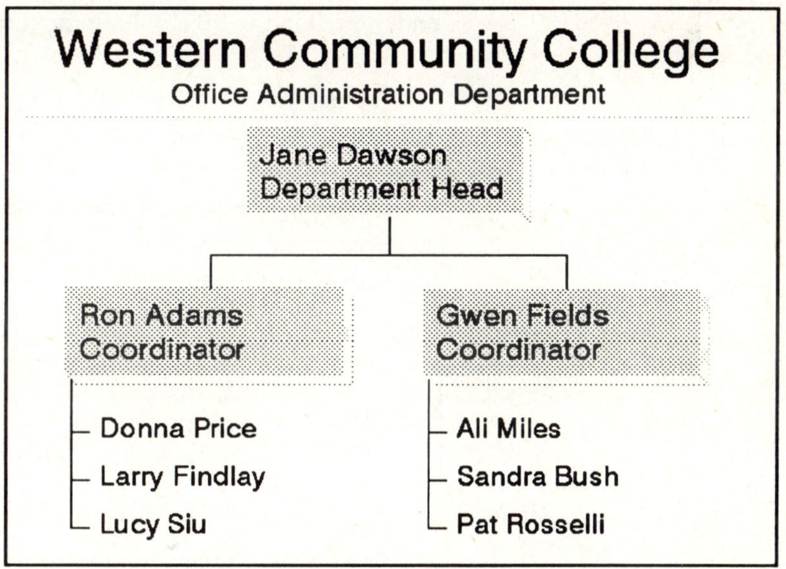

Notice how the names of the instructors do not appear in boxes and that the "Comments" information for the boxes in level two is missing. In the next section, you will change these and a variety of other attributes.

Press **F10** to return to the Chart Edit Screen.

Enhance Your Organization Chart

Your Organization Chart contains all the required data and box levels. Now you need to work on its overall appearance. Here's what you need to do.

Required Enhancements

> → Change the Box Text Alignment
> → Change the Region Frame Style for the Title/Subtitle
> → Enhance the Boxes:
>   - Change the Box Style
>   - Change the Box Fill and Outline Colors
>   - Include the Comments line in the Level Two boxes
>   - Include the Title line in the Level Three boxes
>   - Display Level Three as horizontal boxes

Change Box Text Alignment

You want the text in the boxes to be centered.

1. Press **F8** for **Options.**
2. Press **2** for **Text Attributes.**

The Text Attributes Screen appears. Note that your cursor is currently resting under the **9** in the **Size** column next to **Title.**

1. Press **Tab** two times to move to the **Alignment** column.
2. Press your ↓ arrow to move your cursor opposite **Box Name.**
3. Press **F3** for **Choices.**
4. Cursor to **Center** and press **Enter.**
5. Press your ↓ arrow once so that your cursor is opposite **Box Title.**
6. Press **C** for **Center.**
7. Press your ↓ arrow once more and choose **Center** for **Box Comment.**

> **NOTE:**   You cannot change the size of the box text or the size of the boxes themselves in an Organization Chart.

8. Press **F10** to return to the Chart Edit Screen.

Text Attributes Complete   ☐

Enhance Your Title/Subtitle

You want to enclose the Title/Subtitle in an octagonal frame.

Frame Style

1. Press **F8** for **Options.**
2. Press **3** for **Appearance.** The Appearance Menu appears.
3. Press your ↓ arrow to position your cursor opposite **Region Frame Style** in the **Titles** column. **Line** is currently highlighted.
4. Press **F3** for **Choices.**
5. Cursor up to **Octagonal** and press **Enter.**
6. Press **F10** to return to the Chart Edit Screen.

Chart Appearance Enhanced   ☐

Enhance Your Boxes   You want to enclose your boxes with octagonal frames, change the Box Fill and Outline colors, show your Comments line, and display level three as horizontal boxes.

Box Style
1. Press **F8** for **Options.**
2. Press **5** for **Box Options.** The Box Options Pop-Up appears.
3. Your cursor is currently positioned next to **Style.**
4. Press **F3** for **Choices.**
5. Cursor up to **Octagonal** and press **Enter.**

Frame Fill Color
1. Press your ↓ arrow to position your cursor next to **Fill Color.**
2. Press **F3** for **Choices.**
3. Cursor up to **Background** (shown as black) and press **Enter.**

NOTE: The chart boxes will print white.

Frame Outline Color
1. Press your ↓ arrow to position your cursor next to **Outline Color.**
2. Press **F3** for **Choices.**
3. Cursor to **White: Text** and press **Enter.**

Comments Line
1. Press your ↓ arrow to position your cursor opposite **Show Comment.**
2. Press **Y** for **Yes.**

Level Three: Show Title
1. Press your ↓ arrow to position your cursor opposite **Show Title** in the **Last Level** selection.
2. Press **Y** for **Yes.**

Level Three: Box Format
1. Press your ↓ arrow to position your cursor opposite **Arrangement** in the **Last Level** selection.
2. Press **F3** for **Choices.**
3. Cursor to **Horizontal** and press **Enter.**
4. Press **F10** to return to your Chart Edit Screen.

Box Options Complete   ☐

Display Chart ▶   Press **F2** to display your Chart and compare it to the following illustration:

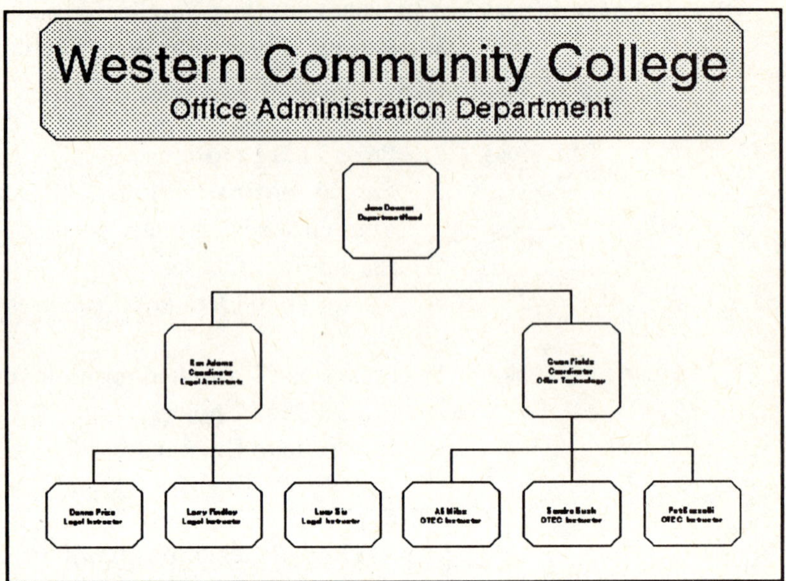

Press **Enter** to return to your Chart Edit Screen.

Save and Print Your Organization Chart

You will save your Organization Chart on your data disk and then access the Output command to print your chart. Once you are satisfied with your Chart, you can either exit from Harvard Graphics or get started on Activity 3.

Save
1. Press **F6** for **Main Menu.**
2. Press **4** for **File** and then **4** for **Save Chart.**

The Save Chart Menu appears. Your cursor is currently positioned next to **Filename.** The default Directory (usually C:\HG3\DATA) is displayed. You will save your file on a data disk in Drive A or B.

1. Press your ↑ arrow to move opposite **Directory.**
2. Type *a:* or *b:* and then press **Delete** to erase the old Directory.
3. Press **Enter.**
4. At **Filename,** type *Orgchrt1* and press **Enter.**
5. At **Description,** type *Organization Chart #1: Lesson 7.*

Your Save Chart Screen should look like this:

```
┌─────────────────────────────────────────────────┐
│                   Save Chart                    │
│                                                 │
│  Directory:      a:\                            │
│                                                 │
│  Filename:       Orgchrt1                       │
│                                                 │
│  Description:    Organization Chart #1: Lesson 7│
│                                                 │
│  Add to current presentation:     No            │
│                                                 │
└─────────────────────────────────────────────────┘
```

6.   Press **F10** to save and return to the Organization Chart Edit Screen.

Organization Chart 1 Saved

Print

1.   Press **F6** for **Main Menu.**
2.   Press **5** for **Output.**
3.   Press **Enter** to accept **Printer 1.**
4.   Press **F2** to view how your document will appear in printed form.

> **NOTE:**   If you do not like the look of your Chart, press **ESC** to return
> to the Chart Edit Screen. Access the **F8 Options Menu** to
> change your Chart's **Appearance (3)** or **Box Options (5).**

5.   If you are satisfied with the look of your Chart, press **F10** twice to accept
     the Default Settings and print your Chart.

The Output to Printer Screen appears. Your Organization Chart has now been
sent to the printer. Wait until the Output to Printer Screen disappears and you
are returned to your Organization Chart Edit Screen.

Organization Chart 1 Printed

You now have three options:

- Exit Harvard Graphics if you are finished with your learning session.
- Clear the current chart.
- Keep the Organization Chart 1 Edit Screen and begin Organization Chart 2.
  When you make the changes to Organization Chart 1 to turn it into Organi-
  zation Chart 2, you will save it with a different name so that Organization
  Chart 1 remains unaffected by the new changes.

Exit Harvard Graphics

1.   Press **F6** for **File.**
2.   Press **E** for **Exit to Main Menu.**
3.   Press **E** again to exit Harvard Graphics.

Clear the Current Chart

1. Press **F6** for **File.**
2. Press **E** for **Exit to Main Menu.**
3 Press **1** for **Create Chart.**
4. Press **8** for **Clear Chart.**

Keep Organization Chart 1 on Screen

If you choose this option, you can continue immediately to Activity 3. Omit the Get Orgchrt1 section and start with Edit Box Text.

ACTIVITY 3   ORGANIZATION CHART 2

For Organization Chart 2, you will change the data in some of the boxes, delete some boxes, remove the octagonal frame around the Title and Subtitle, and change the type size of the Title and Subtitle. Once you have completed your changes to the Chart itself, you will place it in the Draw Screen to add further enhancements.

Three major steps are required to produce Organization Chart 2.

Step One: Edit Your Chart Data
Step Two: Enhance Your Chart
Step Three: Save and Print Your Chart

Follow the step-by-step instructions to edit and enhance your Organization Chart (see page 223). Remember to place a check mark in the box next to each function you complete.

Edit Your Chart Data

Get Orgchrt1 from Disk

If you have exited out of Harvard Graphics and are starting fresh at your Main Menu, bring Orgchrt1 (saved on your data disk) to the screen as follows:

1. Press **4** for **File** and then **1** for **Get Chart.** The default HG3 Data Directory appears on screen.
2. Type the letter of your data disk drive (*a:* or *b:*) over the current Directory and press **Delete** to erase the extra letters.
3. Press **Enter.**
4. At the list of files on your data disk, choose **Orgchrt1** and press **Enter** twice.

Edit Box Text

Jane Dawson has retired from her position as Department Head and been replaced by Ron Adams, the Coordinator: Legal Assistants. Edit the top box as follows:

Department Head Box

1. Position your cursor on the top box and press **Enter.**

Western Community College
Office Administration Department

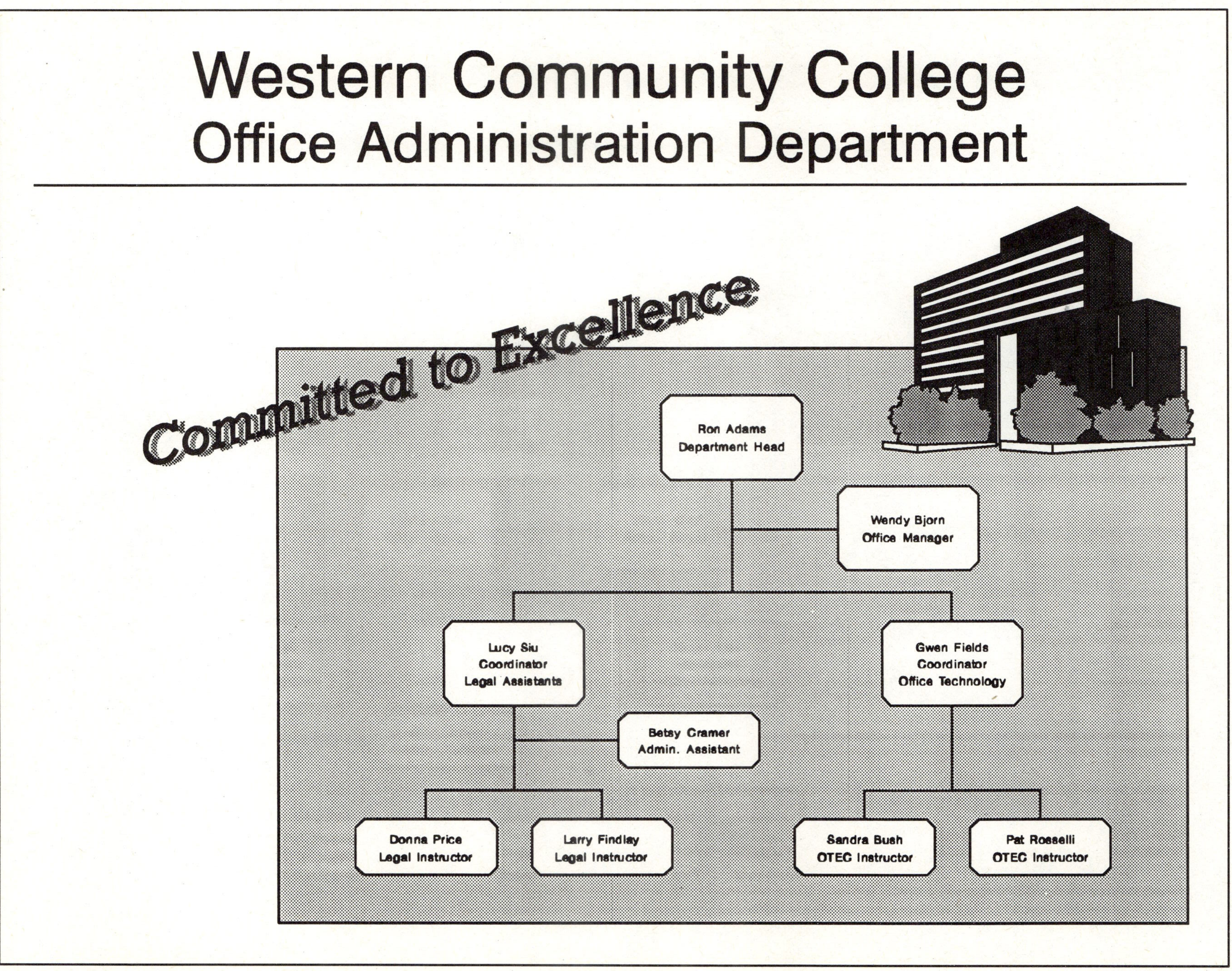

The Add/Edit Box Text Pop-up appears. In this Pop-up, you will replace Jane Dawson with Ron Adams.

2. Next to **Name**, type *Ron Adams* and press **Delete** to erase the remaining letters.
3. Press **Enter** until you are returned to your Chart Edit Screen.

Legal Coordinator's Box

Lucy Siu, one of the Legal Instructors, has been promoted to Coordinator of the Legal Assistants Program.

1. Move your cursor to the left box on level two and press **Enter.**
2. At the Add/Edit Box Text Pop-up, type *Lucy Siu* over *Ron Adams* and press **Delete** to erase the remaining letter.
3. Press **Enter** until you are returned to your Chart Edit Screen.

Box Edits Complete

Delete Boxes

Because of budget cutbacks, a new Legal Instructor to replace Lucy Siu will not be hired. Delete Lucy's box as follows:

Legal Instructor Box

1. Position your cursor on the right box on level two of the Legal Assistants "group" as illustrated:

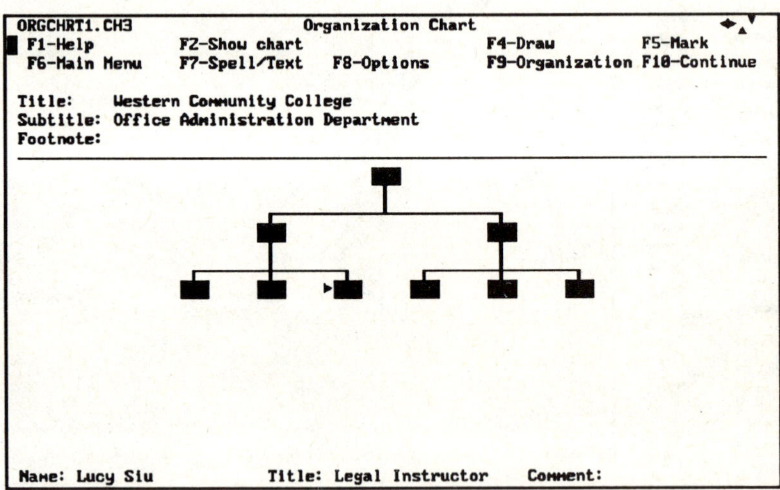

2. Press **Ctrl + Del.**

OTEC Instructor Box

Ali Miles, one of the OTEC Instructors, has left the college. Delete his box.

1. Position your cursor on the left box on level two of the Office Technology group as illustrated:

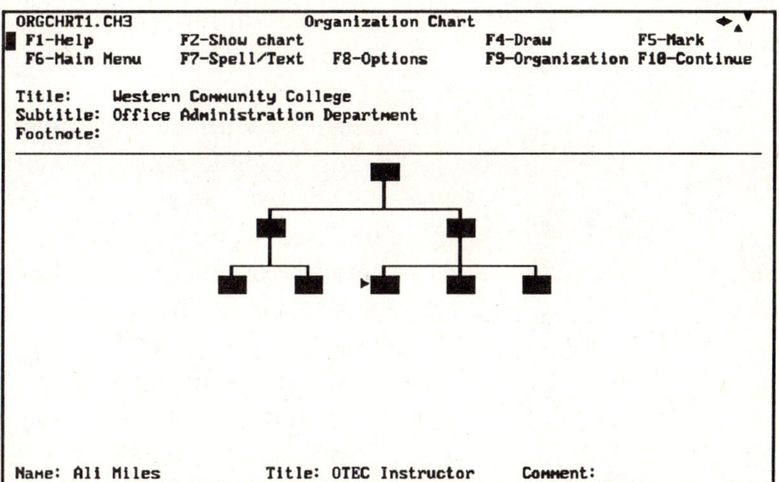

2.   Press **Ctrl + Del.** Note that only two boxes remain.

Your screen should look like this:

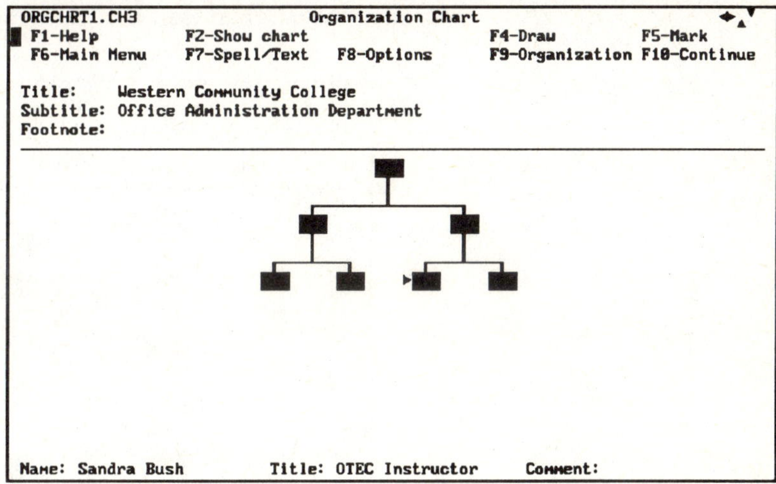

Box Deletions Complete

Add Staff Positions

Two staff positions need to be added to your Organization Chart. A staff position represents a staff member who provides administrative or secretarial support to a principal position. You cannot add boxes to a staff position.

Your Organization Chart requires two staff positions:

- Office Manager to the Department Head
- Administrative Assistant to the Coordinator: Legal Assistants

Staff Position 1

1.   Press your ↑ arrow to move to the Department Head (top) box.
2.   Press **F9** for the **Organization Menu.**
3.   Press **3** for **Add Staff Position.**

4.   Press your ↓ arrow to highlight the new box and press **Enter.**
5.   At the Add/Edit Box Text Pop-up, type

Name: *Wendy Bjorn* (**Enter**)
Title: *Office Manager* (**Enter** twice)

Staff Position 2

1.   Press your ↓ arrow to position your cursor on the Coordinator: Legal Assistants box (left box of level two).
2.   Press **F9** for the **Organization Menu.**
3.   Press **3** for **Add Staff Position.**
4.   Press your ↓ arrow to highlight the new box and press **Enter.**
5.   At the Add/Edit Box Text Pop-up, type

Name: *Betsy Cramer* (**Enter**)
Title: *Admin. Assistant* (**Enter** twice)

Addition of Staff Positions Complete

Compare your Chart Edit Screen to the following illustration:

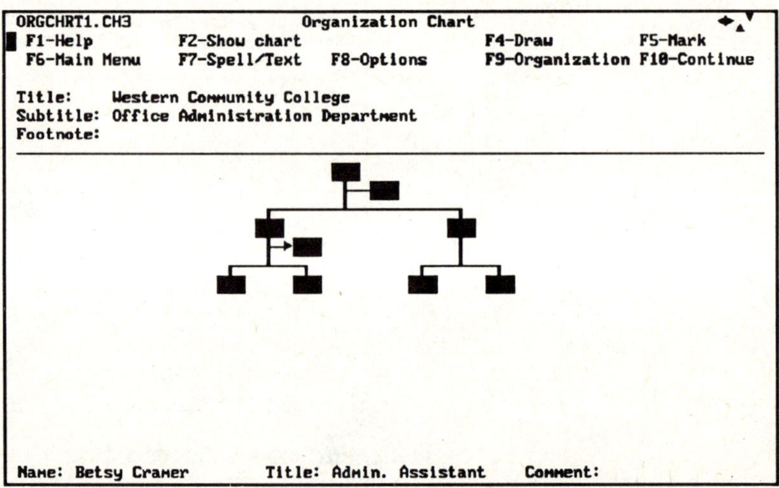

Enhance Chart Appearance

For Organization Chart 2, you need to enlarge your Title and Subtitle, replace the octagonal box with a single line, and remove the frame fill color. In addition, you will enclose the entire chart region with a box and change its fill color. Here's how:

Text Attributes

1.   Press **F8** for **Options.**
2.   At the Options Menu, press **2** for **Text Attributes.** The Text Attributes Menu appears. Your cursor is currently next to **Title** in the **Size** column.
3.   Type *7* and press **Enter.**
4.   Type *6* to change the Subtitle size.
5.   Press **F10** to return to your Chart Edit Screen.

Text Attributes Complete

Chart Appearance

1. Press **F8** for **Options.**
2. Press **3** for **Appearance.**

Title/Subtitle Frame Style

1. Press your ↓ arrow to position your cursor next to **Region Frame Style** in the **Titles** column. **Octagonal** is highlighted.
2. Press **F3** for **Choices.**
3. Cursor to **Line** and press **Enter.**

Chart Frame Style

1. Press **Tab** to move your cursor to **Region Frame Style** in the **Organization** column.
2. Press **F3** for **Choices.**
3. Cursor to **Plain** and press **Enter.**

Chart Frame Outline Color

1. Press your ↓ arrow once to move opposite **Frame Outline Color.**
2. Press **F3** for **Choices.**
3. Cursor to **White: Series 6** and press **Enter.**

Chart Frame Fill Color

1. Press your ↓ arrow once to move opposite **Frame Fill Color.**
2. Press **F3** for **Choices.**
3. Cursor down to **Blue** and press **Enter.**
4. Press **F10** to return to your Chart Edit Screen.

Chart Appearance Enhanced

Box Lines

To ensure a sharp print-out in black and white, you need to change the color of the lines that join the boxes in the Organization Chart.

1. Press **F8** for **Options.**
2. Press **5** for **Box Options.**
3. Press your ↓ arrow to move opposite **Line Color.**
4. Press **F3** for **Choices.**
5. Cursor to **White: Series 6** and press **Enter.** Your box lines will now print black on a black-and-white printer.
6. Press **F10** to return to your Chart Edit Screen.

Box Line Color Changed

Now you are ready to access the Draw Screen so that you can resize the Chart Area and add a symbol and the slanted text.

Enhance Your Chart

Access the Draw Screen

Press **F4** to place your chart in the Draw Screen so that you can resize your Chart Area, add the Office Symbol, and add the slanted text.

The following functions require the use of the mouse. Remember to click the **left** button to select functions and the **right** button to finish functions. If you click the right button twice and return to the Main Menu, just press **3** for **Draw** to return to your Draw Screen.

Resize the Chart Area

In order to resize just the Organization Chart Area, you have to ungroup your Chart.

1. Position your mouse in the middle of the Chart Area and click **left.** Note the orange handles that appear.
2. Click on the ▼ symbol at the bottom of your Draw Screen to access the second level of tools.

Ungroup Tool

1. Click on the **Ungroup Tool.** Handles now appear around both the Title/ Subtitle and the Organization Chart areas.
2. Click **right** to remove the handles.

Now reduce the size of the Chart Area as follows:

1. Click on the Organization Chart Area to select it.
2. Click and hold your **left** mouse button on the top left corner handle.
3. Press **Shift** and drag your mouse down and to the right until the Organization Chart Area is reduced by approximately one-quarter as illustrated:

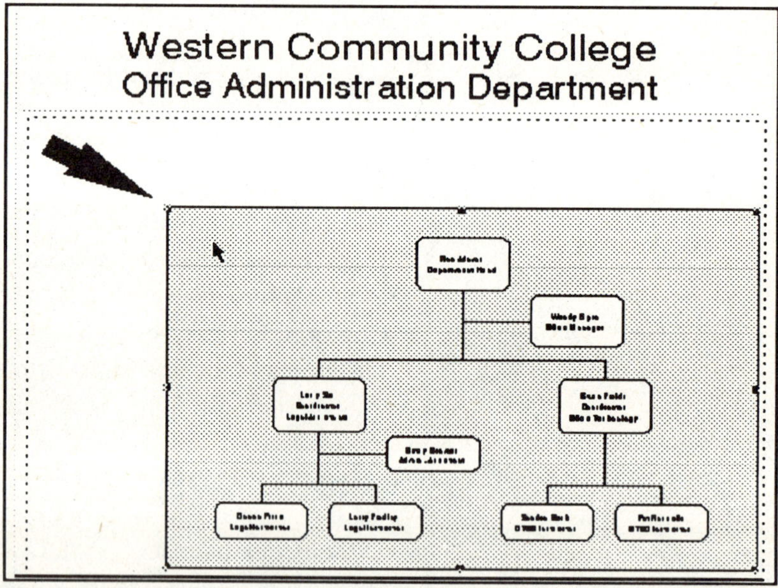

When you are satisfied with the size of your Chart Area, click the **right** button to remove the handles.

Add Building Symbol

Click on the ▲ symbol at the bottom of your Tool Area to access the first level of tools.

1. Click your **left** mouse button on the **Symbol Tool.**
2. Click again on **Get.**

3. At the Symbol Files Screen, press **F8** to sort the files alphabetically.
4. Click on **BUILD3.**
5. Click on the picture of the **Office.**
6. Click on **F10** twice to return to your Draw Screen.

Building Symbol Retrieved

Note that your Office Symbol is enclosed by several orange boxes or *handles*. These handles signify that the building has been selected.

Size   First resize your building as follows:

1. Click on and hold the top left handle.
2. Press **Shift** and your **left** mouse button to reduce the building size by approximately one-quarter.

Move   Now you need to move your building below the Title/Subtitle in the top right section of your drawing.

1. Position your pointer anywhere on the building *except* on one of the handles.
2. Click and hold down your **left** mouse button and position your building as illustrated:

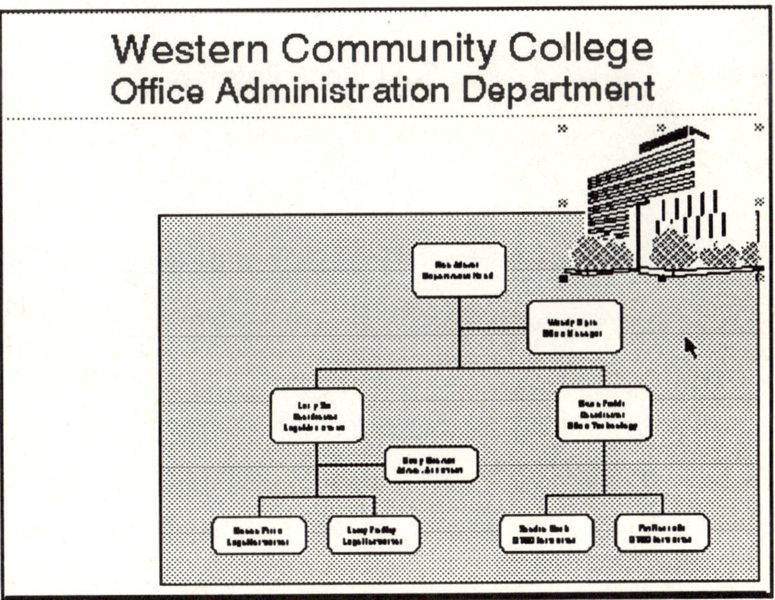

3. Click **right** to remove the handles.

Building Sized and Positioned

Add Your Text Block   Your last task is to add the phrase *Committed to Excellence* and then rotate and position it.

Text Tool

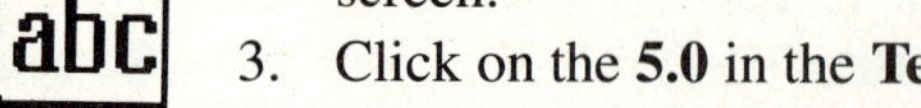

1. Click on the **Text Tool.**
2. Move your mouse up to the Text Attributes Pop-up at the top of your screen.
3. Click on the **5.0** in the **Text Size Ruler.**
4. Type *6.0* and press **Enter.**
5. Click on the **Font** box and choose **Geo Slab 712.**

You need to specify shadow text.

1. Note the row of boxes containing *t*'s in the upper right corner.
2. Click on the shadow *t*.

Now you are ready to type the text.

1. Position the **+** directly below the Title/Subtitle.
2. Click the **left** button and drag your mouse to create a box approximately 4" wide and 1" deep.

Don't worry if your box "runs into" your chart area. You will adjust positioning later.

Enter Text   The Text Pop-up appears.

1. Type *Committed to Excellence.*
2. Press **F10** to return to your Draw Screen.

Text Block Entered

Resize

1. Click on the **Pointer Tool.** Orange handles will appear around your text block.
2. Position your text block as illustrated:

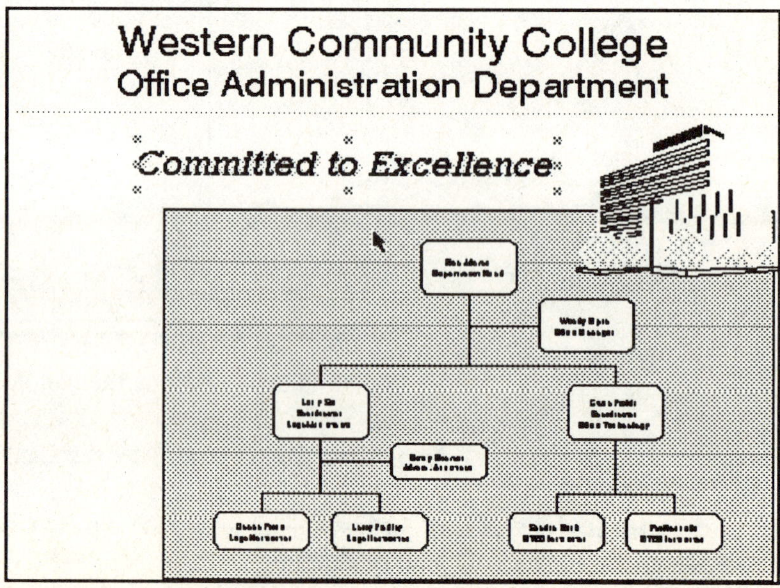

Rotate   Your last step is to rotate the text block across the top left corner of the Organization Chart Area.

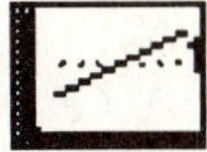

1.   Click on the **Rotate Tool.**
2.   Click on the **0.0** in the **Degrees** box.
3.   Type *15.0* and press **Enter.**
4.   Click on the **Reverse** box.
5.   Click your **right** button to exit Rotate mode.

Text Block Rotated

Reposition   Move your text block into position over the top left corner of your chart area as illustrated:

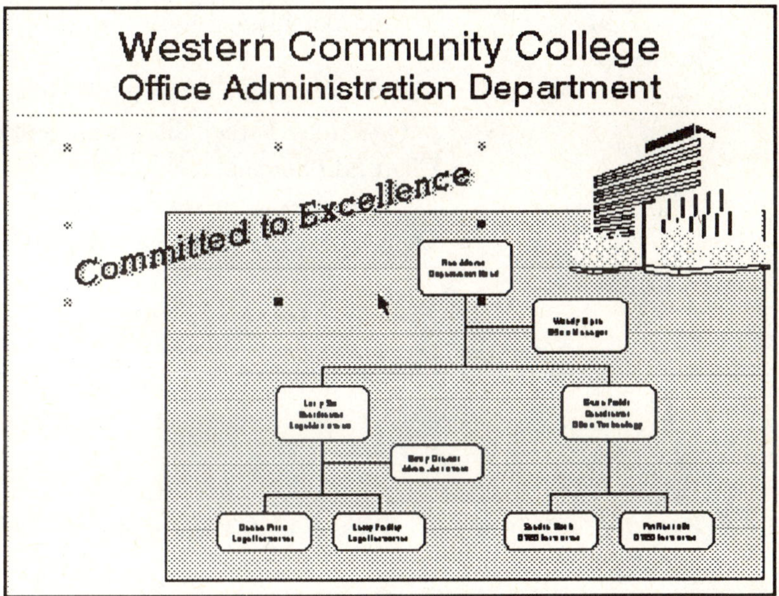

Take a good look at your chart. Are the various elements well balanced and attractive? Use your mouse to adjust the size and position of the various elements until you are satisfied with the overall appearance of Organization Chart 2.

Save and Print Your Chart

You will save Organization Chart 2 on your data disk and then access the Output command to print your chart. Once you are satisfied with your Chart, you can either exit from Harvard Graphics or get started on Activity 4.

Save   1.   Press **F6** for **File.**
2.   Press **2** for **Save Chart.**

The Save Chart Menu appears. Your cursor is currently positioned next to **Filename.** The Directory should be *a:* or *b:*, depending on the drive you used to save Orgchrt1. If your data drive does not appear, press your ↑ arrow to move opposite **Directory** and type your data drive.

1. At **Filename**, type *Orgchrt2* and press **Enter.**
2. At **Description**, type *Organization Chart #2: Lesson 7.*
3. Press **F10** to save and return to the Chart Edit Screen.

Organization Chart 2 Saved   ☐

Print
1. Press **F6** for **File** and **E** for **Exit to Main Menu.**
2. Press **5** for **Output.**
3. Press **Enter** to accept **Printer 1.**
4. Press **F2** to view how your document will appear in printed form.
5. If you are satisfied with the look of your Chart, press **F10** twice to accept the Default Settings.

Your Organization Chart has now been sent to the printer. Wait until the Output to Printer Screen disappears and you are returned to your Organization Chart Edit Screen.

Organization Chart 2 Printed   ☐

You now have two options:

- Exit Harvard Graphics if you are finished with your learning session.
- Clear the current chart and get started on creating your own Organization Chart in Activity 4.

Exit Harvard Graphics
1. Press **E** to exit Harvard Graphics.

Clear the Current Chart
1. Press **1** for **Create Chart.**
2. Press **8** for **Clear Chart.**

ACTIVITY 4   CHALLENGE ASSIGNMENT

Read through the following sections for suggestions on content and then adapt the instructions given for your own material. Use the boxes provided to record material about your Organization Chart.

The Challenge Assignment requires three major steps:

Step One: Select your Company/Organization
Step Two: Plan your Organization Chart information
Step Three: Create and Format Your Organization Chart

First, you need to create a company or an organization that your Organization Chart will represent. For example, you could choose a charitable organization that raises funds for a local Little League. If you choose a charity, remember that at the base of your chart will be a number of boxes for volunteers rather than for staff people.

Enter the name of the company/organization your Chart will represent.

Name of Company/Organization:

Plan Your Chart Information

Now determine the structure of your Organization Chart. Do a rough sketch first—it's much faster to make your main decisions on paper, where you can easily cross out material or make additions.

Number of Levels Place your principal position at the top, then draw the lines down to the next level of boxes and from there to the next level, and so on. Keep the number of levels to three or four *at the most*. Any more levels will become unreadable.

Support Staff Maintain the general shape of a pyramid, but don't be afraid to add in support staff at the sides of boxes. For example, to show that a secretary reports directly to the president but does not supervise the vice presidents, access your **Organization Menu (F9)** and choose **3** for **Add Staff Position.**

Use the following box to make a sketch of your Organization Chart.

Rough sketch of Organization Chart:

Create and Format Your Chart

The following commands and functions are listed to help you create and format your Organization Chart. Once you are satisfied with the format of your Organization Chart, press **F4** to place your Chart in the Draw Screen. Try adding one or two symbols and maybe a text block.

Experiment until you are sure that your Organization Chart displays your information in an efficient—and attractive—format.

Create Chart   At the Main Menu, press **1** for **Create Chart** and **4** for **Organization.**

Enter Text in Boxes
1. Position your cursor on the box and press **Enter.**
2. At the Add/Edit Text Box Pop-up, type the information you wish to include in the box.
3. Press **Enter** to return to your Chart Edit Screen.

Add Boxes
1. Position your cursor on the box *above* where you want the new boxes to appear.
2. Press **Ctrl + Ins.**

Delete Boxes
1. Position your cursor on the box you wish to delete.
2. Press **Ctrl + Del.**

Add Staff Position
1. Position your cursor on the box that requires the staff position.
2. Press **F9** for the **Organization Menu.**
3. Choose **3** for **Add Staff Position.**
4. Move your cursor to the new box and press **Enter.**
5. At the Add/Edit Box Text Pop-up, enter the information for the staff position.

Change Box Options
1. Press **F8** for **Options** and then **5** for **Box Options.**

At the Box Options Menu, you can enhance your boxes as follows:

- Change the box outline style.
- Change the box fill, outline, and line colors.
- Show the Comment line.
- Change the last level to show titles and comments, and to display in horizontal box format.

Text Attributes
1. Press **F8** for **Options** and then **2** for **Text Attributes.**

At the Text Attributes Menu, you can change the size, color, alignment, and font of your text. Remember that you cannot change the size of the text in boxes.

Chart Appearance   1.   Press **F8** for **Options** and then **3** for **Appearance.**

At the Appearance Menu, you can change the region frame style and color for the Title/Subtitle and chart regions.

Draw Screen   Press **F4** to place your chart in the Draw Screen. Press **F4** again if you wish to return to your Chart Edit Screen.

Symbols   Click on the **Symbol Tool** and then again on **Get.** Choose a symbol from the files provided. Click on **F10** to return to the Draw Screen.

Rotate   Click on an item in the Draw Screen and then click on the **Rotate Tool.** Enter the number of degrees to rotate the item and click on the Forward or Reverse boxes *or* click on the **right** handle and drag the mouse up or down.

Save   From the Draw Screen, press **F6** for **File** and then **2** for **Save Chart.** From the Chart Edit Screen, press **F6**, then **4** for **File** and **4** for **Save.** Change to the directory in which you wish to save your file (usually Drive A or B) and then type a filename for your Organization Chart.

Fast Save: Press **Ctrl + S.**

Print   At the Main Menu, choose **5** for **Output**, press **Enter** to accept **Printer 1**, and then **F10.**

Clear Chart   If you wish to start a new chart and have saved your current chart, first exit to the Main Menu. Now choose **1** for **Create Chart** and then **8** for **Clear Chart.** If you haven't saved your current chart, a message will appear. You can then press **ESC** to save your chart before clearing it.

Exit Harvard Graphics   At the Main Menu, press **E** to exit the program.

ACTIVITY 5   LESSON SEVEN REVIEW

Test your understanding of the functions and concepts you learned in Lesson Seven by completing the following Review Questions.

1.   What is the purpose of an Organization Chart?
2.   How do you enter data into a box?
3.   Where must your cursor be positioned to add boxes?
4.   How do you center data within boxes?
5.   How do you access the Box Options Pop-Up?
6.   How do you add a staff position to a box?
7.   Can you change the size of text in a box?

8.   How do you access the Draw Screen?
9.   How do you change the region frame style for the Title/Subtitle?
10.   Make a rough sketch of the Rotate Tool.

SUPPLEMENTARY EXERCISES

Exercise 1   Create an Organization Chart showing the executive positions for a large development company. You determine the name of the company and include the following positions:

- President
- Vice President: Finance
- Vice President: Sales
- Accounting Supervisor
- Legal Counsel
- Sales Manager: Western Division
- Sales Manager: Eastern Division
- Admin. Assistant to the President

Organize the position in a logical way to show reporting relationships. Your Organization Chart will have three levels. Experiment with different text attribute, appearance, and box options.

Exercise 2   Place the Organization Chart you created for Exercise 1 in the Draw Screen and add enhancements such as a company slogan and a symbol. Ungroup your chart and resize and reposition the Organization Area.

GEOGRAPHICAL CHART

FEATURES

- Creating Map Symbols
- Using Group/Ungroup
- Sizing and Moving Chart Areas
- Combining Map and Chart Symbols
- Saving Charts as Symbols
- Using Patterns
- Duplicating Objects
- Using the Align Tool

INTRODUCTION

In Lesson Eight, you will learn how to use maps to communicate data that includes geographical information. Here are the lesson activities:

ACTIVITY 1: Determine the information required for your Geographical Chart.

ACTIVITY 2: Follow the instructions provided to create the Geographical Chart on page 241.

ACTIVITY 3: Follow the instructions given to combine a bar chart with a map as illustrated on page 262.

ACTIVITY 4: Create your own Geographical Chart based on data you have developed.

ACTIVITY 5: Complete the Lesson Review Questions on the use of maps and charts.

ACTIVITY 1 GEOGRAPHICAL CHART INFORMATION

You use a Geographical Chart to highlight information that relates to a variety of locations. Look through any atlas and you will see Geographical Charts showing such data as population density, world crops, etc. In these types of charts, a variety of symbols or colors are placed on a map to communicate the required information.

Business Uses In business graphics, you generally use Geographical Charts in two ways:

1. Shade map areas to show product sales by region.
2. Superimpose a bar chart on a map to show how data vary over three or four broad regions.

Shading Map Areas

Let's look first at an example of a Geographical Chart that uses a map of the United States to make a state-by-state comparison of sales for the Cookie Factory. To create such a Chart, you would display a map of the United States and then fill each state with a pattern that corresponds to a legend specifying high, medium, or low sales.

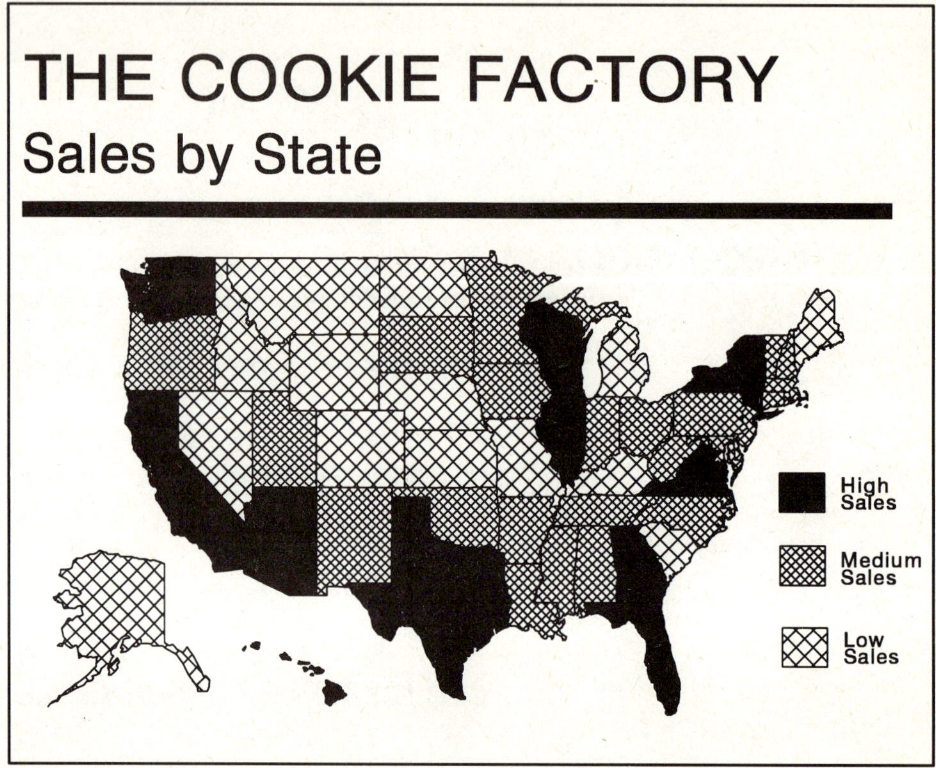

Notice how this type of Chart provides an easy-to-understand summary of regional cookie-eating habits. At a glance, you can see that cookie eating is a high-volume activity in California and Florida but not in Alaska and North Dakota. Of course, the high, medium, and low sales categories also reflect population differences from state to state. Obviously, a high-population state such as New York would have higher sales than a low-population state such as Idaho.

Per Capita Information

To show how many Cookie Factory cookies are consumed *per capita* from state to state, you would change your chart subtitle to "Per Capita Cookie Consumption" and define your color-coded boxes as High Consumption, Medium Consumption, and Low Consumption.

You can imagine all the ways in which you could use a map to show regional differences. All you need is a collection of data, a simple outline map, and an

easy-to-understand legend. To be effective, you need to limit your categories
to four or less.

Superimpose Bar Chart You can also use a map as a backdrop for a bar chart to communicate broad
geographical differences. For example, you could calculate Cookie Factory
sales for each of the three regions of the United States—Western, Central, and
Eastern—and then display this data as three bars placed over a map.

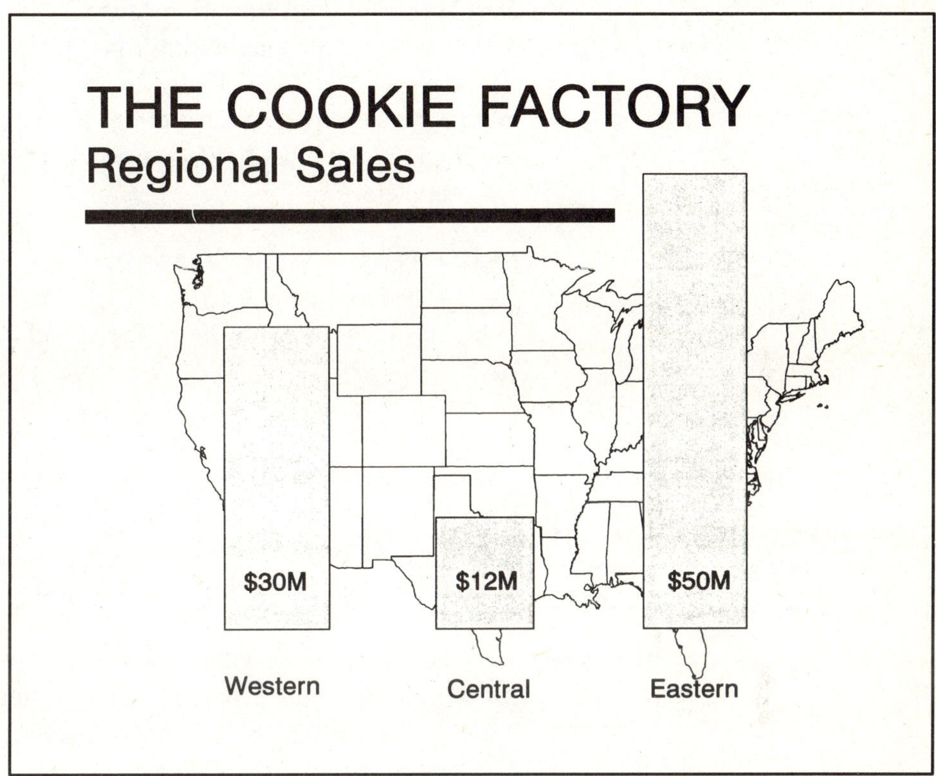

Summary of Activities 2 and 3 For Activities 2 and 3, you will create two Geographical Charts for Panda
Toys—a North American toy manufacturer that specializes in mail-order sales
of quality children's toys. Following its recent expansion into Canada, Panda
Toys has prepared a sales presentation for its Canadian distributors. This presentation will include two Geographical Charts showing the distribution of
sales across Canada.

The Geographical Chart you create in Activity 2 will fill each of Canada's ten
provinces and two territories with patterns that represent high, medium, and
low sales of Panda Toys in 1993.

In Activity 3, you will create a Bar Chart showing the Canadian sales by
region—Western, Central, and Eastern—and then superimpose this Chart on a
blank map of Canada.

ACTIVITY 2   GEOGRAPHICAL CHART 1

Four major steps are required to produce Geographical Chart 1:

Step One:	Enter Your Chart Heading
Step Two:	Create Your Map and Legend
Step Three:	Fill Your Map Areas
Step Four:	Save and Print Your Geographical Chart

Follow the step-by-step instructions to reproduce Geographical Chart 1 (see page 241). Remember to place a check mark in the box next to each function you complete.

Enter Your Chart Heading

You will first access the Draw Screen and enter your Chart heading.

Access Draw   At the Main Menu, press **3** for **Draw.**

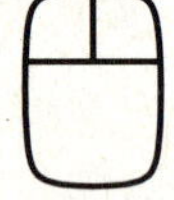

The following functions require the use of the mouse. Remember to click the **left** button to select functions and the **right** button to finish functions. If you click the right button twice, you may return to the Main Menu. If this happens, just press or click on **3** for **Draw** to return to your Draw Screen.

Enter Title
1. Click on the **Text Tool.**
2. Move your mouse up to the Text Attributes Pop-up.
3. Click on the **5.0** in the **Text Size Ruler.**
4. Type *12.0* and press **Enter.**

Now enter the text.
1. Position the **+** at the top left of your screen.
2. Click and hold the **left** mouse button to drag a box across the screen and down about 1".
3. At the Text Pop-up, type *PANDA TOYS.*
4. Press **F10** to exit the Text Pop-up.

Title Position
1. Click on the **Pointer Tool** to select the Title.
2. Position your mouse in the middle of your Title.
3. Click and hold your **left** mouse button and move your Title so that it starts from the top left of your screen as illustrated:

PANDA TOYS
1993 Canadian Sales
High Sales
Medium Sales
Low Sales

4. Click **right** to remove the handles and go on to enter the Subtitle.

Subtitle

1. Click on the **Text Tool.**
2. Click on the **Text Size Ruler** and type *8.0*. Press **Enter.**
3. Position your + under the Title and click **left** to draw a box across the screen and down about 1″.
4. At the Text Pop-up, type *1993 Canadian Sales.*
5. Press **F10** to exit the Pop-up.

Click on the **Pointer** to select your Subtitle and then move your mouse to position the Subtitle under the Title.

Align Title and Subtitle

1. Move your mouse to the Title.
2. Press **Shift** and the **left** mouse button to select the Title. Handles now appear around both the Title and Subtitle.
3. Click on the **Align Tool.**
4. Click on the box labeled **Left.** Compare your screen to the following illustration:

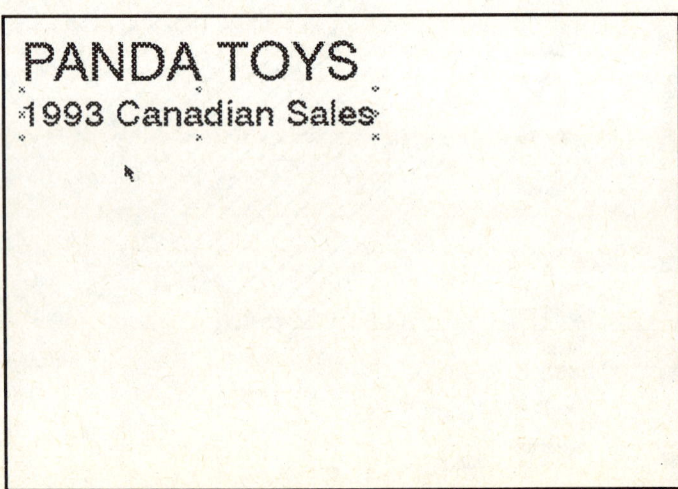

5. Click **right** to remove the handles.

Title/Subtitle Complete   ☐

Create Your Map and Legend

Steps Required   The following steps are required to create your map and Legend:

> → Click on the Symbol Tool to get your map
> → Size and position your map
> → Use the Box and Text Tools to create your Legend

Get Map Symbol   Your first step is to display the list of Symbol Directories and retrieve the map
                         of Canada.

1. Click your **left** mouse button on the **Symbol Tool.**
2. Click again on **Get.**
3. At the Symbol Files Screen, press **F8** to sort the files alphabetically.
4. Click on the ▼ symbol at the top right of your screen to scroll through the
    list of Symbol Directories.
5. Click on **MAPS2**.
6. Click on the map of **Canada** and then click on **F10** twice.

Size and Position Map   Notice how your map appears in the center of your Draw Screen. Your first
                            step is to increase your map size.

Size   1. Click first on the bottom left corner handle and use the **Shift** key to drag
                  your map down to the bottom left corner of your screen.

> **NOTE:**   Using **Shift** to maintain correct proportions is particularly im-
>   portant when you work with maps.

2. Click on the top right corner handle and press **Shift** to slightly increase
    the map size. Your map should look like this:

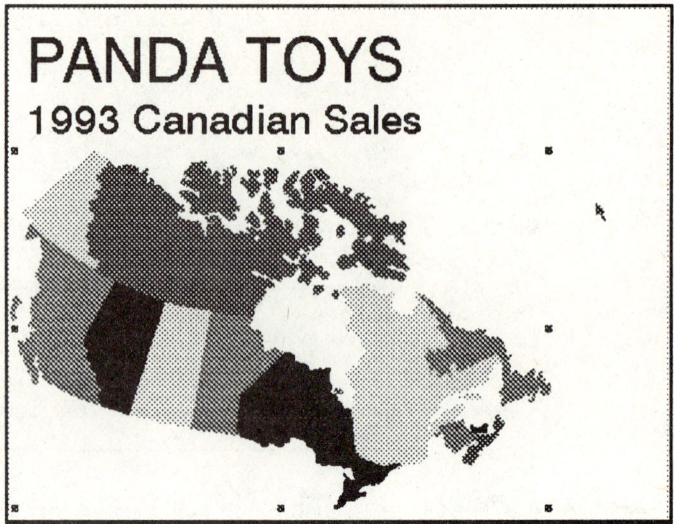

Map Position   1. Position your mouse anywhere on the map *except* on one of the orange
               handles.
               2. Click **left** and move your map about .5" to the right as illustrated:

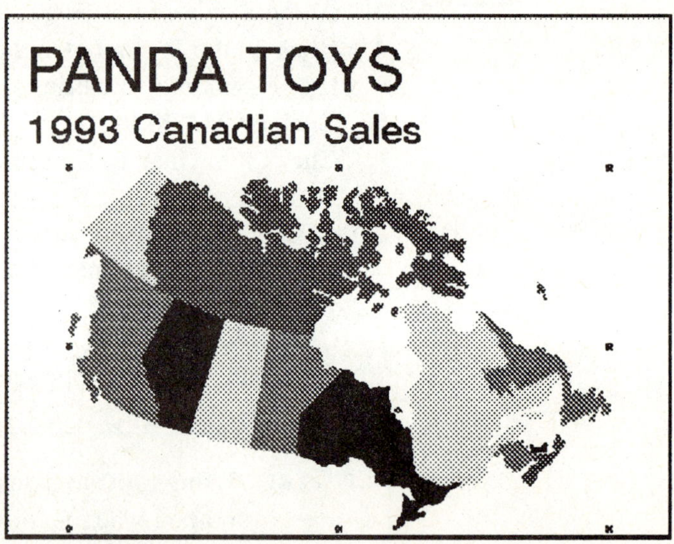

               3. Click **right** to remove the handles.

Map Symbol Sized and Positioned

Create Legend   You need to draw three boxes and create the text for the Legend that appears
                in the top right corner of your Geographical Chart. Create one of the boxes
                and then use the Duplicate Tool to copy it twice.

Box Tool   1. Click your **left** mouse button on the **Box Tool.**

                The Box Options Pop-up appears at the top of your screen and your cursor
                appears as a **+**.

                1. Use your mouse to position the **+** in the top right corner of your screen.

2. Click and release your **left** mouse button.
3. Move your mouse diagonally about one quarter inch; your box should be quite small.
4. Click your **left** mouse button to set the end of the box as illustrated:

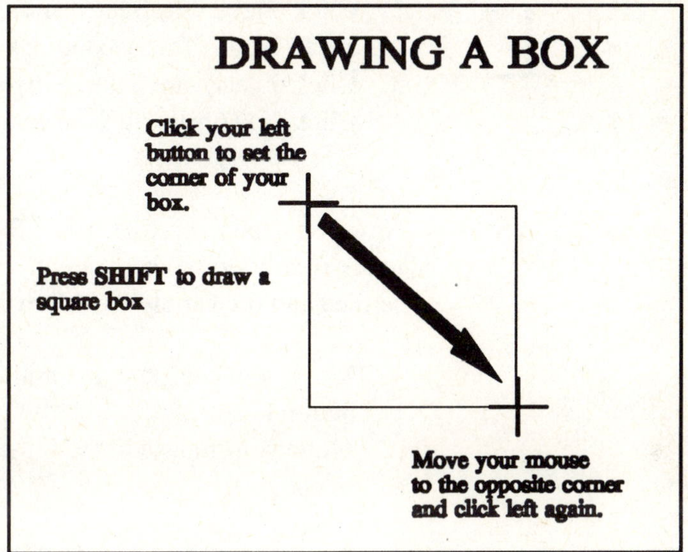

Position your box, if necessary, and compare its size to the following illustration:

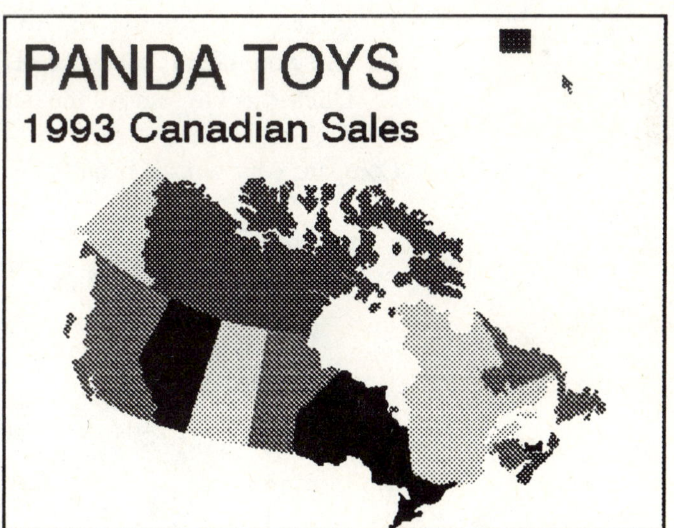

Trouble Note ▶ If your box is too big or not big enough, you can try again as follows:

1. Move your mouse to the top left of your screen and click **left** on the **UNDO Tool.**
2. Try drawing your box again.

Box Drawing Complete   ☐

Box Duplication

To save drawing time and to ensure all three boxes are the same size, you need to *duplicate* the first box twice.

1. Click on the **Pointer Tool** at the top of your Tool Box. The box you just finished drawing is now selected.

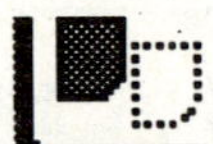

2. Click on the **Duplicate Tool.** Notice how a second box appears on top of the first box. This second box is now selected.
3. Click on and move the second box below the first box.
4. Click the **Duplicate Tool** again. A third box appears under the second box.

Align Boxes

Now you need to use the Align Tool to position the boxes in a straight column. Your bottom box is already selected. Select the other two boxes as described and then apply the **Align Tool.**

1. Move your mouse to the middle box and press **Shift** and your **left** mouse button to select it.
2. Move your mouse to the top box and use the Shift + Mouse method to select it.

Handles now appear around all three boxes.

Now apply the Align Tool.

1. Click on the **Align Tool.**
2. Click on the box labeled **Left.**
3. Click **right** to remove the handles.

Compare your box sizes and positions to the following illustration:

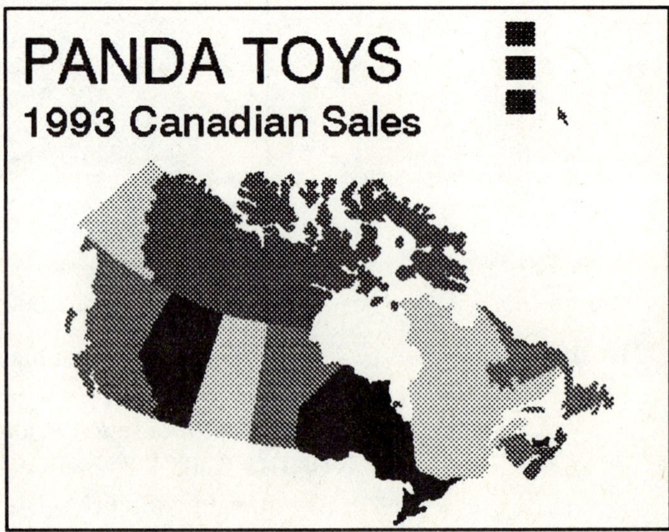

Legend Boxes Complete

Text Creation   To complete your Legend, you now need to enter the text that specifies High, Medium, or Low Sales next to each of the three boxes. First select the Text Tool and change the text size.

Text Size   1.   Click on the **Text Tool.**
2.   Move your mouse above the Draw Screen to the Text Attributes Pop-up.
3.   Click on the number in the **Text Size Ruler.**
4.   Type *3.0* and press **Enter.**

Text Enter   1.   Position the **+** next to your top box.
2.   Click **left** and drag a box to the edge of your screen.
3.   At the Text Pop-up, type *High Sales.*
4.   Press **F10** to exit the Text Pop-up.

Now move your mouse below High Sales and click **left** and drag a box to enter *Medium Sales.* Repeat the process to enter *Low Sales.*

Trouble Note ▶   If *Medium Sales* appears on two lines, click on **Undo** and move your mouse farther left before clicking **left** and drawing the box for the text block.

Legend Text Entered   ☐

Position Text Blocks   You will now use the Space Tool to evenly space the text blocks and the Align Tool to align the text blocks to the left. Start with the Space Tool.

Spacing   1.   Click on the **Pointer** to select the last text block you entered.
2.   Move the text block next to the bottom box.

3.   Use the Shift + Mouse method to select the middle and top text blocks.
4.   Click on the **Space Tool.**
5.   Click on the box that represents **Vertical** spacing.

Left Align   Your three text blocks should still be selected.

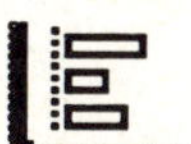

1.   Click on the **Align Tool.**
2.   Click on the box labeled **Left.**
3.   Click **right** to remove the handles.

Compare your Text and box positions to the following illustration:

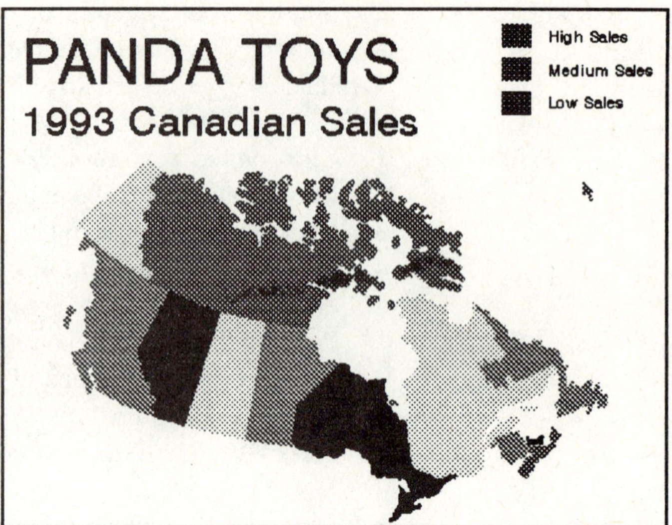

If you are not satisfied with the positioning of your text blocks, select and position them as required. If necessary, apply the **Space** and **Align Tools** again.

Text Block Positioned

Your next step is to group and move the entire Legend as follows:

1. Position your mouse above and to the left of the top box.
2. Click and hold **left** to draw a box around the entire Legend Area.

Notice that orange handles appear around each of the elements. You will now group these elements and reposition the block.

Group   1.   Click on the ▼ symbol to access the second tool level.

A new selection of tools appears. When you want to return to the first selection of tools, you merely click on the ▲ symbol.

2. Click on the **Group Tool.** Notice how orange handles now appear around the entire Legend Area.
3. Click on and position the Legend. Your Draw Screen should now look like this:

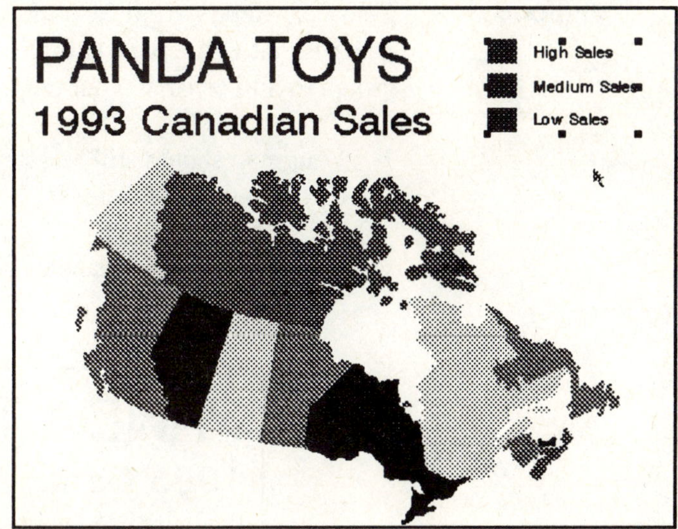

4.   Click **right** to remove the handles.

Legend Positioning Complete

Fill Your Map Areas

At present, the provinces and territories are displayed in several colors. To ensure a sharp print-out in black and white and to show regional sales differences, you will fill each province/territory with one of three patterns.

First, start "fresh" by replacing the existing colors with white and then selecting and filling the individual areas with patterns as instructed.

Color Entire Map

1.   Click on your map to select it.
2.   Click on the **Color Tool.**

Note that the Fill box is already highlighted. You want to change the color displayed to white.

Fill Box

1.   Move your mouse to a **White** box and click **left** to select it. Note that the **Fill** box is now white and that your entire map, except for the lines, appears white.

Line/Text Box   Now change all the lines to yellow.

1.   Click on the **Line/Text** box.
2.   Click on the box colored **Bright Yellow.**
3.   Click **right** to return to your Draw Screen.

Colors Replaced

Ungroup Map

Your next step is to fill each of the provinces/territories with one of the three patterns that will represent high, medium, and low sales. First, use the Ungroup Tool to separate your map into all its various components.

1. Your map should still be selected; if not, click **left** to select it.
2. Click on the **Ungroup Tool.**

Notice how orange handles no,w appear around all the provinces, territories, and islands!

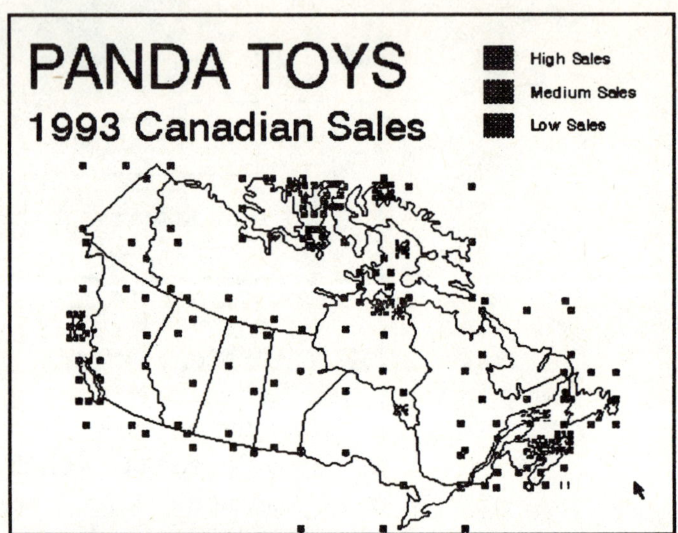

3. Click **right** to remove all the handles.

Each province or territory will be filled with a pattern that represents high, medium, or low sales. Here are the patterns you will use:

High Sales:

Medium Sales:

Low Sales:

You have already filled your entire map with white; therefore, you do not need to fill the High Sales areas. When you print your drawing, the white areas will print black as shown in the illustration on page 241.

Go on now to follow the instructions given to select the Medium Sales areas and fill them with the Check pattern.

> **NOTE:**   Refer to the following map to locate the provinces and territories specified in the instructions.

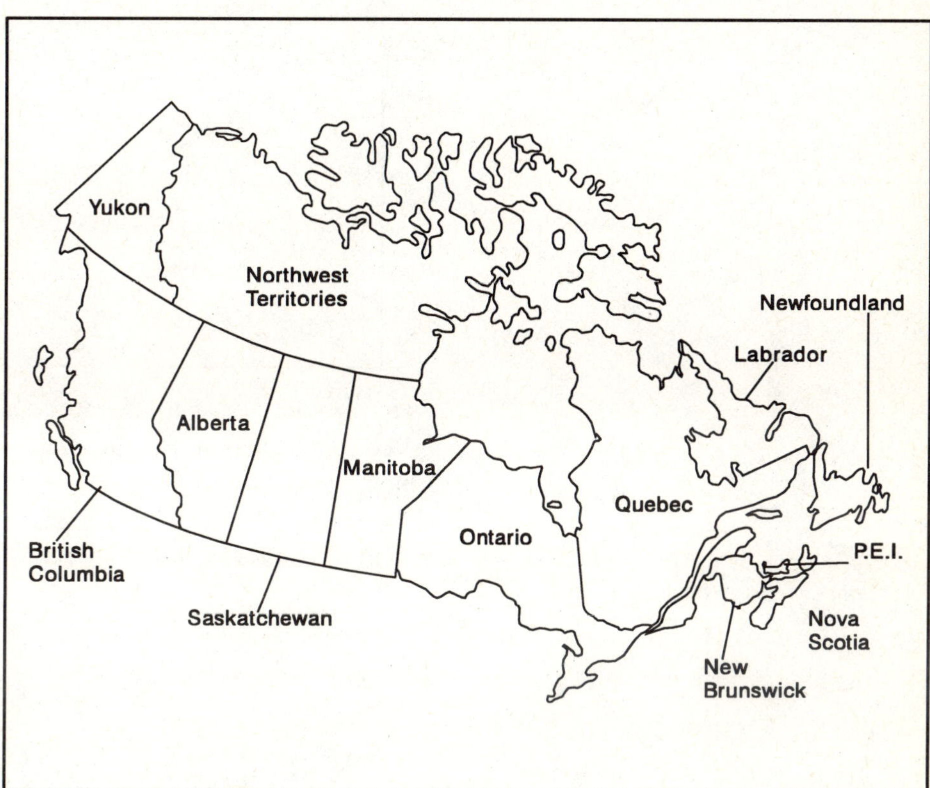

Select Medium Sales Areas   1.   Move your mouse to **Alberta** and click **left** to select it. Your screen should look like this:

2. Now move your mouse to **Manitoba** and select it by pressing **Shift** and your **left** mouse button. Handles now appear around both Alberta and Manitoba.

3. Use the Shift + Mouse method to select **Quebec** and then compare your screen to the following illustration:

Fill Medium Sales Areas   Now you can fill these areas with the Check pattern.

1. Click on the **Color Tool.** The **Fill** box is currently highlighted.
2. Click on the box labeled **None.**
3. Click on the box labeled **Pattern** (below the Line/Text box).

4. Click on a **White** box.

Your Color Pop-up appears as illustrated:

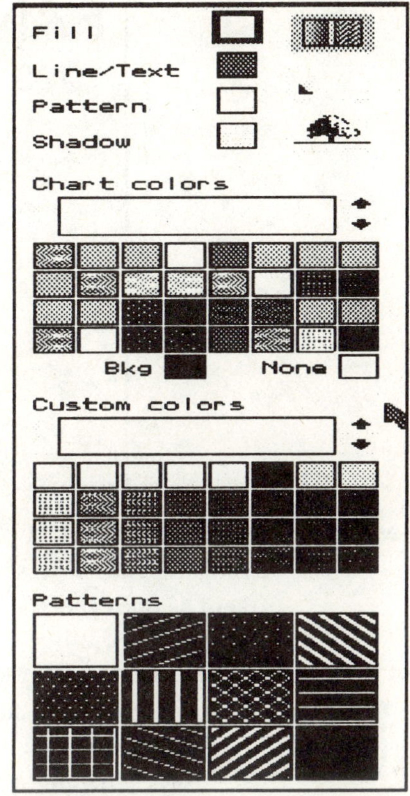

5. Move your mouse down to the patterns displayed at the bottom of the Color Pop-up.

6. Click on the box that looks like this:

7. Click **right** twice to exit the Color Pop-up and remove the handles.

The map areas you have selected are now filled with the Check pattern as illustrated:

Select Low Sales Areas

Now you can select and fill the Low Sales areas with the Diagonal pattern. Your first step is to select and group the northern islands so that you can fill them as one object.

Group Northern Islands

1. Position your mouse above and to the left of the northern islands.
2. Click your **left** button and drag your mouse down and to the right until you have selected all the islands.
3. Press **Shift** and your **left** mouse button to select the mainland section of the Northwest Territories.

Compare your screen to the following illustration:

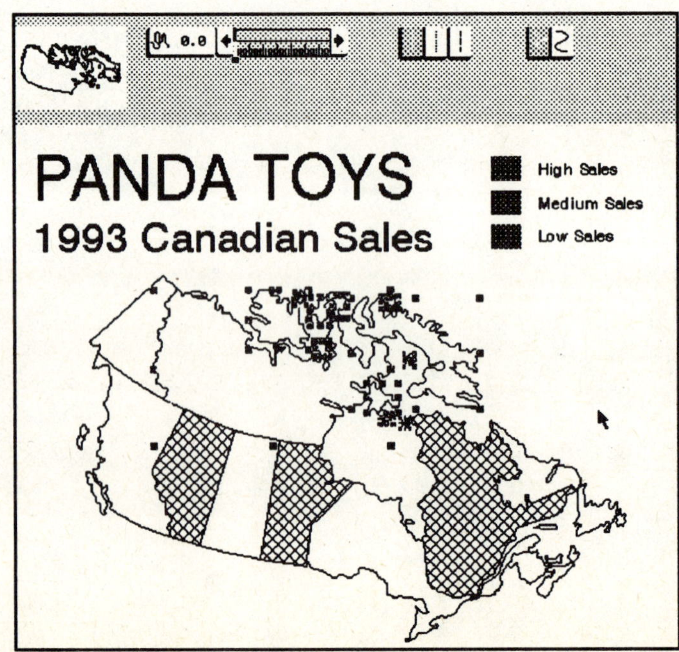

4. Click on the **Group Tool.**

Now you can go on to select the other Low Sales areas as follows:

1. Move your mouse to the **Yukon** (to the left of the Northwest Territories).
2. Press **Shift** and your **left** mouse button to select the Yukon. Handles now appear around both the Northwest Territories and the Yukon.
3. Use the Shift + Mouse method to also select **Saskatchewan, Labrador, Newfoundland, New Brunswick,** and **Prince Edward Island.**

Compare your screen to the following illustration:

Fill Low Sales Areas

Now you can fill these areas with the Diagonal pattern.

1. Click on the **Color Tool**. The **Fill** box is currently highlighted.
2. Click on the box labeled **None.**
3. Click on the box labeled **Pattern** (below the Line/Text box).
4. Click on a **White** box.
5. Move your mouse down to the patterns displayed at the bottom of the Color Pop-up.
6. Click on the box that looks like this:
7. Click **right** twice to exit the Color Pop-up and remove the handles.

The map areas you have selected are now filled with the Diagonal pattern as illustrated:

Map Areas Filled

Before you go on to fill the boxes in the Legend with the appropriate patterns,
take a look at what your Drawing will look like when it is printed.

1. Press **F6** for **File** and **E** for **Exit to Main Menu.**
2. Press **5** for **Output.**
3. Press **Enter** to accept **Printer 1.**
4. Press **F2** to preview your Chart.

Your screen should appear as illustrated:

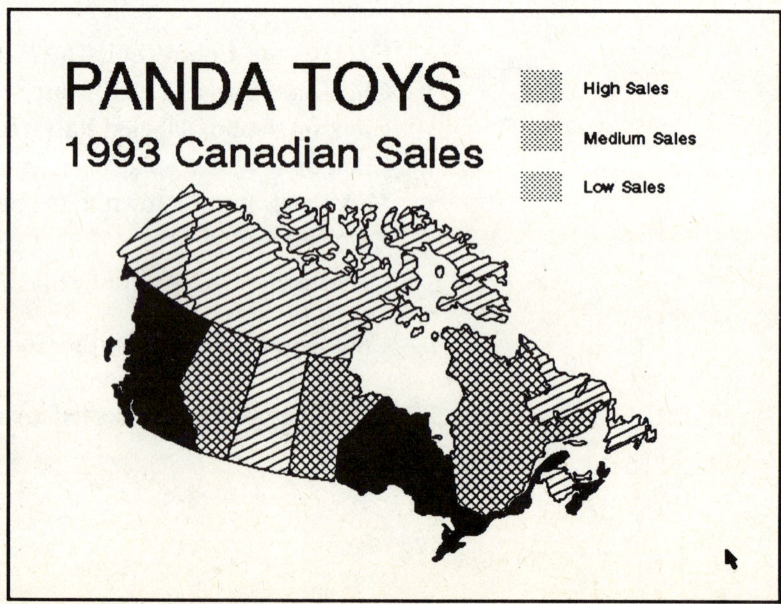

Color Boxes   Now return to the Draw Screen to fill the Legend boxes.

1.   Press **ESC** twice to exit from the Printer Menu.
2.   At the Main Menu, press **3** for **Draw.**

Fill Legend Boxes   You first need to ungroup the Legend.

1.   Click on the Legend to select it.
2.   Click on the **Ungroup Tool** and click **right.**

High Sales Box   1.   Click on the **High Sales** box.
2.   Click on the **Color Tool.**
3.   Select **White** for **Fill Color.**
4.   Click on the **Line/Text** box.
5.   Click on **None.**
6.   Click **right** twice to exit the Color Pop-up and remove the handles from the top box.

Medium Sales Box   1.   Click on the **Medium Sales** box.
2.   Click on the **Color Tool.** The **Fill** box is highlighted.
3.   Click on **Background** for the Fill Color.
4.   Click on the **Line/Text** box and select **Bright Yellow** as the Line/Text color.
5.   Click on the **Pattern** box and select **White** as the pattern color.
6.   Move to the patterns at the bottom of the Color Pop-up and click on the box that looks like this:
7.   Click **right** twice to exit the Color Pop-up and remove the handles.

Low Sales Box   1.   Click on the **Low Sales** box.
2.   Click on the **Color Tool.** The **Fill** box is highlighted.
3.   Click on **Background** for the Fill Color.
4.   Click on the **Line/Text** box and select **Bright Yellow** as the Line/Text color.
5.   Click on the **Pattern** box and select **White** as the pattern color.
6.   Move to the patterns at the bottom of the Color Pop-up and click on the box that looks like this:
7.   Click **right** twice to exit the Color Pop-up and remove the handles.

Compare your screen to the following illustration:

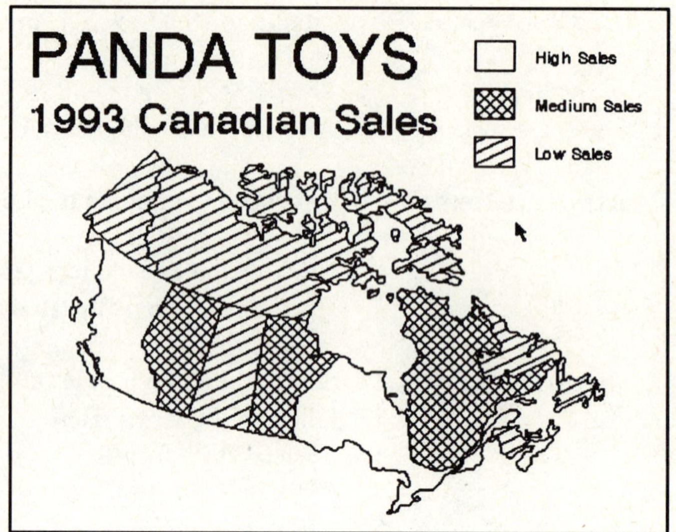

Legend Boxes Filled

Get Symbol   Your last task is to get the Panda Bear Symbol and then size, position, and "flip" it horizontally.

1. Click on the ▲ symbol at the bottom of the Tool Box to access the first tool level.
2. Click your **left** mouse button on the **Symbol Tool.**
3. Click again on **Get.**
4. At the Symbol Files Screen, press **F8** to sort the files alphabetically.
5. Click on **ANIPLANT**.
6. Click on the picture of the **Panda Bear**.
7. Click on **F10** twice to return to your Draw Screen.

Position
1. Click your **left** button on any area of your panda *except* one of the orange handles.
2. Move your mouse to the right of your screen and position your bear under the Legend.

Size
1. Click on one of the corner handles.
2. Press **Shift** and reduce the size of your panda.

Reposition and resize your panda as required so that it appears as illustrated:

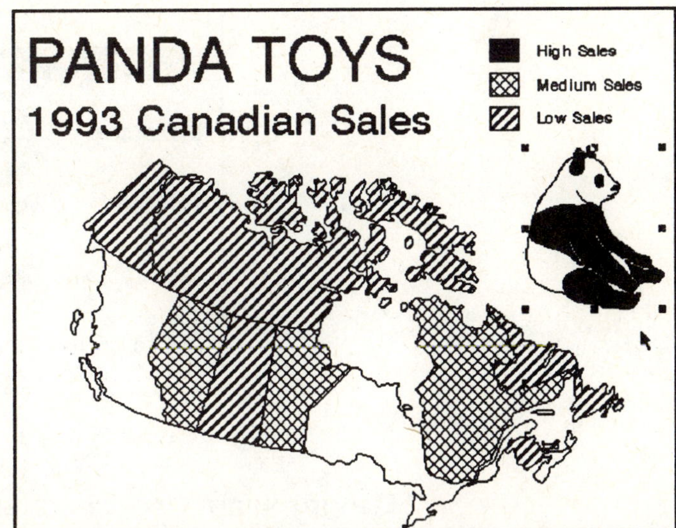

Flip   You want the bear to face the other way. Flip him horizontally as follows:

1. Click on the **Flip Tool** (in the first Tool Box level).
2. Click on the **Horizontal Tool.**
3. Click **right** to remove the handles.

Panda Bear Complete

Save and Print Your Chart

You will save Geographical Chart 1 on your data disk and then access the
Output command to print your chart.

Save   1.   Press **F6** for **File.**
       2.   Press **2** for **Save Chart.**

The Save Chart Menu appears. Your cursor is currently positioned next to
Filename. The default Directory (usually C:\HG3\DATA) is displayed. You
will save your file on a data disk in Drive A or B.

1. Press your ↑ arrow to position your cursor next to **Directory.**
2. Type *a:* or *b:* and then press **Delete** to erase the old Directory.
3. Press **Enter.**
4. At **Filename,** type *Geochrt1* and press **Enter.**
5. At **Description,** type *Geographical Chart #1: Lesson 8.*

Your Save Chart Screen should look like this:

```
┌─────────────────────────────────────────────────┐
│█████████████████████ Save Chart ████████████████│
│                                                   │
│  Directory:      a:\                               │
│                                                   │
│  Filename:       Geochrt1                          │
│                                                   │
│  Description:    Geographical Chart #1: Lesson 8   │
│                                                   │
│  Add to current presentation:     No              │
│                                                   │
└─────────────────────────────────────────────────┘
```

6. Press **F10** to save and return to the Draw Screen.

Geographical Chart 1 Saved

Print

1. Press **F6** for **File** and **E** for **Exit to Main Menu.**
2. Press **5** for **Output.**
3. Press **Enter** to accept **Printer 1.**
4. Press **F2** to view how your document will appear in printed form.
5. If you are satisfied with the look of your Chart, press **F10** twice to accept the Default Settings.

The Output to Printer Screen appears. Your Geographical Chart has now been sent to the printer. Wait until the Output to Printer Screen disappears and you are back at the Main Menu.

Geographical Chart 1 Printed

You now have two options:

- Exit Harvard Graphics if you are finished with your learning session.
- Clear the current chart.

Exit Harvard Graphics

1. At the Main Menu, press **E** to exit Harvard Graphics.

Clear the Current Chart

1. Press **1** for **Create Chart.**
2. Press **8** for **Clear Chart.**

ACTIVITY 3   GEOGRAPHICAL CHART 2

Four major steps are required to produce Geographical Chart 2:

Step One:	Create and Enhance Your Bar Chart
Step Two:	Save Your Bar Chart as a Symbol
Step Three:	Combine Your Bar Chart with a Map Symbol
Step Four:	Save and Print Your Chart

Follow the step-by-step instructions to create Geographical Chart 2 (see page 262). Remember to place a check mark in the box next to each function you complete.

Create and Enhance Your Bar Chart

Create Chart   Your first step is to create the Bar Chart you will superimpose on your Map Symbol.

1.   At the Main Menu, press **1** for **Create Chart.**
2.   Press **3** for **XY Chart.**
3.   Press **1** for **Bar.**

The X Data Type Pop-up appears. Press **F10** to accept **Name** and access your Chart Edit Screen. On your Chart Edit Screen, you will enter *Western, Central,* and *Eastern* as your X-Axis labels.

Enter Title/Subtitle   First, enter your Title and Subtitle.

1.   Type the Title of your Bar Chart in all caps: *PANDA TOYS.* Press **Enter.**
2.   Now type the Subtitle of your Bar Chart in upper/lower case: *1993 Canadian Sales by Region.* Press **Enter** twice.

Title/Subtitle Complete ☐

Enter X Data   Your cursor should be positioned under X-Axis Name.

1.   Type *Western* and press **Enter.**
2.   Type *Central* and press **Enter.**
3.   Type *Eastern.*

Enter Series Data   1.   Press your ↑ arrow and **Tab** to position your cursor in the **Series 1** column opposite *Western.*
2.   Type *10* and press **Enter.**
3.   Type *15* and press **Enter.**
4.   Type *3.*

X-Axis and Series Data Complete ☐

Your Chart Edit Screen should look like this:

PANDA TOYS
$10M
Western
$15M
Central
$3M
Eastern
1993 Canadian Sales by Region

```
                                   XY Chart                                  ◆▴▾
    F1-Help           F2-Show chart                      F4-Draw         F5-Mark
    F6-Main Menu      F7-Spell/Text    F8-Options        F9-XY data      F10-Continue

    Title:      PANDA TOYS
    Subtitle:   1993 Canadian Sales by Region
    Footnote:

    _________________________________ 1 ________ 2 ________ 3 ________ 4 ______
    Data |      X Axis        |
    Pt   |       Name         | Series 1   | Series 2   | Series 3   | Series 4
    _____|____________________|____________|____________|____________|__________
    1      Western              10
    2      Central              15
    3      Eastern              3
    4
    5
    6
    7
    8
    9
    10
    11
    12
```

Required Enhancements

Before you can save your Bar Chart as a Symbol and retrieve it into your Draw Screen to place it over the map of Canada, you need to make the following enhancements:

> → **Text Attributes (2):** Change the Title/Subtitle size
> → **Series (6):** Choose No for Data Labels and Data Table
> → **Legend:** Choose No for Show Legend
> → **Axis Frame (8):** Change the Axis Frame to None
> → **Axis Options (9):** Choose None for Y1 Axis Grid Line Style
> → **Format (A):** Choose No for Show Y1 Axis Labels

You make all the enhancements listed above in the F8 Options Menu. You make these enhancements because you want your Bar Chart to consist only of the Title/Subtitle, the three bars, and the three X-axis labels. You want to delete all other elements such as the Legend, Y-axis labels, and chart grid.

Title/Subtitle Size

1. Press **F8** for **Options.**
2. Press **2** for **Text Attributes** and **1** for **Titles/Footnotes.**
3. Type *11* next to **Title** and press **Enter.**
4. Type *8*.
5. Press **F10** to return to your Chart Edit Screen.

Text Attributes Complete   ☐

Data Labels and Data Table

You don't want to show the data labels or the data table.

1. Press **F8** for **Options** and **6** for Series.
2. Press your ↓ arrow to position your cursor opposite **Data Labels.**
3. Press **N** for **No.**
4. Press your ↓ arrow to position your cursor opposite **Data Table.**
5. Press **N** for **No.**
6. Press **F10** to return to your Chart Edit Screen.

Data Labels/Table Removed

Legend   Remove your Legend.

1. Press **F8** for **Options** and **7** for **Legend.**
2. Press **N** for **No** next to **Show Legend.**
3. Press **F10** to return to your Chart Edit Screen.

Legend Removed

Axis Frame   Delete your Axis Frame.

1. Press **F8** for **Options.**
2. Press **8** for **Axis Frame.**
3. Press **F3** for **Choices.**
4. Cursor to **None** and press **Enter.**
5. Press **F10** to return to your Chart Edit Screen.

Axis Frame Deleted

Axis Options   Change the Grid Line Style to None.

1. Press **F8** for **Options.**
2. Press **9** for **Axis Options.**
3. Press **Tab** to position your cursor in the **Y1 Axis** column.
4. Press your ↓ arrow until your cursor is opposite **Grid Line Style.**
5. Press **F3** for **Choices.**
6. Cursor to **None** and press **Enter.**
7. Press **F10** to return to your Chart Edit Screen.

Axis Grid Removed

Format   Delete your Y Axis.

1. Press **F8** for **Options.**
2. Press **A** for **Format.**
3. Press **Tab** to position your cursor in the **Y1 Axis** column.
4. Press **N** for **No.**
5. Press **F10** to return to your Chart Edit Screen.

Y Axis Deleted

Display Chart ▶   Press **F2** to display your Chart. Your screen should look like this:

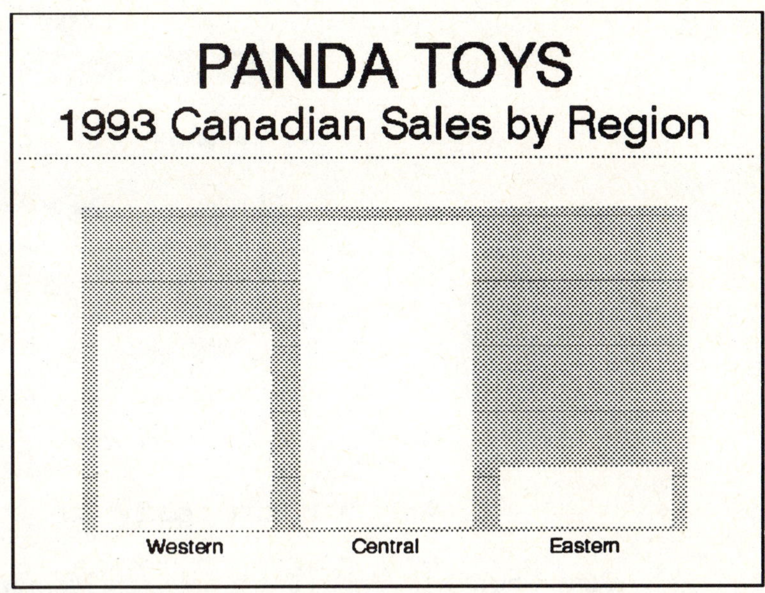

Press **Enter** to return to your Chart Edit Screen.

Save Bar Chart as Symbol

You are now ready to save your Bar Chart as a symbol and then access Draw and get your map of Canada. You save a chart as a symbol when you want to be able to separate its various elements so that you can move or size them individually.

Save as Symbol
1.   Press **F6** for **Main Menu.**
2.   Press **4** for **File** and **6** for **Save as Symbol.**

The Save as Symbol Pop-up appears. Notice how it looks very similar to the Save Menu. Your cursor is currently positioned next to **Filename.**

1.   If necessary, change your Directory to your Drive A or B and press **Enter.**
2.   At **Filename,** type *Geosym* and press **Enter.**
3.   At **Description,** type *Bar Symbol for Geo Chart #2: Lesson 8.*

Your Save Symbol File Menu looks like this:

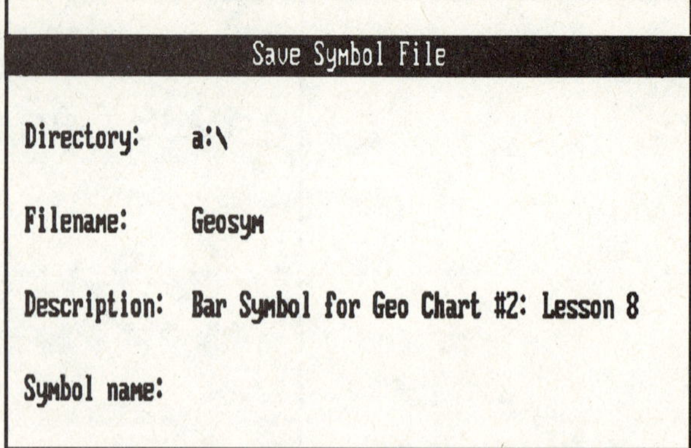

4. Press **F10** to save and return to the Bar Chart Edit Screen.

Bar Chart Saved as Symbol

Clear Chart

1. Press **F6** to return to the **Main Menu.**
2. Press **1** for **Create Chart.**
3. Press **8** for **Clear Chart.**

    You will get the following message: "Your latest changes have not been saved."

4. Press **F10** to confirm; you don't need to save your chart because you have already saved it as a symbol.

Combine Bar Chart with Map Symbol

Access Draw

First, access the Draw Screen from the Main Menu.

1. Press **3** for **Draw.**

The following functions require the use of the mouse. Remember to click the **left** button to select functions and the **right** button to finish functions. If you click the right button twice, you may return to the Main Menu. If this happens, just press or click on **3** for **Draw** to return to your Draw Screen.

Here's what you will do in the Draw Screen:

> → Retrieve the Canada Map Symbol
> → Size and Position the Map Symbol
> → Retrieve your Bar Chart Symbol
> → Ungroup your Bar Chart Symbol
> → Size and move the various Bar Chart elements
> → Add the Bar Labels
> → Get the Panda Bear Symbol

Retrieve Map Symbol

1. Click your **left** mouse button on the **Symbol Tool.**
2. Click again on **Get.**
3. At the Symbol Files Screen, click on **MAPS2.**
4. Click on the map of **Canada** and then click on **F10** twice.

Notice how your map appears in the center of your Draw Screen. Your first step is to increase your map size.

Size

1. Click and hold the bottom left corner handle and press the **Shift** key to drag your map down to the bottom left corner of your screen.

> **NOTE:**   Remember that you use the **Shift** key when you want to main-
> tain the correct proportions of your symbol.

2. Click on the top right corner handle and press **Shift** to further increase the map size.
3. Adjust your sizing and then position your map as indicated in the follow-ing illustration.

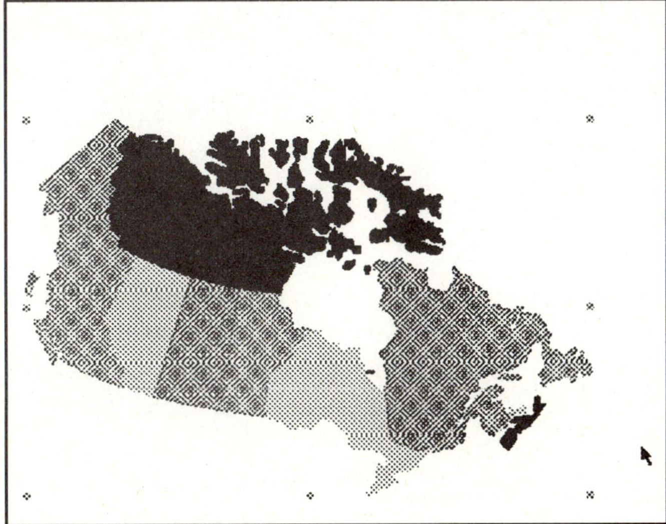

Map Sized and Positioned

Change Map Fill   You need to change the Fill and Line/Text Color of your map so that it will print attractively in black and white.

Color Tool   Your map should still be selected.

1. Click on the **Color Tool.** The **Fill** box is highlighted.
2. Click on one of the **Medium Gray** boxes in the top row of the Custom Color selections. Your entire map now appears gray.
3. Click on the **Line/Text** box.
4. Click on a **White** box (the lines will now print black).
5. Press **F10** to return to the Draw Screen.

Your map now appears as illustrated:

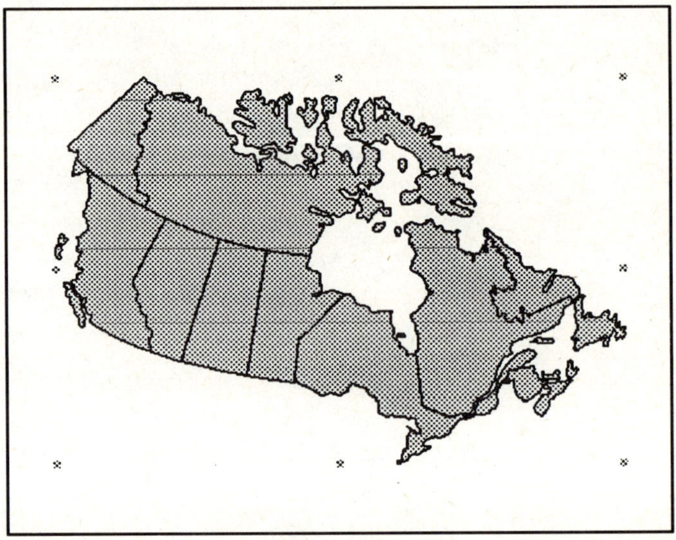

You can now retrieve your Bar Chart Symbol.

Retrieve Bar Chart Symbol   1. Click on the **Symbol Tool.**
2. Click again on **Get.**

The Symbol Directory appears. You will change the directory to your A or B drive and get your Bar Chart Symbol.

1. Place your cursor opposite **Directory** and type *a:* or *b:* to access your data drive.
2. Press **Delete** to erase the extra letters.
3. Cursor to **Geosym** and press **Enter.**
4. Click on the **Geosym** symbol.
5. Click on **F10** twice to return to your Draw Screen.

Notice that orange handles appear around your Bar Chart Symbol to indicate it is selected.

First, you will ungroup your Bar Chart into two sections: Title/Subtitle and Chart Region. You will then ungroup the Title/Subtitle so that you can position your Subtitle at the *bottom* of your Chart and then ungroup your Chart Region so that you can position your bars and X-axis labels on your map.

For the rest of this lesson, you will require constant access to *both* tool levels. To eliminate clicking on the ▼ and ▲ symbols to access the two levels, you can click on the white horizontal bar above the symbols. You will then see both tool levels at once. If you wish to return to a single tool level, press on either the ▼ or ▲ symbol.

Ungroup Title/Subtitle   1.   Click on the **Ungroup Tool.**

Notice how orange handles now appear around three areas of your Bar Chart Symbol: the Title/Subtitle, the Chart Region, and the Legend.

2.   Click **right** to remove all the handles.

You now need to select just the Title/Subtitle and ungroup it.

Select Title/Subtitle   1.   Click on the Title/Subtitle.
2.   Click again on the **Ungroup Tool.**
3.   Click **right** to remove all the handles.

Reposition Subtitle   1.   Click on the Subtitle.
2.   Move the Subtitle to the bottom of your screen. Don't worry that the Subtitle currently obscures the bottom of the Bar Chart.
3.   Click **right** to remove the handles.

Subtitle Positioned   ☐

Delete Line   You need to delete the line under the Title.

1.   Click on the line.
2.   Click on the **Delete Tool.**

Ungroup Chart Region   1.   Click on the Chart Region.

Trouble Note ▶   If you select the Map Symbol by mistake, just click **right**, then position your mouse on a bar and click **left** again.

2.   Move the Chart Region up about .5" as illustrated:

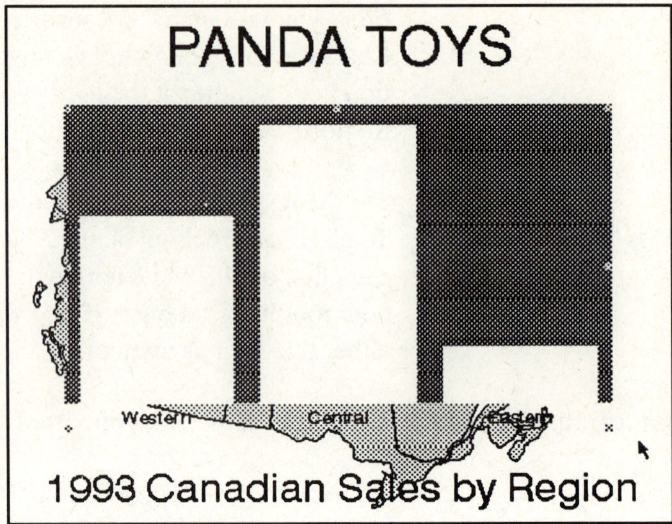

3. Click on the **Ungroup Tool.**
4. Click **right** to remove all the handles.

Bar Chart Moved and Ungrouped

Delete Chart Background

Part of your map is obscured by the Bar Chart background. Delete this background as follows:

1. Position your mouse pointer on the shaded chart background.
2. Click **left** to select the background.
3. Click on the **Delete Tool.**

Chart Background Deleted

Resize Bars

Your bars are too wide. Your next step is to reduce the width of each of the three bars. You will then use your mouse and the Align Tool to reposition the bars and X-Axis titles.

1. Click on the **Western** bar.
2. Click on the middle left handle and drag your box right until your bar is approximately half its original width as illustrated:

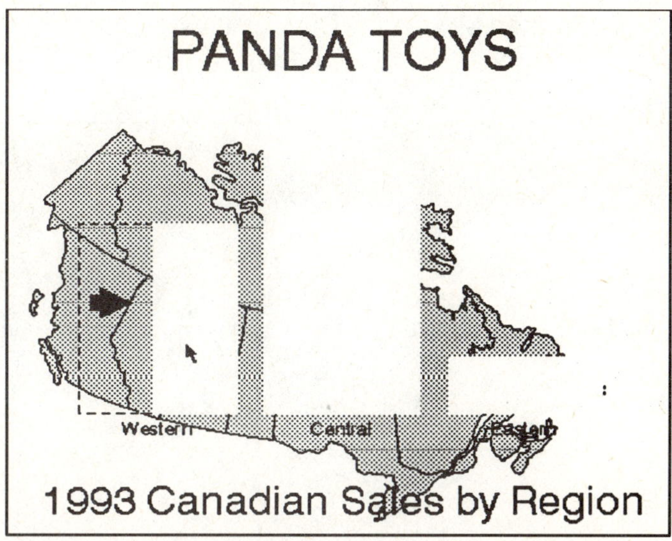

3. Click **right** to remove the handles.
4. Now go on to reduce the width of the Central and Eastern bars. Take your time—you want each of the three bars to be the same width.
5. Click **right** to remove the handles from the last bar you sized.

Bar Widths Reduced ☐

Position X-Axis Labels

To reposition your X-Axis labels, you need to select all three of them at once:

1. Click on the **Western** label.
2. Move your mouse to the **Central** label and press **Shift** and your **left** mouse button to select it. Handles now appear around both labels.
3. Use the Shift + Mouse method to also select the **Eastern** label.
4. Now press and hold your **left** mouse button and move all three labels directly down so that they appear just above the Subtitle as illustrated:

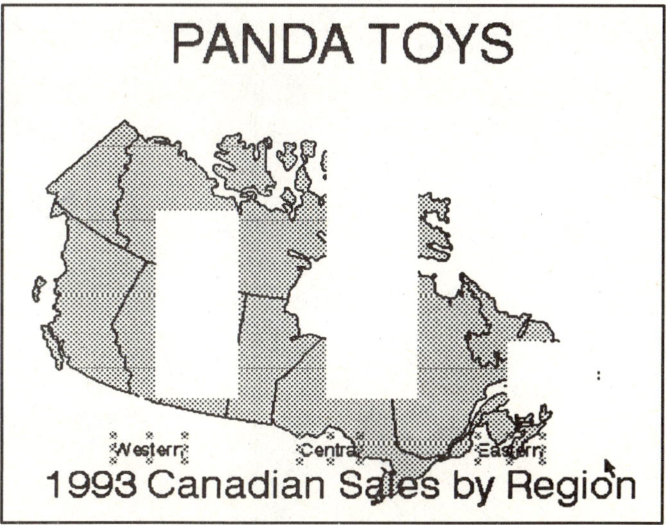

5. Click **right** to remove the handles from the labels.

X-Axis Labels Positioned ☐

Reposition Map   1. Click on the map to select it.
                      2. Move the map up approximately 1" as illustrated:

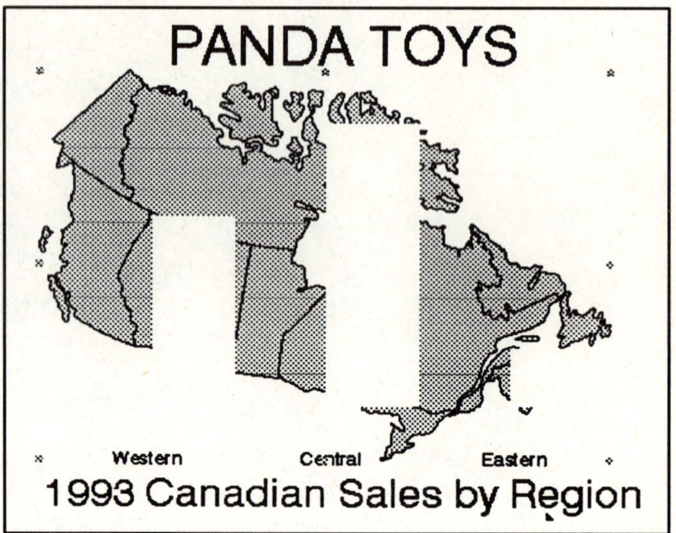

3. Click **right** to remove the handles.

Map Positioned

Position Bars   1. Click on each of the bars in turn to center them above the correct X-axis label. Don't worry about aligning the bottom of each bar—you will use the Align Tool to set a common horizontal position.

Bars Positioned

Align Bars   1. Use the Shift + Mouse method to select all three bars.

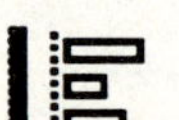

2. Click on the **Align Tool** (first Tool Box level).
3. Click on the **Bottom** box. Your Draw Screen should now look like this:

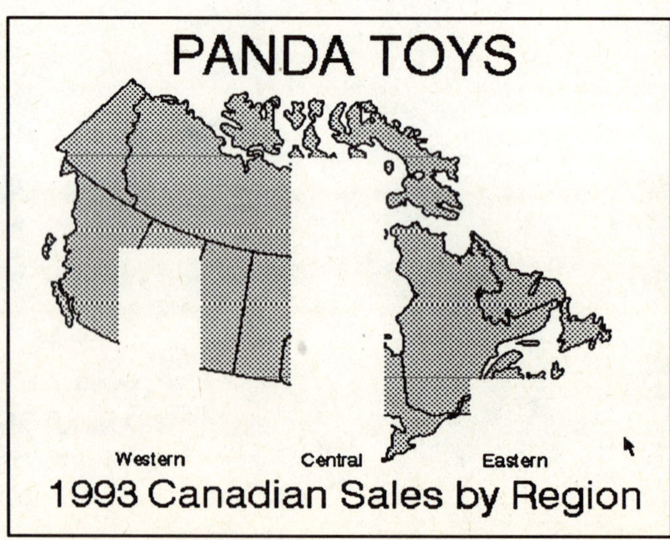

4. Click **right** to remove the handles.

Bars Aligned ☐

Enter Bar Labels

You are almost finished working with your Bar Chart. The last step is to add labels to identify each bar as representing a specific monetary amount such as $3 million, $10 million, etc.

Following are the instructions to enter, color, and position the label for the Western bar. Refer back to these instructions to create the labels for the Central and Eastern bars.

1. Click on the **Text Tool.**
2. Move your mouse up to the Text Attributes Pop-up.
3. Click on the **Text Size Ruler**, type *5.0,* and press **Enter.**
4. Position the **+** in the middle of the Western bar.
5. Click and hold **left** to drag a box about 1" square.
6. At the Text Pop-up type *$10M* and press **F10.**

Change Label Color

You need to change the color of your text to White so that it prints black on a black-and-white printer.

1. Click on the **Pointer** to select the text block.
2. Click on the **Color Tool.**
3. Click on the **Line/Text** box and then click on a **White** box.
4. Click **right** to return to the Draw Screen.

When you enter the labels for the Central and Eastern bars, the text will also appear white.

Position Bar Labels

1. Click on and position the $10M text block towards the bottom of the Western bar.

Now go on to enter and position the Central $15M and Eastern $3M labels.

Bar Labels Entered and Positioned ☐

Align Labels

Align the labels horizontally as follows:

1. Use the **Shift** + Mouse method to select all three labels.
2. Click on the **Align Tool.**
3. Click on the **Bottom** box. Your Draw Screen should now look like this:

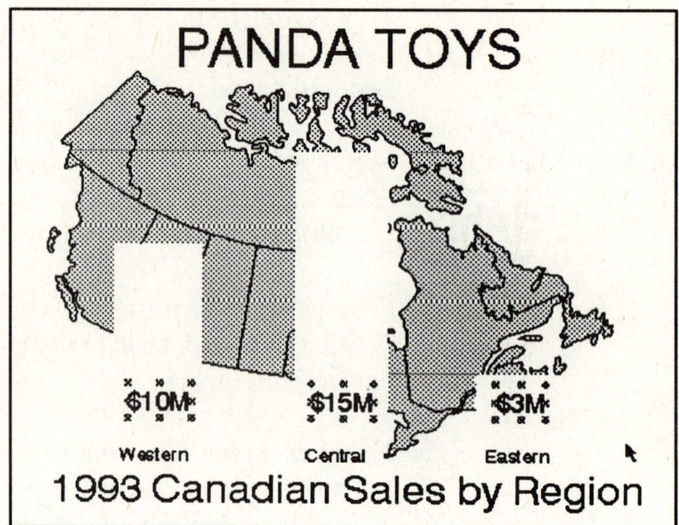

4. Click **right** to remove the handles.

Bar Labels Positioned and Aligned

Add Panda Bear   Now you can get the Panda Bear Symbol and then size, position, and flip it horizontally, as you did for Geographical Chart 1.

Get   1. Click on the **Symbol Tool.**
2. Click again on **Get.**
3. At the Symbol Files Screen, press **F8** to sort the files alphabetically.
4. Click on **ANIPLANT.**
5. Click on the picture of the **Panda Bear.**
6. Click on **F10** twice to return to your Draw Screen.

Position   1. Click your **left** mouse button on any area of your panda *except* one of the orange handles.
2. Position your bear in the top right corner of your screen.

Size   1. Click on one of the corner handles.
2. Press **Shift** and reduce your panda's size. Reposition it if necessary.

Compare your bear's size and position to the following illustration:

Flip

You want the bear to face the other way. Flip it horizontally as follows:

1. Click on the **Flip Tool** (in the first Tool Box level).
2. Click on the **Horizontal Tool.**
3. Click **right** to remove the handles.

Panda Bear Complete

Change Bar Colors

To ensure a sharp print-out, your last task is to change the bar colors to Background and the lines outlining the bars to bright yellow (which prints black).

1. Use the Shift + Mouse method to select all three bars.
2. Click on the **Color Tool.** The **Fill** box is highlighted.
3. Click on the **Background** box.

Note that your bars are now colored black. They will print white on a black-and-white printer.

1. Click on the **Line/Text** box.
2. Click on the box displaying **Bright Yellow.**
3. Click **right** twice to exit the Color Pop-up and remove the handles from the bars.

Compare your screen to the following illustration:

Bar Colors Changed   ☐

Save and Print Your Chart

You will save Geographical Chart 2 on your data disk and then access the
Output command to print your chart.

Save
1. Press **F6** for **File.**
2. Press **2** for **Save Chart.**

The Save Chart Menu appears. Your cursor is currently positioned next to
Filename. Either the default Directory (usually C:\HG3\DATA) or your data
drive is displayed.

1. If necessary, change your Directory to your A or B drive and press **Enter.**
2. At **Filename** type *Geochrt2* and press **Enter.**
3. At **Description** type *Geographical Chart #2: Lesson 8.*
4. Press **F10** to save and return to the Draw Screen.

Geographical Chart 2 Saved   ☐

Print
1. Press **F6** for **File** and **E** for **Exit to Main Menu.**
2. Press **5** for **Output.**
3. Press **Enter** to accept **Printer 1.**

Press **F2** to view how your document will appear in printed form.

> **NOTE:** If you do not like how your chart will appear on your printer, press **ESC** to return to your **Main Menu** and then **3** to access your **Draw Screen.** You can then make any size, positioning, or color fill adjustments necessary.

4. If you are satisfied with the look of your Chart, press **F10** twice to accept the Default Settings.

The Output to Printer Screen appears. Your Geographical Chart has now been sent to the printer. Wait until the Output to Printer Screen disappears and you are back at the Main Menu.

Geographical Chart 2 Printed

You now have two options:

- Exit Harvard Graphics if you are finished with your learning session.
- Clear the current chart.

Exit Harvard Graphics 1. At the Main Menu, press **E** to exit Harvard Graphics.

Clear the Current Chart 1. Press **1** for **Create Chart.**
2. Press **8** for **Clear Chart.**

ACTIVITY 4 CHALLENGE ASSIGNMENT

Read through the following sections for suggestions on content and then adapt the instructions given for your own material. Use the boxes provided to record information about your Geographical Chart.

The Challenge Assignment requires four major steps:

Step One: Select Your Map
Step Two: Determine Your Chart Purpose
Step Three: Plan your Chart Information
Step Four: Create and Format Your Geographical Chart

Select your Map

Harvard Graphics provides you with a large variety of maps to choose from. You could, for example, select the map of Europe and show product sales by country for a company of your choice. To view the maps available, access

your Draw Screen, select the **Symbol Tool,** and take a look at the MAPS1 and
MAPS2 Directories.

Notice that two maps of the United States are available. You use the United
States 1 map when you want your map to appear as a backdrop for a bar chart
as you did for Geographical Chart 2. Choose the United States 2 map if you
want to fill each of the states with colors or patterns that correspond to a Legend as you did in Geographical Chart 1. The sample charts at the beginning of
this lesson show both uses of the United States map.

Write your map selection in the following box.

Map Selection:

Determine Your Chart Purpose

Think of what you wish your reader to learn from looking at your Geographical Chart. For example, the purpose of the chart you prepared for Activity 2
was to show readers that Panda Toys has achieved good sales in provinces
such as British Columbia and Ontario but not in Quebec and Alberta.

Readers could then draw several conclusions, depending on their point of
view. For example, sales personnel may decide to target the provinces with
low sales more vigorously, while Panda Toys retail operators may think of
relocating to a province with high sales.

The purpose of a Geographical Chart showing the number of national parks in
each state would be to encourage foreign travelers to visit the most scenic
areas of the country.

Complete the following sentence to state the purpose of your Geographical
Chart:

The Purpose of My Geographical Chart Is To:

Plan Your Chart Information

Two activities are involved in planning your chart information.

1. Choose your display method.
2. Calculate your chart data.

Display Method

Here are the two display methods you learned in this lesson.

- Use colors or patterns to code map areas by country, state, region, etc.
- Superimpose a Bar Chart over a blank map.

The method you choose will depend upon the requirements of your data. If you want to show sales by state, for example, you would choose Method One. On the other hand, if you want to use a map as a backdrop for a simple Bar Chart, choose Method Two.

Identify your display method in the following box.

<table><tr><td>

Display Method:

</td></tr></table>

Chart Data You need to determine the two or three *data ranges* your map will represent. If, for example, you decide to display map areas in relation to high, medium, and low sales, you need to divide your map areas accordingly. To speed up the planning process, you can print out the map you have chosen and then use colored pens to shade each of the map areas with the color or pattern that corresponds to your data legend.

For both a Bar Chart/Map combination and a Shaded Map, you need to determine the following information:

Bar Chart/Map Combination:
- Bar Series Titles
- Bar Values

Shaded Map:
- Legend Label Titles
- Legend Data Ranges

Here is the chart information for a Bar Chart/Map combination that shows worldwide sales according to three regions: Asia/Pacific, Europe/Africa, and the Americas.

Series Titles	Asia/Pacific	Europe/Africa	Americas
Bar Values	$10M	$50M	$75M

To show the above information on a shaded map, you would specify three label titles: high sales, medium sales, and low sales and the data ranges for each label. For example, you could define high sales as over $10M, medium sales as $5-9M and low sales as under $5M.

Fill in the appropriate spaces in the box below with your chart data.

Legend Series Titles:
Bar Values:

Legend Label Titles:
Label Data Ranges:

Create and Format Your Chart

Refer to the following selection of commands and functions to help you create your Geographical Chart.

Experiment with the size and position of your map, the colors or patterns you choose to fill the map areas, and any additions such as a Bar Chart until you are satisfied that your Geographical Chart communicates your data clearly and with style.

Access the Draw Screen   At the Main Menu, press **3** for **Draw.**

Enter Text
1. Click on the **Text Tool.**
2. Position the **+** at the top left corner of where you want your text to appear.
3. Click **left** and draw a box for your text.
4. At the Text Pop-up, type your text and press **F10.**

Change Fonts/Attributes
1. Move your mouse up to the Text Attributes Pop-up at the top of your screen.
2. Click on the attribute you wish to change; for example, font, size, alignment, etc.

> **NOTE:**   The Text Attributes Pop-up consists of 3 "pages." To access the other two pages, click on the ▼ symbol at the top right of your screen.

Size Text and Symbols
1. Click on the **Pointer** to select your text or symbol.
2. Click and hold your **left** mouse button on one of the corner handles.
3. Press **Shift** and drag your mouse to the size required.

> **NOTE:** Remember that the use of **Shift** when sizing objects is particu-
> larly important when you are working with maps.

Position Text and Symbols
1. Position your mouse anywhere on the text/symbol block *except* on one of
   the orange handles.
2. Click and hold the **left** button to move the block.

Get Symbol
1. Click on the **Symbol Tool** and then click again on **Get.**
2. At the Symbol Directory, press **F8** to sort the files alphabetically, click on
   the appropriate Directory, click on the Symbol you want, and then click
   on **F10** twice to return to your Draw Screen.

Color Fill
1. Click on the area you want to fill.
2. Click on the **Color Tool** and then on the **Fill** box, if it is not already selected. Click on the color you wish to use.

> **NOTE:** Light colors print dark and dark colors print light on a
> black-and-white printer.

Pattern Fill
1. Click on the area you want to fill.
2. Click on the **Color Tool** and then on the **Fill** box, if it is not already selected. Click on **None**.
3. Click on the box labelled **Pattern** (below the **Line/Text** box).
4. Click on a **White** box.
5. Move your mouse down to the patterns displayed at the bottom of the
   Color Pop-up.
6. Click on the pattern you require.
7. Click **right** to exit the Color Pop-up.

Select Several Objects
Method One:
1. Position your mouse pointer on a point above and to the left of the areas
   you wish to select.
2. Click and hold **left** to drag a box around the areas.

Method Two:
1. Click on the first object you wish to select.
2. Move your mouse to the second object and press **Shift** and your **left**
   mouse button. Continue selecting objects by using the Shift + Mouse
   method.

Group/Ungroup   To Group, select two or more objects you wish to group and then click on the **Group Tool.**

To Ungroup, select the object you wish to ungroup and then click on the **Ungroup Tool.**

Flip Tool   1.   Select the object to flip and click on the **Flip Tool.**
2.   Click on either the **Vertical** or **Horizontal** box.

Duplicate Tool   1.   Click on the object you wish to duplicate.
2.   Click on the **Duplicate Tool.**
3.   Position the duplicated object as required.

Align Tool   1.   Select the two or more objects you wish to align.
2.   Click on the **Align Tool** and choose the alignment required (bottom, top, center, etc.)

Save   Press **F6** for **File** and then **2** for **Save Chart.** Change to the directory in which you wish to save your file (usually Drive A or B) and then type a filename for your Geographical Chart.

Fast Save: Press **Ctrl + S.**

Print   At the Main Menu, choose **5** for **Output**, press **Enter** to accept **Printer 1.** Press **F2** to display your Chart *before* sending it to the printer. If you don't like how your Chart will appear, press **ESC** and then **3** to return to your Draw Screen. Once you are satisfied with your Chart, access the Printer Menu and press **F10** to send your Chart to the printer.

Clear Chart   If you wish to start a new Chart and have saved your current Chart, first press **F6** and **E** for **Exit.** Now choose **1** for **Create Chart** and then **8** for **Clear Chart.** If you haven't saved your current Chart, a message will appear. You can then press **ESC** to save your Chart before clearing it.

Exit Harvard Graphics   Press **F6** and **E** for **Exit to Main Menu** and then **E** again to exit the program.

ACTIVITY 5   LESSON EIGHT REVIEW

Test your understanding of the functions and concepts you learned in Lesson Eight by completing the following Review Questions.

1. What are two methods of using maps as charts?
2. Describe how to fill an area with color.
3. List three functions accessed from the Text Attributes Pop-up in Draw.
4. Describe how to group a variety of objects or map areas so that you can fill them with one color.

5. What does the Align Tool do?
6. Describe how to duplicate an object.
7. Describe how to retrieve a chart you have saved as a symbol to the Draw Screen.
8. List three Bar Chart elements to delete in the Bar Chart Edit Screen before adding a Bar Chart to a map.
9. After previewing a Chart from the Print Menu, how do you return to your Draw Screen to make changes?
10. How do you change the line color of an object?

SUPPLEMENTARY EXERCISES

Exercise 1 Create a Geographical Chart of Western Europe that shades the countries according to high, medium, and low sales of a fast-food franchise. You determine the name of the franchise and the fill colors to use.

Exercise 2 Create a three-series Bar Chart showing the American sales of the same franchise according to region: West, Central, and East. Place the Bar Chart over a blank map of the United States and use the Ungroup feature to resize and position the bars and X Axis.

<table>
<tr><td>

LESSON NINE

</td><td>

DIAGRAM

</td></tr>
</table>

FEATURES
- Drawing Lines and Curves
- Using Grids and Grid Snap
- Drawing Boxes and Triangles
- Adding Text
- Using Arrows
- Duplicating Objects

INTRODUCTION

In Lesson Nine, you will use the Harvard Graphics Draw features to create two labeled Diagrams. Here are the lesson activities:

ACTIVITY 1:   Determine the content of your Diagrams.

ACTIVITY 2:   Follow the instructions provided to create the Floor Plan on page 287.

ACTIVITY 3:   Follow the instructions given to create the Process Diagram illustrated on page 303.

ACTIVITY 4:   Create a Diagram based on your own information.

ACTIVITY 5:   Complete the Lesson Review Questions on Drawing and Enhancing Objects.

ACTIVITY 1   DIAGRAM CONTENT

As you learned in the Introduction to Section Three, certain types of information can be communicated best in picture or diagram form. The Organization Chart and the Geographical Chart are bound by certain formatting requirements such as the use of boxes and interconnecting lines or the use of maps. The Diagram form, however, knows no limits beyond the size of your page.

You can create a Diagram to show the parts of a car engine, the steps required to assemble a computer system, or the best route to your house.

A Diagram compresses ideas into picture format. For example, when a new friend asks for directions to your house, your first impulse will probably be to draw a quick diagram of your area—sketching in landmarks such as stores, bridges, and parks, and labeling the street names.

Visualization To make your diagram even clearer, you could add arrows to point out the direction your friend should travel. Such a diagram helps your friend visualize the route. This process of visualization is the goal of an effective Diagram design.

Labeling A workable Diagram should be clearly labeled, easy to understand, and immediately applicable. Here is an example of a Diagram showing the route to the Christmas Tree Farm outside of Cityville, USA:

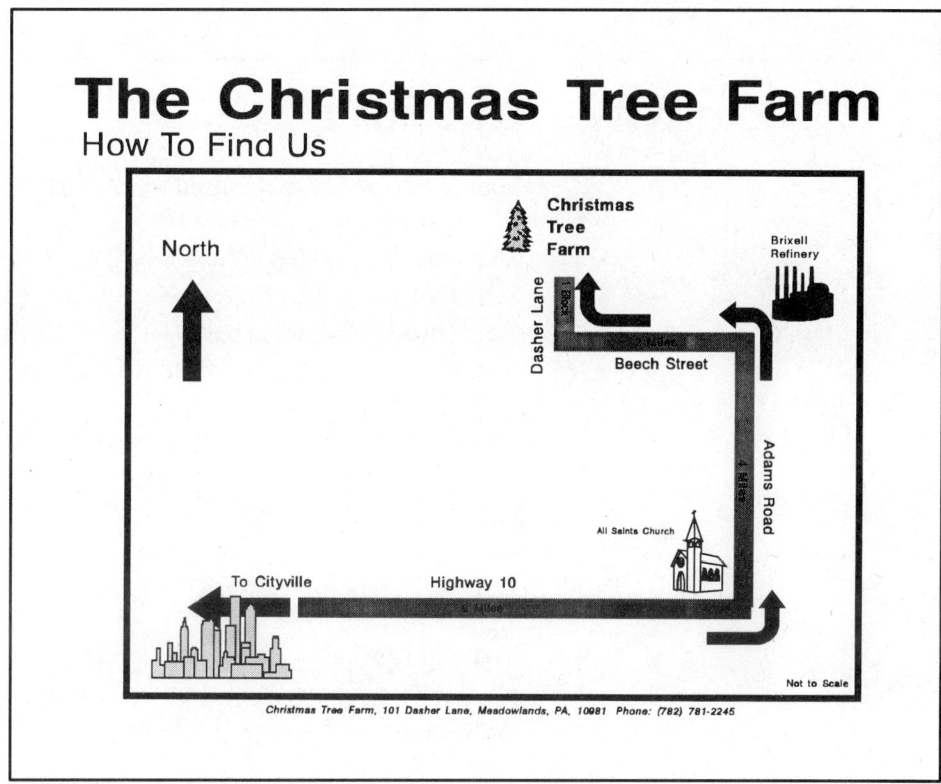

Notice how strong lines are used to display the route along Highway 10 to the Christmas Tree Farm. In addition, symbols are used to show landmarks such as the church and refinery while the use of arrows keeps the traveler on track. A Diagram such as this is meant to provide the user with an easy-to-follow plan—not a scale map. To convert the Diagram to a scale map, you would need to resize all its components to match a specific measurement, such as "1 inch equals 1 mile." This measurement is included at the bottom of the Diagram and referred to as the map *scale*.

A well-constructed Diagram can communicate your message much more quickly than text—particularly when you need your reader to "see" your point immediately.

Summary of Activities 2 and 3 In Activities 2 and 3, you will create two different types of Diagrams for Action Accounting, Ltd.

The Diagram you create in Activity 2 illustrates the floor plan of an office suite just renovated for Action Accounting, Ltd. Dan Stowe, the Personnel Manager for Action Accounting, plans to use this Diagram as part of a presentation for candidates being considered for the position of Vice President, Sales.

For Activity 3, you will create a Process Diagram that shows the six-step hiring process used by Action Accounting to choose the best candidate for the Vice President, Sales position.

ACTIVITY 2   DIAGRAM 1

Four major steps are required to produce Diagram 1.

Step One:	Draw Your Floor Plan Lines
Step Two:	Add Boxes
Step Three:	Add Labels
Step Four:	Save and Print Your Diagram

Follow the step-by-step instructions to reproduce Diagram 1 (see page 287). Remember to place a checkmark in the box next to each function you complete.

Draw Your Floor Plan Lines

You will first access the Draw Screen and then Options to show the grid, apply the Snap feature, and show the Ruler. You will then use the Line Tool to draw the lines of your Floor Plan.

Access Draw   1.   At the Main Menu, press **3** for **Draw.**

Show Grid   Display the grid to help you place your lines precisely where you want them.

1. Press **F8** for **Optionw.**
2. Press **2** for **Grid.**
3. At **Show Grid**, press **Y** for **Yes.**

The default spacing is 1" between all vertical and horizontal points on the grid. For your Diagram, you need to change this spacing to .5".

Grid Spacing   1.   Press your ↓ arrow to position your cursor opposite **Horizontal Spacing.**
2. Type *.5* and press **Enter.** Your cursor is now opposite **Vertical Spacing.**
3. Type *.5* and press **Enter.**

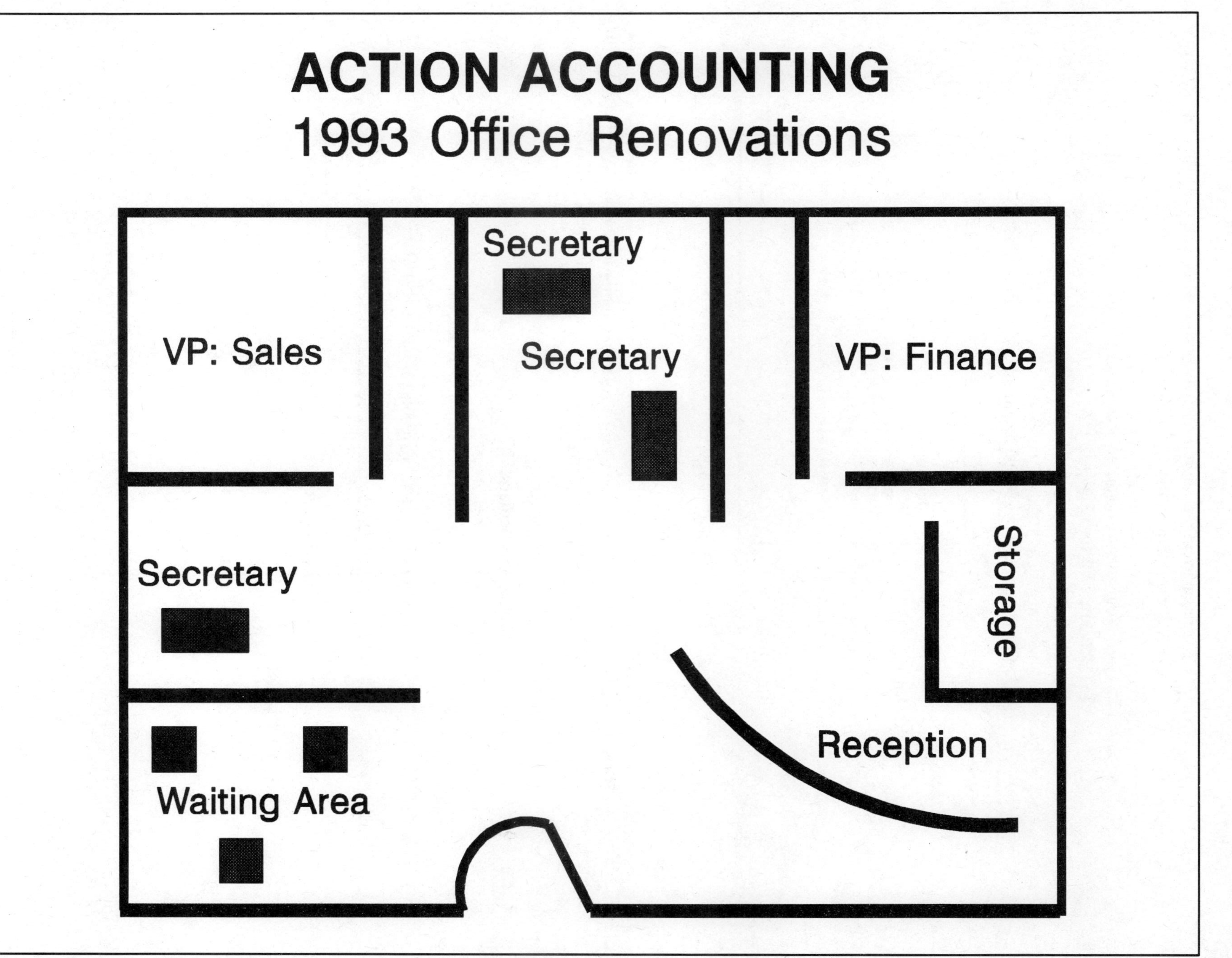

ACTION ACCOUNTING
1993 Office Renovations
VP: Sales
Secretary
Secretary
VP: Finance
Secretary
Storage
Reception
Waiting Area

To draw perfectly straight lines, you will specify Snap To. This feature ensures that every line you draw "snaps" to the nearest grid point.

Snap To

1. Your cursor should be opposite **Snap To.**
2. Press **F3** for **Choices.**
3. Choose **All** and press **Enter.**

Compare your Grid Menu to the following illustration:

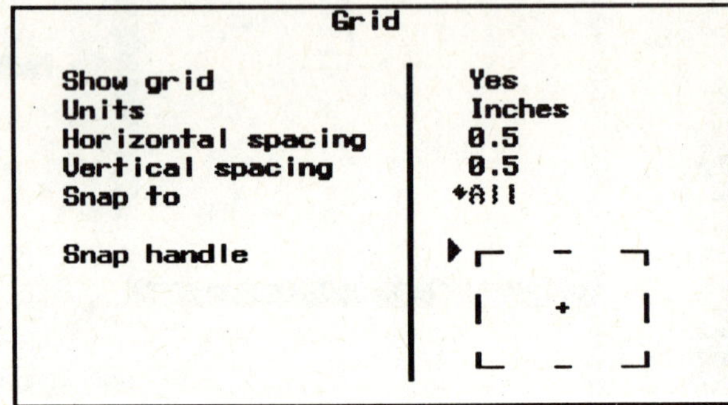

4. Press **F10** to return to your Draw Screen.

Grid Displayed

Show Rulers

The instructions for Diagram 1 refer frequently to horizontal and vertical ruler lines. To understand these references, you need to specify Show Ruler.

1. Press **F8** for **Options.**
2. Press **3** for **Rulers.**
3. Press **Y** for **Yes.**
4. Press **F10** to return to your Draw Screen.

Your Draw Screen now looks like this:

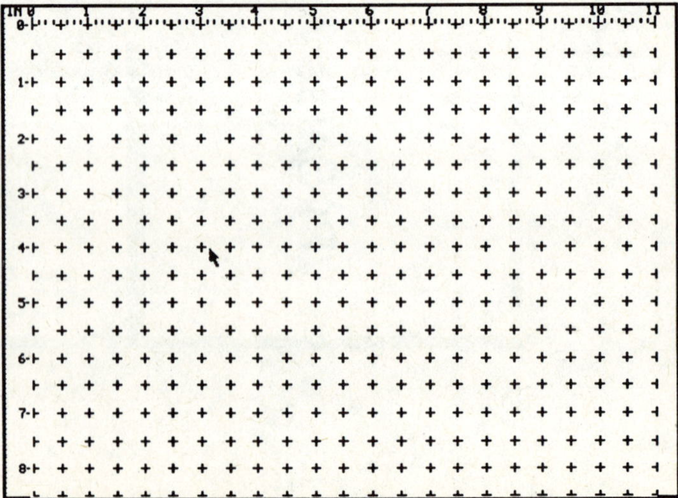

Ruler Displayed

Ruler References Note the numbers along the top and left side of the Draw Screen. In the following instructions, you will see directions such as "Position the + at 3 L and draw a line to 2.5 T."

This direction means that you start your line at the 3 mark on the *left* side of your Draw Screen and continue until you are below the 2.5 mark on the *top* of the grid.

A direction such as "Position your mouse at 8L and 6T" means that you move your mouse down to 8 Left and then horizontally across the screen until you are directly below 6 Top.

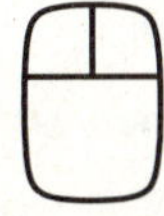

The following functions require the use of the mouse. Remember to click the **left** button to select functions and the **right** button to finish functions. If you click the right button twice, you may return to the Main Menu. If this happens, just press or click on **3** for **Draw** to return to your Draw Screen.

Draw Floor Plan Lines You will first select the Line Tool and then position your mouse at 3L and draw a horizontal line to 2.5T.

Line Tool 1. Click on the **Line Tool.**

Note the Line Attributes Pop-up that appears at the top of your Screen. You need to specify the width of your line.

2. Move your mouse to the **0.0** in the **Size Ruler** at the top of your screen.
3. Click left on the **0.0.**
4. Type *1.5* and press **Enter.**

Color Tool 1. Click on the **Color Tool.**
2. Click on the **Line/Text** box.

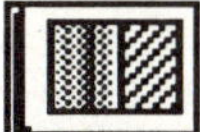

3. Click on the **White** box to set your line color.
4. Click **right** twice to exit the Color Pop-up.

Now you are ready to draw your first line.

Line Tool 1. Click on the **Line Tool** again.
2. Position your pointer at 3L, 0T. Note how a + appears.
3. Click and release the **left** mouse button.
4. Move your mouse horizontally until it is positioned under 2.5T.
5. Click **right** to end the line.
6. Position your + at 3L and 3T and click **left.**

7. Move your mouse up to 3T.
8. Click **right** to end your line.

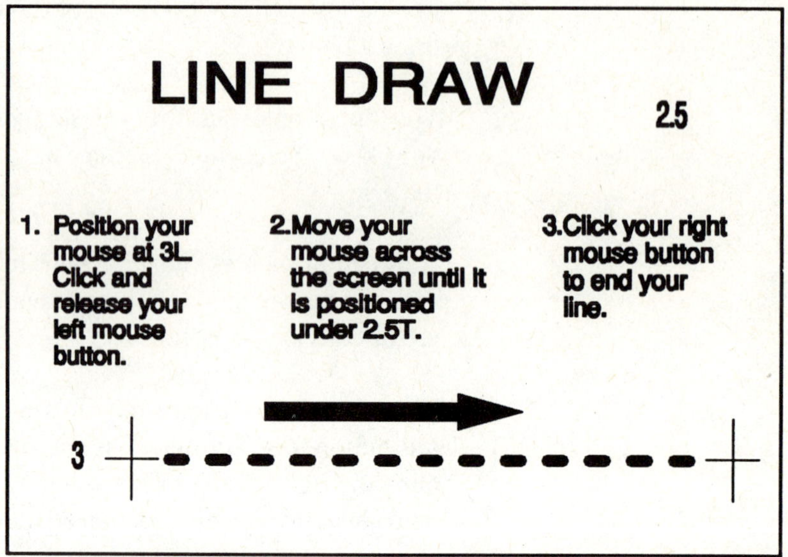

Trouble Note ▶ If your line is incorrectly positioned *immediately* after you click right, you can try again as follows:

1. Move your mouse to the top left of your screen and click left on the **Undo Tool**.
2. Try drawing your line again.

Your screen should look like this:

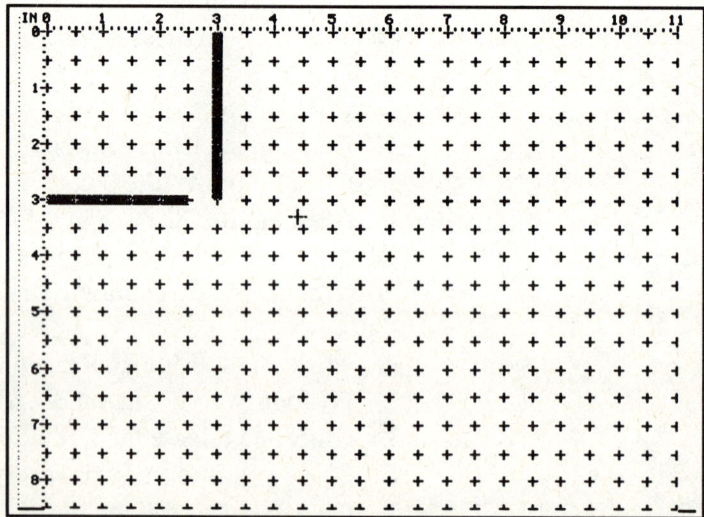

Notice how the use of Grid Snap makes drawing straight lines easy. The Snap feature won't *let* you draw a crooked line!

Are you ready to try the rest of the lines? Study the following illustration and then draw your lines in the positions indicated.

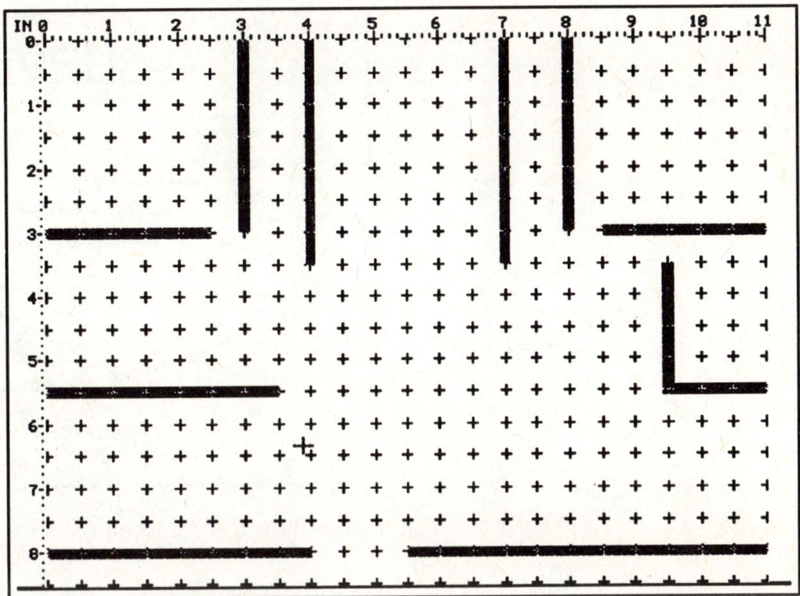

Trouble Note ▶ If your line is incorrectly positioned *immediately* after you click right, you can try again as follows:

1. Move your mouse to the top left of your screen and click **left** on the **Undo Tool**.
2. Try drawing your line again.

If you want to change a line *later*:

1. Click on the **Pointer** to exit Line Draw mode and then click on the line you want to delete.
2. Click on the **Delete Tool**.
3. Click on the **Line Tool** again to redraw your line.

Straight Lines Complete   ☐

Curved Line   You need to draw a curved line to designate the Reception area.

1. Click on the **Curve Tool**.
2. Position your mouse at 5L and 6.5T.
3. Click and release your **left** mouse button.
4. Move your mouse diagonally to 7L and 10.5T.
5. Click and release your **left** mouse button.
6. Move your mouse to the center of the line and pull the mouse down slightly to make your curve.
7. Click **right** to set your curve.

If you are not satisfied with your curve, click on the **Undo Tool** and try again. Study the following illustration:

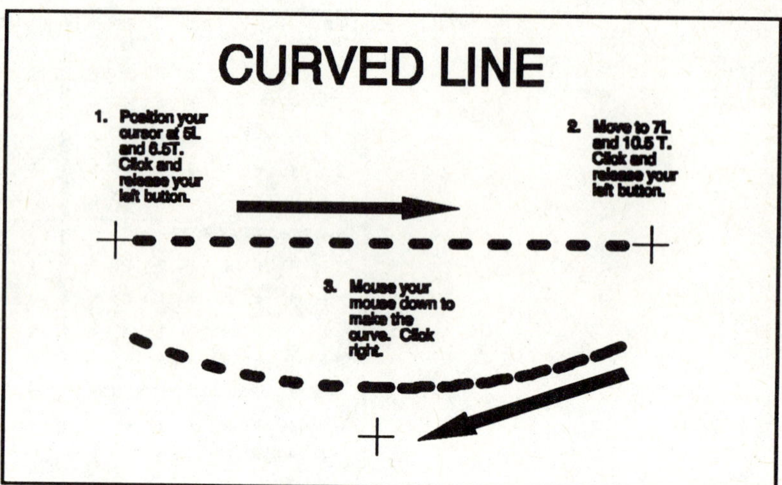

Your curve should look like this:

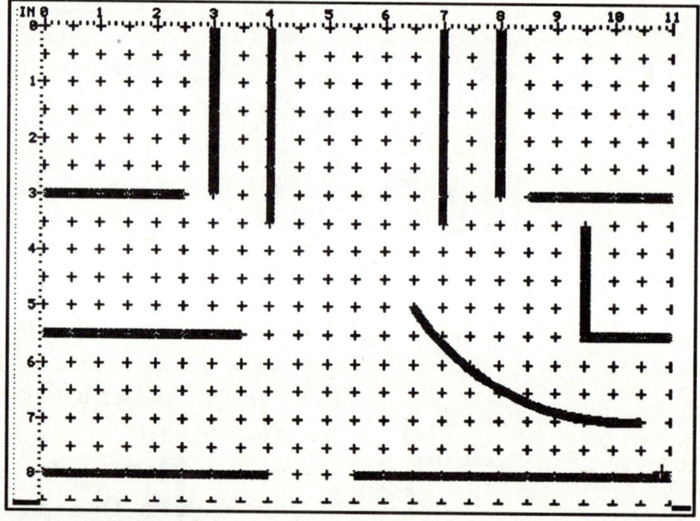

Curved Line Complete

Draw Doorway   You need to join the bottom line with a thinner line and curve to represent a doorway. First, change your line size and then draw the line and curve.

Line Size
1. Click on the **Line Tool.**
2. Click on the **1.5** in the **Line Size Ruler** at the top of your screen.
3. Type *1.0* and press **Enter.**

Diagonal Line
1. Position your cursor at 8L and 5.5T.
2. Click **left** to start your line.
3. Move your mouse up to 7L and 5T.
4. Click **right** to end the line.

Curve 1. Click on the **Curve Tool.**
       2. Position your cursor at 8L and 4T.
       3. Click **left** to start your curve.
       4. Move your mouse up to join your diagonal line.
       5. Click **left** and draw your curve.
       6. Click **right** to end.

Your doorway should look like this:

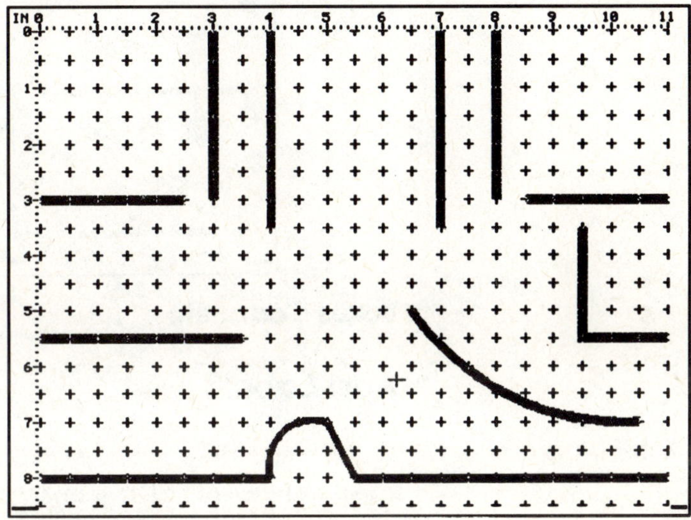

Doorway Complete

Add Boxes

Draw Boxes You can now draw the boxes that represent the secretaries' desks and the waiting area chairs. You first need to change the line size and then select the Box Tool to draw the six boxes required.

Line Size The Line Size you have already selected also affects the outline size of any box you draw. Change this Line Size to 0.0.

1. Click on the **Line Size Ruler** at the top of your screen.
2. Type *0.0* and press **Enter.**

Box 1 1. Click on the **Box Tool.**
       2. Position your cursor on .5L and 4.5T.
       3. Click and release your **left** button.
       4. Move your mouse to 1L and 5.5T.
       5. Click **right** to end the box.

Now draw the other boxes as illustrated:

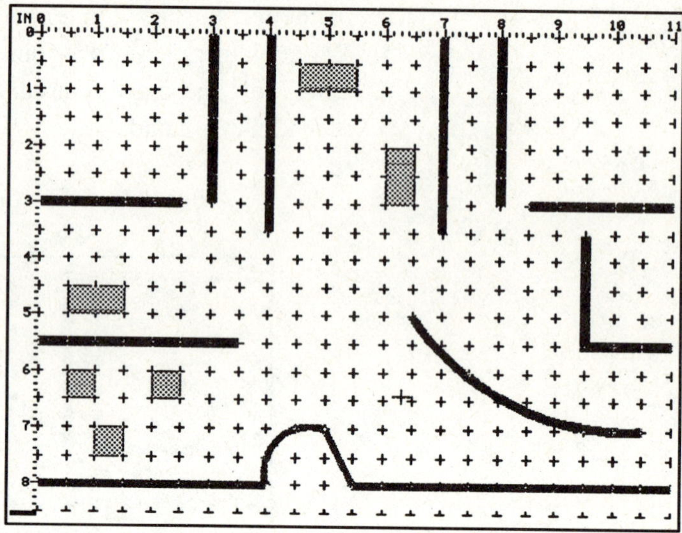

Boxes Complete

Add Labels

Enter Diagram Text You're ready now to label each of the areas of your Diagram and then reduce the size of the entire Diagram to provide room for your Title and Subtitle.

First, you will enter all the labels and then resize and position them to match the illustration of Diagram 1 on page 287.

Text Enter

1. Click on the **Text Tool.** A yellow **+** appears on your screen.
2. Move to the top left office.
3. Click **left** and drag your mouse to draw a good-sized box. Don't worry about running into one of the lines. You can position your text later.
4. At the Text Pop-up, type *VP: Sales.*
5. Press **F10** to place the text in your Draw Screen.

Note that your **+** still appears on your screen. You can now go on to place all the labels in their approximate locations. Don't worry about entering the text blocks in their exact positions. You can reposition the text blocks later. For now, just enter all the labels as illustrated:

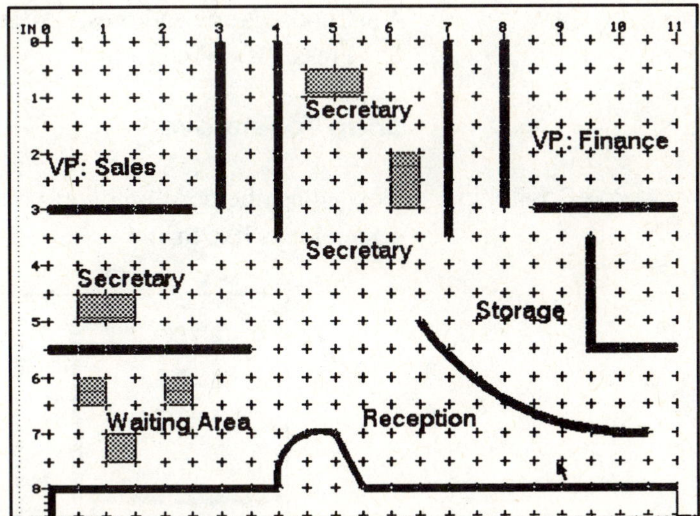

> **NOTE:**   To save keying-in time, you can use the Duplicate Tool to
> copy *Secretary* twice.

Trouble Note 1 ▶ If you receive a message saying your text will not fit where you wish to place it, try again as follows:

1. Move your mouse to the top left of your screen and click on the **Undo Tool.**
2. Move your + to a new location and click **left** to drag a larger box.

Trouble Note 2 ▶ If you notice that a label has been typed incorrectly *after* you have pressed **F10** to exit the Text Pop-up, you can edit the text as follows:

1. Click on the incorrect text to select it; orange handles appear around it.
2. Click on the **Edit Tool.**
3. Click again on **Edit Text.** The Text Pop-up appears.
4. Retype your text and press **F10** twice.

Text Entry Complete   ☐

Size and Position Text   You now need to remove Snap To and rotate the Storage label.

Snap To Remove   You must remove Snap To in order to reposition your text and objects easily.

1. Press **F8** for **Options** and **2** for **Grid.**
2. Press your ↓ arrow to position your cursor opposite **Snap To.**
3. Press **F3** for **Choices.**

4. Choose **None** and press **Enter.**
5. Press **F10** to return to your Draw Screen.

Snap To Removed

Label and Box Positioning

Now adjust the positioning of your labels and boxes, if required, so that your screen looks like this:

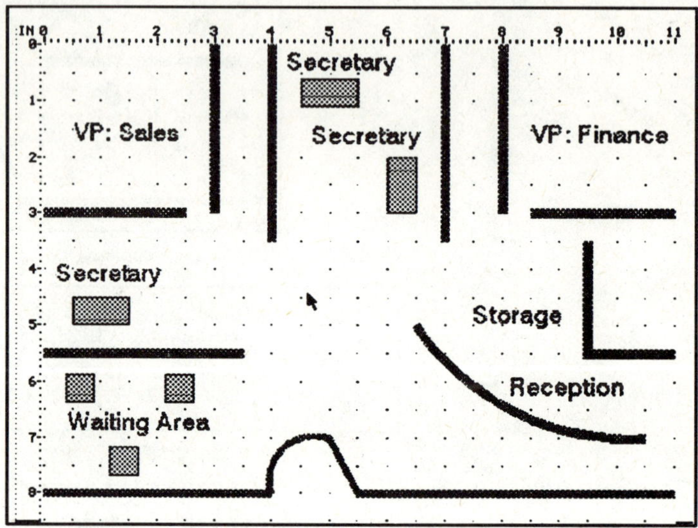

Labels and Boxes Positioned

Storage Label Rotate

You need to *rotate* the Storage label. Here's how.

1. Click on the Storage label to select it.
2. Click on the **Rotate Tool.**
3. Move your mouse to the Degrees box and click on the 0.0.
4. Type *90.0* and press **Enter.**
5. Click on the **Forward** box.
6. Click **right** to exit Rotate mode.

Now position *Storage* in the "room" under *VP: FINANCE* as illustrated:

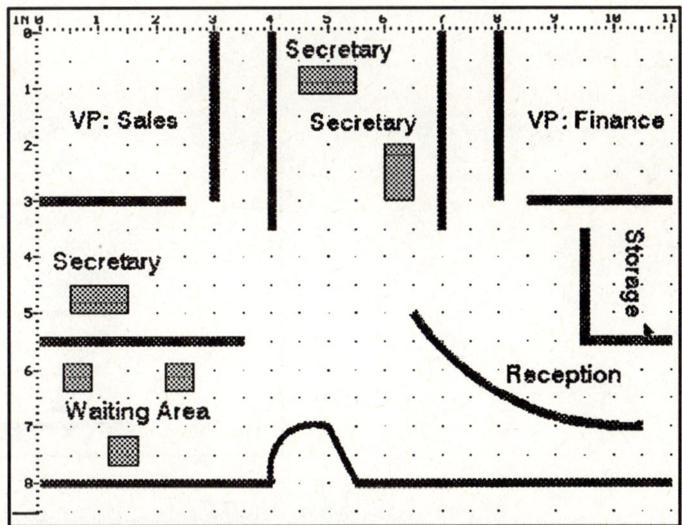

Storage Label Rotated and Positioned

Size and Move Diagram

Before you can type the Title and Subtitle of your Diagram, you need to reduce the size of your Diagram. To do this you will access the Select All feature in F9 (Actions) and then Group all the objects and text in your Diagram into *one* object.

Select All

1. Click on any one of the items in your Diagram.
2. Press **F9** for **Actions.**
3. Press **3** for **Select Objects.** The Select Objects Pop-up appears.
4. Press **F3** for **Choices.**
5. Press **Enter** twice to accept **All.**

Note that orange handles appear around every item in the Diagram.

Group

1. Click on the **Group Tool.**

The entire Diagram is selected as one object. You can now size the whole Diagram at once.

Size

1. Click on the top left handle of your Diagram.
2. Press **Shift** and drag your mouse right and down so that the top left handle is positioned at 1.5 L and 2T as illustrated:

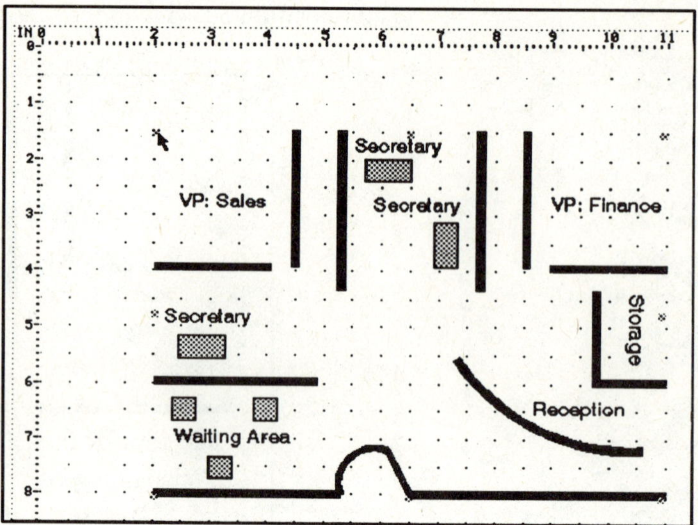

Move   1.   Move the Diagram down to 2L and then left to center it between 1T and 10T as illustrated:

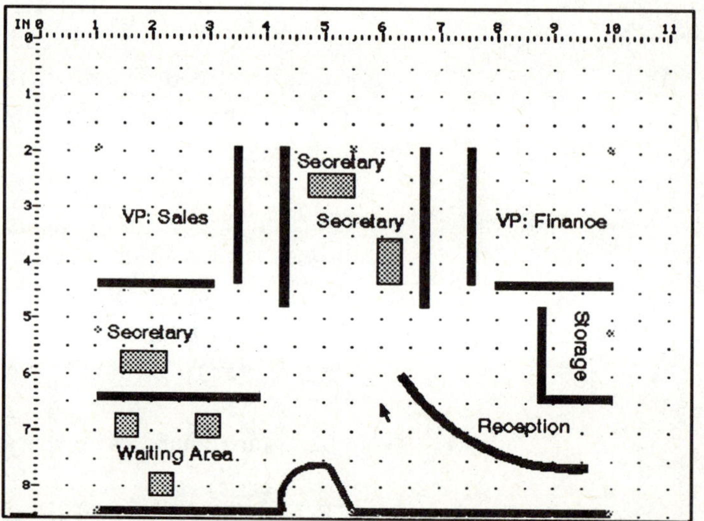

2.   Click **right** to remove the handles.

Diagram Sized and Positioned

Draw Perimeter Lines

Before you go on to enter the Title and Subtitle of your Diagram, you need to enclose the floor plan area with straight lines.

You will draw all three lines at once—just clicking **left** when you need to change the line direction.

> **NOTE:**   Hold your **Shift** key throughout the line draw process to en-
> sure that your lines remain straight.

1. Click on the **Line Tool.**
2. Click on the **Line Size Ruler**, change the size to *1.0,* and press **Enter.**
3. Position your mouse at the end of the line at the bottom left of your
    screen.
4. Click **left** to start the line.
5. Press and hold **Shift** and move your mouse up to 2.1L.
6. Click **left** to change direction and move your mouse across to 10T.
7. Click **left** to change direction again and move your mouse down to meet
    the bottom line. Click **left.**
8. Now click **right** to end the lines.

Trouble Note ▶   If your lines are incorrectly positioned, immediately click on the **Undo Tool**
and try again.

Take your time! Drawing these lines in the correct positions requires precise
mouse movements.

Compare your screen to the following illustration:

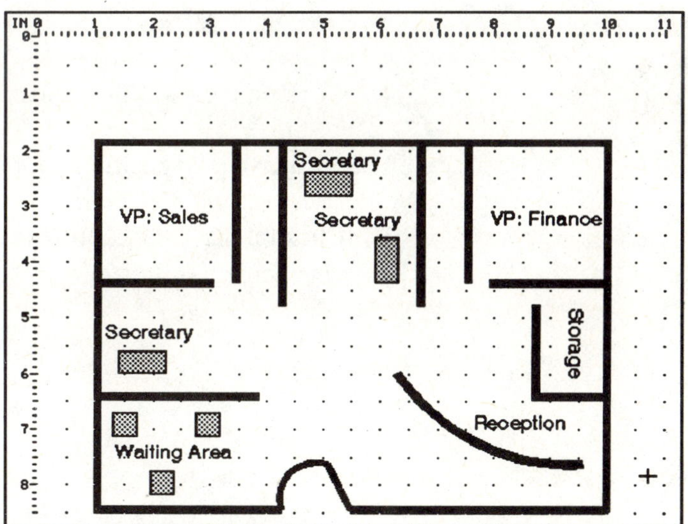

Perimeter Lines Complete   ☐

You can now select the Text Tool to enter the Title and Subtitle of your Diagram.

Enter Title/Subtitle

1. Click on the **Text Tool.**
2. Move your mouse up to the **Text Size Ruler** and click on the **5.0.**
3. Type *6.0* and press **Enter.**

4. Click on the **Style** box and select **Bold.**
5. Position the + at the top left corner of your screen.
6. Click and hold **left** to draw a box that extends across the screen and down about 1".

The Text Enter Pop-up appears. Enter the Title/Subtitle as follows:

1. Type *ACTION ACCOUNTING* and press **Enter.**
2. Type *Office Renovations 1993.*
3. Press your ← arrow to position your mouse on the "O" in *Office.*
4. Press **F5** and move your cursor to the end of the line.
5. Click on the **Style** box and select **Roman.**
6. Press **F10** twice to return to your Draw Screen.

Center Text

You want both your Title and Subtitle to be centered in relation to each other.

1. First click on the **Pointer** to select the text block.
2. Move your mouse up to the Text Attributes Pop-up.
3. Click on the ↓ arrow at the top right of the Pop-up to access the second of the three Text Attributes "pages."

Note the selection of boxes showing different kinds of text alignment.

4. Click on the box that indicates **Centered** text.

Position

Your last task is to position your Title/Subtitle.

1. Click on the Title/Subtitle text block and position it at the top center of your screen as illustrated:

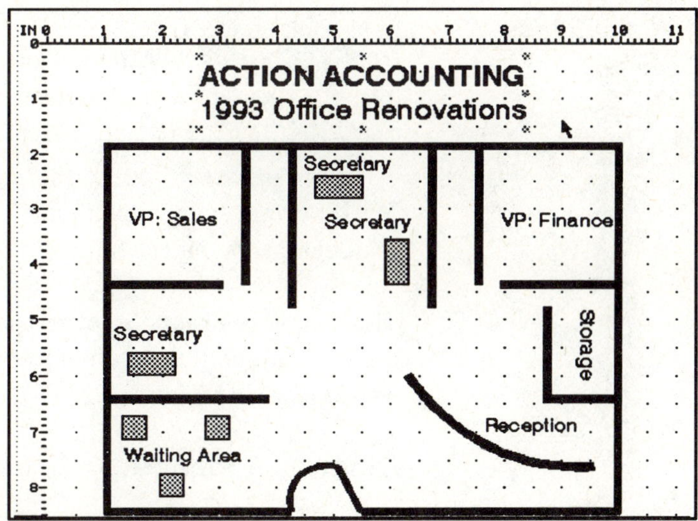

2. Click **right** to remove the handles.

Title/Subtitle Complete

Save and Print Your Diagram

Save your Diagram on your data disk and then access the Output command to print it. Once you are satisfied with your Diagram, you can either exit from Harvard Graphics or start on Activity 3.

Save
1. Press **F6** for **File.**
2. Press **2** for **Save Chart.**

The Save Chart Menu appears. Your cursor is currently positioned next to **Filename.** The default Directory (usually C:\HG3\DATA) is displayed. You will save your file on a data disk in Drive A or B.

1. Press your ↑ arrow to position your cursor opposite **Directory.**
2. Type *a:* or *b:* and then press **Delete** to erase the old Directory.
3. Press **Enter.**
4. At **Filename,** type *Diagram1* and press **Enter.**
5. At **Description,** type *Diagram #1: Lesson 9.*
6. Press **F10** to save and return to the Draw Screen.

Diagram 1 Saved

Print
1. Press **F6** for **File** and **E** for **Exit to Main Menu.**
2. Press **5** for **Output.**
3. Press **Enter** to accept **Printer 1.**
4. Press **F2** to view how your document will appear in printed form.

> **NOTE:**   If you wish to change your Diagram, press **ESC** to return to the Main Menu and then **3** to return to your Draw Screen.

5.   If you are satisfied with the look of your Diagram, press **F10** twice to accept the Default Settings.

The Output to Printer Screen appears. Your Diagram has now been sent to the printer. Wait until the Output to Printer Screen disappears and you are returned to your Main Menu.

Diagram 1 Printed

You now have two options:

- Exit Harvard Graphics if you are finished with your learning session.
- Clear the current diagram and get started on Activity 3.

Exit Harvard Graphics   1.   Press **E** to exit Harvard Graphics.

Clear the Current Chart   1.   Press **1** for **Create Chart**.
2.   Press **8** for **Clear Chart**.

ACTIVITY 3   DIAGRAM 2

For Diagram 2, you will create a Process Diagram to represent the *Six-Step Hiring Process* used by Action Accounting, Ltd. Six major steps are required to produce Diagram 2.

Step One:	Draw, Duplicate, and Position Shapes
Step Two:	Draw an Arrow
Step Three:	Duplicate and Position Arrows
Step Four:	Enter and Position Labels
Step Five:	Enter the Title and Legend
Step Six:	Save and Print your Diagram

Follow the instructions to create Diagram 2 (see page 303). Remember to place a check mark in the box next to each function you complete.

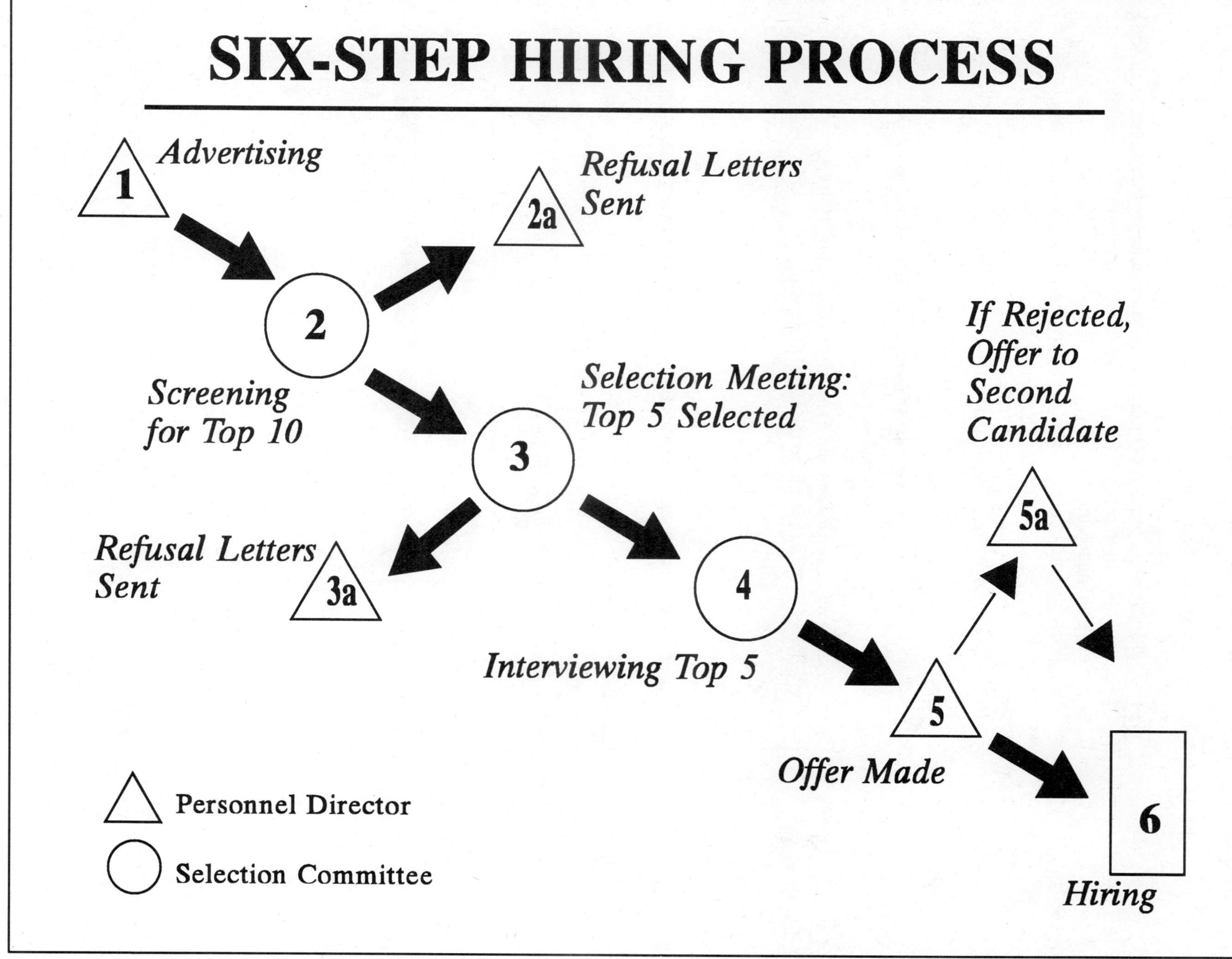

SIX-STEP HIRING PROCESS
1
Advertising
2
2a
Refusal Letters Sent
Screening for Top 10
3
Selection Meeting: Top 5 Selected
Refusal Letters Sent
3a
4
Interviewing Top 5
If Rejected, Offer to Second Candidate
5a
5
Offer Made
6
Hiring
Personnel Director
Selection Committee

Draw, Duplicate, and Position Shapes

Access Draw   At the Main Menu, press **3** for **Draw.**

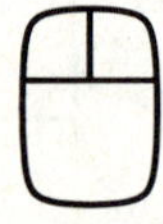

The following functions require the use of the mouse. Remember to click the **left** button to select functions and the **right** button to finish functions. If you click the right button twice, you may return to the Main Menu. If this happens, just press or click on **3** for **Draw** to return to your Draw Screen.

Draw Shapes   Three shapes are required: a triangle, a circle, and a rectangle. You will first draw each of these shapes and then use the Duplicate Tool to copy the triangle four times and the circle twice.

Before you start drawing the shapes, select **Show Ruler** as follows:

1. Press **F8** for **Options.**
2. Press **3** for **Rulers** and **Y** for **Yes** next to **Show Rules.**
3. Press **F10** to return to the Draw Screen.

Now go on to draw the triangle, circle, and rectangle as instructed.

Triangle   1. Click on the **Regular Polygon Tool.**
2. Note the Number of Sides box; *3* should already be entered. If a different number appears, click on the **Number of Sides** box and type *3*.

3. Click **left** to start the triangle.
4. Move your mouse out to increase the triangle size slightly.

Make your triangle quite small as illustrated:

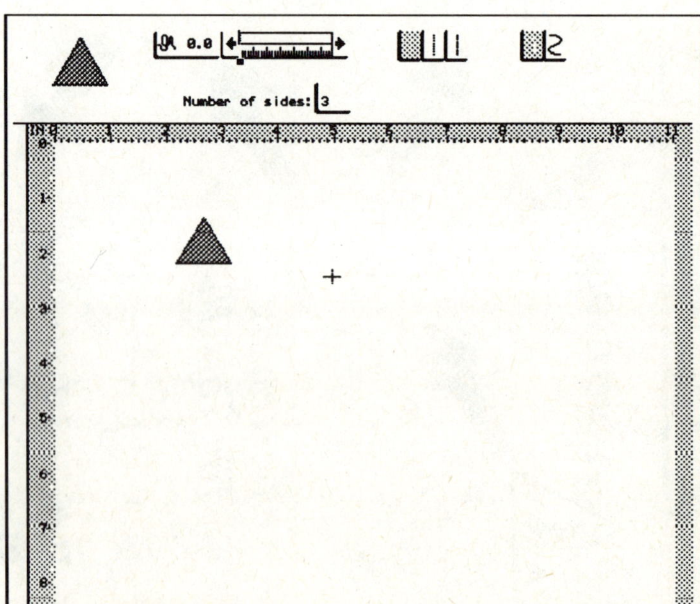

5. Click **right** to end.

Trouble Note ▶ If your triangle is too large, click immediately on the **Undo Tool** at the top left of your Draw Screen and try again. You only have to move your mouse very slightly to achieve the correct sizing.

Triangle Complete

Circle
1. Click on the **Circle Tool.**
2. Press **Shift** and click **left** to start the circle.

> **NOTE:** You *must* press **Shift** to draw a circle; otherwise you will draw an oval.

3. Move your mouse out to increase the circle size slightly.

   Make your circle quite small as illustrated:

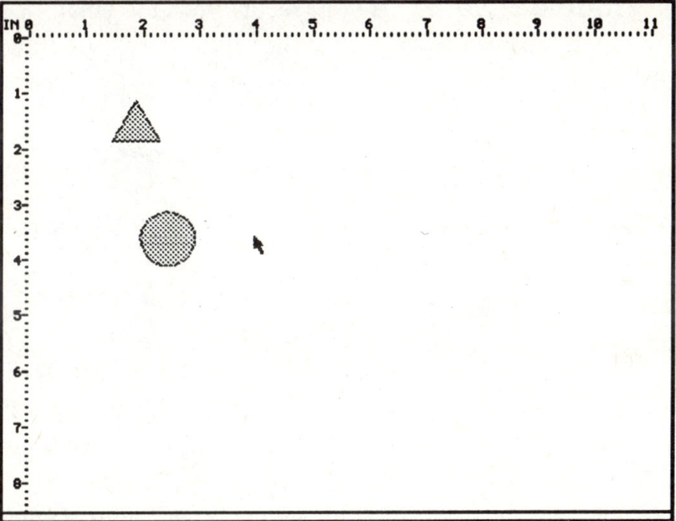

4. Click **right** to end.

Trouble Note ▶ If your circle is too small or too large, click immediately on the **Undo Tool** at the top left of your Draw Screen and try again. You only have to move your mouse very slightly to achieve the correct sizing.

Circle Complete

Rectangle
1. Click on the **Box Tool.**
2. Click **left** and draw a rectangle as illustrated:

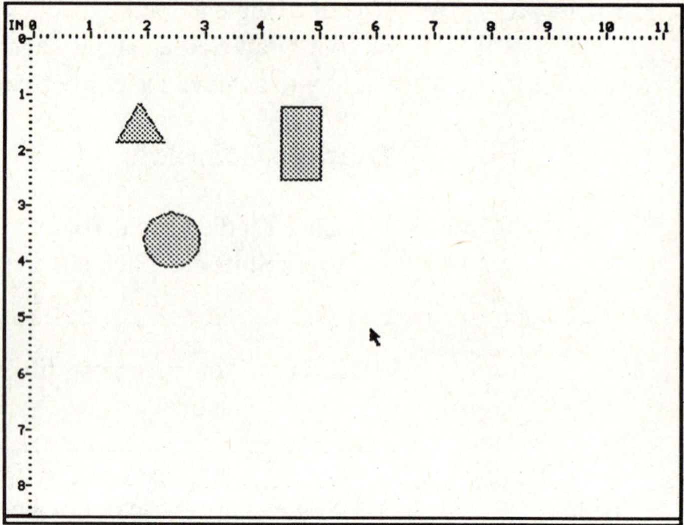

3. Click **right** to end the rectangle.

Trouble Note ▶ If your rectangle is too small or too large, click immediately on the **Undo Tool** at the top left of your Draw Screen and try again. You only have to move your mouse very slightly to achieve the correct sizing.

Rectangle Complete   ☐

Duplicate Shapes Your next step is to duplicate the triangle four times and the circle twice.

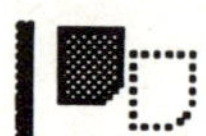

1. Click on the **Pointer Tool.**
2. Click on the **Triangle** to select it.
3. Click on the **Duplicate Tool.**
4. Move the new Triangle away from the first Triangle.
5. Click on the **Duplicate Tool** again.

Duplicate the other two triangles and then go on to duplicate two circles.

Shapes Duplicated   ☐

Position Shapes Use your mouse to position all of the shapes as indicated in the following illustration. Take your time to get the positioning correct so that you won't have to make any positioning adjustments later.

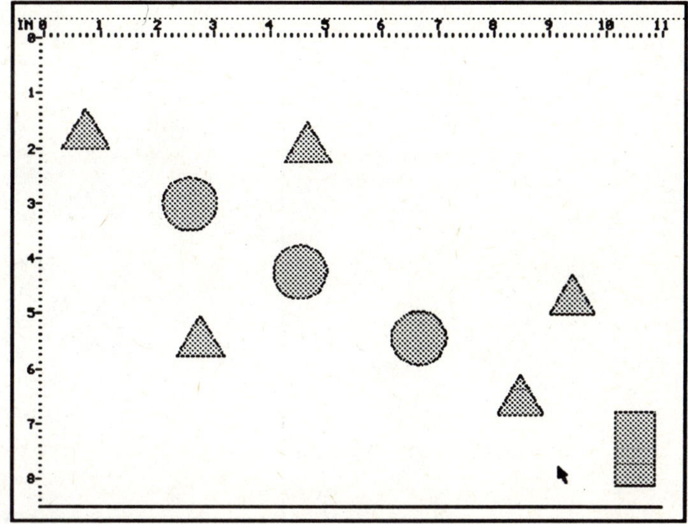

Change Fill Color   You need to change the Fill color of the shapes to None. First, select all the objects on your screen.

1. Press **F9** for **Actions.**
2. Press **3** for **Select Objects**. The Select Objects Pop-up appears.
3. Press **F3** for **Choices.**
4. Press **Enter** twice to accept **All.**

Handles now appear around every object on your screen.

Color Tool   1. Click on the **Color Tool.**
2. Click on the **Fill** box.

3. Click on the box labeled **None.**
4. Click on the **Line/Text** box.
5. Click on a **White** box.
6. Click **right** twice to return to the Draw Screen and remove the handles.

Compare your screen to the following illustration:

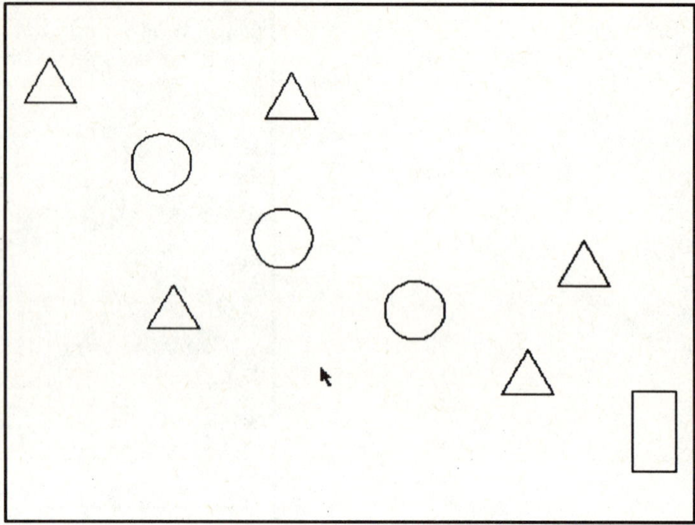

Fill Color Changed

Draw an Arrow

None of the arrows included in the Arrows Symbol Directory are appropriate for this Diagram. You need to draw your own arrow. To give you space to work in, you'll first access the Scratchpad.

Access Scratchpad   1.   Click on the **Scratchpad Tool.**

A blank screen appears. In this screen, you will draw a line and a triangle, join them into an arrow, group them into one object, size the object, and then use the Copy and Paste Tools to place your arrow in the Draw Screen.

Draw Line   1.   Click on the **Line Tool.**
2.   Move your mouse up to the Box Attributes Pop-up.

3.   Click on the number in the **Line Size Ruler.**
4.   Type *2.0* and press **Enter.**

Now draw the line as follows:

1.   Position the + on your Draw Screen.
2.   Click **left** and hold the **Shift** key to draw a straight line about 1" long.
3.   Click **left** and then **right** to end the line.

Draw Triangle   1.   Click on the **Regular Polygon Tool.**
2.   Draw a small triangle as illustrated:

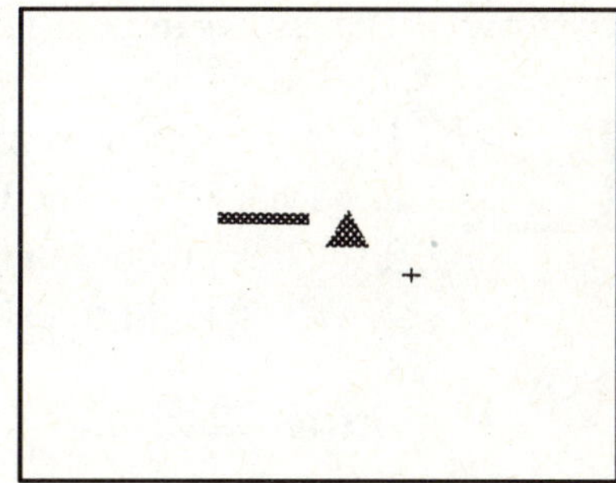

Trouble Note ▶	You may have to try a few times to get the triangle size you want. Just click on the **Undo Tool** if your triangle is too large and try again.

Rotate Triangle

Now you have to rotate your Triangle so that it can be positioned at the end of the line to make an arrow.

1.   Click on the **Pointer** to select the **Triangle.**
2.   Click on the **Rotate Tool.**
3.   Type *90.0* in the Degrees box and press **Enter.**
4.   Click on the **Forward** box.
5.   Click **right** to exit Rotate mode.

Position Triangle

1.   Click on and move your Triangle so that it meets your line.

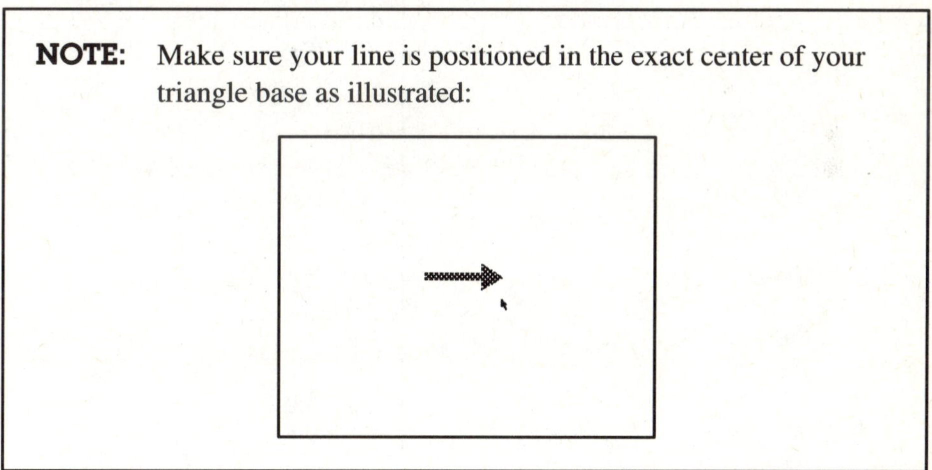

> **NOTE:**   Make sure your line is positioned in the exact center of your triangle base as illustrated:

2.   Click **right** to remove the handles.

Arrow Complete

Group Line and Triangle

Your next step is to group your line and triangle into one object so that you can rotate it before copying and pasting it to your Draw Screen.

1.   Click on a point above and to the left of your line and triangle.
2.   Click **left** and draw a box around both objects to select them.
3.   Click on the **Group Tool** (you may have to access the second tool level).

Rotate Arrow   The arrows in your Diagram are rotated 30°. Rotate your arrow as follows:

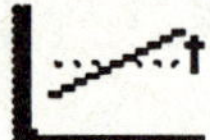

1. Access the first tool level and click on the **Rotate Tool.**
2. Type *30.0* in the Degrees box and press **Enter.**
3. Click on the **Forward** box.
4. Click **right** to exit Rotate mode.

Arrow Rotated

Duplicate and Position Arrows

You can now copy your arrow into the Draw Screen and then duplicate and position the arrows throughout the Process Diagram.

Copy and Paste Arrow   1. Click on the **Copy Tool.**
2. Click on the **Scratchpad** to access your Draw Screen.
3. Click on the **Paste Tool.**

Your arrow now appears in your Draw Screen. Resize and then position your arrow between the top triangle and circle as illustrated:

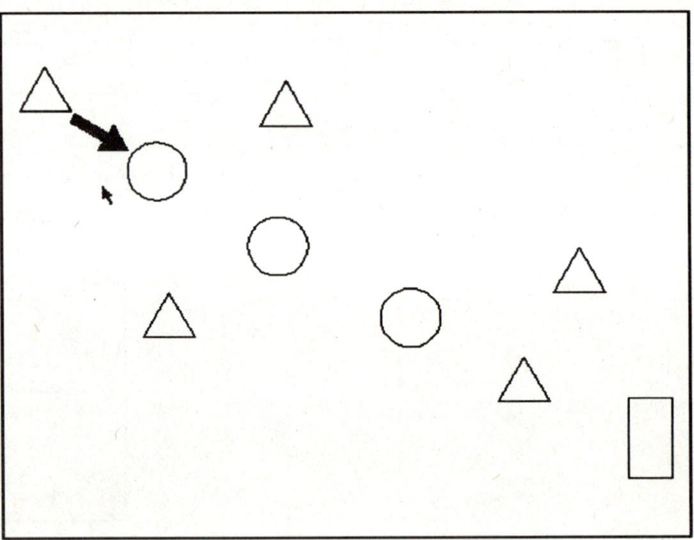

Arrow Positioned

Duplicate Arrows   1. Click on the **Duplicate Tool.**
2. Move the duplicated arrow into position between the first and second circles as illustrated:

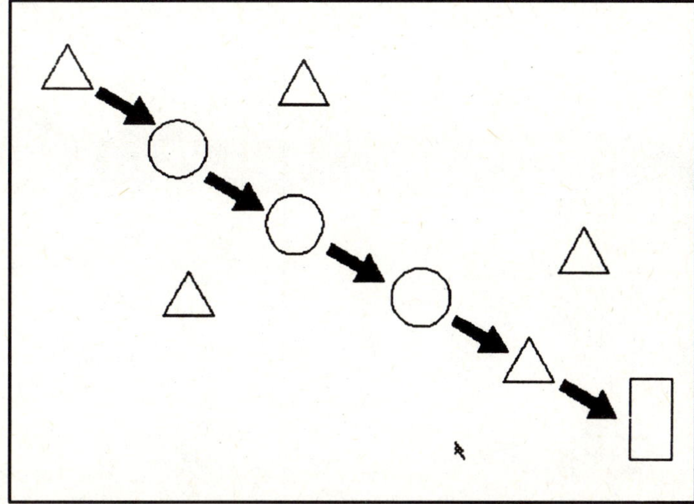

Duplicate three more arrows and position them as illustrated:

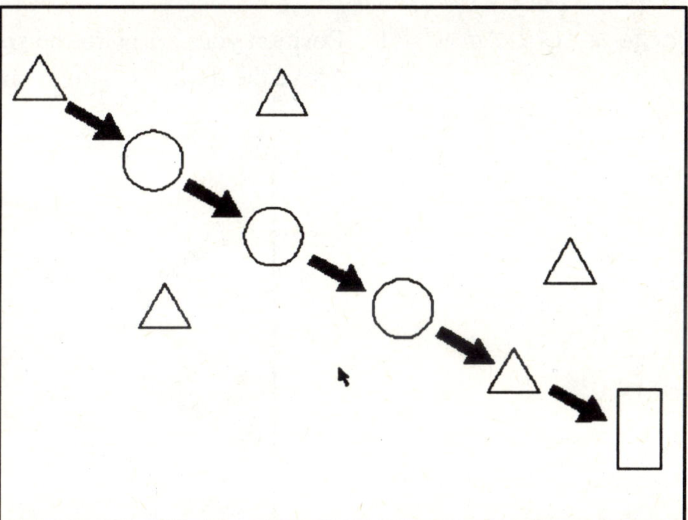

Arrows Duplicated

Duplicate Side Arrows   Now duplicate, rotate, and position the arrows pointing to the two side triangles.

1. Click on and duplicate one more arrow and move it up next to your first circle.
2. Click on the **Rotate Tool.**
3. Click on the right handle that appears and drag your mouse up to rotate the arrow as illustrated:

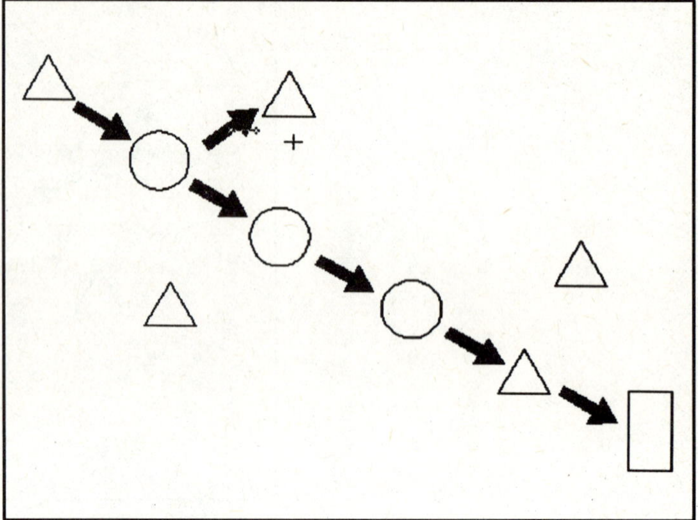

4. Click **right** to exit Rotate mode.

Duplicate Second Arrow   1. Position your arrow in the space and then duplicate it.
2. Move the duplicated arrow into position as illustrated:

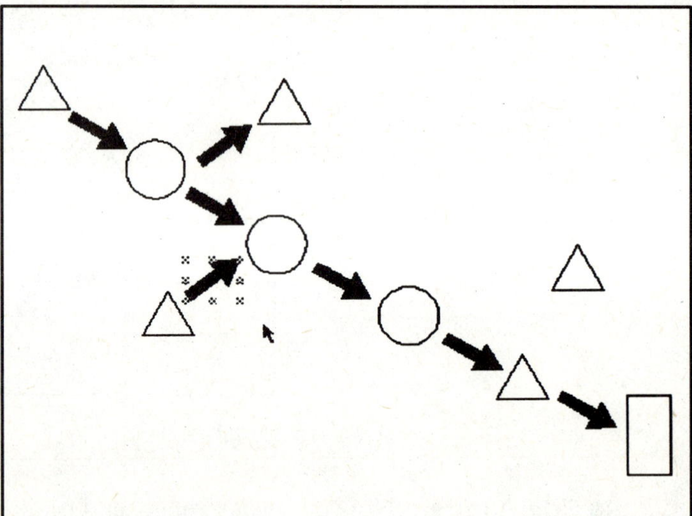

Flip Tool   Change the arrow direction as follows:

1. Click on the **Flip Tool.**
2. Click on the **Vertical** box.
3. Click on the **Flip Tool** again.
4. Click on the **Horizontal** box.
5. Click **right** to remove the handles.

Arrow Flipped

Create Small Arrows

You need to create two more arrows that have smaller lines to indicate that the step pointed to is optional. To change the arrow line size, you will access your Scratchpad again, ungroup the arrow, and then resize the line and triangle.

Ungroup

1. Click on the **Scratchpad.** Your original arrow appears.
2. Click on the **Arrow** to select it.
3. Click on the **Ungroup Tool** to separate the line from the triangle.
4. Click **right** to remove all the handles.

Line Size

1. Click on the **Line.**
2. Move your mouse up to the Line Attributes Pop-up.
3. Click on the number in the **Line Size Ruler.**
4. Type *0.0* and press **Enter.**
5. Click **right** to remove the handles.

Your line size is now reduced.

1. Click on the **Triangle** to select it.
2. Press **Shift** to slightly reduce the size of the triangle.

Reposition your line and triangle if necessary. Your new arrow should look like this:

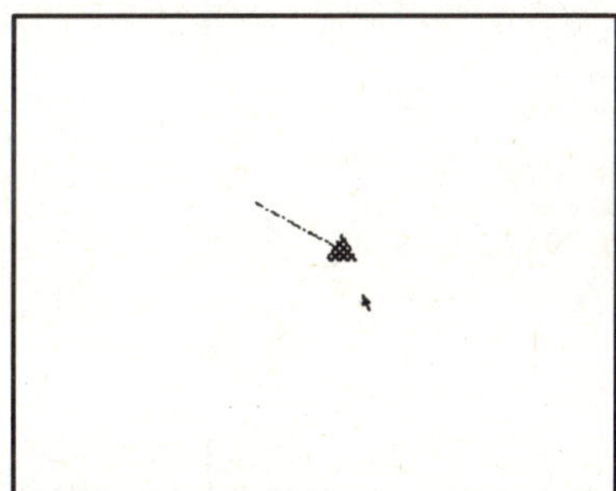

3. Click **right** to remove the handles.

Small Arrow Created

Copy and Paste

1. Click on a point above and to the left of your line and triangle and draw a box to select both.
2. Click on the **Group Tool.**
3. Resize your arrow if necessary.
4. Click on the **Copy Tool.**
5. Click on the **Scratchpad** to access the Draw Screen.
6. Click on the **Paste Tool.**

Position and Rotate Small Arrow

1. Move your arrow above the bottom triangle and resize and position it to fit the space.

2. Click on the **Rotate Tool** and slightly alter the arrow's rotation as illustrated:

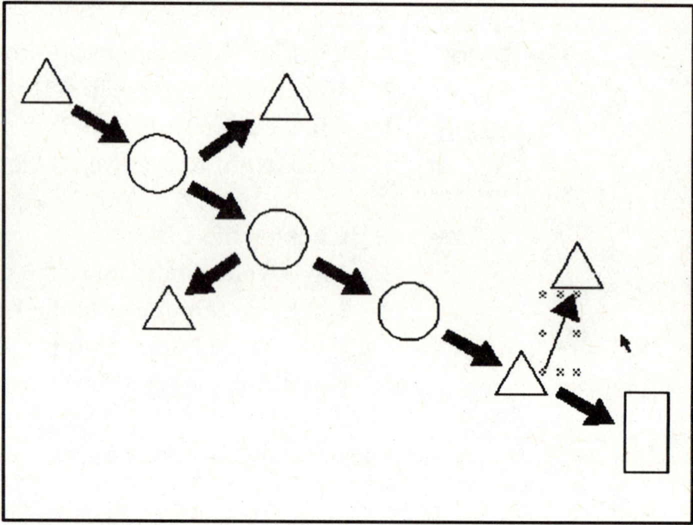

3. Duplicate the arrow and then click on the **Flip Tool** to flip it vertically. Reposition the arrow as illustrated:

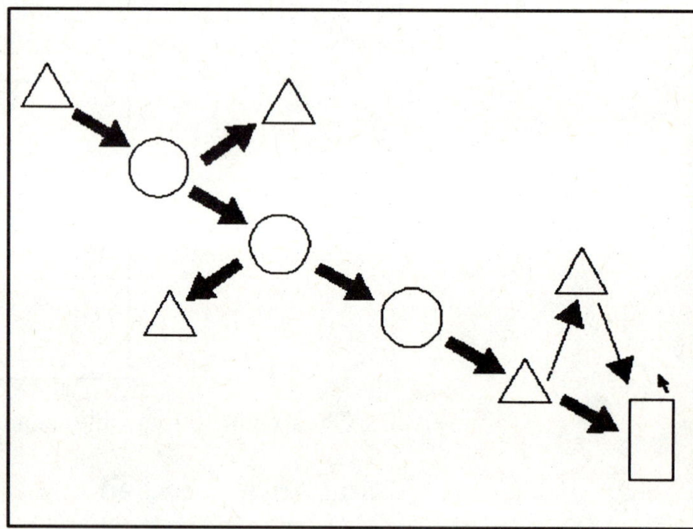

4. Click **right** to remove the handles.

Small Arrows Positioned

Enter and Position Labels

You can now go on to enter the *text labels* for each of the objects in your Diagram. Once your labels are entered and positioned, you will enter the numbers for each of the Diagram objects.

Text Tool   Enter the first label (*Advertising*) as follows:

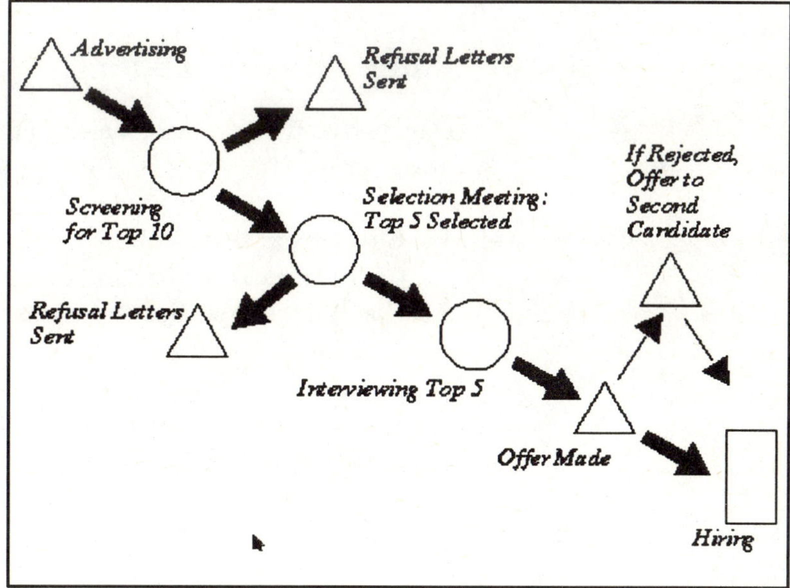

1. Click on the **Text Tool.**
2. Make sure *5.0* appears in your **Text Size Ruler.** If not, type *5.0* and press **Enter.**
3. Click on the **Font** box and choose **Dutch 801.**
4. Click on the **Style** box and choose **Bold Italic.**
5. If you did not exit Harvard Graphics after Activity 2, change the text alignment from center to left by clicking on the bar that displays left alignment.
6. Position the + to the right of your top triangle.
7. Click **left** and drag a box about two inches wide.

> **NOTE:**   Always make your text boxes large to ensure your text will fit.

8. At the Text Enter Pop-up, type *Advertising.*
9. Press **F10** to exit the Text Enter Pop-up.

Now go on to enter the rest of the labels as illustrated below. For labels that take up more than one line, press **Enter** to divide the text. Once you have entered all your text blocks, adjust their positioning as required:

Step Numbers   Use the **Text Tool** to enter a step number on each of the objects. This activity takes some time. After you enter a number, position it correctly before going on to the next number. Refer to the following illustration for guidance:

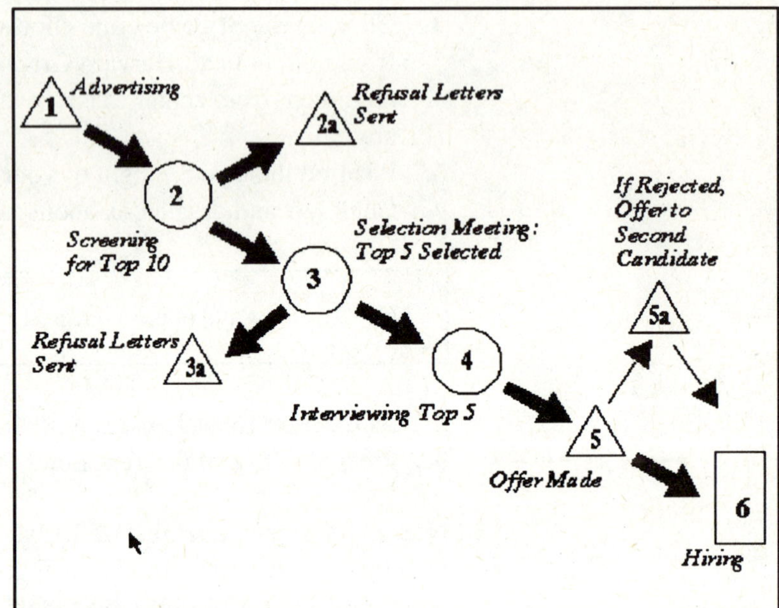

Enter Title and Legend

Only two activities remain: entering the Diagram Title and creating the Diagram Legend.

Create Title
1. Click on the **Text Tool.**
2. Click on the **Text Size Ruler** and change the text size to *8.0.*
3. Click on the **Style** box and change the text style to **Bold.**
4. Position the + at the top left of your screen and draw a box that extends across the screen and down about 1".
5. At the Text Pop-up, type *SIX-STEP HIRING PROCESS.*
6. Press **F10** to exit the Pop-up.

Title Position
1. Click on the **Pointer** and center your Title at the top of your screen as illustrated:

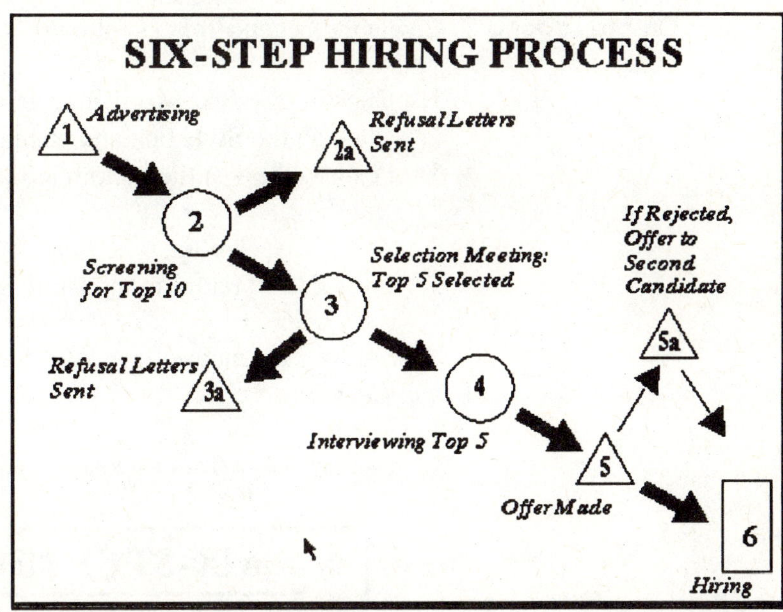

2. Click **right** to remove the handles.

Title Entered   ☐

Draw Line
1. Click on the **Line Tool.**
2. Move to the **Line Size Ruler**, change the line size to *1.0*, and press **Enter.**
3. Position your mouse under and to the left of the Title.
4. Click **left** to start the line.
5. Press and hold **Shift** and move your mouse to the right of the Title.
6. Click **right** to end the line. Compare your line size to the following illustration:

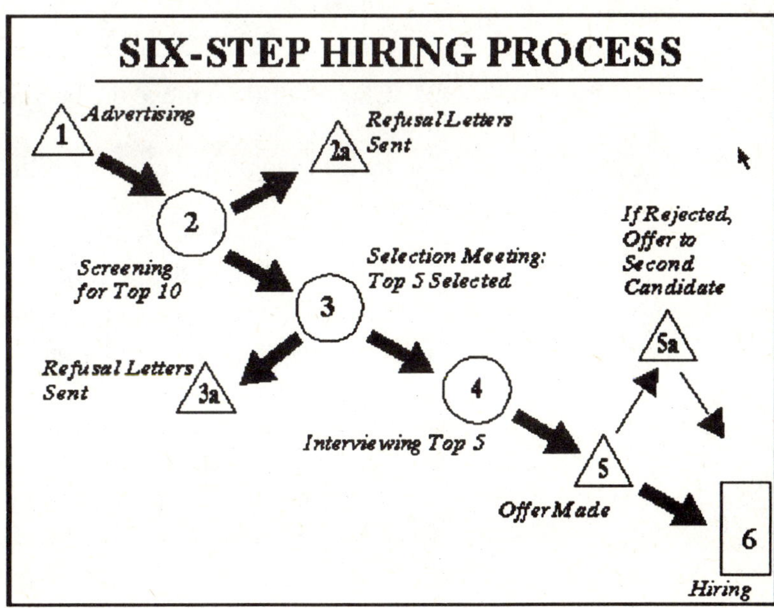

Line Complete   ☐

Create Legend   Create the Legend Text as follows:

1. Click on the **Text Size Ruler** and change the text size to *3.0.*
2. Click on the **Style** box and change the text style to **Roman.**
3. Position the **+** at the bottom left of your screen and draw a box about 3" wide.
4. At the Text Pop-up, type *Personnel Director.*
5. Press **F10** to return to the Draw Screen.

Now move your mouse down and draw another box to enter the text for *Selection Committee.*

1. Use the **Align Tool** to position your text blocks as illustrated:

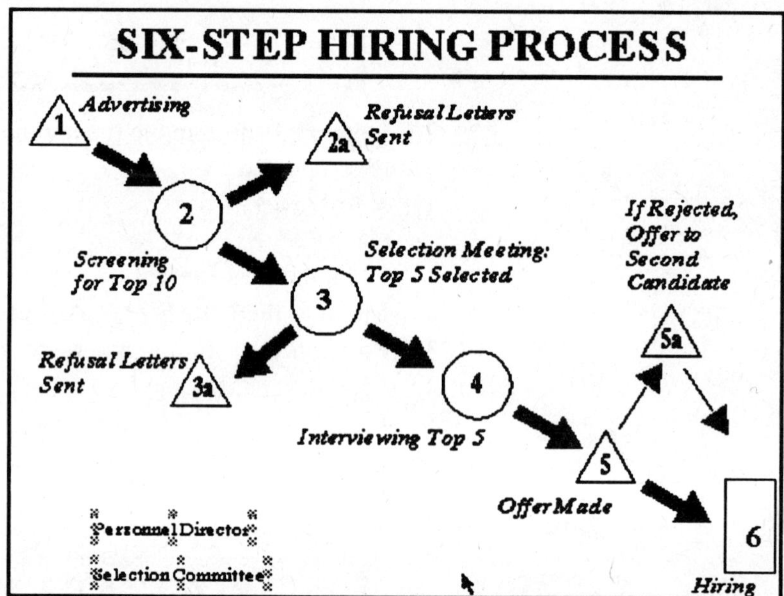

2. Click **right** to remove the handles.

Create the triangle and circle as follows:

1. Click on one of the triangles on your screen.
2. Click on the **Duplicate Tool.**
3. Move the duplicated triangle to the right of *Personnel Director.*
4. Click and hold on a corner handle and press **Shift** to reduce the triangle size slightly.
5. Click on one of the circles on your screen.
6. Click on the **Duplicate Tool.**
7. Move the duplicated circle to the right of *Selection Committee.*
8. Click and hold on a corner handle and press **Shift** to reduce the circle size slightly.

Adjust the positioning of the triangle and circle as illustrated:

Legend Complete ☐

Save and Print Your Diagram

You will save Diagram 2 on your data disk and then access the Output command to print.

Save
1. Press **F6** for **File.**
2. Press **2** for **Save Chart.**

The Save Chart Menu appears. Your cursor is currently positioned next to **Filename.** Either the default Directory (usually C:\HG3\DATA) or your data drive is displayed.

1. If necessary, change your Directory to your A or B drive and press **Enter.**
2. At **Filename**, type *Diagram2* and press **Enter.**
3. At **Description**, type *Diagram #2: Lesson 9.*
4. Press **F10** to return to the Draw Screen.

Diagram 2 Saved ☐

Print
1. Press **F6** for **File** and **E** for **Exit to Main Menu.**
2. Press **5** for **Output.**
3. Press **Enter** to accept **Printer 1.**
4. Press **F2** to view how your document will appear in printed form.

> **NOTE:** If you do not like how your Diagram will appear when printed, press **ESC** to return to your Main Menu and then **3** to access your Draw Screen. You can then make any size, positioning, or color fill adjustments necessary.

5. If you are satisfied with the look of your Diagram, press **F10** twice to accept the Default Settings.

The Output to Printer Screen appears. Your Diagram has now been sent to the printer. Wait until the Output to Printer Screen disappears and you are back at the Main Menu.

Diagram 2 Printed ☐

You now have two options:

- Exit Harvard Graphics if you are finished with your learning session.
- Clear the current chart.

Exit Harvard Graphics   1.   At the Main Menu, press **E** to exit Harvard Graphics.

Clear the Current Chart   1.   Press **1** for **Create Chart**.
2.   Press **8** for **Clear Chart**.

ACTIVITY 4   CHALLENGE ASSIGNMENT

Read through the following sections for suggestions on content and then adapt the instructions given for your own material. Use the boxes provided to record information about your Diagram.

The Challenge Assignment requires three major steps.

Step One: Choose Your Diagram Topic
Step Two: Plan Your Diagram Information
Step Three: Create and Format Your Diagram

Choose Your Diagram Topic

You can create a Diagram to show the steps in a process, directions to a place of business, an abstract idea, a floor plan—the list is endless. In fact, your first task is to *simplify* your topic into elements that you can easily create with the Harvard Graphics Draw features.

Perhaps the best type of Diagram to start with is one that uses geometric shapes to show the steps in a process—as you did with the Process Diagram in Activity 3. Alternatively, you may want to create a simple map that directs your reader to your college, business, or house. Refer to the sample Diagram in Activity 1 for ideas on how to create a map Diagram.

Describe your Diagram topic in the following box.

Diagram Topic:

Plan Your Diagram Information

Your Diagram requires the following elements:

- Geometric Shapes and/or Symbols
- Text Labels

First make a quick sketch of your Diagram. Remember to keep your elements simple and to leave plenty of white space. Once your have determined the overall *look* of your Diagram, complete the following boxes with information on the shapes or symbols and labels required.

> Geometric Shapes:
>
>
> Symbols:

> Text Labels:

Create and Format Your Diagram

Refer to the following selection of commands and functions to help you create your Diagram.

Before you start on your Diagram, jot down a list of the functions you will perform such as create shapes, enter labels, etc. Once you have a clear *plan* in mind, create your Diagram elements and then experiment with different ways of combining, sizing, and positioning them.

Access the Draw Screen   At the Main Menu, press **3** for **Draw.**

Enter Text
1. Click on the **Text Tool.**
2. Position the **+** at the top left corner of where you want your text to appear.
3. Click **left** and draw a box for your text.
4. At the Text Pop-up, type your text and press **F10.**

Change Fonts/Attributes

1. Move your mouse up to the Text Attributes Pop-up at the top of your screen.
2. Click on the attribute you wish to change; for example, font, size, alignment, etc.

> **NOTE:** The Text Attributes Pop-up consists of 3 "pages." To access the other two pages, click on the ▼ symbol at the top right of your screen.

Size Text and Symbols

1. Click on the **Pointer** to select your text or symbol.
2. Click and hold your **left** mouse button on the bottom right handle.
3. Press **Shift** and drag your mouse to the size required.

Position Text and Symbols

1. Position your mouse anywhere on the text/symbol block *except* on one of the orange handles.
2. Click and hold the **left** button to move the block.

Scratchpad

1. Click on the **Scratchpad Tool** to access a blank Draw Screen. You can then experiment with various drawing features before copying and pasting your finished object to your Draw Screen.

Copy and Paste

To copy from the Scratchpad:

1. Click on the **Copy Tool** and then click on the **Scratchpad** to access your Draw Screen.
2. Click on the **Paste Tool.**

Draw Objects

1. Click on the Draw Tool you want (line, curve, oval, polygon, etc.).
2. Change the Attributes of your object (such as line size) in the Attributes Pop-up.
3. Click **left** to start your object and click **right** to end it.

> **NOTE:** To draw a circle, remember to press **Shift** while you drag your mouse. You also press **Shift** if you wish to draw a square with the **Box Tool** or a straight line with the **Line Tool.**

> **NOTE:** Experiment with the Polygon Tools. In the Attributes Pop-up, you can change the line shape from angular to curved to created rounded objects.

Get Symbol
1. Click on the **Symbol Tool** and then click again on **Get.**
2. At the Symbol Directory, press **F8** to sort the files alphabetically, click on the appropriate Directory, click on the symbol you want, and then press **F10** twice to return to your Draw Screen.

Color Fill
1. Click on the area you want to fill.
2. Click on the **Color Tool** and then on the **Fill** box, if it is not already selected. Click on the color you wish to use.

Remember: Light colors print dark and dark colors print light on a black-and-white printer.

Select Several Objects   Method 1:

1. Position your mouse pointer on a point above and to the left of the areas you wish to select.
2. Click and hold **left** to drag a box around the areas.

Method 2:

1. Click on an object you wish to select.
2. Press **Shift** and your **left** mouse button to also select a variety of other objects.

Group/Ungroup
To Group, select two or more objects you wish to group and then click on the **Group Tool.**

To Ungroup, select the object you wish to ungroup and then click on the **Ungroup Tool.**

Flip Tool
1. Select the object to flip and click on the **Flip Tool.**
2. Click on either the **Vertical** or **Horizontal** box.

Duplicate Tool
1. Click on the object you wish to duplicate.
2. Click on the **Duplicate Tool.**
3. Position the duplicated object as required.

Align Tool
Use the **Align Tool** if you want several objects to share the same base point.

1. Select the two or more objects to align.
2. Click on the **Align Tool** and choose the alignment required (bottom, top, center, etc.).

Save
Press **F6** for **File** and then **2** for **Save Chart.** Change to the Directory in which you wish to save your file (usually Drive A or B) and then type a filename for your Diagram.

Fast Save: Press **Ctrl + S** to bypass the Main Menu.

Print   At the Main Menu, choose **5** for **Output**, press **Enter** to accept **Printer 1.**
Press **F2** to display your Diagram *before* sending it to the printer. If you don't
like how your objects appear, press **ESC** and then **3** to return to your Draw
Screen. Once you are satisfied with your Diagram, access the Printer Menu
and press **F10** to send your Diagram to the printer.

Clear Chart   If you wish to start a new Diagram and have saved your current Diagram, first
press **F6** and **E** for **Exit.** Now choose **1** for **Create Chart** and then **8** for
Clear Chart. If you haven't saved your current Diagram, a message will appear. You can then press **ESC** to save your Diagram before clearing it.

Exit Harvard Graphics   Press **F6** and **E** for **Exit to Main Menu** and then **E** again to exit the program.

ACTIVITY 5   LESSON NINE REVIEW

Test your understanding of the functions and concepts you learned in Lesson
Nine by completing the following Review Questions.

1. Describe how to draw a line that is 1.5 points thick.
2. What does Grid Snap to All do?
3. Describe how to Show Ruler.
4. Describe how to draw a curve.
5. How do you select all the objects on your screen?
6. Sketch the Group Tool.
7. Describe how to draw a circle.
8. Why do you use the Shift key to resize objects?
9. What is the purpose of a Process Diagram?
10.   Describe how to draw a triangle.

SUPPLEMENTARY EXERCISES

Exercise 1   Create a Diagram showing the location of a new mall development. You determine the name of the mall and include street names, arrows, and landmark
symbols on your Diagram. Refer to the sample Diagram on page 285 for
ideas.

Exercise 2   Create a Process Diagram showing the steps required to produce a business
report. You determine the number of steps and geometric shapes you wish to
use. Steps include: Researching, Outlining, Obtaining Approval, Writing Draft
1, etc. Designate two positions—the Writer and the Approval Committee—
and identify each position with a different geometric shape. Use arrows to
show how the steps progress.

PRESENTATIONS

Purpose   A presentation displays a series of documents that explain and enhance one basic theme. Text charts, number charts, and pictorial charts are all used to highlight the information presented by a speaker.

To create an effective presentation, you need to become familiar with the following key elements:

- Presentation Methods
- Transition Effects
- Consistent Formats
- Use of Color

Presentation Methods   In Lesson Ten, you will create a computer screen show by displaying all your charts on your computer screen and using the Harvard Graphics transition effects to advance from one chart to the next. Before you learn more about the screen show, however, take a minute to become familiar with the other *presentation methods* you can use to display your documents.

Media	Description
Slide Show	Files are transferred to color slides for projection.
Overheads	Files are made into overhead transparencies for use with an overhead projector.
Projection Pad	Files on a computer screen are transmitted onto an overhead projector for projection onto a large screen.
Screen Show	Files are displayed one after the other on a computer screen using the Harvard Graphics Presentation features.
Flip Charts and Posters	Files are printed and "blown up" for use as flip charts or posters.

In addition to these methods, you can even connect your computer to a VCR and produce computer-generated videos.

The method you choose to display a presentation depends on the equipment you have available and the needs of your audience. For individuals or small groups, a computer screen show can display a presentation quickly and cheaply. Another advantage to using the screen show format is that you can use the transition effects provided by Harvard Graphics.

Transition Effects   A *transition effect* refers to the method used to progress from one screen to the next. For example, you can fade one chart into the next or scroll one chart off the screen while the next chart scrolls onto the screen.

The use of transition effects can enliven a screen show. However, as with all graphics effects, you have to be careful not to include so many transition effect variations in one screen show that your audience starts to feel seasick! In Activity 3 of Lesson Ten, you will use a different transition effect for each of the seven screens in your presentation. These effects are used only to give you an idea of the variations available. For your own presentation, choose only two or three transition effects.

Format   Although a presentation consists of several different types of charts, you will communicate your message most effectively if you use a consistent *format* that links each chart with the one that comes before and the one that follows. Wild variations in format from chart to chart can jar the reader. A consistent format, on the other hand, helps the reader to focus on the *information* in the charts without being distracted by abrupt graphic changes.

You achieve a consistent format by placing one or two elements in the *same location* in every chart. Such elements include a logo, a shaded line, a company name, or a title frame.

Use of Color   When you produce a screen show on a color monitor, you can take advantage of the impact color can have on communicating your message. To use color effectively, you start with a neutral background color such as black (the default setting), blue, or gray and then add accent colors to highlight important information. Be careful not to overload your screen with too many different colors. For example, if you use magenta to highlight a cut pie slice, choose less vibrant colors to fill the other pie slices.

Text colors should contrast strongly with the background color. If you use black as your background color, choose white or yellow for your text colors.

Experiment with different color combinations to achieve the look you want. When you have determined the colors you wish to use, apply them to every chart in your screen show to achieve consistency. For example, if you choose gray as your background color for one chart, you need to ensure that the background of every chart in the screen show is also gray. In Lesson Ten, you will apply the same *palette* to every chart in your screen show.

Section Four Screen Show   In Section Four, you finish your study of Harvard Graphics by creating seven charts and combining them into a Presentation. You can then display your Presentation as a computer screen show complete with a consistent format and interesting transition effects.

<table>
<tr><td>

LESSON TEN

</td><td>

SCREEN SHOW

</td></tr>
</table>

FEATURES
- Using Transition Effects
- Applying Presentation Attributes
- Managing Presentation Files
- Creating Seven Chart Types
- Using Palettes
- Creating a Logo with Evolve

INTRODUCTION

In Lesson Ten, you will combine seven documents into a computer Screen Show. Here are the lesson activities:

ACTIVITY 1: Determine the content of your Screen Show.

ACTIVITY 2: Follow the instructions provided to create the seven documents illustrated on pages 331-337.

ACTIVITY 3: Follow the instructions given to combine the documents into a Presentation and add Transition Effects.

ACTIVITY 4: Create a Screen Show based on your own information.

ACTIVITY 5: Complete the Lesson Review Questions on Presentations and Transition Effects.

ACTIVITY 1   SCREEN SHOW CONTENT

In Activities 2 and 3, you will review many of the features you have learned in *Applying Harvard Graphics* by creating seven charts and then combining them into a Screen Show for the Pacific Artists Association.

John White, the Director of the Pacific Artists Association, plans to use the Screen Show as part of a presentation for his Volunteer Orientation Program. As a nonprofit organization, the Pacific Artists Association depends upon volunteers to help operate the Association's art gallery and organize 15 yearly exhibitions of paintings by community artists.

Screen Show Charts   The following table outlines the type and content of each of the seven charts required for the Screen Show.

Chart Type	Chart Content
Title Chart	Presentation Title: Volunteer Orientation
Bullet Chart 1	Outline of Presentation Content
Organization Chart	Diagram of Association Staff Organization
Pie Chart 1	Breakdown of Association Operating Costs
Pie Chart 2	Exhibition Costs.Link to Pie Chart 1
Bar Chart	Exhibition Attendance over Five Years
Bullet Chart 2	Bullet Chart Summary of Association Goals

In Activity 2, you will enter the data required for each of these charts. In Activity 3, you will create a special background that includes a logo. You can then use the Presentation features to apply both the background you created and consistent text attributes to each of the charts and specify the transition effects required for your Screen Show presentation.

Color Requirements

The Screen Show you produce in Lesson Ten is designed for effective presentation on a color screen. References to color combinations are made throughout Activities 2 and 3 to give you the opportunity to see how color can be used to highlight a presentation. If you are working on a monochrome screen, you may wish to substitute patterns for colors, as you learned in Lesson Four on Pie Charts.

Note that the sample charts printed on the following pages do not appear exactly as they will when displayed on a color monitor. Adjustments have been made to ensure a sharp black-and-white print-out.

ACTIVITY 2   SCREEN SHOW CHARTS

Seven major steps are required to produce the Screen Show Charts:

Step One:	Create the Title Chart
Step Two:	Create Bullet Chart 1
Step Three:	Create the Organization Chart
Step Four:	Create Pie Chart 1
Step Five:	Create Pie Chart 2 and Link to Pie Chart 1
Step Six:	Create the Bar Chart
Step Seven:	Create Bullet Chart 2

Follow the step-by-step instructions to create the seven Screen Show Charts illustrated on pages 331-337.

Note the small triangle logo that appears in the lower left corner of each of these charts. You will create this logo at the beginning of Activity 3 and add it to all the charts at once when you create your Presentation. On a color monitor, this triangle logo will appear multicolored from orange to dark blue.

Note also that *Pacific Artists Association* appears in the lower right corner of Charts 2-7. You will also specify this heading in Activity 3 when you combine your charts into a Presentation.

For Activity 2, you will only enter the required data for each chart. Formatting concerns, such as text size and font, will be applied at the same time to all the charts (except the Title Chart) in Activity 3.

Pacific Artists Association

VOLUNTEER ORIENTATION

Presented By
John White
Director

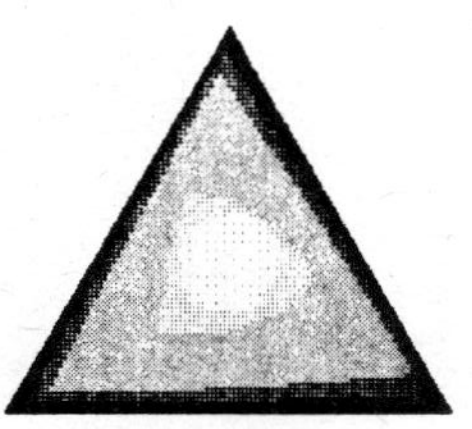

Presentation Outline

▶ Association Organization

▶ Operating Costs

▶ Exhibition Attendance

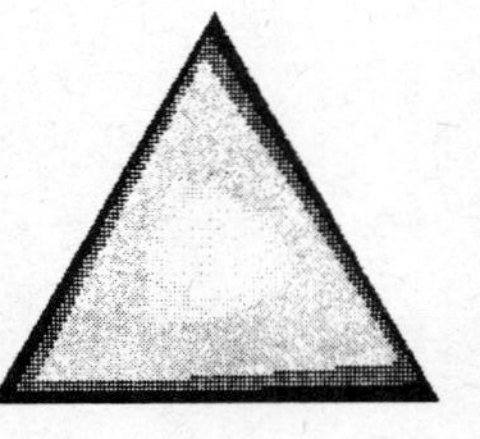

Pacific Artists Association

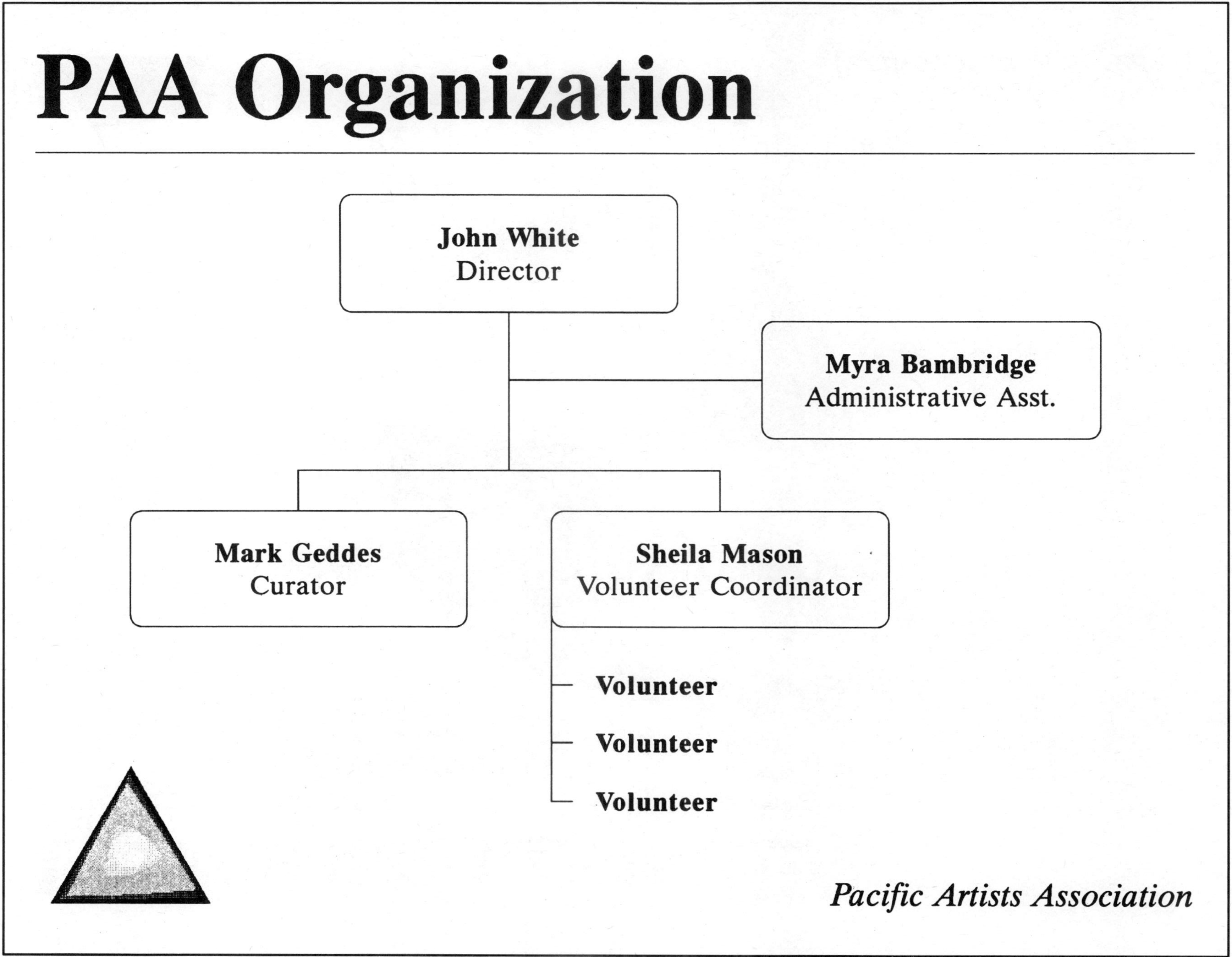

PAA Organization
John White
Director
Myra Bambridge
Administrative Asst.
Mark Geddes
Curator
Sheila Mason
Volunteer Coordinator
Volunteer
Volunteer
Volunteer
Pacific Artists Association

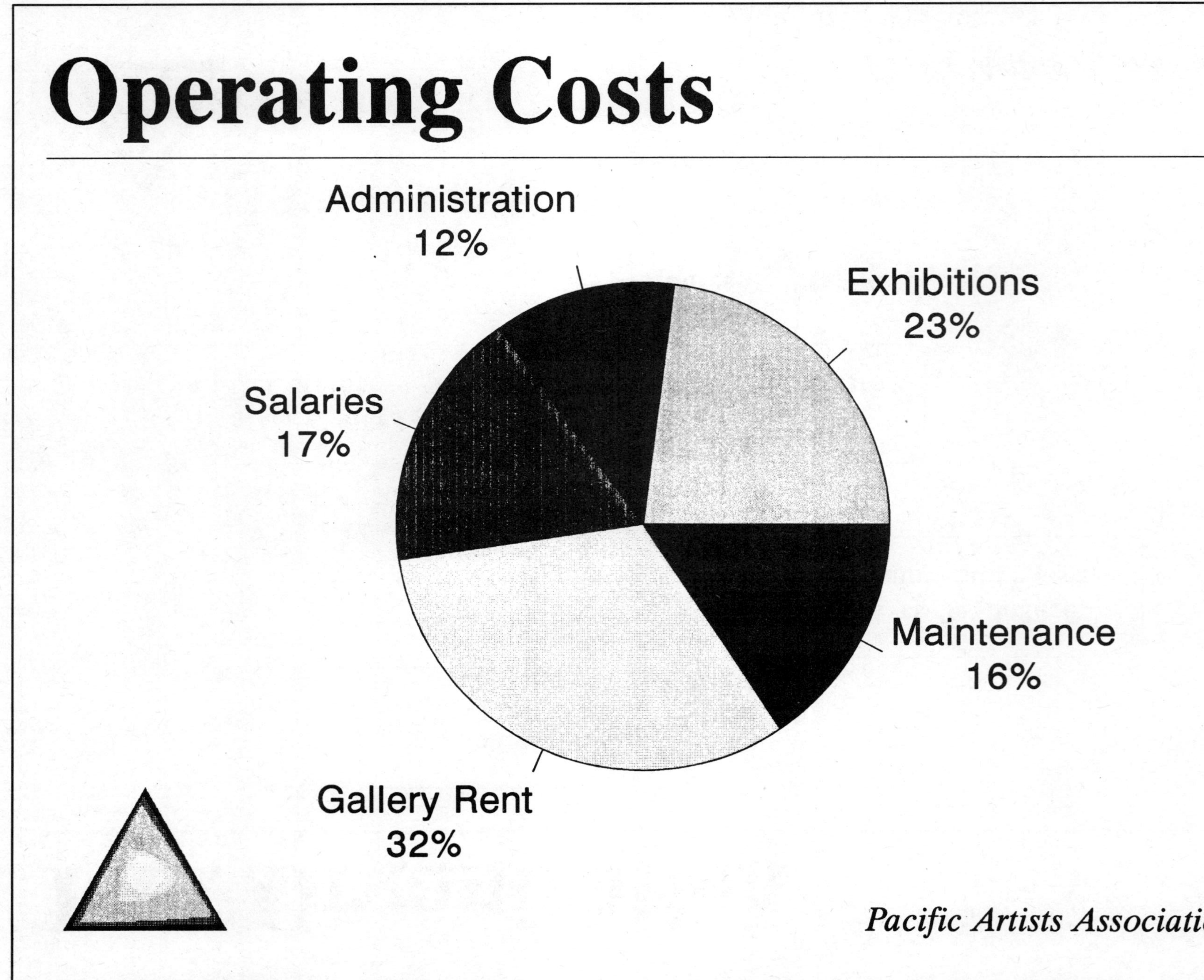

Operating Costs
Administration
12%
Exhibitions
23%
Salaries
17%
Maintenance
16%
Gallery Rent
32%
Pacific Artists Association

Exhibition Costs

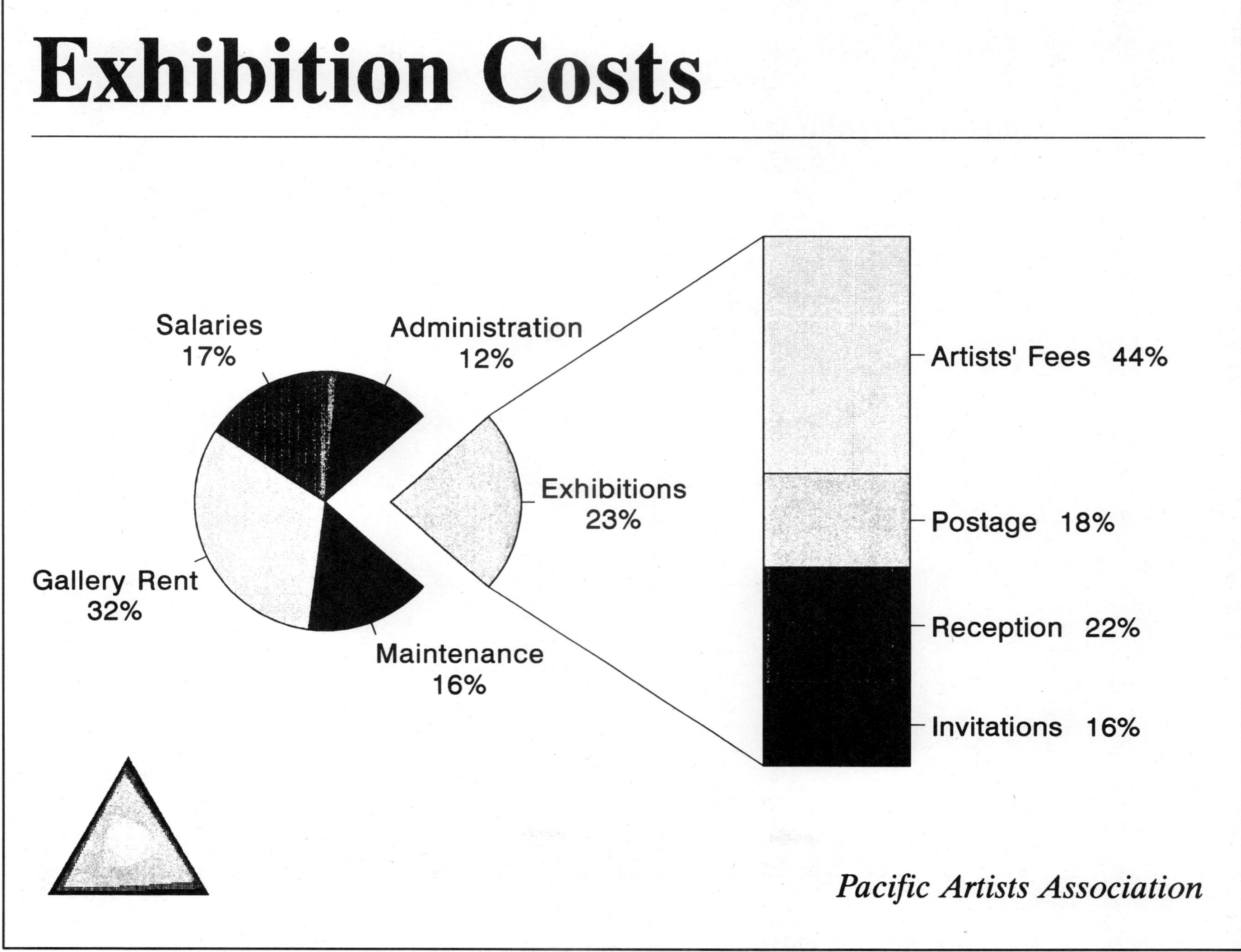

Pacific Artists Association

Exhibition Attendance

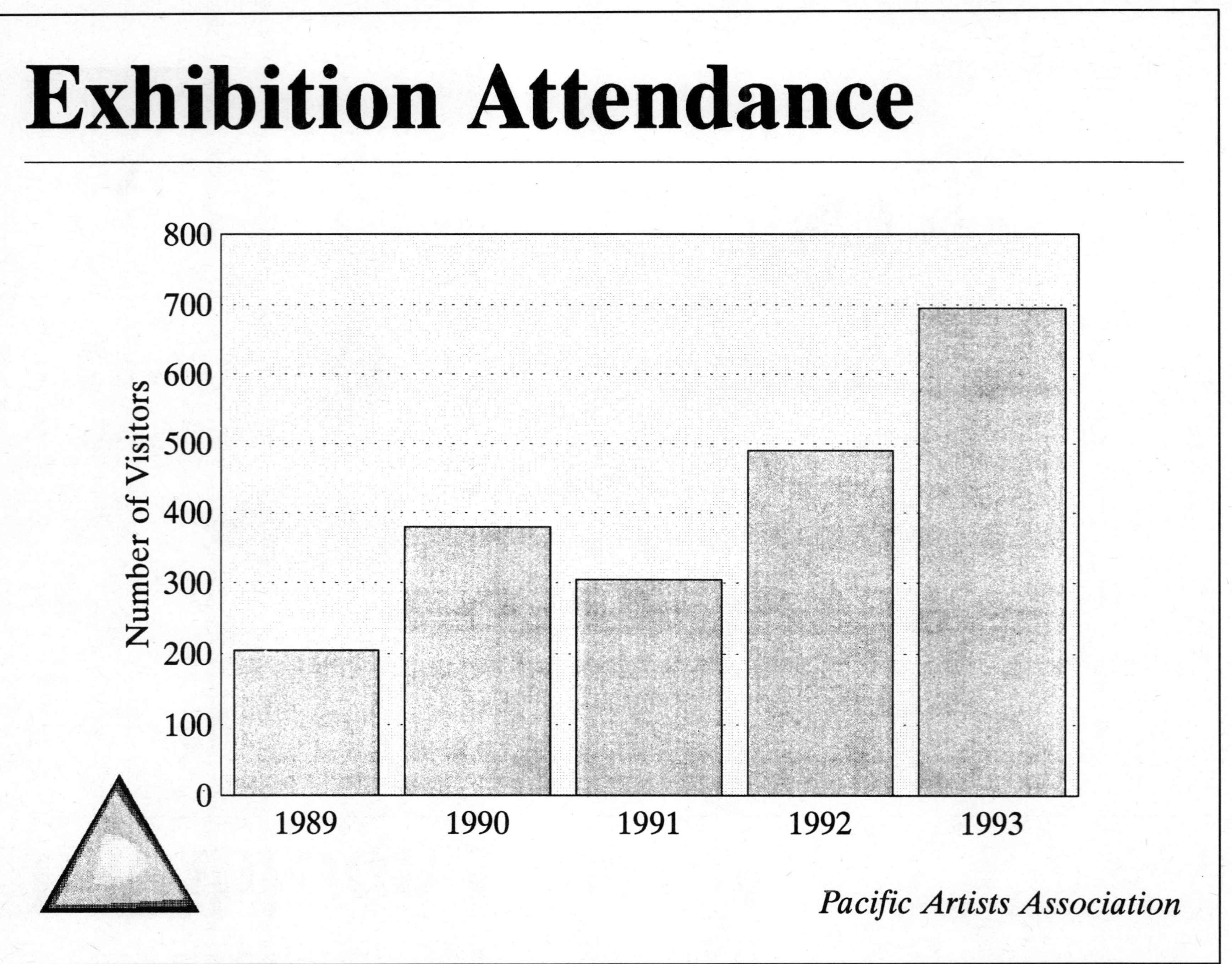

Orientation Summary: Goals

- ▶ Recruit More Volunteers

- ▶ Reduce Exhibition Costs

- ▶ Increase Exhibition Attendance

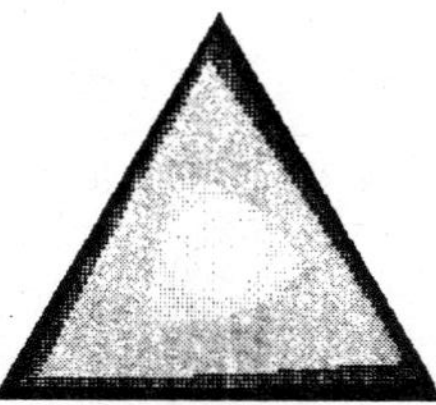

Pacific Artists Association

Create the Title Chart

Create Title Chart
1. At the Main Menu, press **1** for **Create Chart.**
2. Press **1** for **Text Chart.**
3. Press **1** for **Title Chart.**

The Title Chart Data Form appears. Notice that you have three sections: top, middle, and bottom.

Enter Title Data
Type the following information in the areas specified:

Top:	*Pacific Artists Association*
Middle:	*VOLUNTEER* (**Enter**)
	ORIENTATION
Bottom:	*Presented By* (**Enter***)
	John White (**Enter**)
	Director

Your Title Chart Data Form should look like this:

```
SCRTITLE.CH3                        Title Chart
 F1-Help           F2-Show chart                    F4-Draw          F5-Mark
 F6-Main Menu      F7-Spell/Text   F8-Options                        F10-Continue
 ───────────────────────────────── Top ──────────────────────────────────────
 Pacific Artists Association


 ─────────────────────────────── Middle ─────────────────────────────────────
 VOLUNTEER
 ORIENTATION




 ─────────────────────────────── Bottom ─────────────────────────────────────
 Presented By
 John White
 Director
```

Enhance Title Page
You can apply common text attributes such as size, alignment, and font to all the charts in your Screen Show *except* the Title Chart. As a result, you must specify these attributes when you create the Title Chart.

You need to change the font for all the text blocks; the size and alignment of the Top text; and the size, font style, and color of the Middle text.

Top Text
1. Press **F8** for **Options.**
2. Press **1** for **Text Attributes.** Your cursor is positioned in the **Size** column next to **Top.**
3. Type *6* and press **Delete** to erase the *2.*
4. Press **Tab** twice to move to the **Alignment** column.
5. Press **R** for **Right.**
6. Press **Tab** once to move to the **Font Name** column.
7. Press **D** for **Dutch 801.**

8.   Press **Tab** once to move to the **Font Style** column.
9.   Press **I** for **Italics.**

Middle Text

1.   Press **Tab** to position your cursor in the **Size** column next to **Middle.**
2.   Type *12.*
3.   Press **Tab** once to move to the **Color** column.
4.   Press **F3** for **Choices.**
5.   Cursor down to **White Series 6** and press **Enter.**
6.   Press **Tab** twice to move to the **Font Name** column.
7.   Press **D** for **Dutch 801.**
8.   Press **Tab** once to move to the **Font Style** column.
9.   Press **B** for **Bold.**

Bottom Text

1.   Press your ↓ and ← arrows once to position your cursor in the **Font Name** column next to **Bottom.**
2.   Press **D** for **Dutch 801.**

Your Text Attributes Menu should look like this:

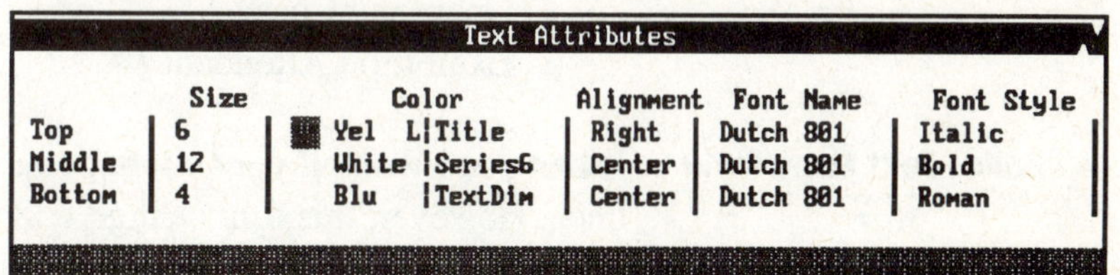

3.   Press **F10** to return to your Chart Edit Screen.

Text Attributes Complete   ☐

Save Title Chart

You will fast-save your Title Chart and answer **Yes** to *Add to Current Presentation.*

1.   Press **Ctrl + S.**
2.   At the Save Chart Menu, type the name of your Directory (usually *a:* or *b:*).
3.   At **Filename,** type *Scrtitle* and press **Enter.**
5.   At **Description,** type *Title Page for Screen Show: Lesson 10* and press **Enter.**
6.   At **Add to Current Presentation,** type **Y** for **Yes.**
7.   Press **F10** to save and return to your Chart Edit Screen.

Title Page Saved   ☐

Clear Chart

1.   Press **F6** for **Main Menu.**
2.   Press **1** for **Create Chart.**
3.   Press **8** for **Clear Chart.**

Go on now to create Bullet Chart 1.

Create Bullet Chart 1

Create Chart

1. At the Main Menu, press **1** for **Create Chart.**
2. Press **1** for **Text Chart.**
3. Press **2** for **Bullet Chart.**

The Bullet Chart Data Form appears.

Enter Title

1. Type the Title of your Bullet Chart: *Presentation Outline.* Press **Enter** three times to move your cursor below the Title/Subtitle line.

A dot representing your first bullet point appears.

Enter Bullet Data

1. Type the following three bullets. Remember to press **Enter** twice after each entry *except* the last entry.

   - Association Organization
   - Operating Costs
   - Exhibition Attendance

Bullet Text Font/Style

When you finish all your charts, you will apply a font to all the chart titles at once. However, this font change will not affect the Bullet Chart text. You need to change the font for your Bullet Chart text as follows:

1. Press **F8** for **Options.**
2. Press **2** for **Text Attributes.**
3. Press your ↓ arrow to move opposite **Bullet Text.**
4. Press **Tab** to move to the **Font Name** column.
5. Press **D** for **Dutch 801.**
6. Press **F10** to return to your Chart Edit Screen.

Bullet Text Font Specified

Change Bullet Options

Now all you need to do is change the bullet type from ● to ▶, the bullet size to large, the bullet color to magenta-red, and the bullet alignment to middle. You make all of these changes in the Bullet Options Menu.

1. Press **F8** for **Options.**
2. Press **5** for **Bullet Options.**

The Bullet Options Menu appears. Your cursor is currently next to **Bullet Type.** Make the following changes:

Bullet Type

1. Press **F3** for **Choices.**
2. Cursor to the ▶ character and press **Enter.**

Bullet Size   1. Press your ↓ arrow once to move opposite **Bullet Size.**
              2. Press **L** for **Large.**

Bullet Color 1. Press your ↓ arrow once to move opposite **Bullet Color.**
              2. Press **F3** for **Choices.**
              3. Cursor down to **Magenta-Red** and press **Enter.**

> **NOTE:** You must choose Magenta-Red **not** Magenta. When you apply
> the new Chart Palette to your Presentation in Activity 3, the
> colors of all your chart elements also change. Throughout Ac-
> tivity 2, the color choices specified are those that will look
> good when used with the new Chart Palette.

Vertical Alignment   You want your Bullet Area to appear centered in the middle of your screen.

1. Press your ↓ arrow to move opposite **Vertical Alignment.**
2. Press **F3** for **Choices.**
3. Cursor to **Middle** and press **Enter.**

Compare your Bullet Options Pop-up to the following illustration:

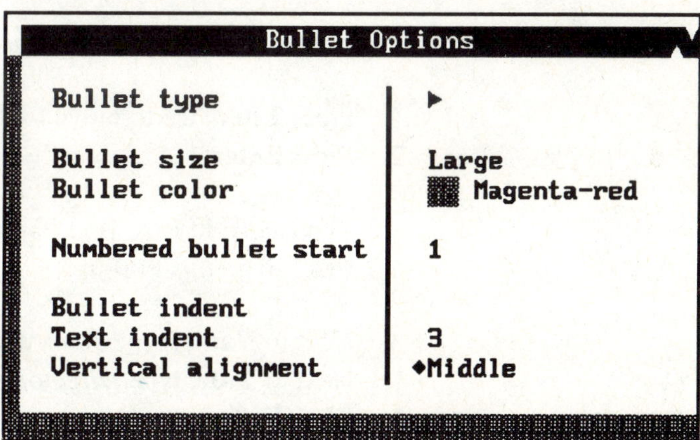

4. Press **F10** to return to your Chart Edit Screen.

Bullet Options Complete

Save Bullet Chart   You will fast-save your Bullet Chart and add it to your Current Presentation.

1. Press **Ctrl + S.**
2. At the Save Chart Menu, type the name of your Directory (usually a:\ or
    b:\), if necessary. If you saved your Title Page on your *a:* or *b:* drive,
    then one of these drives should already appear.
3. At **Filename,** type *Scrbul1* and press **Enter.**

5. At **Description,** type *BulletChart 1 for Screen Show: Lesson 10* and press **Enter.**
6. At **Add to Current Presentation,** type **Y** for **Yes.**
7. Press **F10** to save and return to your Chart Edit **Screen.**

Bullet Chart 1 Saved

Clear Chart
1. Press **F6** for **Main Menu.**
2. Press **1** for **Create Chart.**
3. Press **8** for **Clear Chart.**

Go on now to create the Organization Chart.

Create the Organization Chart

Create Chart
1. At the Main Menu, press **1** for **Create Chart.**
2. Press **4** for **Organization.**

The Organization Chart Data Form appears. You will first enter the Title of your Organization Chart and then create the boxes for the Chart data.

Enter Title
1. Type the Title of your Organization Chart: *Association Organization.* Press **Enter.**

Enter Data in Boxes   Your next step is to type the data required for each of the first three boxes.

Box 1
1. Press **Tab** twice to move to the first box.
2. Press **Enter.**

The Add/Edit Box Text Pop-up appears. You will enter the text for your first box in this Pop-up.

3. Next to **Name,** type *John White* and press **Enter.**
4. Next to **Title,** type *Director* and press **Enter.**
5. Press **F10** to return to your Chart Edit Screen.

Staff Position to Box 1
1. Press **F9** for the **Organization Menu.**
2. Press **3** for **Add Staff Position**.
3. Press your ↓ arrow to move to the new box and press **Enter.**
4. At the Add/Edit Box Text Pop-up, type

   Name: *Myra Bambridge*
   Title: *Administrative Asst.*

5. Press **F10** to return to your Chart Edit Screen.

Box 2
1. Press your ↓ arrow to move to the left box.
2. Press **Enter** to access the Add/Edit Box Text Pop-up.

3. Enter the information for this box as follows:

Name: *Mark Geddes*
Title: *Curator*

4. Press **F10** to return to your Chart Edit Screen.

Box 3   1. Press your arrow to move to the right box.
2. Press **Enter** to access the Add/Edit Box Text Pop-up.
3. Enter the information for this box as follows:

Name: *Sheila Mason*
Title: *Volunteer Coordinator*

4. Press **F10** to return to your Chart Edit Screen.

Add Boxes   You now need to add three boxes below Sheila Mason's box to represent the Volunteers.

To add a box, you first position your cursor on the box *above* where you want the new boxes to appear and then press **Ctrl + Ins.**

1. Your cursor should already be positioned on the right box as illustrated:

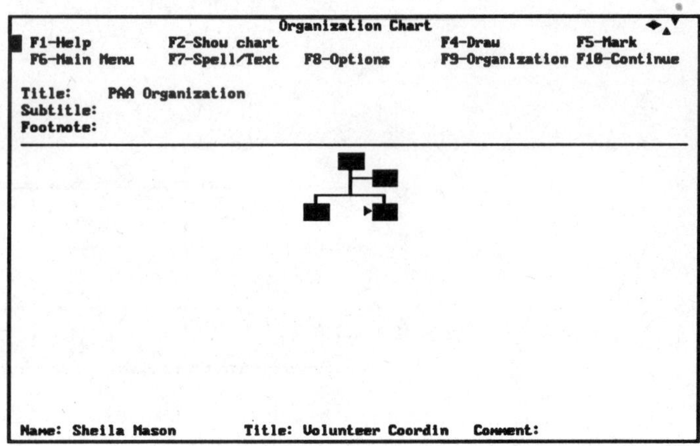

2. Press **Ctrl + Ins**. A new box will appear.
3. Press **Ctrl + Ins** *two* more times.

Your screen should now look like this:

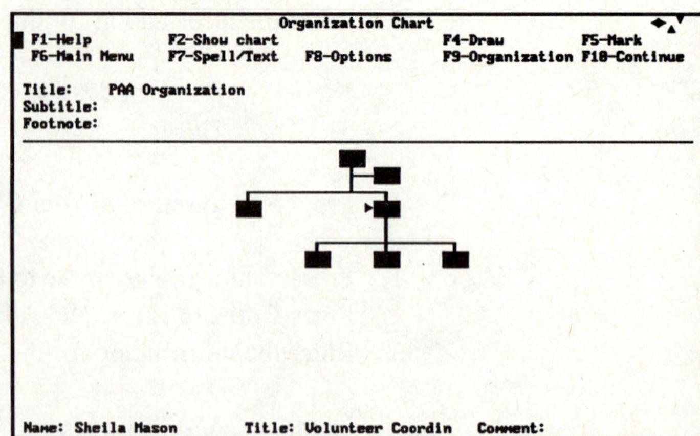

Now enter the word *Volunteer* in each of the three boxes you just created.

1. Position your cursor on the first Volunteer box and press **Enter.**
2. Type *Volunteer* and press **F10** to return to your Chart Edit Screen.

Enter *Volunteer* in each of the remaining two boxes.

Box Data Complete

Box Text Attributes Now change the attributes for the box text as follows:

1. Press **F8** for **Options.**
2. Press **2** for **Text Attributes.**

Make the following changes on the Box Name and Box Title lines:

	Color	Alignment	Font Name	Font Style
Box Name	Yel L Ti	Center	Dutch 801	Bold
Box Title	Yel L Ti	Center	Dutch 801	Roman

3. Press **F10** to return to the Chart Edit Screen.

Box Text Attributes Complete

Box Options Your last step is to change the Box Style to rounded, the Fill color to background, and the line colors to white.

1. Press **F8** for **Options.**
2. Press **5** for **Box Options.**
3. At **Box Style,** press F3 for **Choices** and select **Rounded.**
4. At **Fill Color,** press **B** until **Background** appears.
5. At **Outline Color,** press **W** several times until **White Series 6** appears.
6. At **Line Color,** press **W** several times until **White Series 6** appears.

> **NOTE:** To select a particular color, you can press the first letter of the
> color until the correct selection appears.

Box Options Complete   ☐

Save Organization Chart   Fast-save your Organization Chart and answer **Yes** to *Add to Current Presen-
tation:

1. Press **Ctrl + S.**
2. At the Save Chart Menu, your data drive should already be displayed next
   to Directory.
3. At **Filename**, type *Scrorg* and press **Enter.**
4. At **Description**, type *Org. Chart for Screen Show: Lesson 10* and press
   Enter.
5. At **Add to Current Presentation,** type **Y** for **Yes.**
6. Press **F10** to return to your Chart Edit Screen.

Organization Chart Saved   ☐

Clear Chart
1. Press **F6** for **Main Menu.**
2. Press **1** for **Create Chart.**
3. Press **8** for **Clear Chart.**

Go on now to create Pie Chart 1.

Create Pie Chart 1

Create Chart
1. At the Main Menu, press **1** for **Create Chart.**
2. Press **2** for **Pie.**

Enter Title
1. Type the Title of your Pie Chart *Operating Costs* and press **Enter.**

Enter Slice Data   You need to define each of the five slices of your Pie.

1. Press **Tab** to move your cursor under **Label** next to **Slice 1.**
2. Type *Exhibitions* and press **Enter.**
3. Type *Administration* and press **Enter.**
4. Type *Salaries* and press **Enter.**
5. Type *Gallery Rent* and press **Enter.**
6. Type *Maintenance.*
7. Press **Tab** and your ↑ arrow to move to the **Value** column opposite *Exhibitions.*
8. Type *25* and press **Enter.**
9. Type *13* and press **Enter.**
10. Type *19* and press **Enter.**

11. Type *35* and press **Enter.**
12. Type *17.*

Slice Data Entered

Specify Slice Colors

When you apply a new Chart Palette to your charts in Activity 3, the current slice colors will appear too pale. Change the colors for each slice as follows:

1. Press your ↑ arrow and **Tab** to move to the **Color** column opposite *Exhibitions.*
2. Specify the following colors for each slice:

Exhibitions:	Press **M** until **Magenta-Red** appears.
Administration:	Press **B** until **Blue-Gray** appears.
Salaries:	Press **O** until **Orange** appears.
Gallery Rent:	Press **P** until **Purple** appears.
Maintenance:	Press **Y** until **Yellow-Green** appears.

Your Chart Edit Screen should look like this:

```
                              Pie Chart 1                                  ▲
  F1-Help         F2-Show chart  F3-Choices      F4-Draw        F5-Mark
  F6-Main Menu    F7-Spell/Text  F8-Options      F9-Pie data    F10-Continue

  Title:       Operating Costs
  Subtitle:
  Footnote:
  Pie title:


  Slice        Label            Value     Cut        Color      Pattern

   1     Exhibitions            25        No      █ Magenta-       0
   2     Administration         13        No      █ Blue-gra       1
   3     Salaries               19        No      █ Orange         2
   4     Gallery Rent           35        No      █ Purple         3
   5     Maintenance            17        No      █ Yellow-g       4
   6                                      No        White  |S      5
   7                                      No      █ Cyn   D|S      6
   8                                      No      █ Blu   D|S      7
   9                                      No      █ Cyn   D|S      8
  10                                      No      █ Cyn    |S      9
  11                                      No      █ Yel LL|S      10
  12                                      No        White  |S      11
```

Slice Colors Complete

Label Attributes

You need to specify Light Yellow as the Color and Dutch 801 as the Font for the Labels.

1. Press **F8** for **Options.**
2. Press **2** for **Text Attributes** and **2** for **Labels.**
3. In the **Color** column, press **F3** and choose **Yel L/Y2 Label.**
4. In the **Font Name** column, press **D** for **Dutch 801.**
5. Press **F10** to return to the Chart Edit Screen.

Label Attributes Complete

Show Data as Percents

You want to display your Slice Values as percentages of 100. To do this, you first access Slice Values in the F8 Options Menu and then Show Percents.

Slice Values

1. Press **F8** for **Options.**
2. Press **8** for **Slice Values.**
3. At the Slice Values Menu, press **N** for **No** next to **Show Values.**
4. Press **F10** to return to your Chart Edit Screen.

Show Percents

1. Press **F8** for **Options** and then press **9** for **Slice Percents.**
2. Press **Y** for **Yes** next to **Show Percents.**
3. Press **F10** to return to your Chart Edit Screen.

Percent Data Complete ☐

Save Pie Chart 1

Fast-save Pie Chart 1 and answer **Yes** to *Add to Current Presentation.*

1. Press **Ctrl + S.**
2. At the Save Chart Menu, your data drive should already be displayed next to **Directory.**
3. At **Filename**, type *Scrpie1* and press **Enter.**
4. At **Description**, type *Pie Chart 1 for Screen Show: Lesson 10* and press **Enter.**
5. At **Add to Current Presentation,** type **Y** for **Yes.**
6. Press **F10** to save and return to your Chart Edit Screen.

Pie Chart 1 Saved ☐

Keep your Pie Chart 1 Chart Edit Screen and go on to create Pie Chart 2.

Create Pie Chart 2

Pie Chart 2 will break the Exhibitions slice into four segments to show how exhibition costs break down. You will display this data as a column that is *linked* to your first Pie Chart.

Link Pie Charts 1 and 2

1. Press **F8** for **Options.**
2. Press **5** for **Style.**
3. Press your ↓ arrow to move opposite **Link Pies 1 & 2.**
4. Press **Y** for **Yes.**
5. Press **F10** to return to your Pie Chart Edit Screen.

Cut Exhibition Slice

1. Position your cursor in the **Cut** column opposite **Exhibitions.**
2. Press **Y** for **Yes.**

Enter Pie Chart 2 Data

1. Press **F9** for **Pie Data.**
2. Press **2** for **Pie 2 Data.**

A blank Pie Edit Screen appears. "Pie Chart 2" is displayed at the top of the screen. Change the Title of Pie Chart 2 first and then enter the Chart data.

Title   1. Position your cursor on the "O" in **Operating** and press **Ctrl + Del.**
    2. Type *Exhibition Costs.*

Labels   1. Press **Enter** until your cursor is positioned in the **Label** column next to Slice 1.

Enter the Slice Labels, Values, and Colors as follows:

Label	Value	Color
Invitations	14	Blue–Gray
Reception	20	Orange
Postage	16	Magenta–Red
Artists' Fees	40	Purple

Compare your screen to the following illustration:

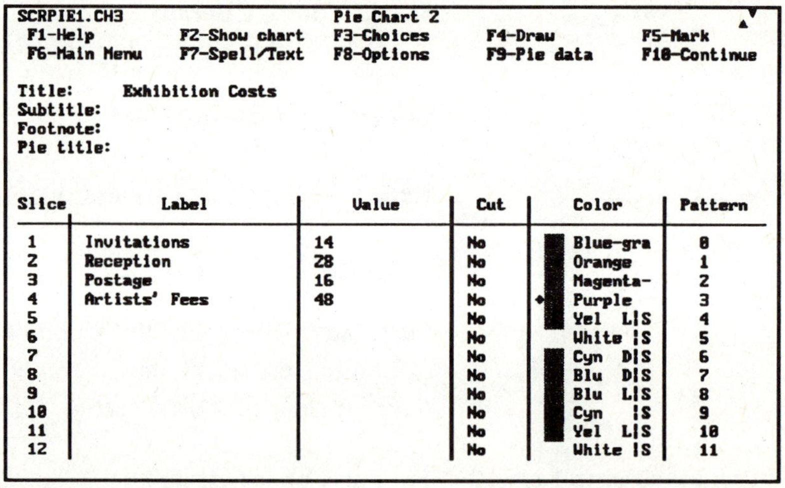

```
SCRPIE1.CH3                        Pie Chart 2                                   ▲
  F1-Help            F2-Show chart  F3-Choices      F4-Draw         F5-Mark
  F6-Main Menu       F7-Spell/Text  F8-Options      F9-Pie data     F10-Continue

  Title:        Exhibition Costs
  Subtitle:
  Footnote:
  Pie title:


  Slice          Label            Value      Cut        Color       Pattern

   1      Invitations            14         No        █ Blue-gra    0
   2      Reception              20         No          Orange      1
   3      Postage                16         No          Magenta-    2
   4      Artists' Fees          40         No  ◆     █ Purple      3
   5                                        No          Yel  L|S    4
   6                                        No          White |S    5
   7                                        No          Cyn  D|S    6
   8                                        No        █ Blu  D|S    7
   9                                        No          Blu  L|S    8
  10                                        No          Cyn   |S    9
  11                                        No        █ Yel  L|S    10
  12                                        No          White |S    11
```

Pie 2 Data Complete   ☐

You now need to change the label text size, display Pie Chart 2 as a column, and show the values as percents.

Change Label Text Size   1. Press **F8** for **Options.**
    2. Press **2** for **Text Attributes** and then press **2** for **Labels.**
    3. Type *3* in the **Size** column next to both **Pie 1 Labels** and **Pie 2 Labels.**
    4. Press **F10** to return to your Pie 2 Edit Screen.

Label Size Specified   ☐

Show Pie 2 as a Column   1. Press **F8** for **Options.**
    2. Press **6** for **Pie Options.**

3. Position your cursor opposite **Show As.**
4. Press **F3** for **Choices.**
5. Cursor to **Column** and press **Enter.**
6. Press **F10** to return to your Pie 2 Edit Screen.

Column Format Specified   ☐

Show Percents
1. Press **F8** for **Options.**
2. Press **8** for **Slice Values.**
3. At the Slice Values Menu, your cursor is positioned opposite **Show Values.** Press **N** for **No.**
4. Press **F10** to return to your Pie 2 Edit Screen.
5. Press **F8** for **Options** and then press **9** for **Slice Percents.**
6. Press **Y** for **Yes** next to **Show Percents.**
7. Press your ↓ arrow to move opposite **Place Percents.**
8. Type **A** for **Adjacent.**
9. Press **F10** to return to your Pie 2 Edit Screen.

Percent Data Complete   ☐

Save Pie Chart 2
1. Fast-save Pie Chart 2 (**Ctrl + S**) and name it *Scrpie2*. Make sure you answer **Yes** at **Add to Current Presentation.**
2. Press **F10** to save and return to your Chart Edit Screen.

Pie Chart 2 Saved   ☐

Clear Chart
1. Press **F6** for **Main Menu.**
2. Press **1** for **Create Chart.**
3. Press **8** for **Clear Chart.**

Go on now to create the Bar Chart.

Create the Bar Chart

Create Chart
1. At the Main Menu, press **1** for **Create Chart.**
2. Press **3** for **XY Chart.**
3. Press **1** for **Bar.**

The X Data Type Pop-up appears. Your cursor is positioned next to **Name**.

1. Press **F3** for **Choices.**
2. Cursor to **Year** and press **Enter.**
3. Press your ↓ arrow to move opposite **Starting With.**
4. Type *1989* and press **Enter.**
5. At **Ending With**, type *1993.*
6. Press **F10** to exit the X Data Pop-up.

Enter Bar Chart Title
1. Type the Title of your Bar Chart: *Exhibition Attendance.* Press **Enter.**

Enter Series Data

Your next step is to enter the attendance figures for each of the five years listed in the X Axis Year column.

1. Position your cursor in the **Series 1** column opposite **1989.**
2. Type *205* and press **Enter.**
3. Fill in the rest of the series information:

1990:	380	1992:	490
1991:	305	1993:	695

Series Data Complete ☐

Label Attributes

1. Press **F8** for **Options.**
2. Press **2** for **Text Attributes** and **2** for **Labels.**
3. Specify **Dutch 801** as the **Font Name** for the X-Axis and the Y1-Axis Labels.
4. Press **F10** to return to your Chart Edit Screen.

Label Attributes Complete ☐

Series Color

Specify magenta-red as the color of each bar displayed in your Bar Chart.

1. Press **F8** for **Options.**
2. Press **6** for **Series.**
3. Press your ↓ arrow to move opposite **Fill Color.**
4. Press **M** until **Magenta-Red** appears.
5. Press **F10** to return to your Chart Edit Screen.

Series Color Defined ☐

Hide Legend

1. Press **F8** for **Options.**
2. Press **7** for **Legend.** Your cursor is opposite **Show Legend.**
3. Press **N** for **No.**
4. Press **F10** to return to your Chart Edit Screen.

Legend Hidden ☐

Y1-Axis Title

1. Press **F8** for **Options.**
2. Press **1** for **Titles/Footnotes.**
3. Press your ↓ arrow to position your cursor opposite **Y1 Axis Title.**
4. Type *Number of Visitors.*
5. Press **F10** to return to your Chart Edit Screen.

Y1-Axis Attributes

1. Press **F8** for **Options.**
2. Press **2** for **Text Attributes** and **1** for **Titles/Footnotes.**

3. Press your ↓ arrow and **Tab** to position your cursor in the **Alignment** column opposite **Y1 Axis Title.**
4. Press **S** for **Side Alignment.**
5. Press **Tab** to move to the **Font Name** column and press **D** for **Dutch 801.**
6. Press **F10** to return to your Chart Edit Screen.

Y1 Axis Enhanced   ☐

Save Bar Chart
1. Fast-save your Bar Chart (**Ctrl + S**) and name it Scrbar. Make sure you answer **Yes** to **Add to Current Presentation**.
2. Press **F10** to save and return to your Chart Edit Screen.

Bar Chart Saved   ☐

Clear Chart
1. Press **F6** for **Main Menu.**
2. Press **1** for **Create Chart.**
3. Press **8** for **Clear Chart.**

Create Bullet Chart 2

Your last chart will function as the Presentation's concluding chart summarizing the goals of the Pacific Artists Association.

Create Chart
1. At the Main Menu, press **1** for **Create Chart.**
2. Press **1** for **Text Chart.**
3. Press **2** for **Bullet Chart.**

The Bullet Chart Data Form appears.

Enter Title
1. Type the Title of your Bullet Chart: *Orientation Summary: Goals.* Press **Enter** three times to move your cursor below the Title/Subtitle line.

A dot representing your first bullet point appears.

Enter Bullet Data
1. Type the following three bullets. Remember to press **Enter** twice after each entry *except* the last entry.

- Recruit More Volunteers
- Reduce Exhibition Costs
- Increase Exhibition Attendance

Bullet Data Complete   ☐

Bullet Text Font/Style
Now change the font for your Bullet Chart text as follows:

1. Press **F8** for **Options.**
2. Press **2** for **Text Attributes.**
3. Press your ↓ arrow to move opposite **Bullet Text.**

4. Press **Tab** to move to the **Font Name** column.
5. Press **D** for **Dutch 801**.
6. Press **F10** to return to your Chart Edit Screen.

Bullet Text Font Specified   ☐

Change Bullet Options   Now all you need to do is change the bullet type from ● to ▶, the bullet size to large, the bullet color to magenta-red, and the bullet alignment to middle. You make all of these changes in the Bullet Options Menu.

1. Press **F8** for **Options**.
2. Press **5** for **Bullet Options**.

The Bullet Options Menu appears. Your cursor is currently next to **Type**. Make the following changes.

Bullet Type
1. Press **F3** for **Choices**.
2. Cursor to the ▶ character and press **Enter**.

Bullet Size
1. Press your ↓ arrow once to move opposite **Bullet Size**.
2. Press **L** for **Large**.

Bullet Color
1. Press your ↓ arrow once to move opposite **Bullet Color**.
2. Press **M** until **Magenta-Red** appears.

Vertical Alignment   You want your Bullet Area to appear centered in the middle of your screen.

1. Press your ↓ arrow to move opposite **Vertical Alignment**.
2. Press **M** for **Middle**.
3. Press **F10** to return to your Chart Edit Screen.

Bullet Options Complete   ☐

Save Bullet Chart
1. Fast-save your Bullet Chart as *Scrbul2* and answer **Yes** to **Add to Current Presentation**.
2. Press **F10** to save and return to your Chart Edit Screen.

Bullet Chart 2 Saved   ☐

Now you can save the seven charts as a Presentation and then go on to Activity 3. There, you will create a Chart background and then access the Presentation Menu to apply presentation attributes, appearance options, and transition effects.

Save Presentation
1. Press **F6** for **Main Menu** and then **6** for **Presentation**.
2. Press **5** for **Save Presentation**.

3. At the Save Presentation Menu, your data drive should already be displayed next to **Directory.**
4. At **Filename**, type *Scrpres* and press **Enter.**
5. At **Description**, type *Screen Show for Lesson 10.*
6. Press **F10** to save and return to your Main **Menu.**

Presentation Saved

Now go on to Activity 3 to create a logo and enhance your Presentation.

ACTIVITY 3 ## SCREEN SHOW PRODUCTION

Four major steps are required to produce your Screen Show:

Step One: Create a Presentation Background
Step Two: Apply Presentation Attributes
Step Three: Add Transition Effects
Step Four: Display Your Screen Show

Create a Presentation Background

A consistent background can be achieved by choosing a particular Chart Palette, including a consistent symbol, or creating a logo that appears in the same position on every chart.

For the charts you developed in Activity 2, you will create a logo that will appear in the bottom left corner of every chart and specify a new Chart Palette.

The triangle logo appearing on the Screen Show charts illustrated on pages 331-337 was created with the Evolve feature. You will first enter the Draw Screen, specify a new Palette, and then draw two shapes and apply the Evolve Tool.

You need to specify the same Palette for your background as you will apply to all the Charts in your Presentation so that you can determine how the colors of your logo will appear.

Access Draw Screen   1. Press **3** for **Draw.**

The following functions require the use of the mouse. Remember to click the **left** button to perform functions and the **right** button to finish functions. If you click the right button twice, you may return to the Main Menu. If this happens, just press or click on **3** for **Draw** to return to your Draw Screen.

Specify a Chart Palette   1. Press **F8** for **Options** and **8** for **Appearance.**

2. Position your cursor opposite **Chart Palette** and press **F3** for **Choices.** The list of Palette Directories appears.
3. Cursor down to **1HDW.PL3** and press **Enter.**
4. Press **F10** to return to the Draw Screen.

Notice that your Draw Screen background now appears dark blue rather than black.

Draw a Triangle

1. Click on the **Regular Polygon Tool.**
2. In the Number of Sides box, *3* should already be entered. If a different number appears, click on the *Number of Sides* box and type *3*.
3. Click **left** to start the triangle.
4. Move your mouse out to increase the triangle size.
5. Click **right** to end.

Compare your triangle size to the following illustration:

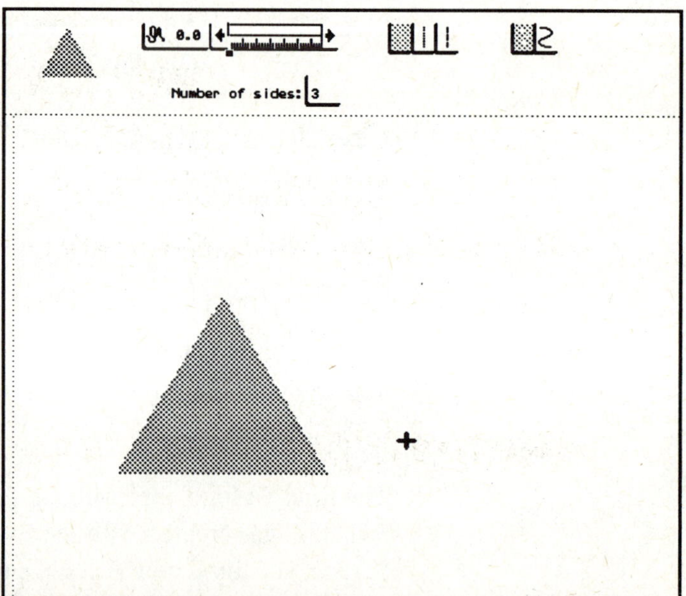

Triangle Color

1. Click on the **Pointer** to select your triangle.
2. Click on the **Color Tool.** The **Fill** box is currently highlighted.
3. Click on an **Orange** box to change the Fill Color.
4. Click on the **Line/Text** box and click on **None.**
5. Click **right** twice to exit the Color Pop-up and remove the handles from around the triangle.

Triangle Complete

Draw Octagon   Now draw your octagon:

1. Click on the **Regular Polygon Tool** again.
2. Click on the **Number of Sides** box, type *8*, and press **Enter.**

You need to change the color of your octagon *before* you draw it on top of the triangle. Otherwise, you will not be able to see the octagon against the background of the triangle.

1. Click on the **Color Tool.** The **Fill** box should be highlighted.
2. Click on a **Bright Blue** box to change the Fill Color.
3. Click **right** twice to exit the Color Pop-up.
4. Click again on the **Regular Polygon Tool.**

Now you can draw your octagon:

1. Position your mouse in the middle of the triangle and click **left** to draw a small octagon.
2. Once you have drawn the octagon, click on the **Pointer** and make any positioning or sizing adjustments necessary.

Your screen should look like this:

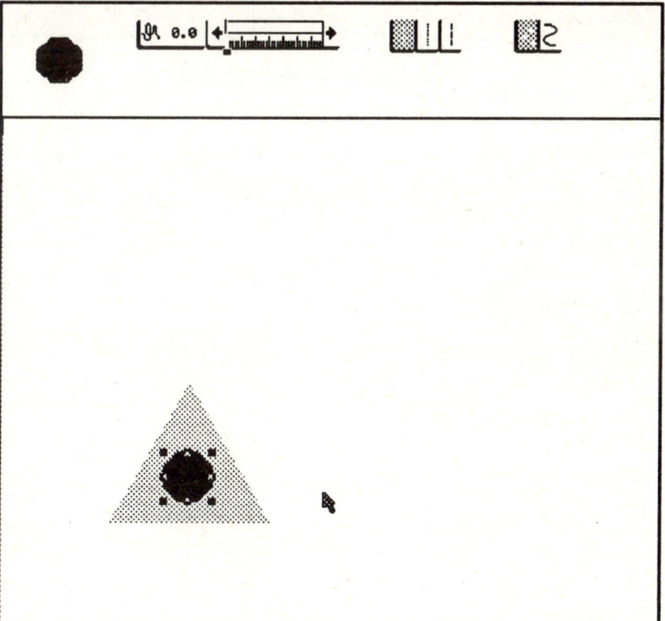

Octagon Complete

Evolve Objects   Now you are ready to apply the Evolve Tool to achieve a very interesting and colorful effect.

1. Your octagon should still be selected. If not, click **left** to select it.
2. Move your mouse to the triangle and press **Shift** and your **left** mouse button to select it. Handles now appear around both the triangle and octagon.
3. Click on the ▼ symbol at the bottom of the Tool Box to view the second level of tools.
4. Click on the **Evolve Tool.**
5. Click again on the **Reverse** box.

Your screen now appears as illustrated:

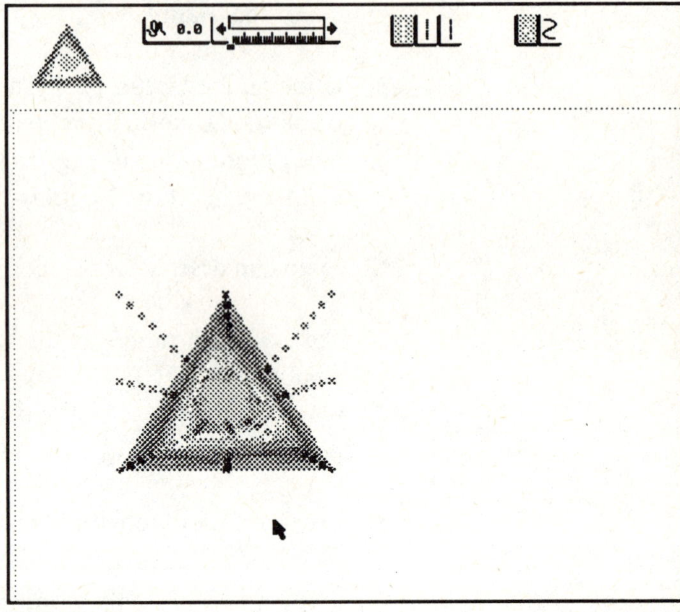

Objects Evolved

Group Objects   1. Click on the **Group Tool** to group the ten elements of your evolved object into one object.
2. Use **Shift** to reduce the triangle's size and then reposition it in the bottom left corner of your screen as illustrated:

Logo Sized and Positioned

Save Background   Your new Chart background is now complete. Press **Ctrl + S** to save your
background and name it *Scrback*. Clear your Drawing and go on now to Apply Presentation Attributes.

Background Saved   ☐

Apply Presentation Attributes

First, retrieve your Presentation and access the Presentation Edit Screen:

Get Presentation   1.   At the Main Menu, press **6** for **Presentation.**

The Presentation Menu appears. If you exited out of Harvard Graphics after
completing Activity 2, get your Presentation as follows:

1.   Press **1** for **Get Presentation.**
2.   Change your Directory to your data drive (*a:* or *b:*) and press **Enter.**
3.   Select *Scrpres* and press **Enter.**
4.   Press **2** for **Edit Presentation.**

If you have *not* exited out of Harvard Graphics, press **2** for **Edit Presentation.**

The Presentation Edit Screen appears. In this screen, you will apply Text Attributes and a Chart Palette and then go on to add Transition Effects.

```
 SCRPRES.SH3                       Edit Presentation
  F1-Help              F2-Preview                    F4-Effects      F5-Mark block
  F6-Main Menu         F7-Add/Edit      F8-Options    F9-HyperShow   F10-Continue

   #      Filename       Type              Description/Directory

 ▶                      DRAW     Background drawing for presentation

   1    SCRTITLE.CH3 TITLE     Title Page for Screen Show: Lesson 10
   2    SCRBUL1 .CH3 BULLET    Bullet Chart for Screen Show: Lesson 10
   3    SCRORG  .CH3 ORG       Org. Chart for Screen Show: Lesson 10
   4    SCRPIE1 .CH3 PIE       Pie Chart 1 for Screen Show: Lesson 10
   5    SCRPIE2 .CH3 PIE       Pie Chart 1 for Screen Show: Lesson 10
   6    SCRBAR  .CH3 XY        Bar Chart for Screen Show: Lesson 10
   7    SCRBUL2 .CH3 BULLET    Bullet Chart 2 for Screen Show Lesson 10
   8
   9
  10
  11
  12
  13
  14
  15
  16
```

Text Attributes   You want each of the charts in your Screen Show to display your logo and use
the same text size, alignment, and font for the Chart Titles. You also want to
display *Pacific Artists Association* in the lower right corner of Charts 2-7.

Harvard Graphics allows you to apply the same Text Attributes to each Chart
except a Title Chart in your Presentation. This feature saves a great deal of
time because you only have to change the Attributes once in the Presentation
Edit screen rather than for each chart individually.

Start with the Footnote.

Enter Footnote

1. Press **F8** for **Options.**
2. Press **1** for **Presentation Titles/Footnotes.** Your cursor appears opposite **Use Presentation Titles.**
3. Press your ↓ arrow twice to position your cursor opposite **Use Presentation Footnotes.**
4. Type **Y** for **Yes.**
5. Press **Tab** to position your cursor opposite **Footnote 1.**
6. Type *Pacific Artists Association.*
7. Press **F10** to return to your Presentation Edit **Screen.**

Footnote Entered   ☐

Presentation Text Attributes

1. Press **F8** for **Options.**
2. Press **2** for **Presentation Text Attributes.**

The Presentation Text Attributes Screen appears. You first need to specify that you want to use Presentation Attributes for your Title and Footnote.

1. Press **Y** for **Yes** next to **Use Presentation Title Attributes.**
2. Press your ↓ arrow twice to move opposite **Use Presentation Footnote Attributes.**
3. Press **Y** for **Yes.**
4. Now specify the Title and Footnote Attributes as follows:

	Size	Color	Alignment	Font Name	Font Style
Title	10	White Series 6	Left	Dutch 801	Bold
Footnote	3.5	no change	Right	Dutch 801	Italic

Your Presentation Text Attributes Screen should look like this:

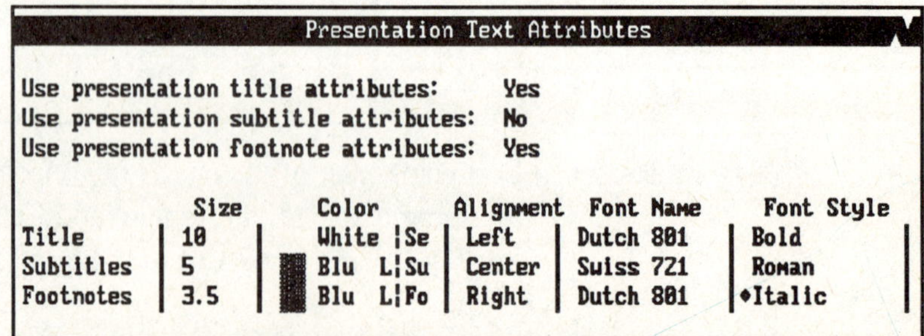

5. Press **F10** to return to your Presentation Edit Screen.

Presentation Text Attributes Complete   ☐

Presentation Appearance   Your last step is to specify a palette for all your charts and retrieve the Chart background you created earlier. When you create your own Screen Show, you may want to experiment with some of the palettes to see how they affect the look of your charts.

Select Palette

1. Press **F8** for **Options.**
2. Press **3** for **Presentation Appearance.**
3. Press **Y** for **Yes** next to **Use Presentation Chart Palette.**
4. Press your ↓ arrow to position your cursor opposite **Presentation Chart Palette.**
5. Press **F3** for **Choices.**
6. Press your ↓ arrow until you see **1HDW.PL3**.
7. Press **Enter** to select this palette.

Select Background

1. Move your cursor opposite **Use Presentation Background Drawing.**
2. Press **Y** for **Yes.**
3. Press your ↓ arrow to position your cursor opposite **Presentation Background Drawing.**
4. Press **F3** for **Choices.**
5. The list of files on your data disk should appear. If necessary, specify your data drive.
6. Cursor to **Scrback** and press **Enter.**

Your Presentation Appearance Menu should like this:

```
┌───────────────── Presentation Appearance ─────────────────┐
│                                                           │
│ Use presentation chart palette:        Yes                │
│ Presentation chart palette:            C:\HG3\PALETTE\1HDW.PL3  │
│                                                           │
│ Use presentation background drawing:   Yes                │
│ Presentation background drawing:       ◆a:\scrback.ch3    │
│                                                           │
└───────────────────────────────────────────────────────────┘
```

7. Press **F10** to return to your Presentation Edit Screen.

Presentation Appearance Enhanced   ☐

Display Chart ▶   Press **F2** to start your Screen Show. To move from one Chart to the next, press any key. To exit from the Screen Show, press **ESC.**

Edit Charts   Make sure your Charts appear as illustrated on pages 331-337. If you wish to change a Chart, press **ESC** to exit the Screen Show and then proceed as follows:

1. Highlight the Chart you wish to change.
2. Press **Ctrl + E** to access the Chart's edit screen.
3. Make the changes required.

4. Fast-save the Chart with **Ctrl + S** and answer **No** to **Add to Current Presentation.**
5. You can then return to your Presentation Edit Screen by pressing **6** at the Main Menu and **2** for **Edit Presentation.**

Add Transition Effects

Now you can determine *how* your charts will be displayed in your Screen Show. Start with the Transition Effects for your Title Chart first.

1. Press your ↑ arrow to highlight **Scrtitle.**
2. Press **F4** for **Effects.**

The Effects Screen appears. In this screen you will specify the transition type in the Draw column, the transition direction in the Arrow column, and the transition speed in the Speed column.

Draw Type
1. Your cursor currently appears in the **Draw** column next to **Scrtitle.**
2. Press **F3** for **Choices.**
3. Cursor to **Scroll** and press **Enter.**

Direction
1. Press **Tab** to move to the **Arrow** column.
2. Press **F3** for **Choices.**
3. Cursor to **Down** and press **Enter.**

Speed
1. Press **Tab** to move to the **Speed** column.
2. Press **F3** for **Choices.**
3. Cursor to **Slow** and press **Enter.**

Now press your ↓ and ← arrows to position your cursor in the **Draw** column next to **Scrbul1**. Go on to enter the effects required for each chart as specified in the following table.

File	Draw	Direction	Speed
Scrbul1	Fade	In	Slow
Scrorg	Open	Out	Slow
Scrpie1	Blinds	Up	Slow
Scrpie2	Wipe	Right	Slow
Scrbar	Iris	In	Slow
Scrbul2	Close	Out	Slow

Your Presentation Edit Screen should look like this:

```
SCRPRES.SH3                      Edit Presentation
 F1-Help            F2-Preview       F3-Choices      F4-Descriptions F5-Mark block
 F6-Main Menu       F7-Add/Edit      F8-Options      F9-HyperShow       F10-Continue

  #  |   Filename   |   Draw   | +↑↓+ | Speed |Time| Erase | +↑↓+ | Speed
     | SCRBACK .CH3 | Replace  |      |       |    |       |      |
 1   | SCRTITLE.CH3 | Scroll   | Down | Slow  |    |       |      |
 2   | SCRBUL1 .CH3 | Fade     | In   | Slow  |    |       |      |
 3   | SCRORG  .CH3 | Open     | Out  | Slow  |    |       |      |
 4   | SCRPIE1 .CH3 | Blinds   | Up   | Slow  |    |       |      |
 5   | SCRPIE2 .CH3 | Wipe     | Right| Slow  |    |       |      |
 6   | SCRBAR  .CH3 | Iris     | In   | Slow  |    |       |      |
►7   | SCRBUL2 .CH3 | Close    | Out  | ◆Slow |    |       |      |
 8
 9
10
11
12
13
14
15
16
```

Transition Effects Complete

Display Your Screen Show

Position your cursor on **Scrtitle** and press **F2** to start your Screen Show. To move from one chart to the next, press any key.

If you want to stop your Screen Show, press **ESC.**

You may decide to change some of the Transition Effects. Simply position your cursor on the file you want to change and press **Tab** to move to the **Draw** column and then **F3** for **Choices.** Choose the effect you want and press **Enter.** You can then press **Tab** to specify a new direction and **Tab** again to specify a different speed.

Experiment with a variety of Transition Effects until you are pleased with the overall impact of your Screen Show.

Add Charts

You can add charts you've produced in other lessons to your current Presentation. Press **F7** to view the **Add/Edit Menu** and choose **1** for **Add Chart.** You can then choose the chart you wish to add from the list of files on your disk. You can also access the Add/Edit Menu to delete a chart or change the order in which charts will appear (**Move Chart**).

Save Presentation

Once you are finished experimenting with the Transition Effects, save your Presentation as follows:

1. Press **F6** for **Main Menu.**
2. Press **6** for **Presentation.**
3. Press **5** for **Save Presentation.**

You can now exit from Harvard Graphics (**E**) or clear your current chart (**1** and **8**) and go on to create your own Screen Show in Activity 4.

ACTIVITY 4   CHALLENGE ASSIGNMENT

Read through the following sections for suggestions on content and then adapt the instructions given for your own material. Use the boxes provided to record information about your Screen Show.

The Challenge Assignment requires four major steps:

Step One:	Determine Your Screen Show Subject
Step Two:	Prepare Your Charts
Step Three:	Edit Your Presentation
Step Four:	Produce Your Screen Show

Determine Your Show Subject

The subject you choose for your Screen Show will affect the chart types you include. Screen Show subjects include a sales proposal, new employee orientation, academic lecture, employee motivation, annual report, etc.

Specify the subject of your Screen Show in the following box.

> Screen Show Subject:

Once you select the subject of your Screen Show, you need to specify the name of the company or organization your Screen Show represents. For example, you could develop a Screen Show designed to motivate sales personnel for a company that manufactures handmade oak furniture.

In the box below, specify the name of your company or organization and write a one-sentence description of its principal business.

> Name of Company/Organization:
>
> Description of Principal Business:

Prepare Your Charts

Your next step is to list the charts you will include in your Screen Show. A typical one-hour presentation can use twenty or thirty charts; however, for the Challenge Assignment, limit the number of charts to ten. To review all that you have learned in *Applying Harvard Graphics,* try to include at least one of each type of chart.

Complete the following table with the name and description of each chart in your Screen Show. List the charts in the order you wish them to appear. You can then go on to create your charts. Remember to save each chart and answer "Yes" to "Add to Current Presentation."

Chart Type	Chart Description
1.	
2.	
3.	
4.	
5.	
6.	
7.	
8.	

Remember to specify the Text Font Name and Style for your Title Charts and for all the text elements except the Title, Subtitle, and Footnotes in your other charts. In addition, if you choose to include charts you've created in Draw, make sure you use the same Font Name and Style for the text as you plan to use for all the other charts.

You can also create a special background for your Presentation. This background could include a logo such as the one you created in Activity 3 or even a simple shaded line at the bottom of the screen. Try creating a variety of chart backgrounds and then applying them to your Presentation charts.

Edit Your Presentation

Once you have created and saved all your charts, press **6** at your Main Menu and then **2** to access the Presentation Edit Screen. Now you can add Presentation Text, Presentation Text Attributes, and a Presentation Appearance.

Press **F8** for **Options** to access the Presentation Options menus and experiment with different looks. Try out a variety of Chart Palettes and press **F2** frequently to preview your charts. To return to your Presentation Edit Screen, just press **ESC.**

Transition Effects

When you are satisfied with the format of your Presentation, add your Transition Effects. Again, experiment with different effects. For example, if you *wipe* one chart left, try wiping the next chart right or *scroll* one chart up and the next chart down. Press **F2** frequently to preview your Screen Show. To move from one chart to the next, press any key. To return to your Presentation Edit Screen, press **ESC.**

Edit Charts

If you decide a chart requires editing, highlight the file and then press **Ctrl + E** or **7** for **Add/Edit** and **7** for **Edit Chart.** After you make the changes you want to the chart, save it, clear it and press **6** at the Main Menu and then **2** to return to your Presentation Edit Screen.

Move, Delete, Insert Files

You can also access the Add/Edit Menu to change the order of your files, delete a file, or add a file from your directory.

Save Presentation

When you are finished with your Screen Show, make sure you save your Presentation.

1. Press **F6** for **Main Menu.**
2. Press **6** for **Presentation.**
3. Press **5** for **Save Presentation.**

Produce Your Screen Show

If possible, try to display your Screen Show for a small audience. Write a brief script to accompany your Show and explain each of the Charts as they appear. When you want to move to a new chart, press any key.

ACTIVITY 5　LESSON TEN REVIEW

Test your understanding of the functions and concepts you learned in Lesson Ten by completing the following Review Questions.

1. List three Presentation methods.
2. Why should each chart in a Presentation conform to the same overall format?
3. What is a Transition Effect?
4. Describe how to apply the same footnote to every chart (except the Title Chart) in a presentation.
5. How do you access the Presentation Edit Screen?
6. Describe the Fade Transition Effect.

7.   How do you apply the same Palette to every chart in a Presentation?
8.   How do you edit a chart from the Presentation Edit Screen?
9.   How do you proceed from one chart to the next in a Screen Show?
10.   What is the Presentation preview key?

ADVANCED FEATURES

Appendix A provides you with two "mini" activities designed to teach you how to use Templates and how to import and export files to and from other programs. Here are the Lesson Activities:

ACTIVITY 1: Follow the instructions provided to create a Template for a Bullet Chart.

ACTIVITY 2: Follow the instructions provided to import and export spreadsheet and graphic files.

ACTIVITY 1   CREATING TEMPLATES

Frequently, you may want several versions of a particular chart type to have the same attributes. For example, you could want each bar chart in a series of bar charts to display the same text font and to include the same logo in a particular location. You could make all of these changes every time you create the chart or you could simplify the process by creating a chart Template.

In a Template, you specify all the settings only once and then retrieve the Template to enter the data required for a specific version of the chart. You can create Templates for all the Harvard Graphics chart types you use most often.

Template Example

For example, you could create a Template for a Pie Chart that specified the title and subtitle as Dutch 801, Bold, and Left-Aligned; the Title Region Frame Style as None; and the Chart Region Frame Style as Octagonal. In addition, you could select a Palette and one of the preset background drawings. Every time you create a Pie Chart requiring these settings, you would first retrieve the Template you created and then add the specific data required for the Pie Chart.

Template Instructions

To familiarize yourself with the process required to create and apply a template, go on now to complete the following instructions for a Bullet Chart Template.

Create Chart

1. Press **1** for **Create Chart** and **1** for **Text Chart.**
2. Press **2** for **Bullet Chart.**

You will make all the changes required in the Bullet Chart Edit Screen. Start with the Text Attributes.

Text Attributes
1. Press **F8** for **Options** and **2** for **Text Attributes.**
2. At the Text Attributes Menu, make the following changes:

	Size	Alignment	Font	Style
Title	10	Left	Geo Slab	Medium
Subtitle	6	Left	Geo Slab	Medium
Bullet Text	7	Left	Geo Slab	Medium

3. Press **F10** to return to the Bullet Chart Edit Screen.

Text Appearance
1. Press **F8** for **Options** and **3** for **Appearance.**
2. At the Appearance Menu, move opposite **Background Drawing** and press **F3** for **Choices.**
3. Select **FRAME1.CH3** and press **Enter.**
4. Press **F10** to return to the Bullet Chart Edit Screen.

Bullet Options
1. Press **F8** for **Options** and **5** for **Bullet Options.**
2. At the Bullet Options Menu, make the following changes:

Bullet Type: ▶
Bullet Size: Large
Vertical Alignment: Middle

3. Press **F10** to return to the Bullet Chart Edit Screen.

Save as Template
Now that you have specified all the settings you require for your Bullet Chart, you need to save your chart as a Template. You can then retrieve this Template and use it to create as many new Bullet Charts as you need—each Chart with the same settings.

1. Press **F6** to return to the **Main Menu.**
2. Press **4** for **File** and **5** for **Save as Template.**
3. At the Save Template Menu, your cursor is currently positioned next to **Filename.** The default Directory (usually C:\HG3\DATA) is displayed. Save your template on a data disk in Drive A or B.
4. Press your ↑ arrow to position your cursor on **Directory.**
5. Type *a:* or *b:* and then press **Delete** to erase the old Directory.
6. Press **Enter.** Your cursor is now opposite **Filename.**
7. Type *Bullet* and press **Enter.** Harvard Graphics will automatically assign TP3 as the file extension to designate the file as a template.
8. At **Description,** type *Template for Bullet Chart.*

Compare your Save Template screen with the following illustration:

```
┌─────────────────────────────────────────────────┐
│                 Save Template                     │
├─────────────────────────────────────────────────┤
│                                                   │
│  Directory:      a:                               │
│                                                   │
│  Filename:       Bullet                           │
│                                                   │
│  Description:    Template for Bullet Chart        │
│                                                   │
│  Clear values:       No                           │
│                                                   │
│  Import data link:   No                           │
│                                                   │
└─────────────────────────────────────────────────┘
```

9. Press **F10** to save and return to the Bullet Chart Edit Screen.

Apply Template   Once you have saved your chart settings as a Template, you can retrieve the Template and create a Bullet Chart with specific information. Here's how.

1. At the Main Menu, press **4** for **File** and **2** for **Get Template.**
2. If necessary, specify your data drive and Directory and press **Enter.**
3. Cursor to **BULLET.TP3** and press **Enter.**

The Bullet Chart Edit Screen appears. You can now enter the specific information you require for your Bullet Chart and then save it as you would any file.

You will find the Template feature very useful as you increase your awareness of how you can apply Harvard Graphics to your own work. For example, if you frequently use the same attributes over and over in a series of Title Charts for a Presentation, take a moment to create a Template. You will cut down your preparation time and ensure the consistent appearance of each Chart you present.

ACTIVITY 2   IMPORTING AND EXPORTING FILES

Activity 2 introduces you to how Harvard Graphics can *interface* or connect with other programs. The instructions provided cover only the basic Import and Export functions. For more detailed information—particularly about importing database and spreadsheet data—refer to the Harvard Graphics manual that accompanies the program.

Importing   You use the Import function to retrieve data or graphics that you have created in another program into Harvard Graphics. For example, you can create a Harvard Graphics chart from data you have entered in Lotus 1-2-3. You can also add a graphics file created in another program such as Corel Draw to a drawing you've created in Harvard Graphics. The Import function extends your application of the Harvard Graphics features. You can use these features to present data you create in other programs without having to re-enter the data into a Harvard Graphics Edit Screen.

Exporting

You can also export a file you've created in Harvard Graphics into another program such as Aldus Pagemaker or Professional Write. For example, you may wish to use a logo created in Harvard Graphics to enhance a newsletter you've created in Ventura. The Export function allows you to save a Harvard Graphics chart or drawing in a format that other software programs can read.

Practice

To introduce you to the Harvard Graphics Import and Export features, instructions are provided to perform the following tasks:

1. Import a Lotus 1-2-3 graph into a Harvard Graphics chart.
2. Import a CGM Graphics File to Harvard Graphics.
3. Export a PCX Graphics File from Harvard Graphics.

Import from Lotus 1-2-3

You can either import a named graph from Lotus 1-2-3 or you can import only the graph data. The reason *why* you import a Lotus graph into Harvard Graphics is so that you can enhance the Lotus graph with Harvard Graphics features. A simple two-dimensional Pie Graph created in Lotus 1-2-3 can be transformed into a three-dimensional, multicolor Pie Chart complete with shaded background and different fonts in Harvard Graphics.

The following instructions show you how to import a named graph from Lotus 1-2-3 to Harvard Graphics.

1. Create a graph in Lotus 1-2-3 using the /Graph Name Create command. You cannot import the graph if it is created with the /Graph Save command.
2. Access the Harvard Graphics Main Menu.
3. At the Main Menu, press **4** for **File** and **7** for **Import.**

The Import Menu appears:

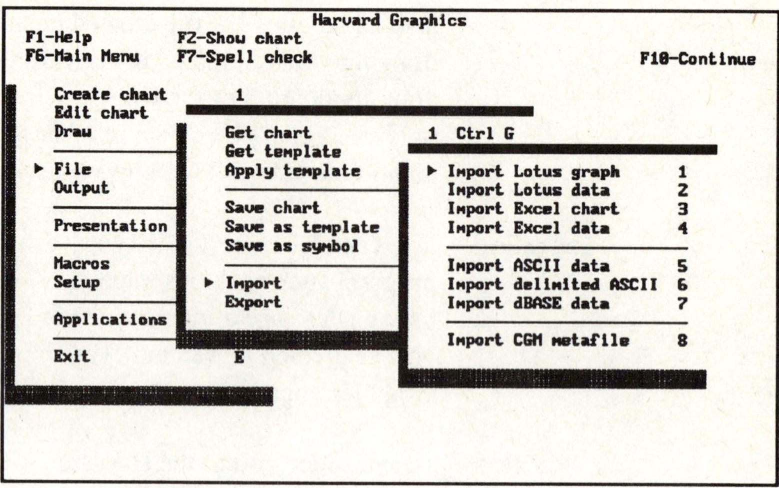

Now all you need to do is choose Import Lotus Graph as follows:

1. Press **1** for **Import Lotus Graph.**
2. A list of the named graphs in the Lotus Worksheet appears on your screen. Cursor to the file you require and press **F10** to import the graph.

> **NOTE:** If the graph you want is not listed, type a new Directory path at **Directory** and press **Enter.**

Your graph should now appear as a Harvard Graphics chart. Press any key to access the Chart Edit Screen. You can now edit, enhance, and save the Chart as you would any Harvard Graphics Chart.

Import Graphics File

To import a graphics file from another graphics program, you must first save the file in CGM format. Refer to the manual accompanying the program you are importing from to determine how to save a file in CGM format.

Once you have saved the file in CGM format, exit from the program and access Harvard Graphics. You can then import the CGM file as follows:

1. At the Main Menu, press **4** for **File.**
2. Press **7** for **Import.**
3. Press **8** for **Import CGM Metafile.**

The file you imported will appear on screen. Press any key to place the new file into your Draw Screen. You can now edit and save the graphics file as you would any Harvard Graphics drawing.

Export .PCX File

Sometimes you may wish to include a chart or drawing you've created in Harvard Graphics in a document you have created with another program such as WordPerfect or PageMaker. To use a Harvard Graphics chart in another program, you need to access the Export command.

1. Retrieve the file you wish to export or create the chart/drawing and save it. For example, access your data drive and retrieve the file named *Barchrt1* from Lesson 5.
2. At the Main Menu, press **4** for **File.**
3. Press **8** for **Export.**

The Export Menu appears. Note the other options you have available:

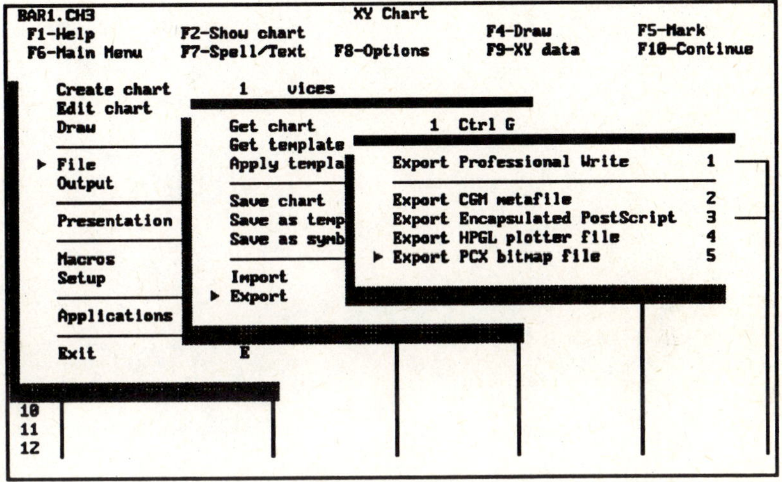

4. Press **5** for **Export PCX Bitmap File.**

The current filename appears. You can change both the filename and the directory, if you wish, and then press **Enter.**

Your Harvard Graphics chart is now saved as a PCX file. The PCX format is one of the most common graphics formats and can be read by most software programs that handle graphics. All you need to do now is retrieve the PCX file into the specific software program you wish to use. How you retrieve the PCX file will depend upon the requirements of the program. For example, to retrieve a PCX file into WordPerfect 5.1 or 6.0, you would need to access the Graphics command (Alt + F9). Refer to the manual that accompanies your software for more detailed information.

INDEX

Accessing program, 2
Advanced features, 366–371
  importing and exporting files, 368–371
  templates, 366–368
Advertising Flyer, 88 (fig.)
  adding Symbols, 80–85
  adding Text in Draw, 75–80
  aligning and positioning Text blocks, 96–97
  applying Group Tool, 82
  choosing product/service/event, 99
  connecting text to curves, 92–94
  connecting text to objects, 87–89, 92–94
  copying text and curves, 94–96
  creating and formatting of, 101–103
  creating curved text and wave lines, 87–98
  creating Starburst Symbol and text, 83–85
  designing, 73–74
  duplicating curves, 91–92
  elements of, 73
  entering text blocks, 75–80
  example of, 74 (fig.)
  pasting, 95
  planning information for, 100–101
  printing, 86
  purpose of, 74, 99
  revising format, 96–97
  rotating and flipping symbols, 80–81, 83–84
  saving, 85–86
  saving and printing, 98
  text for, 74
  using Align Tool, 78, 83, 96
  using Rotate Tool, 93
  using Scratchpad, 87, 95
Alignment
  options, 19 (fig.)
  of text, 18–19
Align Tool, 78, 83, 96, 194, 196, 242–243, 246
Appearance Menu, 5, 53
Area Chart, 167–205, 187 (fig.)
  changing Chart Style, 177
  changing Fill Style to Pattern, 177–178
  changing Region Frame Style, 177
  changing text attributes, 176
    combining Charts, 192–198
    components, 199–201
    converting to Table Chart, 188–189
    creating, 172–175, 173 (fig.)
    creating and formatting of, 202–205
    determining information required, 167–172
    edit and save, 186–188
    enhancing, 175–179
    enhancing Table Chart, 190–191, 192–198
    evolving Symbols, 180–184
    and fast-save of Table Chart, 192
    and Line Chart, 168 and *fig.*
    and mouse use, 192–197
    Overlap style, 169 and *fig.*
    planning information for, 199–201
    printing, 185, 198, 198
    required enhancements of, 176
    saving, 184, 198, 198
    selecting company/organization for, 199
    series data display, 171
    Stacked, 170–171, 170 (fig.)
    styles, 169–170, 199
    using Align Tool, 194–195
    using Group/Ungroup, 183–184
    using Scratchpad, 180–184
    XY data types, 167
Arrows
  creating, 308–314
  using with Diagrams, 308–314
Attributes, 51–52
  alignment, 18–19
  changing, 28–31, 43–44, 117–118, 226, 234–235
  color, 18
  defined, 18
  fonts, 19
  font style, 19–20
  size, 18
Author information, and Title Page, 42–43
Author Text, 31
Axis Frame, 151, 264, 265
  hiding, 151
Axis Options, 264, 265

374   Index

Background, adding to Bullet Chart, 59–60
Background Drawing, 59–60
Backspace key, and correcting errors, 214
Bar Chart, 135–166, 107 (fig.), 136 (fig.), 139 (fig.), 147 (fig.)
   adding and shading symbols, 151–157
   areas of, 135–136
   changing color, 143
   creating, 138–141
   creating and formatting of, 163–165
   creating for Screen Show, 349–351
   determining purpose of, 161
   editing chart data, 146–148
   enhancements for, 149–159
   enhancing Y Axis, 141–143
   entering X Data automatically, 138–140
   and Geographical Chart, 265–275
   hiding Axis Frame, 151
   number of bars for, 137
   planning information for, 161–162
   printing, 145, 160
   programmer symbol and shading, 154–157
   purpose of, 137
   removal of grid lines, 151–152
   resizing bars, 270–271
   saving, 144–145, 159–160
   saving charts as symbols, 152–153
   ungrouping, 158–159
   using the Front Tool, 159
Bar Chart Symbol, 154
Boxes
   adding, 215–216, 234
   adding shaded, 61–65
   adding to Organization Chart, 215–216
   changing Box Options, 234
   changing lines of, 227
   changing style, 219
   deleting, 224–225, 234
   drawing, 61 (fig.), 62 (fig.), 293–294
   duplication, 246
   editing text, 222–224
   enhancing, 219
   entering data in, 214–217
   Legend, 143
   positioning, 65
   shading, 63–64
   Title, 119
Box Line, 64
Box Tool, 8, 61, 244
Bullet Chart, 46–72, 47 (fig.), 49 (fig.), 57 (fig.)
   accessing Draw Screen, 61
   adding Background, 59–60
   adding secondary bullets, 56–58
   adding shaded box, 61–65
   Background Drawing for, 59–60
   changing Bullet Options, 52–53
   changing Fonts and Attributes, 51–52,
   changing Title/Subtitle alignment, 60
   choosing topic for, 67–68
   creating, 48–50
   creating and formatting of, 69–71
   creating and shading Box, 61–65
   creating for Screen Show, 340–342, 351–353
   defined, 47
   Edit Screen, 60 (fig.)
   enhancement of, 53–54
   information required for, 47–48
   Options, 52
   parallel structure for, 68–69
   planning information for, 68–69
   positioning chart area, 65–66
   printing, 55, 67
   required enhancements of, 51, 59
   saving, 54–55, 66
   and text attributes, 51–52
   uses of, 46
Bullet Options, 52–53
Bullet Options Menu, 52
Bullets
   defined, 47
   secondary, 56–58
Bullet Text Frame Fill, 60
Bullet Text Frame Style, 60
Business, Geographical Charts and, 237–238

Camera Symbol, 31–32
Chart Edit Screen, 6, 58 (fig.)
Chart Orientation, 5
Charts. *See also* individual charts by name
   Advertising Flyer, 73–104
   Area, 167–205
   Bar, 107 (fig.), 135–166, 265–275
   Bullet Chart, 46–72
   categories of, 1–2
   changing orientations, 25–27
   creating Pie Charts, 9–11
   creating Templates for, 366–368
   creation of, 4
   defined, 1
   Diagram, 284–324
   Geographical, 237–283
   Line, 169–170
   Number, 105–236
   Organization, 210–236
   Pictorial, 206–324
   Pie, 109 (fig.), 110–134
   Table, 106 (fig.), 188–192, 193–194
   Text Charts, 17–104

types of, 4
type, and content used with Screen Show, 328–329
Circle, drawing, 305
Circle Tool, 7
Color
    effective use with presentations, 327
    of text, 18
Color Tool, 63, 249, 289
Column format, 126
    for Pie Chart, 126
Commands
    F3(Choices), 4, 5, 6
    F8(Options), 4–5, 6
Connect Tool, 92, 94
Copying text, 94–96
Copy Tool, 95, 183
Create Chart Menu, 3, 4
Create Chart option, 4
Cursor/enter method, of selecting menu items, 3, 4
Curved text, 87–94
Curves
    drawing, 89–91
    duplicating, 91–92
Curve Tool, 89, 291

Data, defined, 107–108
Data Points (Series), of Bar Chart, 135, 136
Data ranges, of maps, 279
Delete Tool, 87
Diagram, 284–324, 303 (fig.)
    adding Text, 294–300, 314–318
    choosing topic for, 320
    creating and formatting, 321–324
    creating process, 302–320
    drawing and positioning shapes, 304–307
    drawing Boxes, 293–294
    and drawing floor plans, 286–302
    drawing lines and curves, 286–293, 298–299
    duplicating objects, 304–307, 310–312
    planning information for, 321
    printing, 301–302, 319–320
    saving, 301, 319
    uses of, 284–285
    using arrows, 308–314
    using Grids and Grid Snap, 286–291
Distortion, defined, 108
Document Type, 30–31
Dragging, 8, 11
Drawing
    background, 59–60
    tools, 2
Draw option, 6–7
Draw Screen, 7 and *fig.*
    accessing, 61

Draw Tools, 4
Duplicate Tool, 91, 181, 246

Edit Chart option, 6
Edit Text Tool, 36
Evolve, creating logo with, 353–357
Evolve Tool, 183
Exiting, menus, 6
Exporting files, 369, 370–371, 368–372

Fast Save method, 153
Features, advanced, 366–371
F5 Mark Text feature, 36
F8(Options), 4–5, 4–5
Files
    exporting .PCX files, 370–371
    exporting to other software programs, 369
    importing, 368–370
    importing from Lotus 1-2-3, 369–370
Flip charts, 326
Flip Tool, 83, 197
Floor plans, 287 (fig.)
    drawing, 286–302
Flyer, advertising, 73–104
Fonts
    and Bullet Chart, 51–52
    changing, 28–31, 43–44, 117–118, 226
    Dutch, 28, 29
    sizes and styles of, 19 and *fig.*
Font style(s), types of, 19–20 and *fig.*
Footnotes, entering, 358
Format, and use with presentations, 327
Frames, 20–21 and *fig.*
Front Tool, 159
F3 (Choices), 4, 5, 6
Functions
    finishing, 11
    selecting, 11

Geographical Chart, 237–238 and *fig.*, 241 (fig.), 262 (fig.)
    and Bar Chart, 265–275
    business uses of, 237–238
    chart data for map, 279–280
    combining Map and Chart Symbols, 266–275
    creating, 261
    creating and formatting, 280–282
    creating legend, 244–249
    creating map, 243–244
    creating Map Symbols, 243–249
    data ranges, 279
    duplicating Objects, 246, 282
    entering heading of, 240–243
    methods of display, 279–280
    and per capita information, 238–239

planning information, 278–279
printing, 260, 276–277
purpose of, 278
repositioning labels, 271
repositioning Map, 272
required enhancements, 263–264
resizing bars, 270–271
saving, 259–260, 276
saving Charts as Symbols, 265–266
selecting map for, 277–278
and shaded map areas, 238
sizing and moving Chart Areas, 240–243, 281
used with Bar Chart, 238 (fig.)
using Align Tool, 242–243, 272, 273
using Group/Ungroup, 248, 250, 255, 257, 269–270
using Patterns, 249–259, 281
Graphic elements, 18
Graphic objects, 21
Graphics, presentation, 1
Grid lines, 151–152
Grids, 286–291
Grid Snaps, 288, 290
Group Information area, 82
Group Tool, 95, 183
applying, 82

Horizontal Tool, 197

Importing files, 369–370
Information, planning for Bullet Chart, 68–69
Interface, 368

Keyboard, 3
and accessing menus, 3

Label heading, 10
Labels, for Bar Charts, 271, 273
Landscape orientation, 25, 27
Legend
creating, 244–249
need for, 144
Legend box, 143, 149–150
positioning of, 149–150
Line Chart, vs. Area Chart, 168–169
Lines
creating wave, 87–98
curved, drawing, 89–91
drawing, 286–293, 298–299
drawing straight and curved, 286–293, 298–299
duplicating curved, 91–92
Line Tool, 289
Logo, creation of, 353–357
Lotus 1-2-3, importing files from, 369–370

Main Menu, 2–3 and *fig.*
Maps (Geographical Chart), 237–283
creating, 243–244
for Geographical Chart, 238, 277–278
and use of Shift key, 243
Map Symbols, creating, 243–249
Menus, 2–7
Appearance, 5 and *fig.*, 53
Bullet Options, 52
commands, 4–6
Create Chart, 3, 4
exiting, 6
Main, 2–3 and *fig.*
Options, 4–5
selecting items from, 3–4
Methods, of presentations, 326
Mouse
and use with Draw Tools, 4
dragging, 11
finishing functions with, 11
selecting functions with, 11
techniques for using, 8 (fig.)
use with Area Chart, 192–197
use with Diagram, 289
using, 7–8, 240–243
Mouse method, of selecting menu items, 3–4

Number Charts, 105–236
Area Chart, 167–205
Bar Chart, 135–166
Pie Chart, 110–134
required terms for, 107–109
vs. table chart, 106–107 and *fig.*, 106(fig.)
Number method, of selecting menu items, 3, 4

Objects, 7
duplicating, 246, 282, 304–307, 310–312
Options
Bullet Chart, 52
Create Chart, 3
Draw, 3
Edit Chart, 3
Options Menu, 4–5 and *fig.*
Organization, of text, 14–16
Organization Chart, 210–236, 211 (fig.), 213 (fig.), 223 (fig.)
adding Boxes, 215–216, 234
adding Symbols, 228–229
changing box lines, 227
changing Box Options, 234
changing Box Style, 219
changing Fonts and Attributes, 226
creating, 212–217, 342–345
creating and editing, 212–217

creating and formatting, 233–235
deleting Boxes, 224–225, 234
editing data, 222–227
enhancing, 217–219
entering data, 214–217
limitations of, 211
lines of communication for, 211
planning information for, 233
printing, 221, 232
required enhancements for, 217
resizing Chart Area, 228
rotating text, 229–231, 235
saving, 220–221, 231–232
shape of, 211
Orientations
   Chart, 5–6
   Landscape, 5, 25, 27
   Portrait, 5, 25
Overheads, 326
Overlap Area Chart, 169 and *fig.*
Overview, of text, 1–2

Palette, 70, 327
   using, 353–357
Parallel structure, 68–69
Paste Tool, 95, 183
Patterns, for Pie Chart, 119–120 and *fig.*, 126–127
   using with Geographical Chart, 249–259, 281
Per Capita information, and Geographical Charts, 238–239
Percents, using 126
Pictorial Charts, 206–324, 208 (fig.)
   defined, 207
   Diagram, 284–324
   format of, 208
   Geographical, 237–283
   Organization, 210–236
   purpose of, 207–208 and *fig*
   types, 208–209
Pie Chart, 110–134, 109(fig.)
   adding 3-D effects, 119
   adding symbols, 128–129 and *fig.*
   adding Title Boxes, 119
   changing fonts and attributes, 117–118
   changing values to percents, 126
   and column format, 126
   creating, 9–11
   creating and editing, 113–116, 114 (fig.)
   creating and formatting of, 132–133
   creating for Screen Show, 345–349
   cutting "Slice," 120
   data uses for, 110–111 and *fig.*
   determining purpose of, 130–131
   linking two charts, 123, 124 (fig.)
   planning information for, 131–132

   printing, 122, 129–130
   saving, 121–122, 129
   selecting company/organization, 130
   and slice emphasis, 111, 112 (fig.)
   using patterns, 119–120 and *fig.*, 126–127
Pie Chart Edit Screen, 9
Plane Symbol, 80–81
Pointer Tool, 12, 28, 36, 63, 230, 246
Portrait Format, 43
Portrait orientation, 25
Posters, 326
Presentation attributes, applying, 357–360
Presentation background, creating, 353–357
Presentation graphics, 1
Presentations, 325–365
   format use and, 327
   methods of, 326
   purpose of, 326
   Screen Show method, 328–365
   transition effects for, 327
   and use of color, 327
Printer(s)
   and black-and-white print-outs, 9
   and color print-outs, 9
Printing
   Advertising Flyer, 86, 98
   Area Chart, 185, 198
   Bar Chart, 145, 160, 276–277
   Bullet Chart, 67
   Diagram, 301–302, 319–320
   Geographical Chart, 260
   Organization Chart, 221, 232
   Pie Chart, 122, 129–130
   Title Page, 33–34, 40–41
Programmer Symbol, 154–157
   positioning, 155
   retrieving, 154
   shading, 155–157
Project approach, 14–15
   of text, 14–15
Projection pad, 326

Quick Practice
   creating Pie Chart, 9–11
   using mouse to enter text and retrieve symbol, 11

Rectangle, drawing, 305–306
Regular Polygon Tool, 304
Rotate Tool, 84, 93, 197, 231

Saving
   Advertising Flyer, 85–86, 98
   Area Chart, 184, 198
   Bar Chart, 144–145, 159–160, 276

Bullet Chart, 66
Diagram, 301, 319
fast-save, of Table Chart, 192
Fast Save method, 153
Geographical Chart, 259–260
Organization Chart, 220–221, 231–232
Pie Chart, 121–122, 129
Title Page, 32–33, 41
Scale, of maps, 285
Scratchpad, 87, 95
Scratchpad Tool, 180
Screen Show, 326, 328–365
    applying presentation attributes, 357–360
    charts for, 331 (fig.), 332 (fig.), 333 (fig.), 334 (fig.), 335
        (fig.), 336 (fig.), 337 (fig.)
    creating a Presentation Background, 353–357
    creating Bar Chart, 349–351
    creating Bullet Chart 1, 340–342
    creating Bullet Chart 2, 351–353
    creating logo with Evolve, 353–357
    creating Organization Chart, 342–345
    creating Pie Chart 1, 345–347
    creating Pie Chart 2, 347–349
    creating Title Chart, 338–339
    determining subject, 362
    editing presentation, 363–364
    managing presentation files, 361
    preparing Charts, 363
    producing Show, 364
    types of charts used, 328–329
    using Palettes, 353–357
    using transition effects, 360–361
Secondary bullets, definition of, 56
Series, 109
    of Bar Chart, 135, 136
    data points as, 135, 136
    multiple, 136–137
Series Data, for Bar Chart, 163
Series Titles, of Bar Chart, 162
Service Description, 56
Shaded box, 51–65
Shade Tool, 63
Shapes
    circle, drawing, 305
    duplicating, 306
    positioning, 307
    rectangle, drawing, 305–306
    triangle, drawing, 304–305
Shift key, 38
    use of, 181, 182, 184
Size, of text, 18
Slice labels, for Pie Chart, 115
Slice values, 10
    for Pie Chart, 115–116

Slide shows, 326
Software programs
    and exporting files, 369
    purpose of, 1
Space Tool, 247
Stacked Area Chart, 170–171, 170 (fig.)
Starburst Symbol, 83–84
Subtitle information, and Title Page, 42
Swiss 721 font, 19
Symbol Directories, 13
Symbols, 7, 11, 21
    adding to Organization Chart, 228–229
    adding to Pie Chart, 128–129
    adding to Title Page, 38–40
    Bar Chart as, 154, 265–266
    combining Map and Chart, 266–275
    Information, 80–81
    Map, creating, 243–249
    Programmer, 154–157
    rotating and flipping of, 80–81, 83–84
    saving Charts as, 265–266
Symbol Tool, 11, 13–14, 80, 154, 180, 228

Table Chart, 106 (fig.), 188–192, 193–194
Templates
    applying, 368
    creating, 366–368
Text
    adding in Draw, 25–32, 75–80
    adding to Diagram, 294–300, 314–318
    alignment, 18–19
    blocks, aligning of, 96
    blocks, positioning of, 96–97
    centering, 36–37
    centering for Title Page, 36–37
    color, 18
    connecting to curves, 92–94
    connecting to objects, 87–89, 92–94
    copying to Advertising Flyer, 94–96
    creating curved, 87–98
    editing, 34–37
    editing for Title Page, 36
    entering blocks of, 75–80
    fonts, 19
    font style, 19–20
    frames, 20
    marking, 36
    moving, 11–12
    positioning, 37
    positioning, for Title Page, 37
    rotating, 229–231, 235
    size, 19
    sizing, 37
    spacing of, 247

Text Attributes, changing, 234–235
Text Attributes Pop-up, 280
Text blocks, for advertising Flyer, 75–80
Text Charts, 17–104
    Advertising Flyer, 73–104
    Bullet, 46–72
    title page for, 22–45
Text overview, 1–2
Text Tool, 11–12, 27, 28, 75, 195, 230
3-D effects, for Pie Chart, 119
Title
    changing size, 29
    establishing position, 29
Title Boxes, 119
Title Chart, creating, 338–339
Title information, and Title Page, 42
Title Page, 22–45, 23 (fig.), 24 (fig.), 26 (fig.), 35 (fig.)
    adapting to another document, 34–41
    adding and sizing Symbols, 31–32, 38–40
    adding new symbol, 38–40
    adding Text in Draw, 25–32
    Author Text, 31
    and Camera Symbol, 31–32
    centering text, 36–37
    changing chart orientation, 25–27
    changing Fonts and Attributes, 28–31, 43–44
    changing format of, 27
    creating, 25–34
    creating and formatting, 43–45
    Document Type, 30–31
    editing text, 34–37
    entering and formatting text, 27–28
    information on, 42–43
    marking Text, 35–36
    positioning text, 38
    printing, 33–34, 40–41
    purpose of, 22–25
    saving, 32–33, 40
    sizing text, 38
    trouble note for, 28
    using Portrait Format, 25–27, 43
    using Zoom, 38–40
Tool Box, 92
Tools, 7–9. *See also* Draw tools; tools by name;
    Align, 194, 196, 242–243, 246
    Box, 61, 244
    Circle, 7
    Color, 63, 249
    Connect, 92
    Copy, 95, 183

Curve, 89, 89
Delete, 87
Duplicate, 91, 181, 246
Edit Text, 36
Evolve, 183
Flip, 83, 197
Front, 158
Group, 82, 95, 183
Horizontal, 197
Paste, 95, 183
Pointer, 12, 28, 63, 230, 246
Rotate, 84, 93, 197, 231
Scratchpad, 87, 180
selecting, 7–8
Shade, 63
Space, 247
Symbol, 13, 13–14, 80, 154, 180, 228
Text, 12, 27, 28, 75, 195, 230
trouble note for, 8
Undo, 28, 81, 245
Ungroup, 55, 158, 228
uses of, 7
Zoom, 44
Topic, choosing for Bullet Chart, 67–68
Transition effect, 327
Triangle, drawing, 304–305
2D style, of Area Chart, 186

Undo Tool, 28, 81, 245, 291, 292
Ungroup Tool, 65, 158, 228

Values, 109
Variables, defined, 108
Videos, computer-generated, 326
Visualization, and Diagram, 285

Wave Lines, curved text and, 87–94

X-Axis
    of Bar Chart, 135, 136
    entering data for, 138–140
X-Axis Labels, 162

Y-Axis
    of Bar Chart, 135, 136
    enhancing, 141–143
Y-Axis Title, 162–163

Zoom Tool, 38 and *fig.*